The Normative Foundations of European Competition Law

The Normative Foundations of European Competition Law

Assessing the Goals of Antitrust through the Lens of Legal Philosophy

Oles Andriychuk

University of Stirling, UK

Edward Elgar PUBLISHING

Cheltenham, UK • Northampton, MA, USA

Published by
Edward Elgar Publishing Limited
The Lypiatts
15 Lansdown Road
Cheltenham
Glos GL50 2JA
UK

Edward Elgar Publishing, Inc.
William Pratt House
9 Dewey Court
Northampton
Massachusetts 01060
USA

A catalogue record for this book
is available from the British Library

Library of Congress Control Number: 2017933402

This book is available electronically in the **Elgar**online
Law subject collection
DOI 10.4337/9781786436078

ISBN 978 1 78643 606 1 (cased)
ISBN 978 1 78643 607 8 (eBook)

Typeset by Servis Filmsetting Ltd, Stockport, Cheshire
Printed on FSC approved paper
Printed and bound in Great Britain by Marston Book Services Ltd, Oxfordshire

Contents

Preface

Everybody agrees that competition policy is beneficial for the economy. We all know that competition helps keep prices down and stimulates innovation, growth and consumer choice. Yet it is here where the consensus dissolves. Various visions on the very phenomenon of competition as well as its role in a broader set of economic policies have *competed* fiercely for many decades. The area of competition law, economics and policy is known for its hot discussions among the proponents of different views and theories. This book is focused on the most existential aspects of these conflicts, presuming the beneficial essence of them. It has several key objectives and offers several key messages.

The main argument of this book is that the economic (alongside political and cultural) aspect of competition constitutes the essence of democratic governance and as such should be treated as an autonomous political goal. It should not be always subordinated to the benchmark of efficiency or any other economic value, by which we often evaluate the performance of competition policy and even define its legitimacy. The book explains why competition deserves its regulatory protection not only when reliable evidence of its positive economic impact exists. It will be demonstrated that the current reductionist trend of narrowing down the category of competition to its economically beneficial outcomes exclusively is conceptually confusing, methodologically misleading and ideologically wrong. Semantically, the very gist of competition is embedded in the Smithian notion of the invisible hand. Competition by definition implies such subjective elements as spontaneity, unpredictability, contest, rivalry and luck. It would be naïve to argue that any sustainable economic governance can rely *solely* on the rationale of the invisible hand. Yet it is also naïve to attempt to transform the whole spectrum of competition's attributes to the measurable yardstick of economic calculus. And it is equally naïve to narrow its scope to welfare-oriented goals exclusively. *Visualising* the *invisible* hand is an intriguing exercise, but the exercise is futile by definition.

The above-mentioned argument will be investigated from various points of view. The argument cannot be put forward in isolation and requires a number of ancillary supportive claims. Each chapter of this book develops one or two such claims. Schematically, the algorithm is as follows: (1) tracing the evolution of economic thoughts on competition; (2) showing when exactly (and why) the dominant neoclassical perception of competition overshot the mark; (3) consulting other disciplines (namely, philosophy and legal theory) in the search for a concurrent non-economic theory of (economic) competition; (4) comparing the economic incarnation of competition with its political and cultural incarnations; (5) putting forward a normative hypothesis, which consolidates current European competition law with the philosophical theories of competition and its jurisprudential apparatus; (6) smoothing most of the regulatory turbulence emerging from such a proposal by exploring the mechanics of balancing; (7) demonstrating its practical implications.

The book begins with a historical overview of the phenomenon of competition as perceived by different economic schools and theories. It summarises the common trends and offers an explanation of why no mainstream (equilibrium-based) economic theory of competition is sufficient to explain the whole spectrum of attributes of the competitive process, let alone to offer reliable tools for its further improvement. At the very outset, it is important to stress the obvious: the book is not critical of economics as such. Furthermore, the leading role of economics in the area is not even challenged. The book is critical only of *monopolisation* of the wisdom of competition by the discipline of economics. The criticism is not hostile, but constructive. Several effective methodological mechanisms for mitigating the exclusivity of economics will be offered in different parts of the book and then synthesised into a complete theory of dialectical competition in its conclusion. For example, an analysis of the phenomenon of interdisciplinarity and its application in the area of competition policy will help us to understand paradigmatic algorithms of the relationship between different disciplines. The clash between law and economics is not unique. Law faces similar clashes with other disciplines. For example, ethics *invades* the area of law in the realm of legal theory. The book offers analysis of very interesting parallels in the relationship of law with economics as seen in the area of competition policy and law with morality as seen in legal theory. Exploring these similarities will help us to understand better the regulatory essence of competition policy as well as to disprove some misleading assumptions, which are popular in the contemporary vision of competition policy. The centre of gravity of competition policy should be shifted from values, which are external/peripheral to the very phenomenon of competition (i.e. welfare, growth, integration or innovation), to the issues that are at its very core: namely, the competitive process. The book tests the hypothesis that the main reason why mainstream economic theories tend to under-appreciate the autonomous character and normative significance of the competitive process is based on linguistic confusion. These theories (wrongly) equate the concept of competitive process with the phonetically identical concept of perfect competition. Then they subordinate the former to the latter, considering the process as such as (i) unmeasurable; (ii) redundant and (iii) meaningless. And after such subordination is justified and accepted they replace one category with the other; and then the others (where being procompetitive nowadays means being to the benefit of consumers, growth, innovation etc.). The concept of perfect competition, as we know, is a mere model. It is not a value; it is a hypothetical assumption, a mathematical fiction, whereas the concept of competitive process, conversely, is an ideological belief in entrepreneurial freedom as discovery procedure. These two concepts share nothing but the name 'competition' and one should not define the other.

The next chapter traces the evolution of competition law, economics and policy in the US and EU. Unlike the previous chapter, this one addresses the history of regulatory mechanisms of competition policy rather than looking at how the phenomenon of competition is understood by economics. It is more descriptive than analytical. It basically reminds the readers of the milestones of the development of competition policy, focusing mainly on the issues, which are discussed in the following chapters of the book. Methodologically, this chapter is comparative. It first compares various schools of competition policy; and then it compares the visions of competition policy as perceived on both sides of the Atlantic. The theory offered in this book is to a large extent based on the premises that in one form or another have been used by various authors/regulators of the past. Yet, most of them nowadays are considered as obsolete or radical. By analysing the history of views on competition, this chapter reveals the key pitfalls of such theories offering effective solution/mitigation of these obstacles. Despite exploring all major schools of contemporary competition policy, attention is devoted mainly to Ordoliberalism. This set of theories today is often caricatured and marginalised. Being in general supportive of its key premises, the book, however, does not aim to offer an apologetic vision of Neo-Ordoliberalism, trying rather to extract and conceptualise further those components of Ordoliberalism that are necessary for developing an original theory of competition policy, the theory of dialectical competition. The same can be said about the Austrian (and Hayekian) schools of competition: some central arguments and observations on the phenomenon of competition are internalised by this book, yet the key normative proposition about unregulated competition qua spontaneous order is accepted in very revised and mitigated form.

After looking in Chapter 2 at the perception of competition in economics and after providing an overview in Chapter 3 of the development of the key regulatory schools of competition policy, Chapter 4 offers an analysis of the very phenomenon of competition. While Chapter 2 was mainly critical, apagogical and discursive and Chapter 3 mainly descriptive and comparative, the next one can be described as analytical, normative and constitutive. It is in a sense one of the main components of the book. Several important tasks are accomplished in the chapter. First, it analyses the phenomenon of competition from the point of view of philosophy. The problem of the competitive process attracted the attention of political, philosophical and legal thought long before the very discipline of economics emerged. Some of the views on competition developed by these disciplines are very relevant today, even though most of them are completely ignored by the dominant competition policy discourse. The chapter begins with a philosophical overview of the ideas on competition from Antiquity to the present day, focusing mainly on those aspects of the phenomenon which can and should be internalised by the domain of competition policy. Another important task of this chapter is to explain the nature of competition by looking at two of its philosophical 'twins': *dialectics* and *freedom*. Many philosophers have offered very detailed and analytically perfect theories on both phenomena. The knowledge generated in these disciplines will be internalised, 'translated' and contextualised. The task of this part of the chapter thus is to enrich the views on (economic) competition, which are often seen in the domain of competition policy as dominant (if not exclusive), while in reality they represent only a (peripheral) part of the theory of competition *sensu largo*. The chapter has two other objectives: it offers a comparison between the economic part of the phenomenon of competition and its political and cultural parts, arguing that the latter two are conceptually and normatively similar to the economic one, while they are almost never perceived comparatively. The comparison of these three incarnations of competition reveals many intriguing similarities and one drastic difference. It is exactly this difference which underpins the normative proposal of the book. Both in politics (election) and culture (free speech) the competitive process is protected for two main reasons: (i) because it is efficient and (ii) because it is a matter of ideological choice, made by society. In other words, we believe in elections and free speech not (only) because they (always) deliver the best results, but (also) because they are two important ingredients of liberal democracy *sensu largo*. Neither elections nor free speech guarantee the best performance: we tolerate elements of populism in politics and hate speech in culture. It is not the case with economic competition inasmuch as it remains totally subordinate to efficiency. The practice is tolerated/ encouraged only when it is economically efficient. Furthermore, the term 'efficiency' is often replaced by the term 'competition'. It is not uncommon nowadays to argue that the practice is procompetitive only if it provides positive outcomes for consumers/welfare/growth etc. even though from the perspective of formal logic such a syllogism is a complete fallacy. This analysis enables a normative statement to be made that competition is the distinctive feature of liberal democracy. The theoretical part of this statement forms the foundation of the normative proposal offered in the book. This proposal will be explored in the conclusion, where all components of the theory of dialectical competition are reduced to common denominator and summarised.

Prima facie the normative proposal offered in Chapter 4 of the book may appear radical and unrealistic. If true, these two attributes would make the task of the whole book rather speculative and futile. To avoid this misleading conclusion, Chapter 5 develops a very detailed and scrupulous theory of balancing. The key hypothesis here is that the idea of a normative hierarchy of competition in the pantheon of societal values in liberal democracy does not exempt competition from trade-offs on the regulatory level. In other words, competitive process can remain at the top of the political, economic and cultural values of any liberal democracy, but it can never be protected in its entirety. Compromises are needed; choices are unavoidable. Sometimes, the choices are tragic. The task of this chapter thus is to explore the mechanics of balancing, which is used by any regulatory power/decision-maker in any democratic country. The book offers a number of systematised observations about the phenomenon of balancing, explaining not only the very nature of compromise, but also conceptualising the communicative process between the advocates of different values and those who make decisions. This analysis is made on the 'objective' level of constellation of regulatory values as well as on the 'subjective' level, where these values *compete* with each other to be prioritised by the decision-maker. In other words, this chapter analyses the details of the mechanism of balancing and explains why competition policy, while focusing on the competitive process, does not isolate itself from other legitimate regulatory values – including such important values as welfare, growth, market integration or innovation.

After analysing these components of the theory of dialectical competition, the book offers a number of examples where competition policy should benefit from a rich and comprehensive domain of legal theory. The dominant view that competition is mainly the realm of economics is reductionist. Legal theory discusses a number of problems relevant to today's competition policy. The solutions developed by this discipline are almost never discussed in the area of competition policy. Chapter 6 seeks to remedy this situation, offering a sketchy overview of the problems and the debates in legal theory, which could help to understand better the problems discussed in the area of competition law. The task of this chapter is to build the bridges between two disciplines that are rather ignorant of each other: the theory of law and the economic theory of competition policy. The book does not argue that legal theory should *replace* economic analysis. It argues that legal theory should not be ignored in analysing the concept of economic competition in general, and particularly when discussing its legal regulation.

The last chapter of the book has two main objectives. It first offers a summative representation of the proposed theory of dialectical competition. Secondly, it explains how the key theoretical premises developed in the book could be applied in practice. It does not offer a comprehensive 'translation' of the whole matrix of legal problems to the theory of dialectical competition, but uses paradigmatic cases as examples of applicability and effectiveness of the theory in European legal practice.

Acknowledgements

I am sincerely grateful to those who shared their views and ideas during our countless discussions on the nature of competition law at various domestic and international fora. My gratitude primarily goes to Hannes Ullrich, Giuliano Amato, Pinar Akman, Philippe Coppens, Andreas Heinemann, Morten Hviid, Dov Jacobs, Ioannis Lianos, Giorgio Monti, Tetyana Pavlush, Axelle Reiter, Wojciech Sadurski, Giovanni Sartor, Heike Schweitzer, Daithí Mac Síthigh, Francisco De la Purta, Viktor Hryhorovych Andriychuk and Catherine Waddams. I am also indebted to my colleagues, friends and family in Stirling, Kyiv, Lutsk, Norwich, Florence and Prague for their help in the preparation of this book, and in particular to my parents Nataliya and Mykhailo, my wife Tetyana and my dearest godmother and grandparents, who have been waiting for this study to be accomplished. I would also like to thank my publisher and in particular Ben Booth, Iram Satti, Catherine Cumming and Amber Watts for their very professional approach to the whole project as well as the anonymous reviewers for helpful suggestions and constructive criticism. I am very grateful to the institutions which at different times have shaped my research identity: Volyn University (Lutsk, Ukraine), Ukrainian Academy of Foreign Trade (Kyiv, Ukraine), Charles University (Prague, the Czech Republic), European University Institute (Florence, Italy), the ESRC Centre for Competition Policy, UEA (Norwich, UK) and University of Stirling (UK). The final part of the research has been supported by the British Academy/Leverhulme small grants scheme and was undertaken during research leave granted by the University of Stirling.

Table of cases and legislation

EUROPEAN UNION

Communications, Guidance and Notices

Decisions

Regulations

Reports

Treaties and Consolidated Versions of Treaties

UNITED STATES

1. Introduction

In the last two decades European competition law has undergone a paradigmatic transformation, which in the literature, is known as *the more economic approach*. Having originally been designed and applied predominantly by lawyers, competition law is largely perceived nowadays as a realm of economics, with a strong influence of empirical statistical methods. As a contemporary *methodological* motto of European competition policy, the more economic approach, indeed, significantly advanced the discipline. The quantitative analysis and econometric models enabled more complex and sophisticated research into the behaviour of market actors, contributing to the achievement of the *normative* motto of European competition law: consumer welfare. The language of economics and the ethos of consumer welfare both constitute the core of contemporary European competition law.

Not contesting the methodological significance of economics or the normative importance of consumer welfare, and not intending to offer a reactionary counterpoint to the evolution of European competition law, this book instead seeks to provide a jurisprudential account of the European competition law discourse. The term jurisprudence is taken in this proposal broadly, covering the fields of legal theory, sociology of law and legal philosophy.

The primary objective of the jurisprudential account of competition is to *translate* the contemporary agenda of European antitrust from the language of economics into that of law. The philosophical aspect of this project has two equally important components: the first relates to competition *law*, while the second concerns the very phenomenon of competition itself. The former is primarily of a methodological nature. It contemplates the problems of European competition law through the prism of jurisprudence. The essence of the latter is mainly normative. It analyses the competitive process as a philosophical category, understanding by it a dynamic motion, embedded in the laws of dialectics, which generates a constant *multilogue* between the agents involved. Both aspects have important comparative and interdisciplinary components. The philosophical analysis of (a) *European* (b) *competition* and (c) *law* would be never accomplished if it concentrated solely on the latter two aspects of the problem. Therefore, the suggested elements (i.e. 'law' and 'competition') are explored against their *European* background. The objectives of the EU as reflected in the Treaty on European Union; the Treaty on the Functioning of the European Union (TFEU); case law; and judicial, political and doctrinal sources, are all seen as a common denominator of this project.

Having its conceptual roots in a deontological (non-consequentialist) approach to competition,[1] the normative aspects of this book should, however, be disassociated from the following two intuitive misunderstandings, which can be accordingly labelled as (i) *revisionism* and (ii) *syncretism.*

(i) Non-revisionism. The book *is* interested in the history of European competition law, and it *does* operationalise some important elements of the older doctrines, but it does *not* seek to revive any purely deontological theories of antitrust, acknowledging the inevitability of economic analysis of contemporary competition policy. Its aim is different: it seeks to provide a contemporary jurisprudential discourse for the analysis of competition law. The discourse is missing, inasmuch as in the current framework the very reference to *legal doctrine* in the context of competition law is ubiquitously perceived as a *legalistic doctrinarism.* The role of lawyers tends to be reduced to their technical expertise: how to communicate the economic *truth* to the legally (narrow-)minded judges. In this sense, the task of this book is to enrich the contemporary analysis of competition by implementing into it the valuable theoretical insights deduced from the jurisprudence. The insights are latently present, but they are seldom actualised in the domain of competition law. The following dilemma occurs: any attempt to implement the abundant experience of jurisprudence to the realm of competition policy faces the necessity to contemplate the specificity of the area, and one of such specificities is that the regulation of economic competition should not be based on anything but the economic rationale, which in turn rejects the richness of jurisprudence, as the latter brings different methodological apparatus and normative solutions to the economic problems. This book is committed to bridging these two realms.

(ii) Non-syncretism: The suggested bridging between the law and economics cannot form a happy medium: this *quae sunt Caesaris,*

---

[1] This terminology has been transposed from legal philosophy to competition law in Oles Andriychuk, 'Rediscovering the Spirit of Competition: On the Normative Value of the Competitive Process', Competition Law Journal, Vol. 6, No. 3, 2010.

> *Caesari* approach has failed and the current situation in antitrust is the consequence of such methodological holism. The dilemmatic nature of the problem cannot be solved by cherry-picking the best bits of economics and law. Such an uncritical *merger* would caricature the idea of interdisciplinarity. The epistemic borders of the disciplines cannot be eliminated. Instead, different accounts of the explored phenomena should be available. The book intentionally focuses on a jurisprudential account, being interested in the economic approaches only insofar as they are seen as *explananda* and not as *explanans*. This jurisprudential purism does not claim exclusivity, but it does claim universality: the non-exclusivity clause implies that alternative solutions for the competition problems are acknowledged; the universality clause means that a jurisprudential approach is able to offer a comprehensive account of the subject. Most of the discussions in the economic literature on the issues of competition policy have direct analogies in jurisprudential debates. These analogies, however, have not been systematically operationalised so far. The difference between the economic and the legal analysis is that the former is being widely used by both lawyers and economists, while the latter is available in the realm of competition only *ad marginem*, for purely formal purposes and most often ad hoc. The sporadic operationalisation of jurisprudence cannot make up the lacuna and often can, conversely, diminish its reliability. The methodological hypothesis is hence that, apart from economics, the discourse of competition law should benefit from the comprehensive implementation of the important aspects of jurisprudence into it. Such implementation does not eliminate the interdisciplinary aspects of the research inasmuch as the very phenomenon of competition is by its nature interdisciplinary (see the normative background of the research). In addition, in order to succeed, the jurisprudential account of competition law should be fully up to date on the economic merits of the issue, but such understanding of the economic aspects of competition should not eliminate its juristic nature. In other words, the main materials of the suggested bridge are norms-and-rights and not costs-and-benefits.

Any study on the nature of competition law inevitably requires the analysis of its three main components, namely: (i) the specificity of the phenomenon of competition itself; (ii) the essence of the law taken as a set of particular social norms; and (iii) political, economic and cultural interests of society which inherently predetermine application of any law. The first dimension reflects the *internal* nature of competition; the second dimension explores the *formal* requirements for its existence; the third dimension analyses on the *external* level the scope of its interaction with other societal interests in general as well as the scope of application, protection and promotion of competition in particular. From the systemic point of view these three aspects of competition law are both inseparably linked and mutually dependent. In practice they are hardly distinguishable at all, so long as the general preconditions of the *effective* performance of economic system (iii) require a coherent application of antitrust *law* (ii) which in its turn influences the very understanding of the *phenomenon* of competition (i).

Unlike in practice, from the positive, analytical, perspective the issues of the essence of competition, the nature of law and the broader interests of society are not necessarily strictly correlated to one another. Each of these three aspects of competition law can be explored in isolation. Arguably, this synthetic separation of 'competition', 'law' and its 'efficiency' can yield on the methodological side, inasmuch as this exercise helps to understand each of the three aspects of competition law in a deeper and more neutral way.

The structure of this study is designed in a way which reflects the three-dimensional nature of competition law as mentioned above. It implies that competition law will be explored from the *internal* perspective of competition; from the *formal* perspective of the law; and from the *external* perspective of politics. All three narratives are 'foreign languages' for one another. Therefore the issues related to their interaction will be specifically addressed too. The development of different narratives is a synthetic theoretical exercise. This implies that in order to maintain the consistency of each of the three dimensions, some arguments are presented in a refined, unconditional and uncritical manner. This reflects the methodology of the book. At some points it intentionally 'dives inside the boxes', striving to develop the logic of their functioning from an internal perspective only.

This 'inside the box thinking' can be criticised for its inability to look at the 'broader picture'. The issues of the 'broader picture', its constellation and the functioning of its elements are explored separately; they do not serve here their ordinary task of being a practical counterpoint to the theoretical analysis. They are not perceived as synchronisers or harmonisers of the internal self-centricity of the three narratives of competition law. Such 'broader picture' issues as 'common sense', 'practicality', 'general interests' or 'efficiency' will, on the contrary, be explored 'narrowly', as factors which are constantly influencing the internal functioning of different narratives, impelling them to abandon their self-centricity for the benefits of the general system. These 'broader picture' issues do not predetermine the purpose of this book, and they are not perceived as a common denominator or raison d'être for the existence of the internal narratives. The ability of the 'broader picture' issues to influence the internal narratives or the decision-making process in general is recognised and respected. Yet due to their *practical*, ad hoc nature, any *systematisation* in this respect is problematic and unrepresentative for the methodology which has been selected for this research. It is beyond its limits to explore the statistical or any other empirical instruments which are arguably able to systematise these factors. For this reason empiricism will be addressed as a phenomenon and will not be applied as a method or a universal remedy as it often appears to be from the practical perspective.

The following three terms require some preliminary clarification: *competitive process*; *welfare* and *social market economy*. At this point it should only be pointed out that the term 'competitive process' is ambivalent and does not fit perfectly for the theory of antitrust, and in particular for the purposes of the book. Linguistically its double meaning can cause misunderstanding. 'Competitive' is the adjective of both 'competition' and 'competitiveness', which, despite their similar etymological roots, characterise two different phenomena. In its first meaning, 'competitive' implies 'involving rivalry', in other words, the process which is central for competition itself. Its second meaning, however, is 'sufficiently low in price or high in quality to be successful against commercial rivals', or it reflects a mere *ability* to compete and does not require the existence of competition as such. While the term 'competitive process' itself makes sense predominantly in its first reading, such derivative phrases as 'competitive markets' or 'competitive environment' can have both meanings. For instance, the term 'competitive economy' can mean both the economy with competition as well as the economy which is strong enough to compete on the international level. The latter can be achieved without competition and to its detriment. It has been suggested elsewhere to use the term 'competitory',[2] which reflects the semantics of the term 'competition' more appropriately, however due to uncommonness thereof priority is afforded to the more usual term. The specificity of the term 'welfare' will be addressed in more details in the relevant chapter (4). It suffices to say now that in most of the cases it will be used in its generic, broad meaning, which implies health, happiness, prosperity and well-being in general. The meaning of the term 'social market economy' is also context dependent and it is also explored in Section 3.2.1, which analyses the origins of the European concept of competition. As a more general term it is used to describe the model in

---

2 Oles Andriychuk, 'Dialectical Antitrust: An Alternative Insight into the Methodology of the EC Competition Law Analysis in a Period of Economic Downturn', European Competition Law Review, Vol. 31, No. 4, 2010, p. 155.

which private market incentives are circumscribed by more general social public concerns, trying to coexist in a mutually enhancing way.

It will be argued that all the main approaches to antitrust policy and law can be divided in this respect into two rival groups. The pragmatic schools claim that the main or the central goal of competition should be measured by its broader impact on economic life. They perceive competition in its instrumental, applied sense and will be labelled 'utilitarian' or 'consequentialist'.[3] These approaches will be juxtaposed with those doctrines which claim that the competitive process itself constitutes an important societal value and should be protected regardless of (or at least without strong conjunction with) the economic outcomes which it can eventually deliver for society. These views are marked by the term 'deontological' (also known as the axiomatic[4] human rights-based approach). In other words, for the utilitarian schools the competitive process represents *a means*, whereas for the deontologists it constitutes *an end*.

The *rivalry* between these two approaches to competition is characterised by three interrelated elements which require some clarification. (1) Although the book tends to reflect all the main arguments and doctrinal points of different antitrust schools, it intentionally underlines – sometimes in an explicitly synthetic manner – these differences *between* and, conversely, does not fully explore the doctrinal discrepancies *within*, the two approaches. This method is used in order to illuminate the central point of the suggested taxonomy, which is the role of the competitive process in the economic life of society. It leaves on the periphery all other possible criteria for classification of different antitrust schools. (2) As will be argued below, it is acknowledged that all reasonable schools of law, economics and politics in one way or another recognise the importance of welfare and are in this sense utilitarian. Otherwise, the social legitimacy of these visions, let alone the seriousness of their authors, would be rightly challenged. The deontologists do not claim that the values or rules should be protected *only* for their own sake, as a kind of religious dogma. The rule-centred models are enhanced because they are finally beneficial for society, individuals or welfare. The genuine difference between the utilitarians and the deontologists is not that the former promote welfare and the latter

[3] Oles Andriychuk, 'Rediscovering the Spirit of Competition: On the Normative Value of the Competitive Process', Competition Law Journal, Vol. 6, No. 3, 2010.

[4] Roger Zäch and Adrian Künzler, 'Efficiency or Freedom to Compete? Towards an Axiomatic Theory of Competition Law', Zeitschrift für Wettbewerbsrecht, Vol. 7, No. 3, 2009, pp. 269–288.

do not. This statement will be correct *only* if these schools are scrutinised on the same level of abstraction: if under the *same* set of circumstances (institutional, factual, behavioural etc.) a certain action which is prohibited by formal rules should still be authorised or not. Only at this level is the comparison appropriate and might the statement be correct. The reason why the deontologists prefer rules over the eventual effectiveness of breaking them is finally predetermined exactly by the interests of common welfare but on the higher level of generalisation. This most general welfare-centred imperative is factored out of considerations altogether by the deontologists due to its repetitiveness and triviality. They concentrate their attention exactly on the situations when formal rules conflict with immediate interests of society or individuals, implying that the obedience to the rules is itself in the long-term interests of society and individuals. Therefore the deontological approach is often 'uncritically criticised' for its rigidity, formality and lack of sympathy to the *real* interests of society. The more detailed analysis of correlation between rules, principles and policies will be offered in the chapter which explores legal foundations of competition law. (3) The rivalry between the two approaches to the role of the competitive process in economic life is also articulated so explicitly in order to prove the effectiveness of the dialectical method of research. Its epistemological purpose is to instrumentalise the hidden potential of the productive conflict between the two subjects of interaction in order to generate added knowledge of the object of this research.

Despite the significant ideological, historical and methodological discrepancies of different deontological approaches to competition, they can supplement each other with respect to the general increase of the role of the competitive process in society. These schools perform their analysis concentrating on different elements of the phenomenon of competition and its interaction with other societal values and they operate with different theoretical premises and apparatus. In spite of this, however, the similarities of the deontological schools are more important than their differences for the theses which the book develops. An attempt is made to synthesise the main theoretical claims of the deontological schools in order to develop a more comprehensive argument in favour of protection and promotion of competition. This research acknowledges the *negative externalities* of such theoretical 'merger', recognising that the normative and ideological discrepancies between these schools combined with different historical contexts in which their arguments were developed require that the problem of their eventual synthesis be addressed with care.

The main hypothesis with regard to the issue of the normative importance of competition is that the competitive process as a social and natural phenomenon constitutes the essence of liberal democracy, which is perceived for the purposes of the book as a form of political self-organisation of people which bases their main common values on the principles of individual liberty, autonomy and humanism. The political aspects of competition are encompassed in the idea of elections, where different political parties *compete* with one another using their political programmes for the constituency. In the context of cultural relations, the idea of competition is embedded in the notion of free speech and pluralism. These values reflect the metaphor of the marketplace of ideas, in which different individual opinions and collective positions are freely circulated within society. The more diverse the society, the bigger the discrepancy between these ideas. This implies that they have to *compete* with each other for public and private acceptance in cultural spheres. In a broader context the same model can be traced in such areas as religion, psychoanalysis, sports and jurisprudence. Each of these four discourses is discussed in the respective sections of Chapter 4.

An independent public value of competition should not be taken as an absolute. Competition alone is neither a sufficient nor even a desirable means of economic and social governance. In a broader regulatory context it should be perceived only as one of many legitimate public goals and one among several ways to enhance societal welfare. The fact that competition cannot be taken as a universal remedy does not imply, however, that methodologically it should be perceived only in its applied instrumentalised sense. Its methodological disentanglement from other public values enables better understanding of its distinctive features, which are peculiar only to it and cannot be substituted by other societal phenomena.

This hypothesis is substantiated by application to the antitrust analysis of some comparative elements, perceiving economic competition from the perspective of psychology and psychoanalysis. The argument is that the competitive process should be treated as a driving force for entrepreneurial activities as 'a type of energy';[5] its enhancement implies provision of conditions which either increase the desire to compete or facilitate the very process of competition. The comparison with psychoanalysis is relevant in respect of its treatment of the problem of *libido* (psychic energy emanating from the individual) which, for the purposes of this research, is analogous to the entrepreneurial spirit of economic discovery. Although *libido* and natural instincts of a human being are never sufficient to develop a harmonious individuality, at the same time they are indispensable components of this creative process. *Libido* should be limited, but not

---

[5] Herbert J. Hovenkamp, 'The Antitrust Movement and the Rise of Industrial Organization', Texas Law Review, Vol. 68, No. 1, 1989, p. 144.

abandoned. It should be contextualised but not eliminated. The life of any human being which is governed solely by his instincts is unmanageable; no society can tolerate it even in principle. It is also meaningless, however, when the instincts are fully subordinated to purely rational interests of the individual or society in general. The second scenario can occur in antitrust when decision-makers try to eliminate the spontaneous order of the competitive instincts by circumscribing them to the rational interests of society entirely.

The book proceeds as follows. Following the general overview of the main topics in this introductory chapter, Chapter 2 looks at the historical evolution of the concept of competition and explores the phenomenon of competition from the perspective of economic theory. The third chapter analyses the conceptual foundations of the US and EU competition laws. The fourth chapter addresses the main theoretical background of the competitive process, comparing the role of competition in political, cultural and economic systems and developing the normative premises of the research. The fifth chapter concentrates on mechanics of balancing, which reflects the main methodological aspects of coexistence of competition with other economic and social values. In the sixth chapter the phenomenon of competition is explored from the broader legal theoretical perspective, contextualising the competitive process with the main theoretical problems of jurisprudence. It concentrates upon the jurisprudential aspects of the problem of balancing, trying to apply the techniques developed in the previous chapter to the legal discourse, with the purpose of demonstrating the significance of the competitive process not only in economic, political and cultural aspects, but also for the law itself. The final chapter explains the normative proposal which this analysis puts forward, explores its practical implications and summarises the main finding of the overall research.

2. The evolution of the economic concept of competition

For the first time the concept of competition was articulated with sufficient methodological precision as an important aspect of free market economy. However, long before the classicists, competition was perceived as an internal attribute and indispensable part of the economic process. The origins of the ideas of competition spring from two conceptual roots: natural sciences and social sciences. Both descend from the Ancient Greek and Roman philosophy and are embedded in several discourses: competition and the process of natural selection; competition and liberalism; competition and welfare. This chapter highlights the evolution of the main aspects of economic competition.

Due to its natural embeddedness into the broader idea of freedom, the concept of competition is not a linear development. Unlike such disciplines as physics, chemistry, medicine and most of the humanities, the philosophical problems of freedom and coercion represent a self-sufficient abstract area of knowledge which does not require the pre-existence of previously generated information in order to develop its arguments. It derives to a large extent from the individual experience and does not necessarily have to be based on the findings of its predecessors. This implies that the ideas of economic liberty can be articulated better in one historical period than in the others and the fluctuation of this intellectual development depends rather on a particular historical context than on the isolated evolution of the phenomenon itself, on the political and economic environment rather than on the intellectual continuity of the subject. In other words, apart from the secondary nuances, there is no such idea on freedom, which could not be generated in any particular period of time or which would absolutely depend on the discoveries of the previous generations. For this reason the cyclical, self-centred concepts (unlike the linear ones) can be analysed from the historical perspective either descriptively or constructively. The *descriptive* perspective would require a narrow definition of the period and territory of the studies and should confine the factual context which essentially defines the subject at issue. The *constructed* model, on the contrary, syncretises the ideas and the contexts, building up a narrative which, for the sake of consistency, intentionally prioritises one aspect over the others, providing an illusion of the linear, gradual development of the concept of economic freedom. In other words, the task of the former is to provide the *facts*, while the latter provides *stories*. The former is descriptive and objective, the latter is synthetic and subjective. The following sections take the second approach.

The traditional historiography of economic competition begins with tracing some economic ideas of ancient philosophy, going through the medieval period to early modernity, concentrating on the Enlightenment followed by the neoclassical and contemporary schools. This book will also follow this path without implying, however, the linearity of the development of the concept of economic competition. This retrospective overview therefore does not purport to serve as a comprehensive survey of the chronological development of the ideas of competition. Its task is to emphasise an intellectual connection between the origins of economic competition and the ideas of political liberty, necessary for the development of the normative argument of this research about the quintessential nature of the competitive process for the political system of liberal democracies.

2.1 ANCIENT ROOTS OF THE ECONOMIC CONCEPT OF COMPETITION

Ancient Greek and Roman thought have developed the premises for all the main contemporary intellectual doctrines of freedom, paying greater attention, however, to its individual or political aspects rather than economic ones. The general spirit of competition was perceived as 'the essential element in ancient Greek and especially Athenian culture'.[1] The process of rivalry is widely described in the antique mythology. The very idea of the Olympic Games can symbolically be taken as the quintessence of their respect for competition. However, the economic dimension of freedom was not articulated explicitly. Most of the thinkers of that time are characterised by their static views on competition. Economics and markets were perceived within the framework of strong government, which designed the rules and applied them for the benefit of society. For obvious historic reasons, the written sources generated at that time are rather sporadic and indirect.

---

[1] Bernard Knox, 'Always To Be Best: The Competitive Spirit in Ancient Greek Culture', The Professor John C. Rouman Classical Lecture Series, University of New Hampshire, Durham, 1999, www.helleniccomserve.com/images/Knox%20 Lecture.pdf, accessed on 4 August 2010, p. 1.

The concept of competition was understood rather in a social than in an economic context. This has been predetermined by the development of dialectical thinking and the creation of the concept of *eris* ('strife', 'discord') as reflected inter alia in the poems of Hesiod, which can be perceived as a prototype of competition.[2] Hesiod distinguishes between good and bad conflicts – the former should be promoted, the latter, reflected also in Greek mythology as the Golden apple of discord, should be avoided. He regards 'good conflicts' as 'a vital entrepreneurial force that often permits the surmounting of the big problems the shortage of resources poses'.[3] Thucydides was one of the first thinkers who applied in his economic reasoning the ideas of equilibrium, which has become the dominant rationale of understanding competition for neoclassical economics.[4] Xenophon was among the founders of the concept of economy of scale, public investments and the simulation of trade.[5] The ideas of market exchange were supported by the Sophists.

The ideas of Plato are more relevant to the philosophical foundations of dialectical competition and together with the concept of *eris* are explored in Chapter 4.1. Plato was the first to introduce the notion of free market of ideas.[6] In a narrow economic sense his ideas are relevant to the issues of public administration of the economy, the division of labour and the correlation between individual morality, rationality and economic efficiency, which jointly constitute a successful algorithm of economic performance.[7] Some authors disagree with the traditional perception of Plato's contribution to the idea of division of labour, submitting that 'while Plato recognizes both the economic and political benefits

---

2 William G. Thalmann, '"The Most Divinely Approved and Political Discord": Thinking about Conflict in the Developing Polis', Classical Antiquity, Vol. 23, No. 2, 2004, p. 359.

3 Jesus Huerta de Soto, 'Economic Thought in Ancient Greece', Mises Daily, 15 September 2010.

4 Todd Lowry, 'The Economic and Jurisprudential Ideas of the Ancient Greeks: Our Heritage from Hellenic Thought', in Todd Lowry and Barry Gordon (eds.), *Ancient and Medieval Economic Ideas and Concepts of Social Justice*, Brill Publishing, Leiden, 1998, p. 13.

5 ibid, p. 20.

6 William F. Campbell, 'The Free Market for Goods and the Free Market for Ideas in the Platonic Dialogues', History of Political Economy, Vol. 17, No. 2, 1985, p. 187.

7 Todd Lowry, 'The Economic and Jurisprudential Ideas of the Ancient Greeks: Our Heritage from Hellenic Thought', in Todd Lowry and Barry Gordon (eds.), *Ancient and Medieval Economic Ideas and Concepts of Social Justice*, Brill Publishing, Leiden, 1998, pp. 23–25.

of the division of labour, he ultimately critiques this form of economic arrangement'.[8] The reason for this criticism is based in Plato's preference for individual way of self-management, which would be undermined with the introduction of a conveyer belt-style of generation of wealth. In either case the contribution itself to the development of the idea of the division of labour in Plato's Dialogues is accepted by both parties to the discussion. Similarly, the main economic theses of Socrates' epistemology are also ethically centred. For Socrates, as Petrochilos observes, 'the study of economic issues becomes the study of the proper place of economic problems in relation to the human will'.[9]

For Aristotle the task of economic policy is in happiness maximisation, and Aristotelian thinking in this respect can be perceived as the beginning of the utilitarian perception of *good* competition, reflected inter alia in the notion of 'just price as a generalised norm'.[10] Aristotle's views are often criticised by the prominent economists for being too general.[11] This criticism, however, is usually based on misleading methodological premises, which assess the ancient texts by the yardstick of the contemporary apparatus.[12] Many economic historians, conversely, consider Aristotle's economic heritage to be '[t]he economically provocative analytic writing

---

[8] Daniel Silvermintz, 'Plato's Supposed Defense of the Division of Labor: A Reexamination of the Role of Job Specialization in the *Republic*', History of Political Economy, Vol. 42, No. 4, 2010, p. 767.

[9] George A. Petrochilos, '*Kalokagathia*: The Ethical Basis of Hellenic Political Economy and Its Influence from Plato to Ruskin and Sen', History of Political Economy, Vol. 34, No. 3, 2002, p. 600.

[10] David J. Gerber, 'Prometheus Born: Shaping the Relationship Between Law and Economic Conduct', St. Louis University Law Journal, Vol. 38, No. 3, 1994, pp. 717–720.

[11] Joseph A. Schumpeter, *History of Economic Analysis*, Routledge, London, 1994, p. 57: '[Aristotle's economic analysis was . . .] if such a thing may be said without offense of so great figure . . . decorous, pedestrian, slightly mediocre and more than slightly pompous common sense'. This rather unusual wording should be taken perhaps with a bit of irony, fairly common at that time. The review of Schumpeter's work written by the Chicago School economist Jacob Viner states, for instance, that: '[t]here is, as we shall see, much in this book which is redundant, irrelevant, cryptic, strongly biased, paradoxical, or otherwise unhelpful or even harmful to understanding. When all this is set aside, there still remains enough to constitute, by a wide margin, the most constructive, the most original, the most learned, and the most brilliant contribution to the history of the analytical phases of our discipline which has even been made' (Jacob Viner, 'Schumpeter's History of Economic Analysis', The American Economic Review, Vol. 44, No. 5, 1954, pp. 894–895).

[12] William Kern, 'Returning to the Aristotelian Paradigm: Daly and Schumacher', History of Political Economy, Vol. 15, No. 4, 1983, p. 506.

in ancient Greece'.[13] Others submit that the very existence of the economy as part of human knowledge before Aristotle is doubtful, attributing to Aristotle the very discovery of the subject,[14] acknowledging his intellectual contribution inter alia to the area of monetary policy and in particular his thesis on commoditisation of money.[15] In fact it was Aristotle who for the first time used the term 'monopoly' (though in a context which is different to the contemporary meaning).[16]

One of the main differences between the Greek and Roman traditions was the existence in Rome of a very mature system of contracts which constituted an important part of Roman law. Some Roman statutes regulated the establishment of excessive prices (e.g. *Edictum De Pretiis Rerum Venalium*), which reveals the concerns with competition problems, though the primary task of pre-competition regulation at that time was maintaining economic homogeneity between different parts of the Roman empire (a goal which is not that dissimilar to our contemporary 'market integration' task of competition law). This institutional framework played an important role in the transition from antiquity via scholasticism and natural philosophy to the classical economic theories and therefore the 'parallel ascent of Roman law and capitalism is indisputable'.[17] The economic aspects of competition were embedded in the notion of the stable system of markets, regulated by the state, which also provided predictability and uniformity of the application of law. In spite of the strong influence of Stoicism with its emphasis on the internal evaluation of content, 'the wise man alone is rich' (Cicero) and 'in what suffices no one is poor' (Plutarch) mottos, the economic concepts developed in Ancient Rome were analytically separated from morality. Historically, Roman law played a pivotal role in the development of the market process, which gradually evolved via the medieval period[18] into one of the important preconditions for the development of classical ideas on competition.

---

[13] Todd Lowry, 'Ancient and Medieval Economics', in Warren J. Samuels, Jeff E. Biddle, John B. Davis (eds.), *A Companion to The History of Economic Thought*, Blackwell Publishing, Oxford, 2003, p. 20.

[14] Karl Polanyi, 'Aristotle Discovers the Economy', in George Dalton (ed.), *Primitive, Archaic, and Modern Economics*, Doubleday, Garden City, 1968, pp. 78–115.

[15] Max Alter, 'Aristotle and the Metallist Tradition: A Note', History of Political Economy, Vol. 14, No. 2, 1982, p. 559.

[16] Raymond De Roover, 'Monopoly Theory Prior to Adam Smith: A Revision', The Quarterly Journal of Economics, Vol. 65, No. 4, 1951, p. 492.

[17] Odd Langholm, 'Economic Freedom in Scholastic Thought', History of Political Economy, Vol. 14, No. 2, 1982, p. 260.

[18] David J. Gerber, 'Prometheus Born: Shaping the Relationship Between Law and Economic Conduct', St. Louis University Law Journal, Vol. 38, No. 3, 1994,

The Ancient Greek and Roman – as well as the early Christian – thinkers contributed to the theorising of economic problems by developing the philosophical, scientific and cultural fundamentals for many generations ahead.[19] Their contribution in economic analysis, however, was not as remarkable as in other areas of social and natural sciences. Unlike in other areas of human knowledge, which often base not only their principles, but also their terminology on the Greek and Roman heritage, economic theory does it only indirectly.[20] This can be explained by the fact that most of the ancient economists were primarily philosophers. Economic theory was not separated from philosophy and public administration. In addition, the division among the secular and religious spheres of knowledge was not as explicit at that time as it became after the Renaissance. The ancient philosophers therefore were, to a large extent, predetermined by the ethical ideas of individual life, often developed as prescriptive normative systems, in which trade and the entrepreneurial spirit of individuals was often associated with a trade-off between living a morally and religiously good life and living a prosperous life. The commitment of individual interests to these societal values of the higher order has been perceived as a more important task than generation of material wealth.

As Perrotta observes, 'in all pre-modern Western thought, hostility to increased consumption is nearly always linked to or confused with the condemnation of the desire to get rich'.[21] This is partially explained by the agrarian nature of their economies, which implies the closed static nature

---

pp. 690–691: 'By the eleventh century the corpus of Roman law had been largely forgotten in the West, . . . but in about 1075 in . . . Bologna the texts of Roman law . . . began to be systematically and intensively studied as part of the process of responding to commercialisation and urbanisation'.

19 David J. Gerber, 'Prometheus Born: Shaping the Relationship Between Law and Economic Conduct', St. Louis University Law Journal, Vol. 38, No. 3, 1994, p. 691: 'The objective of Roman law study was . . . to generate an enlightened body of knowledge about how to order society'.

20 Joseph A. Schumpeter, *History of Economic Analysis*, Routledge, London, 1994, p. 52: '[R]udimentary economic analysis is a minor element . . . in the inheritance that has been left to us by our cultural ancestors, the ancient Greeks. [Unlike their mathematics and geometry, their astronomy, mechanics, optics] their economics failed to attain independent status or even a distinctive label: their *Oeconomicus* (οἶκος, house, and νόμος law or rule) meant only the practical wisdom of household management. . . . They merged their pieces of economic reasoning with their general philosophy and rarely dealt with an economic topic for its own sake'.

21 Cosimo Perrotta, 'The Legacy of the Past: Ancient Economic Thought on Wealth and Development', The European Journal of the History of Economic Thought, Vol. 10, No. 2, 2003, p. 180.

of their production cycle. The agrarian mindset dominated even polis mentality. According to Silvermintz's interpretation of Xenophon, '[e]ven in a city as developed as Athens, the self-sufficient farm . . . remained the dominant economic unit during this period'.[22] This is the reason why even such *utilitarian* schools of ancient thought as Hedonists and Epicureans emphasised an internal, self-generated benchmark of measuring pleasure and were not as much interested in the public aspects of economic life. Indeed the internal measure of things is very characteristic of the Greek perception of happiness, which considers that both poverty and wealth are 'inner dimensions of man'.[23] Therefore the intellectual contribution of that period to the development of economic aspects of competition has been made rather indirectly by articulating philosophical aspects of this phenomenon.

2.2 THE IDEAS OF ECONOMIC COMPETITION BEFORE THE LATE 18TH CENTURY

The role of the competitive process in economic life was not articulated very explicitly in the writings of the scholars of this long period following antiquity. The evolution of economic theory was rather slow and indirect; this period, however, played its own important role too.[24] The medieval mindset was predetermined by the monistic perception of the universe with its strong monarchic and religious imperatives. The term 'economy' was still used predominantly in its original Greek 'housekeeping' sense, applicable mostly to the commercial bookkeeping context and other applied arithmetic areas. Before the rise of capitalism, the role of the universities as places for generating innovative ideas in economic thinking was rather scholastic and apologetic than inventive and critical. This,

[22] Daniel Silvermintz, 'Plato's Supposed Defense of the Division of Labor: A Reexamination of the Role of Job Specialization in the *Republic*', History of Political Economy, Vol. 42, No. 4, 2010, p. 761.

[23] Cosimo Perrotta, 'The Legacy of the Past: Ancient Economic Thought on Wealth and Development', The European Journal of the History of Economic Thought, Vol. 10, No. 2, 2003, p. 191: 'So the real way to avoid poverty (i.e. the sense of privation) and to obtain wealth (i.e. to feel satisfied) is to limit one's needs and one's desires'.

[24] David Levy, 'Rational Choice and Morality: Economics and Classical Philosophy', History of Political Economy, Vol. 14, No. 1, 1982, p. 1: 'Although a study of pre-Smithian economics is often regarded as decorative at best, it illuminates very well the methodological framework of modern economic theory, i.e., how theory is related to reality'.

however, does not diminish the role of academia as well as such Western institutions as religion, ethics and philosophy in influencing the development of the principles of market economy.[25]

Proto-utilitarian economic reasoning can be found in the works of St. Thomas Aquinas, particularly in his perception of private property. In a rather Aristotelian spirit he considered the institution of private possession to be desirable for society in general, because of the natural ability of people to be more careful with their own property than with public property. The writings of St. Thomas Aquinas as well as other scholiasts against the background of the broader philosophical ideas developed by moral philosophers created an intellectual premise for the development of economic liberalism.[26]

Respect for private property jointly with the development of relatively large-scale companies led to the establishment of more mature industrial relationships. The idea of the competitive process evolved naturally with the increase in demand and with the extension of potential markets. However, this process evolved rather sporadically. At the initial stages it was predetermined by '"monopolistic" policies and business practices that were one of the chief topics of the economic literature of that period'.[27] It was the first time that the ideas of monopoly were critically examined by economic scholarship.[28] Almost immediately with the development of the phenomenon of monopolies, the term received a negative connotation. As Schumpeter observes, 'monopoly came to denote almost anything that a man disliked about capitalist practice'.[29] Therefore, the ideas of competition evolved in this respect as a negative concept, which explains the strength and dominance of the *preventive* interpretation of competition

---

[25] David J. Gerber, 'Prometheus Born: Shaping the Relationship Between Law and Economic Conduct', St. Louis University Law Journal, Vol. 38, No. 3, 1994, p. 675: '[The relationship between law and economic conduct] was generated in response to the first great wave of market forces that transformed European society during the twelfth and thirteenth centuries'.

[26] Wilhelm Röpke, 'Liberalism and Christianity', Modern Age, Vol. 1, No. 2, 1957, pp. 129–130: 'A précis of liberalism could be written using only the orations of Cicero, the *Corpus Juris*, and the *Summa* of Aquinas; it would be vividly contemporary'.

[27] Joseph A. Schumpeter, *History of Economic Analysis*, Routledge, London, 1994, p. 150.

[28] David J. Gerber, 'Prometheus Born: Shaping the Relationship Between Law and Economic Conduct', St. Louis University Law Journal, Vol. 38, No. 3, 1994, p. 723.

[29] Joseph A. Schumpeter, *History of Economic Analysis*, Routledge, London, 1994, p. 155.

law and the rise of its *proactive* aspects only as a justification of *liberalisation* policies and authorisation of mergers in contemporary antitrust.

The transitory stage from the feudal to capitalistic perception of the economy was accompanied by broader cultural transformations. This period was characterised by further elaboration of the idea of economic freedom, which was considered as a natural way to achieve good economic performance. For instance, for the physiocrats who insisted on self-sufficiency of the agrarian economic model, the institute of private property and economic liberty (freedom of exchange, of entry and of competition)[30] were among the main prerequisites of economic governance. Viner observes that the intellectual heritage of physiocrats was 'a curious blend of the myth of a beneficent physical order of nature, of Hobbesism, of Cumberland's and Cartesian rationalism, and of some fresh and important economic analysis of the coordinating, harmonizing, and organizing function of free competition'.[31] Unlike traditional utilitarian reasoning, the physiocracy is a combination of welfare and imperative-based 'ought' arguments.[32] Their views on the relations between states and markets were rather laissez-faire, and their perception of competition was respectively natural and organic. Christensen, analysing the ideas of one of the precursors of the physiocracy, Pierre Le Pesant, sieur de Boisguilbert, observes his 'powerful recognition of the beneficial effects of economic competition. But competition's positive role depends on the active hand of nature, which alone can bring order to the whole'.[33] The ideas of physiocrats can be seen in this respect as a reference to the natural, organic elements of competition and the invisible hand of the markets.

The general hostility towards monopolies was not only of an ethical or practical nature. As the development of the mercantilist ideas reveals, it was also very pragmatic, selective and Machiavellian (in as much as Machiavelli himself is associated with the mercantilist tradition in politics). Thus, according to the mercantilists, the monopolies were harmful only on the domestic level. At the international stage they were beneficial and

---

30 Joseph J. Spengler, 'The Physiocrats and Say's Law of Markets. II', The Journal of Political Economy, Vol. 53, No. 4, 1945, p. 328.

31 Jacob Viner, 'The Intellectual History of Laissez-Faire', Journal of Law and Economics, Vol. 3, No. 1, 1960, p. 59.

32 Warren J. Samuels, 'The Physiocratic Theory of Economic Policy', The Quarterly Journal of Economics, Vol. 76, No. 1, 1962, p. 148.

33 Paul P. Christensen, 'Epicurean and Stoic Sources for Boisguilbert's Physiological and Hippocratic Vision of Nature and Economics', History of Political Economy, Vol. 35, No. 5 (annual supplement), 2003, p. 125.

required the support of the state.[34] The mercantilist approach (reflected later on in the concept of *dirigisme*)[35] embraces the dominance of the interests of state at the international level, as well as the cartelised structure of the main industries at the domestic level with strong emphasis on collective interests over the interests of individuals. At the national level monopolies and restrictive practices were encouraged due to their potential protectionist effects. The economic power of guilds implied strong control mechanisms over the principles of competition.[36] Monopolies were also tolerated in the area of intellectual property.[37] The economic essence of guilds can be seen as a compromise between the monopoly and free competition. Although often tolerated, '[c]ity governments generally opposed the monopolistic practices of guilds'.[38] It has been accepted that the cartelised industries enable sufficient protection of their participants against the interference of the state.[39] However, as Dabbah indicates,[40] in some countries, especially in the UK, the negative perception of monopoly can be traced back at least to the late 16th century. Jones notes that '[t]he history of Anglo-Saxon peoples discloses an undying hostility toward monopoly'.[41]

---

34 William H. Page, 'Ideological Conflict and the Origins of Antitrust Policy', Tulane Law Review, Vol. 66, No. 1, 1991, p. 25: 'The mercantilist system that Adam Smith attacked in 1776 . . . was strongly interventionalist in international trade; and in private commercial relations'.

35 David J. Gerber and Richard Azarnia, 'Dirigisme and the Challenge of Competition Law in France', Cardozo Journal of International & Comparative Law, Vol. 9, No. 1, 1995, p. 11.

36 Thomas B. Nachbar, 'Monopoly, Mercantilism & the Politics of Regulation', University of Virginia Law School, Public Law and Legal Theory Working Paper Series, No. 32, 2005, p. 6.

37 An Act concerning Monopolies and Dispensations with Penal Laws and the forfeitures thereof, 1624, 21 Jac.I, c.3.

38 David J. Gerber, 'Prometheus Born: Shaping the Relationship Between Law and Economic Conduct', St. Louis University Law Journal, Vol. 38, No. 3, 1994, p. 730.

39 Thomas B. Nachbar, 'Monopoly, Mercantilism & the Politics of Regulation', University of Virginia Law School, Public Law and Legal Theory Working Paper Series, No. 32, 2005, pp. 43–44: 'Closed markets were such a widely accepted part of the economic structure – and so different was the economic theory from today's dominant laissez-faire tradition – that those who were accused of being monopolists frequently defended themselves on the ground that they were actually oligopolists'.

40 Maher M. Dabbah, *The Internationalisation of Antitrust Policy*, Cambridge University Press, Cambridge, 2003, p. 32.

41 Franklin D. Jones, 'Historical Development of the Law of Business Competition', The Yale Law Journal, Vol. 35, No. 8, 1926, p. 905.

The period reviewed covers over a thousand years, reflecting many intellectual traditions, contexts and landscapes. Its main task was to provide some historical background concerning the times which preceded the development of classical economic theories of liberalism with their specific approach to the issues of individual economic freedom and competition. The dominating evolutionary narrative on the historical development of competition often limits this process to the reduction of power of the state.[42] The history of economic thought does prove that these two processes are in direct correlation and to a large extent are in causal relations too. However, this does not cover the whole spectrum of interconnections between state and competition. As has been shown, there are also some examples of an active state encouraging competition, promoting its economic virtue for the benefits of the citizens.

In spite of the concurrent evolution of the ideas of natural law, social contract and humanism, the development of the economic aspects of competition has proceeded rather sporadically and with no or minimal reference to natural rights. This can serve as an argument in favour of the *creationist* as opposed to the *evolutionary* view on the development of competition. Creationists argue that the ideas of economic freedom are not natural, organic (as is the case with the first generation of human rights), but rather reflect a certain evolutionary stage of human economic relations. The ideas of economic competition were 'discovered' and praised among the quintessential economic freedoms not necessarily due to their natural inevitability, but jointly with the establishment of the principles of humanistic ethics with its strong adherence to the ideas of individualism. This process reflects the historical maturity of those societies which discovered and adopted these ideas. The strong elements of spontaneity of the competitive process were first protected, supported and encouraged by the institutional systems of the societies in which the authority of state was limited but strong. The ideas of protection of freedom therefore can be developed not exclusively within the laissez-faire tradition. The protection of individual freedom can also be considered within the framework of active government too. An *either-or* perception of the state–market relationship often proves to be ideologically speculative and does not reflect the historical evolution of the market institutions. Such reductionist positions are often harmful for competition itself, portraying this phenomenon

---

42 Michael Perelman, 'Classical Political Economy and Primitive Accumulation: the Case of Smith and Steuart', History of Political Economy, Vol. 15, No. 3, 1983, p. 451: 'The story of classical political economy is often told as the tale of the gradual recognition of the eternal truths of laissez-faire.'

as a direct analogy with Social Darwinism and describing its supporters as representatives of 'the fittest'. This *zero-sum* contraposition[43] limits the ability to promote the ideas of free competition on a broader societal level and can be held partly responsible for the situation in which the ideological rigidity of the concept of competition impelled the substitution of its original individualistic meaning by the benchmark of consumer or total welfare performed in order to provide some social *convertibility* of the concept among the broader values of liberal democracies. The next historical period reflects one of the most fruitful stages of evolution of the modern perception of economic competition and provides a conceptual background for the polyvalent nature of competition highlighted in this section.

2.3 THE ROLE OF COMPETITION IN THE CLASSICAL ECONOMIC THEORIES

This period is characterised by the development of theoretical foundations of economic competition, which were contextualised vis-à-vis the regulatory frameworks afterwards via the first generation of competition laws. The ideas of free markets were developing in two different dimensions: domestic and international. These were not necessarily in conformity with each other. Those who advocated free international trade originated predominantly from the countries with an economically successful colonial past or the countries in which the dominant industries were on a very competitive level vis-à-vis their foreign counterparts. These ideas were fairly pragmatic. For the supporters of free trade and competition on the domestic level the ideas of economic progress represented only one – although decisive – part of the argument. The second was based on the ethical premises of individual freedom and human rights developed by the great philosophers and political activists of that time in particular Mill, Bentham and Locke. The ethical premises of free market do not negate their eventual positive impact on the economy, but this impact is secondary and ancillary. The evolution of the ideas of free competition therefore

---

43 Jeremy Bentham, 'Anarchical Fallacies: Being an examination of the Declaration of Rights issued during the French Revolution', 1843 http://oll.libertyfund.org/titles/bentham-the-works-of-jeremy-bentham-vol-2, accessed on 12 March 2011, par. 340: 'As against the coercion applicable by individual to individual, no liberty can be given to one man but in proportion as it is taken from another. All coercive laws, therefore . . . and in particular all laws creative of liberty, are, as far as they go, abrogative of liberty'.

should be perceived as a combination of both utilitarian and deontological movements, which despite their conflicting nature often reinvigorate each other. The utilitarian perception of competition should not be reduced to the ideas of utilitarian philosophy developed by the great English and Scottish philosophers of that time.[44] Some parts of the philosophy of utilitarianism encompass strong deontological imperatives/obligations and imply that the achievement of utility/happiness can sometimes be made via their temporal limitation or reduction. In general, as Budzinski puts it, 'in classical economics, the notion of competition remains rather intuitive and close to its semantic understanding'.[45]

The main narrative of classical economic liberalism, with its powerful metaphor of the 'invisible hand', was provided by Smith in his landmark *An Inquiry into the Nature and Causes of the Wealth of Nations*,[46] though he himself, being primarily a philosopher, acknowledged more his first, rather general piece *The Theory of Moral Sentiments*.[47] According to Skinner, 'Smith recognised that pursuit of wealth and "place" was a basic human drive that would involve sacrifices likely to be supported by the approval of the spectator'.[48] This human feature had become an implicit motto of a bourgeois ideology. One of the main attributes of Smith's ideology was creating by synthesizing. He was in this respect '*the* great eclectic. He drew upon all previous knowledge in developing his doctrine of a harmonious order in nature manifesting itself through the instincts of the individual man'.[49] The analogy between societal and biological

---

[44] Schumpeter in his peculiar strict and fairly unreserved manner describes the essence of utilitarianism as follows: 'Evidently, the "calculus of pleasure and pain" and the principle of "greatest happiness for the greatest number" do not, in themselves, assert anything about specifically philosophical or epistemological problems, though they are capable of producing an ethical doctrine. The reason why this speculative deficiency of utilitarianism was not more keenly felt was that utilitarians found what they wanted ready at hand in the empiricist tradition of the Locke-Hume type' (Joseph A. Schumpeter, *History of Economic Analysis*, Routledge, London, 1994, pp. 407–408).

[45] Oliver Budzinski, 'Monoculture versus Diversity in Competition Economics', Cambridge Journal of Economics, Vol. 32, No. 2, 2008, p. 297.

[46] Adam Smith, *An Inquiry into the Nature and Causes of the Wealth of Nations*, Edwin Cannan (ed.), Methuen & Co, London, 1904.

[47] Adam Smith, *The Theory of Moral Sentiments*, Prometheus Books, Amherst, 2000.

[48] Andrew S. Skinner, 'Adam Smith (1723–1790): Theories of Political Economy', in Warren J. Samuels, Jeff E. Biddle, John B. Davis (eds.), *A Companion to The History of Economic Thought*, Blackwell Publishing, Oxford, 2003, p. 96.

[49] Jacob Viner, 'Adam Smith and Laissez Faire', The Journal of Political Economy, Vol. 35, No. 2, 1927, p. 199.

self-maintaining organisms implies that the 'deistic notion of a "natural order"'[50] was the basis of Smith's perception of the competitive process. In the pre-classical period the beneficial aspects of the *ability* to compete were predominantly discussed in the vertical 'state–individual' dimension. The horizontal aspects of the problem (competition *between* individuals) which constitute the core of antitrust were mentioned only sporadically. In the classical period the horizontal narrative of competition was discussed more widely. Smith suggests that the 'price of monopoly is upon every occasion the highest which can be got. The natural price, or the price of free competition, on the contrary, is the lowest which can be taken, not upon every occasion, indeed, but for any considerable time together',[51] considering all the restrictions of competition as having an effect similar to the price of monopolies (though to a proportionally smaller extent). Competition is perceived as 'an inherently lively process',[52] with clear parallels to the rivalry where the incentives of competitors stimulate the actor to advance his skills and techniques.

Smith develops his ideas on competition in his famous passage that '[p]eople of the same trade seldom meet together . . . but the conversation ends in a conspiracy against the public, or in some contrivance to raise prices'.[53] Mill was of a similar view too.[54] Eucken agrees: '[w]hy should three bakers in a 13th century town compete with one another'?[55] However, in the second part of the same paragraph Smith suggests that it is 'impossible indeed to prevent such meetings, by any law which either could be executed, or would be consistent with liberty and justice. But though the law cannot hinder people of the same trade from sometimes

---

50 Wolfgang Kerber and Ulrich Schwalbe, 'Economic Principles of Competition Law', in Günther Hirsch, Frank Montag and Franz Jürgen Säcker (eds.), *Competition Law: European Community Practice and Procedure – Article-by-Article Commentary*, Sweet & Maxwell, London, 2008, p. 217.

51 Adam Smith, *An Inquiry into the Nature and Causes of the Wealth of Nations*, Vol. 2, Edwin Cannan (ed.), Methuen & Co, London, 1904, p. 8.

52 Oliver Budzinski, 'Monoculture versus Diversity in Competition Economics', Cambridge Journal of Economics, Vol. 32, No. 2, 2008, p. 297.

53 Adam Smith, *An Inquiry into the Nature and Causes of the Wealth of Nations*, Vol. 1, Edwin Cannan (ed.), Methuen & Co, London, 1904, p. 130.

54 John S. Mill, *Principles of Political Economy*, University of Toronto Press, 1965, p. 142: 'Where competitors are so few they always end up agreeing not to compete'.

55 Walter Eucken, 'Die Wettbewerbsordnung und ihre Verwirklichung', Jahrbuch für die Ordnung von Wirtschaft und Gesellschaft, Vol. 2, 1949, cited in Christian Ahlborn, Carsten Grave (trans.), Walter Eucken, 'The Competitive Order and its Implementation', Competition Policy International, Vol. 2, No. 2, 2006, p. 222.

assembling together, it ought to do nothing to facilitate such assemblies; much less to render them necessary.'[56] This implies that the quintessential role of the freedom of contract as a part of the broader freedom to compete had been recognised at that time. The harmfulness of cartels is balanced with the rights of free economic associations, implying that the latter *can* prevail over the former. Obviously, this outcome of the balancing act reflects the situation in 19th-century capitalist societies. Nowadays the balancing pendulum moves significantly towards prohibition of such anticompetitive conduct.

In regard to the term *justice* used by Smith in this passage, the dominant view is that Smith refers to the *commutative*, meritocratic aspect of justice, leaving aside issues related to the *distributive*, egalitarian justice.[57] Others recognising that Smith pays particular attention to the commutative elements of justice submit that at the same time 'distributive justice emerges as an important normative concern in his political economy',[58] explaining that Smith perceived the ideas of distributive justice as an important distinction between his theory and those of feudalism and mercantilism, which on the contrary support the commutative aspects of justice. The reference to the commutative aspects of justice as an obstacle to prohibition of cartels would imply strong adherence to the ideas of individual freedom of contract. The distributive justice interpretation, conversely, would emphasise the substantial importance of communitarian interests, related to competition – of both utilitarian (as being most effective) and deontological (as being fair to the real and potential competitors) nature. The former takes competition as freedom from state regulation, the latter perceives it rather as a freedom from collusive practices and abuse of dominance related to the weaker economic actors. Smith in general was sceptical of the ability of the state to regulate competition. The monopoly problem was reduced by him to two main instances: guild corporations and the great stock exchange trading companies.[59]

The ideas of marginal utility developed in the 19th century by English

---

[56] Adam Smith, *An Inquiry into the Nature and Causes of the Wealth of Nations*, Vol. 1, Edwin Cannan (ed.), Methuen & Co, London, 1904, p. 130.

[57] Knud Haakonssen, *The Science of a Legislator: The Natural Jurisprudence of David Hume and Adam Smith*, Cambridge University Press, Cambridge, 1981, p. 99.

[58] Jeffrey T. Young and Barry Gordon, 'Distributive Justice as a Normative Criterion in Adam Smith's Political Economy', History of Political Economy, Vol. 28, No. 1, 1996, p. 24.

[59] George J. Stigler, 'The Economists and the Problem of Monopoly', The American Economic Review, Vol. 72, No. 2, 1982, p. 1.

and Austrian marginalists significantly extended the perception of the market process. The ideas of marginalists were based on the utilitarian foundations of Bentham, who conceptualised the benchmark of the utility in respect to happiness. According to one of the founders of English marginalism, Jevons, the main principle of marginalist theory is 'the coefficient of utility', which can vary depending on the subjective preferences of the individual and is therefore volatile. Jevons submits that '[a]mount of utility corresponds to amount of pleasure produced. But the continued uniform application of a useful object to the senses or the desires will not commonly produce uniform amounts of pleasure.'[60] The principle of marginal utility became one of the important topics in which different *subjectivist* and *inductive* economic schools disagreed with the *universal* and *deductive* principles of mainstream equilibrium economics.

The development of the concept of marginal utility is of particular importance to the problem of balancing of different values. The dilemmas of in-/commensurability of values are represented in the economic domain through the problem of marginal utility. The theory reveals that not only do values possess *objective* attributes, but their rate is rather volatile and can change depending on ad hoc context. Jevons universalises this economic law to 'each kind of object and more or less to each individual'[61] and suggests that the coefficient of utility can be mathematically calculated. He proposes in this respect the theory of exchange which is deduced from the 'laws of utility', suggesting that despite its incalculability on the individual level the coefficient utility is deducible according to the principles of statistics by the method of average.

Addressing the problem of quantification, Jevons recognises that utility reflects *quality* of things, emphasising, however, that this quality is not '*inherent quality*'.[62] He perceives it rather as '*a circumstance of things* arising out of their relation to man's requirements'.[63] This relativises the idea of objective quality of utility, 'the fruit ungathered for want of consumers, have no utility at all'.[64] The act of political balancing between different values can be perceived from this perspective as a precise definition of which portion of utility constitutes the highest value and cannot be

---

60 William S. Jevons, 'Brief Account of a General Mathematical Theory of Political Economy', Journal of the Royal Statistical Society, Vol. 29, No. 3, 1866, p. 283.

61 ibid.

62 William S. Jevons, *The Theory of Political Economy*, Macmillan and Co., London, 1888, p. 43 (emphasis in the original).

63 ibid.

64 ibid.

sacrificed for the benefits of other values in the situation of the necessity to make constant choices between them. It is important that each utility has its own *internal* scale of measurement which can be contextualised only as a second consecutive step. From this perspective, the competitive process itself cannot be measured by its positive effects for consumers, because this is already a second step, the step of balancing, not the step of definition.

The application of the principle of marginal utility to the balancing act has also been explored by another prominent economist of that time, Marshall, who stressed the importance of the 'balancing of advantages' in the theory of decision-making.[65] Marshall elaborates the thesis of balancing, paying attention to the internal nature of value. Unlike Jevons, his reliance on a mathematical explanation of the problems of marginal utility was not as unequivocal. The relevance of these principles as developed by the marginalists goes beyond pure economic analysis and experimental economics, covering also political aspects of the decision-making process. Since marginal utility is not constant, it cannot represent the value as a whole, which implies that marginal utility embraces only a fluctuating, external aspect of the value, which often does not reflect the essence of the value as such.

Another branch of marginalism was developed by the founders of the Austrian school of economic analysis. It articulated the emphasis of the marginalists on the subjective aspect of decision-making, exploring such categories as limited knowledge, time and uncertainty. These subjective, unpredictable characteristics of the markets to some extent mitigate each other, creating a self-governed economic order (known also by Hayek's term *spontaneous order*). The marginalist theories develop substantial arguments against the concept of an active state, revealing that relationships at the individual level are better governed directly by their actors rather than by a big state. The economic law of competition between individuals is considered by the Austrians to be the only reasonable treatment for dealing with all these asymmetries.

A view on the nature of economic competition which can be seen as an alternative insight on its development in the liberal tradition was presented by Marx. He disentangled competition from its purely individualistic exchange aspects, submitting that the provisions for the existence of competition should not be limited to the absence of governmental or private constraints and the availability of a significant number of buyers and

[65] Peter Groenewegen, 'English Marginalism: Jevons, Marshall, Pigou', in Warren J. Samuels, Jeff E. Biddle and John B. Davis (eds.), *A Companion to The History of Economic Thought*, Blackwell Publishing, Oxford, 2003, p. 251.

sellers on the market. For Marx competition was embedded in a 'labour–capital' dimension, which implies that competition between companies is only a derivative of the primary stage of competition – competition between labour force and capital. Due to the fact that labour forces are impossible to monopolise, the idea of protecting competition was seen as meaningless because there is nothing which can significantly encroach into it. From this doctrinal stage there were two potential directions for the following development of the theory of competition: laissez-faire and planned economy with conglomeration of private property under public economic control. Because genuine competition is competition between labour and capital, competition between producers (i.e. competition within the capital sector) does not represent a real value for the state, being a redundant and unnecessary act of particularism. Therefore states should not spend their resources on the limitation of freedom of contracts, enabling free unrestricted competition (laissez-faire) because there is no value in protecting competition between capitals. This aspect of competition is seen as redundant and instead of reconciling the interests of supply and demand it creates bigger conflicts within capitals. Therefore states should act in the interests of labour. According to this approach, the higher the concentration of capital, the better the positions of labour regarding its competition with capital and therefore such practices as nationalisation, expropriation and planned economy are in conformity with this scenario, enabling accumulation of property in the centralised collective authority.

Marx perceived the phenomena of competition and monopoly in their correlation, submitting that '[i]n present-day economic life you will find, not only competition and monopoly, but also their synthesis'.[66] This connection reveals that competition invigorates monopolies (the fittest eventually achieve dominance) and monopolies constitute the driving force for competition 'which sets the economic mechanism in motion'[67] (being the subjective purpose of the participants of competition). These ideas are consonant with the libertarian perceptions of the potential competition being as important as the real one. While the positions of two parts are diametrical, the premises are comparable (they seem to agree upon what to disagree). Marx claims that one phenomenon is impossible without the other and that those who want 'competition without the

[66] Karl Marx, 'Letter to Pavel Vasilyevich Annenkov', in *Marx Engels Collected Works*, Vol. 38, International Publishers, 1975, http://www.hekmatist.com/Marx%20Engles/Marx%20&%20Engels%20Collected%20Works%20Volume%2038_%20Ka%20-%20Karl%20Marx.pdf, accessed 1 December 2010.

[67] Robert Liefmann, 'Monopoly and Competition as the Basis of a Government Trust Policy', Quarterly Journal of Economics, Vol. 29, No. 2, 1915, p. 323.

pernicious consequences of competition . . . all want the impossible, i.e. the conditions of bourgeois existence without the necessary consequences of those conditions'.[68] Apart from the historically problematic aspects of Marx's alternative, it is also disputable conceptually, since by perceiving the natural *dilemmatic* conflict he tries essentially to *solve* it, rather than to put it on a higher dialectical level, introducing the balancing between the mechanics of competition and the non-market interests, which itself continues the natural competitive process in a broader conceptual sense. Marx's contrapuntal views, however, provide a significant antithesis for the embrace of the phenomenon of competition as a self-sufficient mechanism for regulation of economic, as well as political and cultural aspects of societal relations.

One of the most influential methodological prerequisites of modern antitrust theory has its conceptual roots in the doctrine of historicism. Alongside positive and normative analysis, the historical approach constitutes the indispensable part of the theory of competition. Due to its methodological nature, the doctrine of historicism is universal in its application, though in its substantive part, conversely, it stresses the importance of particularities, contexts and societal institutions,[69] and overall emphasises the inductive method of analysis. The development of German, French and English historical schools of economics as well as jurisprudence reveals the understanding of the necessity of taking into account the significant influence of the historical and cultural context on theorisation of economic affairs. This approach juxtaposes the common trend towards universalisation and mathematisation of economic knowledge, which played a pivotal role in the development of contemporary economics,[70] having direct repercussions on the perception of competition

---

68 Letter from Marx to Pavel Vasilyevich Annenkov, in *Marx Engels Collected Works*, Vol. 38, International Publishers, 1975, http://www.hekmatist.com/Marx%20Engles/Marx%20&%20Engels%20Collected%20Works%20Volume%2038_%20Ka%20-%20Karl%20Marx.pdf, accessed 1 December 2010.

69 Herbert J. Hovenkamp, 'The First Great Law & Economics Movement', Stanford Law Review, Vol. 42, No. 4, 1990, p. 1014: 'The institutionalists believed that ideology, technology, history, habit, previous investment, and lack of information or difficulty in communication drive both individual human motivation and institutional structure. According to the institutionalists, economics could not generalize about the behavior of business firms or other organizations, or even about the influence of particular sets of legal concepts such as contract or property. Each had its own motives and working rules, which required individual study'.

70 Avery W. Katz, 'Positivism and the Separation of Law and Economics', Michigan Law Review, Vol. 94, No. 7, 1996, p. 2242: 'Mathematical modelling has

and market process.[71] One of the main postulates of the historical schools is that 'individuals are influenced by motives that cannot be quantitatively measured'.[72]

This period is also characterised by the subsequent theorisation and systematisation of economic knowledge in general and the ideas of competition specifically. The development by Torrens and Ricardo of the principle of comparative advantage was an additional argument in favour of free international trade as well as competition. It relativises the advantages of the fittest, creating conditions for harmonious development. Therefore, on the domestic level, the application of this principle increases collective long-term considerations over the individual expectations of immediate gains. Competition policy receives within this framework the necessary theoretical background for justification of collective actions directed to the designing of economic rules, which, apart from recognising the fundamentals of private property and freedom of contract, enable real and potential participation in the competitive game for many companies which would be prevented from it otherwise without the principle of comparative advantage.

The history of economic thought also categorises the variety of other schools and approaches to the concept of competition in the classical economic period. This book addresses only those which are operationalised in the substantive part of the development of its main argument. Due to the fact that most of the problems related to competition in the post-classical period require cross-examination of their perception of the concept of competition and in order to avoid compendium-style observations of various schools and approaches developed mostly within neoclassical and institutional narratives, the chronological method applied in this section is substituted in the following by subject analysis of the area itself.

---

served the discipline well by allowing both theoretical and empirical arguments to be put forward with greater clarity, to be checked for error more reliably, and to be analogized and generalized more easily'.

71 Ioannis Lianos, 'Lost In Translation? Towards a Theory of Economic Transplants', Current Legal Problems, Vol. 62, No. 1, 2009, p. 353: 'The alliance of mathematical economics and neoclassical price theory in the 1950s, with the development of a mathematical proof of the general equilibrium theory, still dominates, in some respects, the field – at least economic theory applying in competition law'.

72 Helge Peukert, 'Walter Eucken (1891–1950) and the Historical School', in Peter Koslowski (ed.), *The Theory of Capitalism in the German Economic Tradition: Historism, Ordo-liberalism, Critical Theory, Solidarism*, Springer, Hannover, 2000, p. 94.

2.4 PERFECT COMPETITION VS. COMPETITIVE PROCESS

Now we are approaching the question which constitutes perhaps the quintessence of the conflict between neoclassical and dynamic understandings of competition. The hypothesis is that each mainstream economic perception of competition policy is deeply rooted in understanding of competition in terms of equilibrium economics.[73] The idea of equilibrium in economics is the methodological starting point. Without accepting it, no understanding of the discipline is possible.[74] All instances in which equilibrium is modified by external forces are automatically counterbalanced by other forces. The logic of equilibrium can tolerate all complexities. It is the language of economics.[75] One could basically say that the principle of equilibrium constitutes the *archetype* of economic reasoning.

Economic thinking is inherently mathematical. The rationale of economic equilibrium has been applied in economic theory long before the emergence of equilibrium economics. The theorisation of the concept dates from the 19th century and Walras was one of the main figures in the development of the pure quantity-based rationale of economics. Free competition played an important role in his modelling, because it has been seen as an inductive way for individuals to adjust their interests to the interests of society. Free competition was perceived as a means to achieve harmonious cooperation between suppliers and consumers where each of these actors fine-tunes the economic system by pursuing individual interests and reacting rationally to market conditions. The mathematical perception of market processes significantly advanced the static aspects of competition. At the same time 'dynamic and evolutionary aspects of competition, which had been inherent to classical theory, were neglected for a considerable time'.[76]

[73] Oliver Budzinski, 'Monoculture versus Diversity in Competition Economics', Cambridge Journal of Economics, Vol. 32, No. 2, 2008, p. 297.

[74] Claus Thomasberger, 'The Two Utopias of Economics: Human Freedom and the Mechanism of Competition', http://people.f3.htw-berlin.de/Professoren/Thomasberger/pdf/11_The-Strange-Triumph-of-the-Neoliberal-Credo.pdf, accessed on 4 February 2011, p. 6: 'The Equilibrium Model or the utopia of the self-regulating system has the character of an ideal-type construct, a hypothesis, which does not tell us anything about economic reality'.

[75] Israel M. Kirzner, 'Entrepreneurial Discovery and the Competitive Market Process: An Austrian Approach', Journal of Economic Literature, Vol. 35, No. 1, 1997, p. 64: 'In the neoclassical world, decision makers know what they are ignorant about. One is never surprised'.

[76] Oliver Budzinski, 'Monoculture versus Diversity in Competition Economics', Cambridge Journal of Economics, Vol. 32, No. 2, 2008, p. 298.

The term 'free competition' is used in equilibrium economics in a specific manner. It is not an ideological plea for economic freedom of market actors. Freedom in this context means rather such a condition for determining price, in which market players are not restrained by their will. In other words, it is seen as a mechanism ensuring that market decisions are taken rationally and 'organically'. The idea of freedom in equilibrium economics is of methodological rather than normative character. Freedom is protected in order to maintain equilibrium. It is subordinated to equilibrium. It is accepted only as its precondition. Freedom as *status* is replaced by freedom as *condition*. It does not mean that this model is critical of normative understanding of freedom, rather it means its complete indifference regarding that vision of freedom. Critics of equilibrium economics argue that it does not tolerate subjectivity, unpredictability and the entrepreneurial spirit of profit maximisation.

The notion of perfect competition corresponds to the equilibrium condition. It shares nothing but spelling with the notion of competitive process. Perfect competition is a purely hypothetical situation in theory: it is an imaginary point when demand meets supply. McNulty explains that '[c]ompetition came to mean, with the mathematical economists, a hypothetically realized situation in which business rivalry, or competition in the Smithian sense, was ruled out by definition'.[77] Or as Kirzner puts it, 'the act of choice consists in nothing more than computing the solution *already implicit* in the data'.[78] So basically, the notion of equilibrium 'not only allowed for very important insights and advances in economic theory, it also changed the meaning of the term competition in comparison to classical economics'.[79] Such an unfortunate conflation of these two absolutely irrelevant to each other categories causes a great deal of confusion and blurs the understanding of the competitive process in the contemporary neoclassical antitrust world.[80]

For this reason, the notion of perfect competition should be understood

---

77 Paul J. McNulty, 'A Note on the History of Perfect Competition', The Journal of Political Economy, Vol. 75, No. 4, 1967, p. 398.

78 Israel M. Kirzner, *How Markets Work: Disequilibrium, Entrepreneurship and Discovery*, Institute of Economic Affairs, London, 2000, p. 31, (emphasis in the original).

79 Oliver Budzinski, 'Monoculture versus Diversity in Competition Economics', Cambridge Journal of Economics, Vol. 32, No. 2, 2008, p. 298.

80 Furthermore, neoclassical economists developed the notion of perfect competition as an attempt to better comprehend the idea of competition through a more advanced methodology. That is why this perception of competition does not argue against classical views, but 'merely' perceive them as obsolete and rudimentary.

and used only as a theoretical mechanism with no ideological or even substantive connotation. Perfect competition does not offer any elements of dynamism or rivalry. It is by definition static. And precisely because of this the idea of competition in antitrust is perceived as value-neutral. A similar perception of the concept of perfect competition is reflected in the Ordoliberal notion of 'complete competition', to indicate a position 'in which no firm in a market has power to coerce other firms in that market'.[81] These two notions are essentially indistinguishable:[82] for some authors they are identical,[83] for others the only difference between them lies 'in the rejection [by Ordoliberalism] of the neoclassical hypothesis of homogeneity of goods and agents'.[84] The Ordoliberal version does, however, hold some elements of the *practical* dimension, which may imply that the concept of complete competition contains some normative elements, while the state of perfect competition is rather a methodological premise, adopted primarily for analytical purposes[85] and 'having only didactic value'.[86] In addition these concepts are different, since the notion of complete competition entails elements of market dynamism and rivalry,[87] while the perfect competition scenario

---

81 David J. Gerber, 'Constitutionalizing the Economy: German Neo-Liberalism, Competition Law and the "New" Europe', The American Journal of Comparative Law, Vol. 42, No. 1, 1994, p. 43.

82 Christian Ahlborn and Carsten Grave, 'Walter Eucken and Ordoliberalism: An Introduction from a Consumer Welfare Perspective', Competition Policy International, Vol. 2, No. 2, 2006, p. 200.

83 Pinar Akman, 'Searching for the Long-Lost Soul of Article 82EC', Oxford Journal of Legal Studies, Vol. 29, No. 2, 2009, p. 275: 'Eucken's "complete competition" was indeed "perfect competition"'.

84 Sylvian Broyer, 'German Contemporary Analyses of Economic Order: Standard Ordnungstheorie, Ordoliberalism and Ordnungsökonimik in Perspective', in Agnès Labrousse and Jean-Daniel Weisz (eds.), *Institutional Economics in France and Germany: German Ordoliberalism versus the French Regulation School,* Springer, Berlin, 2001, p. 109.

85 Edward N. Megay, 'Anti-Pluralist Liberalism: The German Neoliberals', Political Science Quarterly, Vol. 85, No. 3, 1970, p. 430: 'Böhm reluctantly acknowledges that denial of power is possible only through governmental restrictions upon the freedom . . . of powerful members of the society when he admits that an economic order providing and maintaining complete (not perfect) competition requires a great deal of governmental coercion and control'.

86 Phedon Nicolaides, 'An Essay on Economics and Competition Law of the European Community', Legal Issues of Economic Integration, Vol. 27, No. 1, 2000, p. 13.

87 Walter Eucken, 'Die Wettbewerbsordnung und ihre Verwirklichung', Jahrbuch für die Ordnung von Wirtschaft und Gesellschaft, Vol. 2, 1949, cited in Christian Ahlborn, Carsten Grave (trans.), Walter Eucken, 'The Competitive

is rather static.[88] It goes without saying that the theoretical significance of the concept of perfect competition is beyond doubt. The problem for antitrust emerges only when one concept is interpreted in terms of the other. Such a situation can be called *homonymy*. As we know, homonymy occurs when two different notions share spelling but have a different meaning.[89] Most of the homonymies are identified automatically (river bank vs. financial bank) and cause no confusion. However, when they are used in the same area, they can often be misleading. This is exactly the situation with the terms 'competitive process' and 'perfect competition'. The situation becomes even more problematic if the concepts originate from the same roots.[90]

It is hard to disagree with Hayek that 'competition is important only because and insofar as its outcomes are unpredictable and on the whole different from those that anyone would have been able to consciously strive for [and] its salutary effects must manifest themselves by frustrating certain intentions and disappointing certain expectations'.[91]

Order and its Implementation', Competition Policy International, Vol. 2, No. 2, 2006, pp. 228–229: 'Complete competition has rightly been compared to a race. It is not a battle man-to-man but a race run in parallel. It is not impediment or injurious competition, but rather performance competition'.

88 Wernhard Möschel, 'Competition Policy from an Ordo Point of View', in Alan Peacock and Hans Willgerodt (eds.), *German Neo-Liberals, and the Social Market Economy*, The Macmillan Press, London, 1989, p. 146: 'The scholars of Ordo-liberalism have also used economic models for the description of their ideas, for instance, the model of perfect competition as it was developed in the traditional theory of competition. . . . Such models, however, served only for the description of general effects of a market system, illustrating them in what might be called a chemically pure form. That did not imply, however, that those partly unreal premises were to be integrated as goals into practical competition policy'.

89 Stanley L. Paulson prefers the term 'isomorphism' (Stanley L. Paulson, 'Introduction', in Stanley L. Paulson and Bonnie Litschewski Paulson (eds.), *Normativity and Norms: Critical Perspectives on Kelsenian Themes*, Clarendon Press, Oxford, 1998, p. xli).

90 Oles Andriychuk, 'Exclusive Legal Positivism and Legal Autopoiesis: Towards a Theory of Dialectical Positivism', Rechtstheorie, Vol. 46, No. 1, 2015, pp. 44–48; Oles Andriychuk, 'The Concept of Perfect Competition as the Law of Economics: Addressing the Homonymy Problem', Northern Ireland Legal Quarterly, Vol. 62, No. 4, 2011.

91 Friedrich A. von Hayek, 'Competition as a Discovery Procedure', The Quarterly Journal of Austrian Economics, Vol. 5, No. 3, 2002, p. 9.

2.5 CONCLUSIONS

The purpose of this chapter has been twofold. Its primary objective has been to provide a roadmap of the evolution of the basic economic idea of competition, tracing its origins back to the Ancient Greek and Roman cultures, through the medieval period to classical economic thinking. Although the idea of economic competition has traditionally been considered a fairly synthetic concept, developed in the late 19th century and adopted only in the 20th century, its preconditions had already been discussed long before. The history of economic thought shows that economic competition is by no means an indispensable component of economic governance. Likewise, democracy, which is also a context-dependent concept, evolves only in societies and cultures historically prepared for this value choice. Hence, competition should not be perceived as an exclusively utilitarian result-oriented phenomenon. Arguably, competition does not always create welfare, and there might be more efficient economic models to increase growth or the scope of consumer choices than perfect competition. Its main constitutional importance – and this is the main normative argument of this book – does not lie so much in its effectiveness as in the ethical value it represents for society. Arguments in favour of the deontological and ethical dimensions of competition are discussed in the following chapters. Different intellectual traditions address the ethical dimensions of competition from various angles. This research conceptualises these thoughts into a constitutional theory of competition, which is based inter alia on philosophical ideas developed in Ancient Greece.

The second part of this chapter explored the basic economic concepts which have become theoretical prerequisites for the major antitrust schools. These concepts have been analysed mainly from a historical perspective. Accordingly, the main task of this chapter was to explore the historical and theoretical background to competition. These aspects were fundamental to the development of the main premises of the major modern antitrust law schools that emerged in the 20th century in the US and Europe.

3. Doctrinal foundations of competition law

This chapter analyses the theoretical background to the principal competing understandings of the role that antitrust law should play in protecting and promoting competition. *Unlike* the previous chapter, it contains an important new dimension: competition is not perceived only from the internal perspective of economics, but also through the regulatory lens of law. *Like* the previous chapter, its primary task is to provide a critical overview of the main evolutionary trends in antitrust theory. Its discourse remains predominantly historical, unlike the approach taken in the following chapter, which illustrates the main theoretical prerequisites necessary for the development of normative arguments concerning the constitutionalisation of the competitive process. The argument as such is explored mostly in the subsequent chapters.

Although the length to which the evolutionary development of competition is explored might suggest otherwise, the historical method of interpretation does not constitute one of the main instruments of this research. The intentionalism which refers to the original positions of those who *adopted* the law is a helpful analytical tool to understand the context of legislative debates, but their intentions should not be perceived as a source of ultimate authority. On the contrary, dynamic legal concepts such as competition are constantly evolving together with the development of economic relations and the relevant theoretical framework. Therefore this book rejects the approach which often dominates antitrust analysis, according to which '[t]he appeal to history [serves as] the proof of the existence of inescapable law'.[1] In contrast, the analysis of competition law should focus on innovative perceptions of the phenomenon, even if they presuppose an understanding of its historical development. In a word, the historical analysis should not predetermine its normative counterpart.

---

1 William P. LaPiana, 'The Legal Culture of the Formative Period in Sherman Act Jurisprudence', New York Law School Law Review, Vol. 35, No. 4, 1990, p. 843.

3.1 EVOLUTION OF COMPETITION LAW FROM THE US PERSPECTIVE

The theoretical polemic over the role of the competitive process started in Europe before spreading to the US in the 20th century, for various historical reasons, including the rapid development of the economy[2] and universities[3] in the US. As Morgan explains in her remarkable research on the history of economic competition in the US, '[American economists of that period] had inherited a body of ideas, but they were no longer tied down by the authority of past European thinkers'.[4] The discussion on the wording and interpretation of US antitrust legislation was predetermined by fierce theoretical debates, predominantly among economists, on the essence of the competitive process. Although the history of economic thought reveals the significance of competition-related problems during the classical period, the concept as such was relatively new and underdeveloped to the extent that it 'did not begin to receive explicit and systematic attention in the main stream of economics until 1871'.[5] Some authors submit that the specific conditions for the development of antitrust are predetermined by an uneasy relationship between the American colonies

---

[2] Mary S. Morgan, 'Competing Notions of "Competition" in Late Nineteenth-Century American Economics', History of Political Economy, Vol. 25, No. 4, 1993, p. 564: 'The period after the Civil War and up to around 1900 was an era of massive structural change in the U.S. economy. In a period of rapid growth throughout all sectors, the economy was transformed from a predominantly agricultural economy to a state of highly developed industrial capitalism within a period of about 30–40 years'.

[3] William J. Barber, 'American Economics to 1900', in Warren J. Samuels, Jeff E. Biddle and John B. Davis (eds.), *A Companion to The History of Economic Thought*, Blackwell Publishing, Oxford, 2003, p. 231: 'To judge by the distribution of Nobel Prizes in economics over the past three decades or so, it would appear that American economics – for good or ill – has come to occupy a position of world pre-eminence. This has not always been so. To the contrary, if we roll the clock back to consider the "state of the art" during the first century of the nation's existence, the United States was largely on the periphery of major intellectual developments in the discipline. Indeed, when the country's centennial was celebrated in 1876, American economists had an inferiority complex. Writing on this occasion, Harvard's Charles F. Dunbar – the first American to be accorded the title "Professor of Political Economy" – observed that American scholarship as yet had contributed nothing to fundamental economic knowledge'.

[4] Mary S. Morgan, 'Competing Notions of "Competition" in Late Nineteenth-Century American Economics', History of Political Economy, Vol. 25, No. 4, 1993, p. 566.

[5] George J. Stigler, 'Perfect Competition, Historically Contemplated', The Journal of Political Economy, Vol. 65, No. 1, 1957, p. 1.

and their 'mother' countries.[6] In the political sphere the rapid development of monopolies and the cartelisation of big industries raised concerns both at the state and federal levels. The rapid development of trusts was one of the consequences of the existing discrepancy between political and economic democracy in the US at that time. As Brietzke observes, 'America was virtually the only country to achieve democracy before passing over the economic development "hump"',[7] and trusts followed the increase in economic power.

The American legal culture is designed by and largely subordinated to the courts' case law. In some sense, 'the whole history of antitrust policy can be read as the judicial quest for a working definition of competition'.[8] The specificity of judicial reasoning, which is predetermined by a combination of strong legal argumentation and explicit policy concerns for common interests, introduces to the debates on the nature of competition and its regulation an important new narrative: the narrative of law with all its own rules and logic, with an apparatus developed over the centuries, normative values and argumentative schemes that are very different from the economic way of thinking. Competition law is the area where legal and economic discourses meet and interact in the most intensive manner. This creates a potential for misunderstanding basic concepts, which are perceived differently from the internal perspective of each discipline. The history of antitrust reveals that these clashes constitute one of the main difficulties for the evolution of the concept of competition.

The rapid growth of big industries was the outcome of the development of capitalism in late 19th-century America. Opposition to trade restraints belongs to the tradition that the US legal system inherited from old English case law.[9] Initiatives to regulate monopolisation and

---

6 Edward H. Levi, 'The Antitrust Laws and Monopoly', The University of Chicago Law Review, Vol. 14, No. 2, 1947, p. 155: 'The right of every man to engage in business free of restrictions not imposed by law, the necessity to guard against exorbitant prices, and opposition to governmental grants to favorites – these are the first themes of the Anglo-American tradition against monopolies. The colonies developed an additional theme and one always popular. They were opposed to other people's monopolies and restrictions on trade imposed upon them from afar'.

7 Paul H. Brietzke, 'The Constitutionalisation of Antitrust: Jefferson, Madison, Hamilton and Thomas C. Arthur', Valparaiso University Law Review, Vol. 22, No. 2, 1988, p. 283.

8 Donald Dewey, 'The Economic Theory of Antitrust: Science or Religion?', Virginia Law Review, Vol. 50, No. 3, 1964, p. 414.

9 George J. Stigler, 'The Origin of the Sherman Act', The Journal of Legal Studies, Vol. 14, No. 1, 1985, p. 7.

collusion between major actors, as well as related judicial decisions, first appeared at state level and different states embraced different priorities, visions and approaches in their antitrust statutes.[10] The first wave of antitrust proposals stemmed from powerful agrarian lobbies in western and southern states[11] and was strongly opposed as the very phenomenon of trusts was directly associated with significant economic growth, this being one of its important components. The antitrust Bill became another reason for the opposition between two camps: Jeffersonians (who defend the interests of small business) and Hamiltonians (the protagonists of big corporate capital).[12] Furthermore, for a long time trusts 'were a form of salvation'.[13] Thereby the very *inefficiency* of trusts, cartels and monopolies which is so widely accepted today was not only questioned by trusts participants and lobbies, but also by some argumentative economic evidence, developed inter alia by conservative parts of the media. In addition, the omnipotent present-day reliance on consumer welfare was not on the agenda;[14] though some authors suggest (not without irony, perhaps) otherwise.[15]

---

[10] Rudolph J. R. Peritz, *Competition Policy in America: History, Rhetoric, Law*, Oxford University Press, Oxford, 1996, pp. 9–10.

[11] Hans Thorelli, *The Federal Antitrust Policy: Origination of an American Tradition*, Johns Hopkins University Press, Baltimore, 1955, p. 143.

[12] Paul H. Brietzke, 'The Constitutionalisation of Antitrust: Jefferson, Madison, Hamilton and Thomas C. Arthur', Valparaiso University Law Review, Vol. 22, No. 2, 1988, pp. 276–278: '[A] history of antitrust law should . . . be an economic history. Such a history would be simplistic if it reduced everything to a struggle between agrarian and industrial interests, between ideological Jeffersons and ideological Hamiltons. But a properly-qualified analysis of antitrust is as based on the ideas of these worries. . . . The Jeffersonian desire is to defuse wealth and power, to protect "small, local, responsible" businesses from "large, politically irresponsible, absentee-owned, and possibly corrupt giants" . . . The Hamiltonian ideal found its modern organizational home in the large corporations organized after the Civil War and, later, in trade associations, in elite business schools and their ideology of "managerialism" . . . in Wall Street law firms, and most recently in the Chicago School of law and economics'.

[13] Herbert J. Hovenkamp, 'The Antitrust Movement and the Rise of Industrial Organization', Texas Law Review, Vol. 68, No. 1, 1989, p. 145.

[14] Rudolph J. Peritz, 'A Counter-History of Antitrust Law', Duke Law Journal, Vol. 39, No. 2, 1990, p. 274: 'In contrast to today's overdetermined focus on consumers, their [the Congress of 1888] notion of industrial liberty included a sense of the public as both competitors and employees of the new large combinations of capital'.

[15] Eleanor M. Fox, 'The Battle for the Soul of Antitrust', California Law Review, Vol. 75, No. 3, 1987, pp. 918–919: 'Chicagoans assert an ahistorical view of antitrust. . . . They declare that the only significant goal of the Congress

One of the main arguments against the introduction of antitrust legislation was the economic belief, supported by many economists and political activists, that competition is tied to the 'needless duplication of facilities, overproduction, and higher transportation costs'.[16] As Clark observed, economists were generally reluctant to allow for the introduction of antitrust legislation.[17] Yet, negative public opinion towards trusts eventually compelled Congress to depart from the existing status quo, deeply embedded in fundamental American values such as freedom of contract ('industrial liberty'[18]) as well as the general mercantilist hostility to the principles of competition (the word was commonly used by opponents to the Bill with the qualified 'ruinous'). As Yankwich indicates, there were 14 antitrust Bills introduced at the time in the House of Representatives.[19] It shows that even those who were concerned about the increasing power of monopolies and trusts did not agree on the best way to regulate them. References to freedom and (natural) individual rights dominated the whole history of antitrust debates. The ensuing arguments are double-faced and can be used to defend the liberty of either those who act in an anticompetitive way or those who are prevented from acting due to anticompetitive restrictions. This is the reason why the concept of freedom is explored separately in the chapters on the philosophical and legal foundations of competition.

3.1.1 The Rule of Reason vs. *the Reason of Rule*

After the adoption of antitrust laws the focus of political, economic debates on competition shifted from Congress to the judicial authorities. In one of the early cases concerning competition[20] the US Supreme Court

---

that passed the Sherman Act was to enhance consumer welfare . . . Otherwise, Chicagoans ignore the historical goals of antitrust, claiming that Congress, by framing the statutes as vague prescriptions, thereby delegated power to the courts to use Chicago's efficiency model'.

16 Herbert J. Hovenkamp, 'The Antitrust Movement and the Rise of Industrial Organization', Texas Law Review, Vol. 68, No. 1, 198s9, p. 145.

17 John B. Clark, *The Federal Trust Policy*, Johns Hopkins University Press, Baltimore, 1931, p. 89.

18 Rudolph J. R. Peritz, 'The "Rule of Reason" in Antitrust Law: Property Logic in Restraint of Competition', Hastings Law Journal, Vol. 40, No. 2, 1989, p. 291.

19 Leon R. Yankwich, 'Competition, Real or Soft – Or What Have You? Observations on Competition and Antitrust Policy', American Bar Association Section of Antitrust Law Proceedings at the Annual Meeting, 1952, p. 126.

20 *Northern Securities Co. v. United States*, 193 U.S. 197 (1904).

established 'the principle of competition that became the lynchpin of antitrust policy'.[21] It had been argued in court that '[c]ompetition drives the weak to the wall, the fittest survive, but the greatest good to the greatest number results'.[22] Following the decision in *Parker v. Brown*, the aim of the main federal antitrust laws (Sherman Act 1890, Clayton Act 1914, Federal Trade Commission Act 1914 and Robinson-Patman Act 1936) was to 'suppress combinations to restrain competition and attempts to monopolize by individuals and corporations'.[23] The importance of the first antitrust legislation has been very much acknowledged by the US courts. Some decisions considered it to be 'comparable to that found to be desirable in constitutional provisions'.[24] Later on the Sherman Act was famously associated by the US Supreme Court with 'the Magna Carta of free enterprise',[25] implying that competition laws are important guarantees for individual economic freedom.[26] As Säcker observes, '[a]nyone who is familiar with the history of the origin of antitrust policy, and with the Sherman Act, knows that the starting-point was the need to combat economic power. . . . Protecting freedom from the extension of power is the objective of American antitrust legislation.'[27] This implies that, from the very beginning of antitrust policy, efficiency justifications were seen neither as the sole goal of competition nor as a sufficient ground for its restriction.

An important issue related to the interpretation of the requirements of Section 1 of the Sherman Act, which prohibited *all* contracts restricting trade. The supporters of a literal interpretation referred inter alia to the fact that the Bill which introduced the rule of reason into the US legislation had been explicitly rejected by Congress in 1909,[28] others pointed out

---

21 Stephen Martin, 'The Goals of Antitrust Policy', in Wayne D. Collins (ed.), *Issues in Competition Law and Policy*, American Bar Association Publishing, Chicago, 2008, p. 20.

22 *United States v. Joint Traffic Ass'n*, 171 U.S. 505 (1898).

23 *Parker v. Brown*, 317 U.S. 341, 351 (1943).

24 *Appalachian Coals, Inc. v. United States*, 288 U.S. 344, 360–361 (1933).

25 *United States v. Topco Assocs., Inc.*, 405 U.S. 596, 611 (1972).

26 ibid: '[Antitrust laws] are as important to the preservation of economic freedom and our free enterprise system as the Bill of Rights is to the protection of our fundamental personal freedoms'.

27 Franz Jürgen Säcker, 'Legal Foundations of Competition', in Günther Hirsch, Frank Montag and Franz Jürgen Säcker (eds.), *Competition Law: European Community Practice and Procedure – Article-by-Article Commentary*, Sweet & Maxwell, London, 2008, p. 9.

28 George W. Stocking, 'The Rule of Reason, Workable Competition, and the Legality of Trade Association Activities', The University of Chicago Law Review, Vol. 21, No. 4, 1954, p. 529.

to the inability to prohibit *all* such contracts and the necessity to apply the *rule of reason*.[29] In the same vein, they submitted that, in spite of its wording, Section 2 of the Sherman Act bans monopolisation only as an act of unreasonable acquisition and/or maintenance of monopoly and not the possession of a monopoly as such.[30] As in other areas of law in which the concept has been already applied[31] (and constitutional law in particular) the rule of reason debates shifted the antitrust debates from the wording of legal texts to the rationality of economic processes. In addition, many forms of anticompetitive conduct were traditionally tolerated by the case law. Such practices as resale price maintenance or exclusive dealing were, on the contrary, seen by classical economists as 'nothing more than the consequence of a firm's decision whether to produce some essential product or service internally or to purchase it externally by general or exclusive contract'.[32]

The rule of reason was one of the proxies that enabled the economic and legal disciplines to establish an intensive communicative process. It is argued that notorious difficulties with the rule of reason such as 'its open-endedness, its incoherence, its unrealizeability'[33] do not preclude reasoning about competition law in a purely legal way. The existence of the rule of reason is indispensable for constitutional analysis. The dogmatic and literal interpretation of constitutional provisions might be desirable, but it is unenforceable. In relation to the rule of reason, the US Supreme Court observes that the Sherman Act 'does not go into detailed definitions which might either work injury to legitimate enterprise or through particularization defeat its purposes by providing loopholes for escape. The restrictions the act imposes are not mechanical or artificial. Its general phrases . . . set up the essential standard of reasonableness'.[34] The Congress debates over the Sherman Act also included this view and Senator Sherman himself submitted in his proposal that it was 'difficult to define in legal language

---

29 *Standard Oil Co. of New Jersey v. United States*, 221 U.S. 1, 63 (1911): 'the language of the statute embraces every contract, combination, etc., in restraint of trade, and hence its text leaves no room for the exercise of judgment, but simply imposes the plain duty of applying its prohibitions to every case within its literal language'.

30 *United States v. American Tobacco Co.*, 221 U.S. 106 (1911).

31 Robert H. Bork, 'The Rule of Reason and the Per Se Concept: Price Fixing and Market Division', The Yale Law Journal, Vol. 75, No. 3, 1966, p. 376.

32 Herbert J. Hovenkamp, 'The Antitrust Movement and the Rise of Industrial Organization', Texas Law Review, Vol. 68, No. 1, 1989, p. 157.

33 Rudolph J. R. Peritz, 'A Counter-History of Antitrust Law', Duke Law Journal, Vol. 39, No. 2, 1990, p. 265.

34 *Appalachian Coals, Inc. v. United States*, 288 U.S. 344, 360–361 (1933).

the precise line between lawful and unlawful combinations. This must be left for the courts to determine in each particular case. All that we, as lawmakers, can do is to declare general principles, and . . . the courts will apply them so as to carry out the meaning of the law'.[35] In other words, from the pragmatic perspective, '[t]he structure and performance of important sections of the American economy are simply too important to be left to per se rules'.[36] However, as Peritz observes, 'the sensible recognition of a technical need for a "rule of reason" . . . ended in normative chaos, with the "rule of reason" out of control'.[37] Accordingly, as Christiansen and Kerber suggest, analysis under the rule of reason benchmark has become 'effectively open-ended'.[38]

From the doctrinal perspective, legal interpretation, implied in the rule of reason rationale, constitutes one of the central topics of contemporary analytical jurisprudence, and despite the openness of law towards other disciplines, this does not imply that legal thinking acknowledges its inability to address economic problems from an intra-disciplinary perspective. Formalism and literalism are important but not exclusive methods of legal analysis; furthermore they are not only important in law: economics similarly depends on theorems, axioms and generalised formulas. Hence, the discussion between formalists and realists in legal theory should not be taken as a conflict between lawyers and economists. *Realism* reflects the necessity to adapt static rules to the dynamism of real life and is not less *real* for jurisprudence than for economics or politics. As a known constitutional theorist of that time, Tiedeman, observes, the general structure of most legal texts requires interpretation,[39] which itself is a significant deviation from legal formalism.

The opposite view considers interpretation as a vindication of the literal meaning of texts or, at least, an affirmation of the wording of the

---

[35] 21 CONGR. EC.2 460 (1890).

[36] Donald Dewey, 'The Economic Theory of Antitrust: Science or Religion?', Virginia Law Review, Vol. 50, No. 3, 1964, p. 434.

[37] Rudolph J. Peritz, 'A Counter-History of Antitrust Law', Duke Law Journal, Vol. 39, No. 2, 1990, p. 279.

[38] Arndt Christiansen and Wolfgang Kerber, 'Competition Policy with Optimally Differentiated Rules Instead of "Per se Rules vs. Rule of Reason"', Marburg Papers on Economics, No. 6, 2006, p. 4.

[39] Christopher G. Tiedeman, *The Unwritten Constitution of the United States: A Philosophical Inquiry into the Fundamentals of American Constitutional Law*, G.P. Putnam's Sons, New York, 1890, p. 43: the 'Federal Constitution contains only a declaration of the fundamental and most general principles of constitutional law. . . . [T]he flesh and blood of the [US] Constitution, instead of its skeleton, is . . . unwritten'.

law. Otherwise it would not require too many creative efforts for this *frivolous* style of legal reasoning, to prove or condemn *everything* based on a randomly taken positive norm. In relation to antitrust, opposition to an interpretive jurisprudence was and remains significant. It developed different lines of reasoning. First, the literalists refer to the principle of the separation of powers, which the delegation of a quasi-legislative competence to judges (most of whom are unelected by the public) would allegedly undermine. Another powerful argument refers to the danger for legal certainty and the increase in the length of proceedings, because it would require 'prolonged economic investigation into the entire history of the industry involved, . . . – an inquiry so often wholly fruitless when undertaken'.[40] As Arthur argues, a broad application of the interpretative techniques creates 'a body of antitrust law that rivals only constitutional law in indeterminacy',[41] suggesting also that from the contextual perspective the Sherman Act included fairly concrete and specific provisions which should be observed and applied by the courts.[42] Arguably, this makes litigation more costly. Some authors are sceptical in general about the use of economic formulas in legal antitrust analysis and submit that these are often 'metaphors of their time and culture, and their truths fail when conditions change'.[43] The later jurisprudence of the US Supreme Court was also sceptical about the rule of reason. Following the *Topco* decision, '[o]ur inability to weigh, in any meaningful sense, destruction of competition in one sector of the economy against promotion of competition in another sector is one important reason we have formulated per se rules'.[44] This approach can be counterbalanced by the 21st century's view of the US Supreme Court, expressed in the *Leegin* case.[45] According to this understanding of the notion of rule of reason, it is not considered anymore as a mere tool for the reauthorisation of otherwise prohibited agreements, but rather as a way to eliminate anticompetitive transactions.[46]

The application of the concept of the rule of reason has been gradually expanding over the last hundred years, covering broad areas of allegedly

---

40 *Northern Pacific Railway Co. v. United States*, 356 U.S. 1, 5 (1958).

41 Thomas C. Arthur, 'Farewell to the Sea of Doubt: Jettisoning the Constitutional Sherman Act', California Law Review, Vol. 74, No. 2, 1986, p. 268.

42 ibid, p. 270.

43 Frederick M. Rowe, 'The Decline of Antitrust and the Delusions of Models: The Faustian Pact of Law and Economics', Georgetown Law Journal, Vol. 72, No. 4, 1984, p. 1513.

44 *United States v. Topco Assocs., Inc.*, 405 U.S. 596, 611 (1972).

45 *Leegin Creative Leather Products, Inc. v. PSKS, Inc.*, 551 U.S. 877 (2007).

46 ibid: 'The rule of reason is designed and used to eliminate anticompetitive transactions from the market'.

anticompetitive conduct. This shows that the principle of per se rule should not be perceived, or applied, legalistically in a mechanical manner. On the other hand, the doctrinal significance of per se rules should not be undermined by a wide application of the rule of reason. Its theoretical significance is akin to the principle of equilibrium in economics: even those who do not accept its application cannot reject its important epistemological character. The pervasiveness of application of the rule of reason should not be taken, therefore, as evidence for the rejection of per se rules, which remain a fundamental cognitive instrument in legal argumentation.

One of the reasons for the existence of polarised views on US antitrust laws reflects the economic reality of the phenomenon of competition. From the political perspective the detailed specification was also undesirable, since 'to do so would, on the one hand, drastically curtail the freedom of businessmen . . . and, on the other hand, too readily permit unanticipated competitive abuses not specifically singled out and condemned'.[47] This explanation finds its legal-theoretic justification in the relationship between legal rules (imperative commands, 'which are always either fulfilled or not',[48] in an 'all-or-nothing fashion')[49] and legal principles (balancing-based relative commands, 'optimisation requirements').[50] A hypothesis put forward in this book postulates that neither the legislator nor the interpreter is able to decide absolutely which legal norm should be considered as a rule or a principle. Each norm dialectically contains elements of both, which implies that in some cases it is considered as a rule and in others as a principle. The proportion of the imperative and relative elements of each norm is evaluated ad hoc by each legitimate decision-maker in each particular case.[51] The justification of the hypothesis would contribute to a better understanding of the phenomenon of law, as well

---

[47] Jerrold G. van Cise, 'The Future of Per Se in Antitrust Law', Virginia Law Review, Vol. 50, No. 7, 1964, p. 1177.

[48] Robert Alexy, *A Theory of Constitutional Rights*, Oxford University Press, Oxford, 2002, p. 48.

[49] Ronald M. Dworkin, 'The Model of Rules', The University of Chicago Law Review, Vol. 35, No. 1, 1967, p. 25.

[50] Robert Alexy, *A Theory of Constitutional Rights*, Oxford University Press, Oxford, 2002, p. 47.

[51] Aharon Barak, *The Judge in a Democracy*, Princeton University Press, Princeton, 2006, p. 171: 'Balancing between fundamental principles may be principled or ad hoc. Principled balancing determines a weight that is normative, leading to a legal criterion or formula that can be applied in future cases. . . . Ad hoc balancing, by contrast, is not based on a general formula that can be applied in similar cases other than the baseline determination that one should balance the competing principles according to what the circumstances of the case require'.

as to the universalisation of its apparatus, when difficult legal choices are made *within* the legal discourse and without relying on economical or moral alternatives.

There are mid-way proposals to address the clashes between per se rules and the rule of reason. Some renowned authors proposed to substitute the strict legalistic approach of per se rules and the purely consequentialist solution developed in the rule of reason 'with a series of simple filters . . . designed to screen out beneficent conduct and pass only practices that are likely to reduce output and increase price',[52] implying that this technique can absorb the benefits of both traditional approaches, while escaping their shortcomings. More recently proposals were made to substitute rigid antitrust rules with more flexible and therefore efficient legal ontologies called 'standards'. This entails that standards can help to address antitrust problems (as well as more general legal issues)[53] with 'optimal precision',[54] increasing the external accountability and effectiveness of competition law.[55] This research is rooted in the presumption of the futility of any attempt to 'solve' the dilemma created by the opposition between certainty and workability. The problem of the formalism of the per se rules and the consequentialism of the rule of reason cannot be *solved*, but only operationalised. The conflict between the form and the essence of a norm cannot be resolved by introducing a mid-way category of semi-form/semi-essence. One of the reasons for this is that each concretisation of the substance of rules as well as the softening of their binding force presents not only advantages, but also disadvantages.[56] If standards are seen as the technical requirements of a specific field agreed upon by its key participants, they can be accepted, prohibited or ignored by the law. If standards are

---

[52] Frank H. Easterbrook, 'The Limits of Antitrust', Texas Law Review, Vol. 63, No. 1, 1984, p. 40.

[53] Colin S. Diver, 'The Optimal Precision of Administrative Rules', The Yale Law Journal, Vol. 93, No. 1, 1983.

[54] Ken Kress, 'Legal Indeterminacy', California Law Review, Vol. 77, No. 2, 1989, p. 308: '[T]he advantage of standards is that they directly set forth their purposes. . . . [H]owever, they require greater discretion in their application. As a consequence, this discretion often results in uncertainty and arbitrariness'.

[55] Henk Don, Ron Kemp and Jarig Van Sinderen, 'Measuring the Economic Effects of Competition Law Enforcement', De Economist, Vol. 156, No. 4, 2008, p. 341.

[56] Daniel A. Crane, 'Rules Versus Standards in Antitrust Adjudication', Washington and Lee Law Review, Vol. 64, No. 1, 2007, p. 52: 'Whatever the perceived advantages of standards over rules in antitrust, the disadvantages of standards will probably induce a counter-movement back toward rules once the current movement has run its course'.

the specific benchmark of economic theory, they can either be relevant or irrelevant in each particular case. In both situations the standards do not create alternatives to legal rules and they do not define the legal essence of rules.[57] The only plausible scenario is to view standards as concurrent (and softer) authoritative requirements which parties can refer to in order to justify their violation of the rules. The aetiology of this situation is fully covered by legal theory when addressing the problem of correlation between law and morality, as well as between legal rules and legal principles. The problem can also be adequately addressed by the economic apparatus, but by going beyond the limits of the law. In the chapter on the legal theoretical problems of competition, these issues are addressed on their substance (Chapter 6.2). It is only necessary to point out here that the existence of the dichotomised relationship suffices to treat the problem properly. The introduction of any intermediaries complicates the issue more than it helps to explain it. Proposals to mitigate the dilemmatic nature of the conflict may *work* in many areas of antitrust and can in practice be rather *effective*; furthermore, there are persuasive attempts in the law and economics literature to develop different criteria for the measurement of the effectiveness of antitrust rules.[58] There are also studies which show from the economic point of view the relative effectiveness of form-based approaches, suggesting 'optimally differentiated rules' as a solution,[59] as well as legal research promoting the evaluation of legal antitrust rules by cost-benefit analysis.[60] The eventual *effectiveness* of the proposed solutions has a 'sociological', 'external' nature – important for society but not so much for the more theoretical aspects of the problem.

---

[57] Hans Kelsen, *General Theory of Law and State*, Russell & Russell, New York, 1973, p. 6: '[A] pure theory of law in no way opposes the requirement for just law by declaring itself incompetent to answer the question whether a given law is just or not, and in what the essential element of justice consists. A pure theory of law – a science – cannot answer this question because this question cannot be answered scientifically at all'.

[58] Daniel L. Rubinfeld and Peter O. Steiner, 'Quantitative Methods in Antitrust Litigation', Law and Contemporary Problems, Vol. 46, No. 4, 1983.

[59] Arndt Christiansen and Wolfgang Kerber, 'Competition Policy with Optimally Differentiated Rules Instead of "Per se Rules vs. Rule of Reason"', Marburg Papers on Economics, No. 6, 2006, p. 2: '[T]he application of rules instead of focusing on case-by-case analyses can have many advantages (less regulatory costs, rent seeking and knowledge problem)'.

[60] Mark A. Lemley, Christopher R Leslie, 'Categorical Analysis in Antitrust Jurisprudence', Iowa Law Review, Vol. 93, No. 4, 2008, p. 1212: 'We evaluate the costs and benefits of the judicial creation of categories, and contend that the complex of antitrust boxes the courts have created today does more harm than good'.

The reliance on commonsense and inductive empiricism in each particular case is not quantifiable and cannot be apprehended in abstract theoretical considerations. Besides, these empirical studies usually go beyond the legal theoretical domain, and can therefore not be assessed properly from a legal perspective, as they are generally irrelevant to theoretical jurisprudence. Some elements of ineffectiveness and arbitrariness are inevitably present in any formal legal ontology.[61] Arguably, the balancing compromise should be considered mostly at the legislative level during the implementation of the rules and to some extent at the level of their interpretation, and not at the adjudicative level when the rules are applied. As a result, the effectiveness of rules is not a criterion for their validity.

3.1.2 Normative and Methodological Components of Antitrust Doctrine

The interplay between the economic and legal aspects of competition has been significant from the very beginning of the regulation of antitrust by positive legislation and case law. This process has intensified with the increasing institutionalisation of the field. The differences between the economic and legal views on the role of antitrust laws in the regulation of the competitive process are usually covered by three umbrella terms, which generally reflect three major paradigms in the evolution of competition in the 20th century, albeit to a larger extent in the US than in the rest of the world. Initially the theorisation of competition was dominated by the Harvard School, followed by the Chicago and Post-Chicago Schools.

The main principles underlying the public regulation of competition developed and advocated by the representatives of all antitrust traditions can be explored from a normative and methodological perspective. Acknowledging a lack of complete coherency within them, the division of each of them into normative and methodological parts helps to understand their doctrinal roots and the political agenda they embrace. Usually these two components are in harmony, which shows that a school is coherent in its premises. For example, the Chicago School was for quite a long period characterised by its laissez-faire normative component and rule of reason methodology. However, as soon as their normative values transferred from their heterodox to the mainstream status, the Chicagoan methodology of the rule of reason started to gradually shift

---

[61] Duncan Kennedy, 'Legal Formality', The Journal of Legal Studies, Vol. 2, No. 2, 1973, p. 378: '*Formality itself represents a compromise of conflicting claims: The heterogeneity of values and the multiplicity of factual situations, in a world of purposive actors, forces the group to admit an element of the arbitrary and irrational into its governance*' (emphasis in the original).

towards the per se legality of some formally anticompetitive practices. In contrast, the Harvard School was more interventionist normatively and more rule oriented (structure – conduct – performance (S–C–P) rationale) methodologically. The Post-Chicago School, taken as a broader cultural trend, is characterised by its refined (predominantly game-theoretic) methodology[62] and it is predominantly consumer oriented normatively.

The shift from one paradigm of antitrust to the next is usually accompanied by the emergence of internal discrepancies between these two components. As soon as the selected methodology does not produce the expected normative results, the harmony between them disappears. This provides a possibility for re-interpretation of the doctrinal premises of each school against the background of the changing economic and political environment, which enables the emergence of a new dominant school (provided that contextual changes were significant enough and that the new alternative is sufficiently conceptualised) or the dominant school undergoes a significant revision from within by the next generation of scholars. The former creates a *post-* situation, the latter a *neo-* situation. The prevalence of a new school follows the algorithm eloquently described by Hovenkamp[63] in his landmark paper, in which apparently the very term 'Post-Chicago School' was first coined.[64] Conflicts between schools may be perceived as a part of the evolutionary process, beneficial for theory,[65] even if not in practice.

---

[62] Oliver Budzinski, 'Modern Industrial Economics and Competition Policy: Open Problems and Possible Limits', IME Working Paper, No. 93/09, 2009, p. 9: '[M]arket participants play a strategic game, in which each player has some leeway to act and influence the market parameters but, notwithstanding, depends in his or her revenue on its competitors (as well as of the demand side of the market, of course)'.

[63] Herbert J. Hovenkamp, 'Antitrust Policy after Chicago', Michigan Law Review, Vol. 84, No. 2, 1985, p. 215: 'The life of a school of antitrust policy is like the life of a scientific model. . . . First the model experiences a period when only one or a few people dare to propose it. These people may be treated as charlatans by those who work within the consensus model. . . . Later a break-through or discovery, or perhaps a series of discoveries, occurs that both discredits the accepted model and makes the new model seem far more palatable. Then the new model achieves consensus, and most people in the scholarly community try to jump on the wagon – to do research that will validate the model, or that is guided by the framework established by the model'.

[64] Daniel A. Crane, 'Chicago, Post-Chicago, and Neo-Chicago', The University of Chicago Law Review, Vol. 76, No. 4, 2009, p. 1913.

[65] Oliver Budzinski, 'Modern Industrial Economics and Competition Policy: Open Problems and Possible Limits', IME Working Paper, No. 93/09, 2009, p. 19: 'Actually, the controversial industrial-economic treatment of some cases triggered

The emergence of each school first depends on the historical, political and economic context. The context in its kaleidoscopic manner enables the original constellation of the normative and methodological components peculiar to this school. Following the institutional maintenance of these components, the main doctrinal premises of the respective schools emerge. The volatile and temporal nature of this intellectual 'norm-method' alliance should not be perceived as a repairable error. In due course a momentum for the intellectual dominance of each doctrine objectively disappears, which leads to the emergence of a new one. The old schools cannot be maintained in their former shape unless they obtain some ideological elements. This process can transform these *rational* schools into a type of *societal religion*, supported uncritically by the followers as a matter of principle rather than on their merits.

All antitrust schools are in one way or another defined by the combination of the political values they support and the methodological instruments they apply. These two components are indispensable for the establishment of a school of thought. However, their indispensability does not mean that they are not independent and cannot be explored separately – they can. Normative values are mostly developed by political ideologies; methodological issues are predominantly discussed in the academic sphere. Ideologies play a pivotal role in the development of any school, and this *what* element is supplemented by the methodological *how* element. The phenomenon of competition has been almost exclusively perceived as a *how* phenomenon. Different antitrust schools consider normative elements in terms that are not directly relevant to the competitive process itself. Neither pro-government nor pro-market approaches (left-right) include the competitive process within the normative scope of the respective doctrines. Depending on the context these *normative* values might encompass consumer or total welfare, laissez-faire or equal redistribution of resources, but competition always appears as a *methodology* used to achieve these goals. By revealing the constitutional foundations of the competitive process itself it will be possible to shift the process from the methodological to the normative in antitrust doctrines. The conceptual part of this purpose is described in Chapter 4; its operational part is present through the analysis of the nature and forms of the balancing act.

---

fierce academic debates . . . – and, thereby, drove theory development (in most cases without eventually resolving the conflicts)'.

3.1.3 Harvard School, S–C–P Paradigm, the Concept of Workable Competition

The normative values espoused by the Harvard School reflect the idea that competition laws must encompass and correspond to all the major macroeconomic policies. Therefore competition itself should be treated through the prism of more general and significant economic problems. Its methodology derives from the conception that the regulation of competition should be based on strong assumptions as to the institutional nature of each industry. This antitrust tradition bases its premises on the 'classical market-morphologically oriented price theory'.[66] Thereby the Harvard tradition on antitrust policy is characterised by the S–C–P algorithm, the self-explanatory nature of which shows that the *structure* of competition within a certain market and the role of a company in this structure predetermine a certain *conduct* of the company and its competitors, which in its turn reflects the *performance* of individual companies as well as the industry in general – and this, again, should ideally have some influence on the structure of the industry (creating the effect nature in this dynamic process: S↔C↔P↔S).[67] This approach uses advanced statistical empirical methods in order to determine the correlation between market structure and performance. The most important cases that reflect the rationale of the Harvard School and can be seen as '[t]he zenith of S–C–P-style antitrust law'[68] are the *Brown Shoe* case,[69] the *Philadelphia National Bank* case,[70] and the *Von's Grocery* case.[71]

---

[66] Franz Jürgen Säcker, 'Legal Foundations of Competition', in Günther Hirsch, Frank Montag and Franz Jürgen Säcker (eds.), *Competition Law: European Community Practice and Procedure – Article-by-Article Commentary*, Sweet & Maxwell, London, 2008, p. 12.

[67] Wolfgang Kerber and Ulrich Schwalbe, 'Economic Principles of Competition Law', in Günther Hirsch, Frank Montag and Franz Jürgen Säcker (eds.), *Competition Law: European Community Practice and Procedure – Article-by-Article Commentary*, Sweet & Maxwell, London, 2008, pp. 220–221: 'In the beginning, the S–C–P paradigm was based upon the clear causal hypothesis that market structures influence the behaviour (conduct) of the competing firms, which, in turn, leads to a certain market performance. . . . [Afterwards,] [a]ttention was drawn to feedback effects from market conduct and performance to market structure, and a partial endogeneity of market structures suggested'.

[68] Nicola Giocoli, 'Competition versus Property Rights: American Antitrust Law, the Freiburg School, and the Early Years of European Competition Policy', Journal of Competition Law and Economics, Vol. 5, No. 4, 2009, p. 756.

[69] *Brown Shoe Co., Inc. v. United States*, 370 U.S. 294 (1962).

[70] *United States v. Philadelphia Nat'l Bank*, 374 U.S. 321 (1963).

[71] *United States v. Von's Grocery Co.*, 384 U.S. 270 (1966).

The evolution of the Harvard School tradition coincided with the development of the economic concept of workable competition. According to Sosnick, the term is best understood as 'an attempt to indicate what practically attainable states of affairs are socially desirable in individual capitalistic markets'.[72] The term was originally coined in the 1930s in the US. It reflects the attempt to adjust the main methodological premise of perfect competition to the increased significance of empirical tools in economics. The concept of workable competition is theoretically rooted in the idea of imperfect competition as developed right after the establishment of the model of perfect competition. The premises of perfect competition were not rejected as a theoretical model, but it was considered that in practice they cannot reflect the real state of affairs due to the multiple negative effects of the model's unknown parameters.

According to Clark, who was one of the founders of the concept, '[w]here one of the conditions of perfect competition is absent, the presence of others may lead to greater rather than less imperfection'.[73] Acknowledging the inductive, context-dependent nature of any industry and any market, Clark systematised the most common factors (standardisation of products; number of producers; method of price-making; market information; geographical factors; control of output; variation of costs and flexibility of product capacity) that influence competition and provided a classification of different deviations from the model of perfect competition: pure (rigorous, unmitigated) competition; imperfect pure competition; modified (intermediate, hybrid) competition; and monopolistic competition.[74] The aim of the alternative, more moderate and empirical theory was to develop the most desirable formats of real competition rather than to assess its performance solely according to the perfect competition benchmark and to propose some parameters which could help in evaluating the workability of competition.

There was no consensus on the measurement of the *workability* of competition. Different approaches entail different criteria and benchmarks of success. Markham observed that 'the term workable competition defies precise definition',[75] tracing the connection of the term 'workable competition' back to its intellectual predecessor 'perfect competition' with

---

72 Stephen H. Sosnick, 'A Critique of Concepts of Workable Competition', The Quarterly Journal of Economics, Vol. 72, No. 3, 1958, p. 380.

73 John M. Clark, 'Toward a Concept of Workable Competition', The American Economic Review, Vol. 30, No. 2, 1940, p. 241.

74 ibid, pp. 244–245.

75 Jesse W. Markham, 'An Alternative Approach to the Concept of Workable Competition', The American Economic Review, Vol. 40, No. 3, 1950, p. 349.

all its practical weaknesses. The Chicago School proponents criticise the concept for being 'suspicious of almost every industrial practice',[76] suggesting that the very existence of the concept is a consequence of the development of the theory of monopolistic competition.[77] Some US cases prove that this criticism was more than a mere rhetorical tool.[78] Säcker provides a systematic overview of possible workability benchmarks,[79] describing and referencing the following four types: market structure; market phase; market conduct; and market results; while acknowledging that some authors suggest different combinations of the four. Sosnick produced one of the most detailed surveys of the possible combinations between the requirements of the structure, conduct and performance of the industry. He noticed the different patterns and priorities which have been given by different authors with regard to each of the three components, comparing them and evaluating critically the main combinations between the elements of workable competition, and suggested two different criteria for the following analysis. First, these criteria 'demand a satisfactory situation in different combinations of the three categories – just performance, or both conduct and structure, etc. and, within a mutually chosen category, in different combinations of its component elements or dimensions'.[80] The second criterion requires an internal evaluation of different achievements for each dimension and proportions thereof. The last of the three dimensions of the S–C–P paradigm (performance) is the most politically

---

[76] Frank H. Easterbrook, 'Workable Antitrust Policy', Michigan Law Review, Vol. 84, No. 8, 1986, p. 1696.

[77] George W. Stocking, 'The Rule of Reason, Workable Competition, and the Legality of Trade Association Activities', The University of Chicago Law Review, Vol. 21, No. 4, 1954, pp. 535–536: 'Chamberlin is primarily a theorist and as such has been only incidentally concerned with policy, but the policy implications of his theory of monopolistic competition are clear. . . . But economists are a resourceful lot. Having created a dilemma, they resolved it. They did so by developing the concept of workable competition'.

[78] Dissenting opinion of Justice Douglas in *United States v. Columbia Steel Co.*, 334 U.S. 495, 535–536 (1948): 'The philosophy of the Sherman Act is that . . . [i]ndustrial power should be decentralized. It should be scattered into many hands so that the fortunes of the people will not be dependent on the whim or caprice, the political prejudices, the emotional stability of a few self-appointed men. The fact that they are not vicious men but respectable and social-minded is irrelevant'.

[79] Franz Jürgen Säcker, 'Legal Foundations of Competition', in Günther Hirsch, Frank Montag and Franz Jürgen Säcker (eds.), *Competition Law: European Community Practice and Procedure – Article-by-Article Commentary*, Sweet & Maxwell, London, 2008, pp. 11–12.

[80] Stephen H. Sosnick, 'A Critique of Concepts of Workable Competition', The Quarterly Journal of Economics, Vol. 72, No. 3, 1958, p. 381.

sensitive. As a result, it has often been seen as a benchmark for the success of the remaining two, as a matter of ultimate importance. In contrast, the structure and the conduct are usually seen as merely 'necessary' and not 'sufficient' components of the workability of competition. This implies that 'unless the concept of workable competition is to be an instrument of public policy, there is little reason for differentiating between workable and pure competition',[81] which means that the concept is closely connected to the value judgements of the decision-makers. Therefore, the condition of 'workability is relative to various subjective judgements'.[82] By solving the problematic aspects of 'ideal conditions' which are relevant to the concept of perfect competition, the concept of workable competition creates the problem of uncertainty encompassed in the parameters of its workability themselves.[83] As other critics suggest, the concept itself 'fails to indicate how much competition is required to satisfy its pragmatic demands'.[84] In general, according to Hovenkamp, the concept can be perceived as 'an early attempt to create an economic model that took into account such real world market imperfections as economies of scale, information failures, and transaction costs'[85] in order to encourage by means of legal rules and administrative control the market to perform in a similar way as in the model of perfect competition.

Säcker differentiates at least two theoretical traditions in this respect: according to one opinion the workability of competition is measured by market *results*; according to the opposite view it is assessed by market behaviour only.[86] This taxonomy reflects the pendulum nature[87] of the *form-* and *effect*-based assessments of the performance of the

---

[81] Jesse W. Markham, 'An Alternative Approach to the Concept of Workable Competition', The American Economic Review, Vol. 40, No. 3, 1950, p. 361.

[82] Stephen H. Sosnick, 'A Critique of Concepts of Workable Competition', The Quarterly Journal of Economics, Vol. 72, No. 3, 1958, p. 412.

[83] ibid, p. 411: 'The workable-or-unworkable dichotomy . . . still fails to distinguish different degrees of under- or over-fulfilment . . . This would involve a series of categories, including "workable," "almost workable," and "largely unworkable." Such labels should readily be abandoned, however, if the object is merely a fuller description of a suboptimal situation'.

[84] Walter Adams, 'The "Rule of Reason": Workable Competition or Workable Monopoly?', The Yale Law Journal, Vol. 63, No. 3, 1954, p. 364.

[85] Herbert J. Hovenkamp, 'Antitrust Policy after Chicago', Michigan Law Review, Vol. 84, No. 2, 1985, p. 222.

[86] Franz Jürgen Säcker, 'Legal Foundations of Competition', in Günther Hirsch, Frank Montag and Franz Jürgen Säcker (eds.), *Competition Law: European Community Practice and Procedure – Article-by-Article Commentary*, Sweet & Maxwell, London, 2008, pp. 11–12.

[87] Daniel A. Crane, 'Rules Versus Standards in Antitrust Adjudication',

competitive process.[88] Taken separately, the effect-based approach helps to solve the problems of workability, but it cannot address the problem of predictability; the form-based approach delivers the opposite results: it is predictable but creates many externalities. The further development of the theory of competition law reveals that these two approaches dominate the mainstream antitrust discourses interchangeably and they dialectically need each other in order to develop their doctrinal claims.

Another important feature of the Harvard School is its perception of competition within a broader regulatory framework. Competition is not considered as an ultimate economic goal, but it constantly *interacts* with such public interests as welfare, growth or international competitiveness. On the one hand such a 'multigoal approach that can include any type of (desired) goals',[89] by considering competition as an intermediate goal, relativises the peculiarity and economic value of competition. On the other hand it permits one to correlate the interests of competition with other significant public benefits without a *fusion* of the different concepts. This fusion occurs in the models where competition is declared to be the ultimate or absolute goal, since the methodological ignorance of other related economic interests does not eliminate their existence and influence in real life. Thus, the balancing occurs not at the external level (competition vs. welfare), but internally, when competition is defined in a way which includes elements of other economic values (competition as welfare). Such an internal balancing dilutes the conceptual meaning of competition and erodes its semantic consistency. The effect-oriented approach to competition policy can be accepted insofar as it does not interfere with the *meaning* of competition, but merely considers its *external* societal importance as insufficient in comparison to other economic values.

Over the last three decades in the US and over a slightly shorter period in Europe, the effect-based approach was seen as the best solution. Nicolaides suggests that the competitive process itself is indefinable, which explains why the economic rationale is based on practical outcomes.[90]

Washington and Lee Law Review, Vol. 64, No. 1, 2007, p. 2: 'If history is a reliable teacher, the pendulum will eventually swing back toward rules'.

[88] Herbert J. Hovenkamp, 'Antitrust Policy after Chicago', Michigan Law Review, Vol. 84, No. 2, 1985, p. 213: 'If one hundred years of federal antitrust policy have taught us anything, it is that antitrust is both political and cyclical'.

[89] Oliver Budzinski, 'Monoculture versus Diversity in Competition Economics', Cambridge Journal of Economics, Vol. 32, No. 2, 2008, p. 299.

[90] Phedon Nicolaides, 'An Essay on Economics and Competition Law of the European Community', Legal Issues of Economic Integration, Vol. 27, No. 1, 2000, pp. 15–16: 'Neither the number of firms, nor the presence and size of profits are indicators of ability to compete in the market. . . . Only a calculation of

The *victory* of the effect-based approach is arguable and can become Pyrrhic unless the relationship between the two 'wings' of antitrust is not considered as a mutual dependence. This dialectical interconnection is still visible at the methodological level when the two approaches develop their arguments *a contrario*, criticising the opposite view. The internal interdependence between the form and the effect is unbreakable at the ontological level. As soon as one of its parts is perceived as an obstacle or a mere rudiment of antitrust (as is sometimes the case with the present-day perception of the form-based approach),[91] the theory of competition goes into a cycle facing the same conceptual challenges which it was unsuccessfully trying to solve over the whole historical development of antitrust, and which – as Chapter 4 demonstrates – are irresolvable by definition and should be internalised within the debates.

3.1.4 Shaping the Scope of the Goal(s) of Antitrust

The normative argument of the Harvard School that 'competition policy should pursue a bundle of aims (multi-goal approach), which ultimately, are the results of political decisions'[92] can be justified from the premises of this book, even if with some reservation. The issue for this purpose should be separated into two parts: (i) methodological and (ii) jurisdictional. The former relates to the recognition of the connection of different economic, social and political problems which regulators often try to solve at the cost of other important problems. This perpetual intersection of different legitimate objectives has been observed and recognised by the Harvard School and it is accepted by this research as well. However, the reservation has to do with the jurisdictional premise that the entire scope of all societal interests which could be influenced by competition policy should constitute the goal of this policy. In this respect the book suggests the opposite path: antitrust law should stand within its realm, concentrating

---

[competition's] final impact on allocative and technical efficiency can tell whether a certain practice is anti-competitive in the sense of reducing efficiency (and thus reducing social welfare). . . . The character of the agreement is not as important as the effect on the market'.

91 Richard Whish, '*Intel v Commission*: Keep Calm and Carry on!', Journal of European Competition Law & Practice, Vol. 6, No. 1, 2015, p. 1: 'The expression "form-based" is always used pejoratively, but laws by their very nature have "form"'.

92 Wolfgang Kerber and Ulrich Schwalbe, 'Economic Principles of Competition Law', in Günther Hirsch, Frank Montag and Franz Jürgen Säcker (eds.), *Competition Law: European Community Practice and Procedure – Article-by-Article Commentary*, Sweet & Maxwell, London, 2008, p. 222.

exclusively (or at least primarily) upon the problems related to the protection and promotion of competition. Other relevant economic and social objectives should constitute the centre of gravity for other policies: consumer, industrial, federalist, social security and so on. These policies are closely connected, and they may share their legal institutional framework, but they should be analytically separated. The operational, functional aspects of this argument as well as the risk of arbitrariness[93] which this approach contains are explored in the chapter on balancing, in which it is shown how the narrowly defined public policies (and competition *sensu stricto* is also one of them) interact on the regulatory level in order to be prioritised by the decision-makers (Chapter 5.3.4). At this stage, however, it is important to recognise that the Harvard School defended the necessity of balancing, while acknowledging its failure to separate competition as an independent parameter in this balancing.

Prima facie, the Chicagoans – the intellectual successors and the main opponents of the Harvard School – have managed to address the problem of the multifaceted nature of competition policy, narrowing its main goal to efficiency and total welfare. However, the Chicago School did not manage to single out competition as a separate public value and emphasised the desirable outcomes of competition rather than the process itself. This conceptual 'merger' of the competitive process with economic efficiency provided a rich methodological soil for the following internalisation of such utilitarian public values as consumer welfare into the core of antitrust analysis, eliminating the natural borders between different societal values and perceiving the organic conflicts between them as a negative externality which always needs to be resolved in favour of the welfare of consumers.

3.1.5 The Chicago School

The way in which problems of competition and its legal regulation were addressed by the representatives of the Harvard School was challenged by many authors from different perspectives. Economists predominantly criticised the S–C–P paradigm, lawyers and policy-makers – the ideological premises of the Harvard School.[94] Since the 1960s the political and eco-

---

93 ibid: 'From the legal perspective, the normative openness of the concept of the Harvard School has some appeal, because this leaves scope for the legislator (and the courts) to decide on the aims of competition policy. In economics, however, this openness was criticised because of the risk of arbitrariness with regard to the aims of competition policy'.

94 Robert H. Bork and Ward S. Bowman, Jr., 'The Crisis in Antitrust', Columbia Law Review, Vol. 65, No. 3, 1965, pp. 363–364: 'From its inception with the passage

nomic circumstances prepared the ground for the development of a new paradigm in antitrust scholarship and practice, which reached its peak in the 1980s. Its various insights concerning the role of regulation in competition policy and the perception of the phenomenon of competition as such were conceptually integrated under the term Chicago School. Its main characteristics were reduced by Coate and Fischer to 'first that antitrust is primarily a question of economics; and second that economics *is* neoclassical price theory'.[95] According to Easterbrook, the Chicago School's legacy is 'thoroughgoing skepticism – doubts about the use of abstract models, about the wisdom of legal rules designed to move the economy closer to a model of atomistic competition'[96] as well as a critical approach to the idea that the main natural purpose of firms is to cartelise a market. Unlike the Harvard School, the Chicagoans perceived the changes in the structure of the markets as an indication of 'a development towards superior, i.e. more efficient, solutions and not an accumulation of anticompetitive market power'.[97] It should be noticed, however, that inasmuch as the neoclassical apparatus required the Chicagoans to focus 'much more on individual preferences and decision making than did classical economics',[98] this condition was not fully coherent with the normative non-intervention narrative, inherited from classical economics. The incoherency is based on the conditional, relative character of non-intervention in the Chicago tradition. The conditionality implies that the neoclassical reasoning could potentially abandon the non-intervention imperative if the latter were found not to be the optimal solution for the individual preferences. This may explain why the standard of consumer welfare, which was originally developed and used by the Chicago School as a pro-defendant tool, has been so easily utilised by their ideological opponents,[99] which applied the same standard to justify more regulatory interventions. Unlike the Harvard School, the Chicagoan

---

of the Sherman Act . . . in 1890, antitrust has vacillated between the policy of preserving competition and the policy of preserving competitors from their more energetic and efficient rivals. It is the rapid acceleration of the latter "protectionist" trends in antitrust that has brought on the present crisis. Anti-free-market forces now have the upper hand and are steadily broadening and consolidating their victory'.

95 Malcolm B. Coate and Jeffrey H. Fischer, 'Can Post-Chicago Economics Survive *Daubert*?', Akron Law Review, Vol. 34, No. 4, 2001, p. 796.

96 Frank H. Easterbrook, 'Workable Antitrust Policy', Michigan Law Review, Vol. 84, No. 8, 1986, p. 1698.

97 Oliver Budzinski, 'Monoculture versus Diversity in Competition Economics', Cambridge Journal of Economics, Vol. 32, No. 2, 2008, p. 300.

98 Daniel M. Hausman, 'Economic Methodology in a Nutshell', The Journal of Economic Perspectives, Vol. 3, No. 2, 1989, p. 117.

99 Oles Andriychuk, 'Dialectical Antitrust: An Alternative Insight into the

approach reduces the goal of antitrust policy to competition, but it perceives competition in terms of total or consumer welfare.

Despite strong methodological and substantive opposition between the Chicago and Harvard Schools, the former in some sense continues the work of the latter,[100] developing, reinterpreting and applying certain aspects of the concept of workable competition.[101] The relativity of the doctrinal distinctions between the schools can be also explained by the fact that 'there is no central creedal authority to delimit orthodoxy and heresy'.[102] With the passing of time their ideological and methodological differences became even less visible.[103] In some cases the effect-based premises of the concept have been used by the Chicago School in order to reveal the necessity of abandoning legalistic formalism in antitrust; in others the Chicago School itself supports the form-based approach, suggesting per se legality of certain commercial practices which were originally perceived as anticompetitive. These similarities reflect strong interconnections in the

---

Methodology of the EC Competition Law Analysis in a Period of Economic Downturn', European Competition Law Review, Vol. 31, No. 4, 2010, p. 159.

[100] There were also many (usually fairly synthetic) attempts to provide a monolithic narrative of the development of antitrust, which abandon the Harvard–Chicago dichotomy, suggesting that 'the courts and agencies should adopt a "third way" that builds upon the insights of both Schools' (Thomas A. Piraino, 'Reconciling the Harvard and Chicago Schools: A New Antitrust Approach for the 21st Century', Indiana Law Journal, Vol. 82, No. 2, 2007, p. 347).

[101] Richard A. Posner, 'The Rule of Reason and the Economic Approach: Reflections on the *Sylvania* Decision', The University of Chicago Law Review, Vol. 45, No. 1, 1977, p. 2: 'My interest in *Sylvania* is based not only on the fact that it is one of the most discussed antitrust decisions of recent years. I briefed and argued the *Schwinn* case for the government. Subsequently, my views on the proper treatment of restrictions in distribution under the antitrust laws took a 180-degree turn, and the article [Richard A. Posner, 'Antitrust Policy and the Supreme Court: An Analysis of the Restricted Distribution, Horizontal Merger and Potential Competition Decisions', Vol. 75, No. 2, 1975.] expressing my new thinking was heavily cited by the majority in *Sylvania*'.

[102] Daniel A. Crane, 'Chicago, Post-Chicago, and Neo-Chicago', The University of Chicago Law Review, Vol. 76, No. 4, 2009, p. 1915. Crane follows on, supplementing his metaphor with another one: '[i]ntellectual "schools" tend to be "Protestant" rather than "Catholic"' (ibid., p. 1915).

[103] Herbert J. Hovenkamp, 'Antitrust and the Costs of Movement', University of Iowa Legal Studies Research Paper, 12, 2010, p. 8: 'Today, structuralist orthodoxy and the S-C-P paradigm are dead and not likely to rise again. The "orthodox" Chicago School is perhaps not quite as dead, but it certainly has not produced the kind of excitement that it did forty or fifty years ago. It has become commonplace to say that the Harvard School has gradually moved to the right and the Chicago School to the left, with the result that the two are almost indistinguishable on most issues'.

subject area of antitrust as well as continuity in economic thinking based on the equilibrium model. It should not overshadow the major differences between these two schools. In a word, it is not submitted that these schools are essentially identical, but that the perception of their absolute difference must be relativised.

One of the main judicial decisions which paved the way to a broad recognition of the premises of the Chicago School in antitrust scholarship and practice was the *Sylvania* case[104] in which the US Supreme Court dismissed per se illegalities of vertical territorial restrictions, overruling the former well-established *Dr. Miles*[105] and *Schwinn*[106] doctrines, which conversely recognised the per se illegality of these practices. As Page explains, 'the Supreme Court adopted a major tenet of Chicago analysis when it recognized the free rider problem as a political justification for vertical territorial restrictions'.[107] This was only one of the many landmark cases[108] which interpreted antitrust rules in the Chicago School tradition. In order to maintain continuity the Court seldom overruled its older, more interventionist judgments, preferring rather to re-interpret them in a more laissez-faire manner.[109] One of the main components of the academic and political success of the Chicago School was the fact that its main protagonists were both outstanding academics and very influential political decision-makers, particularly with respect to the judicial branch (which, by its very nature, is more stable and much less influenced by electoral swings).

Historically, one of the main merits of the Chicago School, which is acknowledged by some of its critics, was its 'significant contributions to the law, particularly at a time when antitrust law seemed to have no direction except to expand'.[110] Originally, the school appeared as a law and economics movement in antitrust.[111] The general framework of the

---

104 *Continental T.V., Inc. v. GTE Sylvania, Inc.*, 433 U.S. 36 (1977).

105 *Dr. Miles Medical Co. v. John D. Park & Sons Co.*, 220 U.S. 373 (1911).

106 *United States v. Arnold, Schwinn & Co.*, 388 U.S. 365 (1967).

107 William H. Page, 'Legal Realism and the Shaping of Modern Antitrust', Emory Law Journal, Vol. 44, No. 1, 1995, p. 47.

108 For a not-exhaustive list see e.g. Frank H. Easterbrook, 'Workable Antitrust Policy', Michigan Law Review, Vol. 84, No. 8, 1986, pp. 1698–1699.

109 William H. Page, 'Legal Realism and the Shaping of Modern Antitrust', Emory Law Journal, Vol. 44, No. 1, 1995, p. 51: 'Rather than overrule established precedents, the Court has reinterpreted those precedents in light of Chicago's positive models, integrating the insights of the models with the Warren Court's formal standards'.

110 Eleanor M. Fox, 'Consumer Beware Chicago', Michigan Law Review, Vol. 84, No. 8. 1986, p. 1714.

111 William H. Page, 'The Chicago School and the Evolution of Antitrust: Characterization, Antitrust Injury, and Evidentiary Sufficiency', Virginia Law

Chicago analysis has been diverted from the institutional aspects of antitrust regulation towards the conduct of individual firms. The structural presumptions of the form-based aspect of the S–C–P paradigm have been criticised and an alternative approach which concentrates on individual practices has been proposed instead. The benchmark of the workability of antitrust policy has been oriented towards economic performance: *total* welfare for the core Chicago analysis or *consumer* welfare for its moderate and later versions. Both terms embrace the notion that 'allocative efficiency as defined by the market should be the only goal of the antitrust laws'.[112] According to Easterbrook, '[g]oals based on something other than efficiency (or its close proxy consumers' welfare) really call on judges to redistribute income' – but this task goes beyond their mission and capacity; judges cannot make political choices – because '[j]udges have no metric'.[113] This view is consonant with Hovenkamp's concerns about the Post-Chicago School.[114] Another regulatory premise of the Chicago School is that the cost 'of erroneously finding a practice lawful . . . is likely to be less than the cost of erroneously finding the practice unlawful, since the market will ineluctably erode private monopolistic practices, but inefficient governmental interventions will persist indefinitely'.[115] Further, the prima facie technical economic calculus of wealth maximisation has been perceived as 'the soundest ethical basis for the organization and operation of social institutions'.[116] Ethical concerns are unavoidable even in a pragmatic

---

Review, Vol. 75, No. 7, 1989, p. 1229: 'The Chicago approach is, first of all, a part of the Law and Economics movement at Chicago, . . . which is itself a part of the Chicago School of economics'.

112 Herbert J. Hovenkamp, 'Antitrust Policy after Chicago', Michigan Law Review, Vol. 84, No. 2, 1985, p. 215.

113 Frank H. Easterbrook, 'Workable Antitrust Policy', Michigan Law Review, Vol. 84, No. 8, 1986, pp. 1703–1704.

114 Herbert J. Hovenkamp, 'The Reckoning of Post-Chicago Antitrust', in Antonio Cucinotta, Roberto Pardolesi and Roger Van den Bergh (eds.), *Post-Chicago Developments in Antitrust Law*, Edward Elgar Publishing, Cheltenham, 2002, p. 4: '[T]he biggest danger presented by post-Chicago antitrust economics is not that the variety and likelihood of anticompetitive practices will be exaggerated . . . [T]he biggest danger is that antitrust tribunals will be confronted with antitrust problems that they are not capable of administrating'.

115 William H. Page, 'The Chicago School and the Evolution of Antitrust: Characterization, Antitrust Injury, and Evidentiary Sufficiency', Virginia Law Review, Vol. 75, No. 7, 1989, p. 1243.

116 Richard Schmalbeck, 'The Justice of Economics: An Analysis of Wealth Maximization as a Normative Goal', Columbia Law Review, Vol. 83, No. 2, 1983, p. 488.

cost-benefit calculus.[117] The arguments of Easterbrook have been criticised, inter alia, by Fox, who submitted that the Chicago School is no less selective than any other school in advocating only certain rules.[118] A substantive analysis and criticism of the concept of consumer welfare and its transformation into the paramount goal of antitrust is developed in the relevant part of the research, in which the different approaches to the goals of competition policy and law are explored and compared. At this point it was only necessary to highlight some historical characteristics of the Chicago School.

The areas that raise anticompetitive concerns for the Chicago approach are limited to horizontal hardcore cartels and horizontal mergers with monopolisation effect.[119] According to Hovenkamp,[120] the Chicago School can be characterised by the following features: (i) economic efficiency is the exclusive goal of antitrust; (ii) regardless of the size, most markets are competitive; (iii) the monopolist's high profits tend to attract newcomers, thereby eliminating the problem of abuse of market power; (iv) natural barriers to entry are also not absolute, and most of them are of a hypothetical nature; (v) economies of scale are far more pervasive than was usually thought; (vi) vertical integration and resale price maintenance is almost always efficient, since it is in the interest of both agents to behave competitively; (vii) the primary and sole task of firms is to maximise profits; (viii) regulatory measures should be very well designed in order to avoid primarily Type I errors (false positives; prohibition of something which should not be in fact prohibited);[121] (ix) regulatory intervention

---

117 George J. Stigler, 'Economics or Ethics', The Tanner Lectures on Human Values, Harvard University, 1980, http://tannerlectures.utah.edu/_documents/a-to-z/s/stigler81.pdf, accessed on 14 January 2011, p. 145: 'Of course the ethical questions are inescapable: one must have goals in judging policies, and these goals will certainly have ethical content, however well concealed it may be'.

118 Eleanor M. Fox, 'Consumer Beware Chicago', Michigan Law Review, Vol. 84, No. 8, 1986, p. 1718: 'The difference between Chicago and its critics is not that Chicago offers administrable policy and that its critics offer concepts and balances so complex that antitrust cannot work. Both Chicago and its critics support some rules that are clear and support other rules and inquiries that are more complex. Chicago rejects some perfectly good simple rules'.

119 Oliver Budzinski, 'Monoculture versus Diversity in Competition Economics', Cambridge Journal of Economics, Vol. 32, No. 2, 2008, p. 301.

120 Herbert J. Hovenkamp, *Federal Antitrust Policy: The Law of Competition and Its Practice*, Thomson West, St. Paul, 2005, pp. 62–63.

121 Frank H. Easterbrook, 'Does Antitrust Have a Comparative Advantage?', Harvard Journal of Law & Public Policy, Vol. 23, No. 1, 1999, p. 7: '[A]lthough judges may be able to fix markets when they are monopolized, other social institutions may have a comparative advantage. . . . Competition is the long-run solution

is costly and on average is not capable of improving even those market imperfections which are worth improving; (x) in allocative terms antitrust policy should be politically neutral, because if the total welfare increases, this will benefit the interests of consumers and vulnerable groups in the long run. These characteristics are theoretically consonant with those provided by Page.[122]

Methodologically, the Chicago School does not deal with sophisticated econometrical formulas, typical of the more nuanced economic approach of the Harvard School. They replace strict regulatory intentions and elaborate statistical analysis with a categorical imperative of non-intervention; the necessity for complex economic data is trumped by ideological laissez-faire maxims;[123] the appeal to legal certainty is overruled by reference to economic efficiency; references to competitors' rights are dealt with by the invocation of the interests of consumers. The Chicago School in this respect is more an ideological than a methodological movement: it started by advocating the methodology of the rule of reason, referring to the more differentiated, inductive, case-by-case approach, but eventually started to

---

to monopoly. On rare occasions this may not work. Unless we know that it fails, however, judges ought to apply their talents in other fields, where they have a comparative advantage'.

[122] William H. Page, 'The Chicago School and the Evolution of Antitrust: Characterization, Antitrust Injury, and Evidentiary Sufficiency', Virginia Law Review, Vol. 75, No. 7, 1989, pp. 1230–1231: 'Most descriptions of Chicago antitrust economics also emphasize its reliance on neoclassical price theory, . . . and certainly there are important general bodies of theory that underlie the approach. These more general shared commitments of Chicago scholars include the principle of maximizing behavior and other conventional neoclassical conditions for equilibrium in competition and in noncompetitive market structures that guide Chicago economics generally. . . . The reliance on price theory leads to a preference for determinate models, such as the theory of cartels . . . and the dominant firm pricing model of oligopoly, . . . and to a skepticism of other models of imperfect competition. . . . The reliance on determinate models, of course, affects the interpretation of market characteristics. Concentration, for example, is viewed as anticompetitive to the extent that it facilitates cartelization . . . or dominant firm pricing. . . . Other bodies of theory are also frequently applied in Chicago analyses. These include treatments of price discrimination, . . . the theory of public goods, . . . natural monopoly (including the theory of contestable markets), . . . in formation costs, . . . and the Coase theory of the firm'.

[123] Jonathan B. Baker, 'A Preface to Post-Chicago Antitrust', in Antonio Cucinotta, Roberto Pardolesi and Roger Van den Bergh (eds.), *Post-Chicago Developments in Antitrust Law*, Edward Elgar Publishing, Cheltenham, 2002, p. 68: '[T]he Chicago School became influential as part of a more general social and political reaction in the USA to the role of government, at roughly the same time that neo-conservatism and deregulation became familiar words'.

defend the application of per se rules with respect to the legality of certain practices. Accordingly, it can be perceived rather as a free market school than a purely competition school.[124] This perhaps partly explains its rhetorical elegance, observed, inter alia, by Hovenkamp, who submits that the 'Chicago School of antitrust analysis is the most coherent and elegant ideology that antitrust has ever experienced. . . . One must admire its simplicity, as well as its confidence in markets and its optimism'.[125]

Wealth maximisation and allocative efficiency,[126] the Chicagoan benchmarks for good performance of antitrust policy, enable a benevolent attitude towards most mergers and vertical agreements. Monopolies and cartels only pose a problem for the Chicago School insofar as 'market power leads to distorted prices and quantities, and such an inefficient allocation implies a loss of total welfare'.[127] This means that purely distributional concerns are not relevant to antitrust analysis from this perspective. Barriers to entry are not considered either as a sufficient reason for regulatory intervention. They are perceived rather as a natural evolutionary process, which each market can arrange better than regulators. Thereby the Schumpeterians in their normative[128] assumptions theory of contestability[129] and theory of potential competition[130] – although

---

[124] Eleanor M. Fox, 'Consumer Beware Chicago', Michigan Law Review, Vol. 84, No. 8, 1986, p. 1714: 'The heart of Chicago School is not its model for finding a violation. . . . Chicago is not fighting a war against inefficiency. Chicago is fighting a war for private freedom of action'.

[125] Herbert J. Hovenkamp, 'Post-Chicago Antitrust: A Review and Critique', Columbia Business Law Review, Vol. 16, No. 2, 2001, p. 258.

[126] Though some authors equate the terms *wealth-maximisation* and *allocative efficiency* (Richard S. Markovits, 'Legal Analysis and The Economic Analysis of Allocative Efficiency', Hofstra Law Review, Vol. 8, No. 4, 1980, p. 811), at least their different genealogy enables the synonymic rather than tautological use of these terms.

[127] Wolfgang Kerber and Ulrich Schwalbe, 'Economic Principles of Competition Law', in Günther Hirsch, Frank Montag and Franz Jürgen Säcker (eds.), *Competition Law: European Community Practice and Procedure – Article-by-Article Commentary*, Sweet & Maxwell, London, 2008, p. 223.

[128] These two approaches, however, are not Schumpeterian in their *positive* analysis, since both operate with static models (as Kerber and Schwalbe observe, 'the conditions of perfectly contestable markets with entirely free market entry and exit almost never exist in real markets', ibid, p. 225); they do not include in their models the dimension of technological progress, whereas the Schumpeterian views on competition imply the dynamism of 'creative destruction'.

[129] William J. Baumol, John C. Panzar and Robert D. Willig, 'Contestable Markets: An Uprising in the Theory of Industry Structure', The American Economic Review, Vol. 73, No. 3, 1983.

[130] Robert H. Bork and Ward S. Bowman, Jr., 'The Crisis in Antitrust', Columbia Law Review, Vol. 65, No. 3, 1965, p. 375: 'Too few people understand

technically perceived as independent economic doctrines – actually ground their ideological roots in the Chicago School tradition too[131] – or the other way around.

Unlike the Harvard School, the Chicago theorists acknowledge the dynamic nature of the competitive process but still apply in their economic models the static methodology of perfect competition and criticise the vast usage of empirical techniques in antitrust analysis, submitting that '[i]f it is too hard for courts to determine what is "efficient" using a simple model, how are courts going to decide cases based on complex, strategic models?';[132] and that the 'purpose of any model is to strip away complications, to make intractable problems manageable, to make things simple enough that we can see how particular variations matter'.[133] The reliance on simple neoclassical economic models is a distinctive feature of the Chicago School, an explanation of its political success. Yet, as Royall argues, 'what many consider to be the crowning achievement of the Chicago School ... may prove to be the cause of its downfall',[134] because these models are not always able to reflect the economic reality adequately. They are rather 'mechanical models drawn by analogy from a Newtonian view of the physical universe'.[135] Other authors accuse economic models of the Chicago School for their selectivity.[136] On the other hand, a similar criticism has been raised against the Post-Chicago,

---

that it is the essential mechanism of competition and its prime virtue that more efficient firms take business away from the less efficient. ... Some businesses will shrink and some will disappear. Competition is an evolutionary process. Evolution requires the extinction of some species as well as the survival of others'.

[131] Oliver Budzinski, 'Monoculture versus Diversity in Competition Economics', Cambridge Journal of Economics, Vol. 32, No. 2, 2008, p. 300.

[132] Frank H. Easterbrook, 'Workable Antitrust Policy', Michigan Law Review, Vol. 84, No. 8, 1986, p. 1700.

[133] ibid, p. 1706.

[134] Sean M. Royall, 'Editor's Note: Symposium Post-Chicago Economics', Antitrust Law Journal, Vol. 63, No. 2, 1995, p. 445.

[135] Lawrence A. Sullivan, 'Economics and More Humanistic Disciplines: What Are the Sources of Wisdom for Antitrust?', University of Pennsylvania Law Review, Vol. 125, No. 6, 1977, p. 1218.

[136] Thomas M. Melsheimer, 'Economics and Ideology: Antitrust in the 1980s', Stanford Law Review, Vol. 42, No. 5, 1990, p. 1335: '[T]he use of economics [by Chicago School proponents] is ideologically selective. If economic learning can assist in labeling a practice procompetitive or, at worst, neutral, then such learning is an appropriate component of the judicial process. If the economic learning, however, causes antitrust concern, it is too cumbersome for judges to handle'.

which has been seen by many as a manageable alternative to the Chicago theory.[137]

Even its doctrinal opponents acknowledge that the 'growing influence of economics on antitrust law can be traced in part to the Chicago School';[138] even though economic analysis has been present in antitrust law from its very beginning,[139] tracing it essentially back to Bentham's utilitarianism.[140] Yet, whereas antitrust 'has always been closely tied to prevailing economic doctrine',[141] the Chicagoans were the most successful in integrating economic reasoning into the legal discourse.[142] In fact, this integration often loses its *inter*disciplinary features, since the very gist of the law and economics movement is to interpret legal institutions through the prism of economic parameters, assuming that the incapacity for self-reflection of the law and its traditional internal apparatus in the absence of some external assistance by economics, which provides the *raison d'être* for the law itself. This subordination of law can hardly be seen as proper interdisciplinarity. This research provides some analysis of the communicative aspects of the problem in the chapter which explores the balancing act (Chapter 5.2, 5.3). Then again, it should be admitted that the ideas

---

137 Malcolm B. Coate, Jeffrey H. Fischer, 'Can Post-Chicago Economics Survive *Daubert*?', Akron Law Review, Vol. 34, No. 4, 2001, pp. 832–833: 'In contrast to Chicago theory, . . . [Post-Chicago economics] offers little, if any, real assistance with which to structure the competitive analysis . . . because they require a broad set of assumptions, some that are explicitly listed by the researcher, while others are tacitly maintained. . . . Therefore, the courts cannot resolve disputes . . . by interpreting the facts in the record. Two conflicting . . . [Post-Chicago] theories may generate entirely different competitive implications not because they judge some facts in the record as important and others as trivial, but because they are based on different virtual fact scenarios'.

138 Louis Kaplow and Carl Shapiro, 'Antitrust', John M. Olin Center for Law, Economics and Business, Discussion Paper No. 575, 2007, p. 1.

139 Louis Kaplow, 'Antitrust, Law & Economics, and the Courts', Law and Contemporary Problems, Vol. 50, No. 4, 1987, pp. 184–187.

140 Louis Kaplow and Steven Shavell, 'Economic Analysis of Law', http://papers.ssrn.com/sol3/papers.cfm?abstract_id5226405, accessed on 19 January 2011, p. 3: 'The field of economic analysis of law may be said to have begun with Bentham'.

141 Herbert J. Hovenkamp, *Federal Antitrust Policy: The Law of Competition and Its Practice*, Thomson West, St. Paul, 2005, p. 60.

142 The emergence of the economic analysis of law has itself been subject to severe criticism, with accusations that '[w]ith its pseudoscientific aura of producing the right answer, the law and economics approach may have appeared irresistible to the uninitiated' (John J. Flynn, James F. Ponsoldt, 'Legal Reasoning and the Jurisprudence of Vertical Restraints: The Limitations of Neoclassical Economic Analysis in the Resolution of Antitrust Disputes', New York University Law Review, Vol. 62, No. 5, 1987, p. 1142).

of the Chicago School remain paramount in many aspects of antitrust economics, policy and law and its role in incorporating economic analysis into the antitrust decision-making process is in general indisputable.[143] The legacy of the Chicago School, like that of all other mainstream antitrust paradigms, 'did two things. First, it gave us much that was useful. Second, it was oversold.'[144]

3.1.6 Consequentialism as a Source of Legal Realism

The Chicago School's methods and principles do not represent the exclusive mode in which economic disciplines address law.[145] Aside from methodological differences, the schools also significantly differ in their normative ideologies.[146] Although the argumentation of the Chicago School is the most representative in terms of how it perceives the correlation between economic efficiency and non-quantifiable societal goods, and is still theoretically among the most influential ones in antitrust, historically it provided neither the first nor the most significant conception of the role of economic analysis in designing the competitive process. Initially economic argumentation was used in antitrust by ideological opponents of the Chicago School – Socio-Legal Studies, Critical Legal Studies and some other *progressive* schools[147] –

---

143 Herbert J. Hovenkamp, 'Antitrust Policy after Chicago', Michigan Law Review, Vol. 84, No. 2, 1985, p. 283: 'The School has placed an emphasis on economic analysis in antitrust jurisprudence that will likely never disappear'.

144 Herbert J. Hovenkamp, 'Post-Chicago Antitrust: A Review and Critique', Columbia Business Law Review, Vol. 16, No. 2, 2001, p. 267.

145 Mercuro (Nicholas Mercuro, 'The Jurisprudential Niche Occupied by Law and Economics', The Journal Jurisprudence, Vol. 2, No. 1, 2009, pp. 72–109.) highlights at least seven economic schools which approach the legal issues. Apart from the Chicago School he lists also public choice theory, institutional law and economics, the new institutional economics, social norms and law and economics, the New Haven school, and Austrian law and economics.

146 John J. Flynn, 'The Misuse of Economic Analysis in Antitrust Litigation', Southwestern University Law Review, Vol. 12, No. 2, 1980, pp. 340–341: '[E]conomic theory is not monolithic. . . . If "economic analysis" is to be given a reasonably comprehensive reading, our range of choices should include the models of, inter alia, the Buddhists, the Marxists, the new-wave radicals, the Austrian analytical school, the neoclassical school, the post-Keynesian, and others. Each significant "school" or tradition of economic theorising is rigorously analytical and at least somewhat persuasive. . . . The truly synthetic analytical superstructure and utterly subjective infrastructure of these several incompatible economic schools, however, cannot be overemphasised. These synthetic and subjective features lead to a multiplicity of coherent but closed systems of thought, each claiming to possess truth'.

147 William H. Page, 'Legal Realism and the Shaping of Modern Antitrust', Emory Law Journal, Vol. 44, No. 1, 1995, p. 2: '[T]wo prominent and often con-

who had a very reserved approach to the ability of markets to correct themselves.[148] In this view, competition policy was considered as a tool for the proper *distribution* of wealth rather than its *generation*.

The reception of economic concepts into the legal discourse was facilitated by developments in legal theory in the first half of the 20th century. The traditional formalist and doctrinaire approaches to the law were successfully contested by *legal realists*, a movement mainly developed in the US, but with some presence in Europe as well. This trend of 'de-mystification' and 'humanisation' of law was based on attempts to rationalise the legal discourse and criticise the infallibility of the authority of the form in law. Its first significant propositions were developed by the American Supreme Court judges Holmes and Cardozo.

Since the main preconditions for legal realism were reactionary rather than purely normative, it was developed mainly as a methodological rather than an ideological theory. As a result, both free market and interventionist principles were embedded into this theory. Balancing was an important part of it.[149] The rise of legal realism was preconditioned by long debates about the indeterminacy of law and the necessity to address legal issues from an interdisciplinary perspective. Ironically, nowadays, it is the latter that claims to be solving the problems of the former. Interdisciplinarity is often considered as the only effective way to address the problem of indeterminacy, ignoring its dilemmatic essence, and thereby transforming itself into another type of legal dogmatism. The main argument of legal realists is that the law should be interpreted in a way which would enable its effective application. This instrumental orientation towards outcomes implies strong philosophical connections with consequentialism. The consequentialist moral-theoretic reasoning plays a pivotal role in the transition of legal-theoretic paradigms from dogmatic, imperative-based formalism to pragmatic, result-oriented realism. Legal realism rejects the autopoietic essence of the law.[150]

---

flicting contemporary schools of legal thought – Law and Economics and Critical Legal Studies – can plausibly claim (or be accused of) descent from realism'.

148 Herbert J. Hovenkamp, 'The First Great Law & Economics Movement', Stanford Law Review, Vol. 42, No. 4, 1990, p. 955: 'In contrast with today's law & economics movement, the first great law & economics movement was dominated by the more liberal ["liberal" in the US context, meaning progressive, left-wing, distributive] American economists'.

149 Richard H. Pildes, 'Avoiding Balancing: The Role of Exclusionary Reasons in Constitutional Law', Hastings Law Journal, Vol. 45, No. 4, 1994, p. 712.

150 Dworkin (Ronald M. Dworkin, 'Law's Ambitions for Itself', Virginia Law Review, Vol. 71, No. 2, 1985, p. 174), being sceptical of both realism and legalism (which he calls positivism) describes the rationale of their proponents

In some sense antitrust emerged as a reaction to the literalist absolute interpretation of the principles grounding freedom of contract and economic activity. This is the historical reason for Bork's *paradoxicality* of antitrust.[151] On the one hand antitrust protects competition as a right to participate in the market process as well as the competitive process as such. On the other hand, competition becomes meaningless in the absence of freedom of economic action. This is the reason why a *realist* interpretation of legal antitrust rules can be consistent with both the laissez-faire Chicago tradition and more interventionist postulates.[152] At the same time similar evolutionary and intentional visions of markets can be defended from non-realist, formalist viewpoints.

3.1.7 The Post-Chicago School

The rapid development of advanced econometrical models and game-theoretic techniques in economics and some political reassessment of the role of regulatory authorities in effective antitrust policy paved the way for the relative decline of the principles and methods developed and advocated by the Chicago School. The variety of theoretical alternatives suggested more refined economic (and other social sciences) solutions for the efficient functioning of the competitive markets. The different visions of the role of market participants, the decision-making process and the estimation of efficient market practices are integrated under the umbrella term 'Post-Chicago School', with the *post* standing for 'the desire for a fresh start'.[153] The historical origins, the adherence to different economic methodologies and the lack of core ideological postulates make it difficult to uncover a monolithic vision of the Post-Chicago School. Svetiev describes at least two powerful traditions (an old, legal, 'civic' one and a new, economic, 'empirical' one) that belong to the Post-

---

in the following way: 'there is no such thing as the law that can have its own ambitions, that can guide the course of its own change. There are only judges who change the law, from time to time, in order to make it better, in their own entirely human view, or simply to repair its gaps enough to decide cases at hand. We do much better, these critics said, to junk the obscurantism, and to insist that the law already in the books, with all its faults and gaps, is the only law we have'.

[151] Robert H. Bork, *The Antitrust Paradox: A Policy at War with Itself*, Basic Books, New York, 1978.

[152] William H. Page, 'Legal Realism and the Shaping of Modern Antitrust', Emory Law Journal, Vol. 44, No. 1, 1995, pp. 43–44.

[153] Karen Petroski, 'Is Post-Positivism Possible?', German Law Journal, Vol. 12, No. 2, 2011, p. 672.

Chicago School.[154] However, certain methodological similarities as well as the relative acceptance of more active regulatory intervention provide enough coherence for taxonomic categorisation and self-identification.[155] The Post-Chicago School shares significant similarities with its intellectual predecessors. One of the most important of these is their perception of economic theory 'as the only lens through which to analyze antitrust issues to the exclusion of other political and social goals'.[156]

It would be simplistic to remark that a main characteristic of the Post-Chicago School is that it is explicitly proactive, though most of the Post-Chicago economists 'despite all kinds of specific disagreements, see a much greater necessity for an active competition policy'.[157] Since its primary concerns are not ideological, but methodological, it can tolerate both laissez-faire and regulatory intervention if they are supported by sound economic evidence. Because the Post-Chicago methods are advanced mainly by econometrics, it tends to emphasise the welfare effect as the clearest yardstick of economic analysis.[158] This 'professionalisation' of antitrust makes the situations where the Post-Chicagoans

---

[154] Yane Svetiev, 'Antitrust Governance: The New Wave of Antitrust', Loyola University Chicago Law Journal, Vol. 38, No.3, 2007, pp. 607–609: '[T]he academic response to the Chicago New Learning in favor of a more robust antitrust policy developed in two broad directions. . . . Antitrust lawyers steeped in the earlier (civic) tradition accepted that in some cases the old antitrust doctrine was consistent with the Chicago insights, and in those cases economic arguments could guide antitrust decision-making. . . . The second line of research was spurred by post-Chicago developments in the economics of industrial organization, with the growth of theoretical and empirical work that models competitive market interactions'.

[155] Oliver Budzinski, 'Modern Industrial Economics and Competition Policy: Open Problems and Possible Limits', IME Working Paper, No. 93/09, 2009, p. 23: 'Where the Chicago School predominantly acknowledged procompetitive efficiency effects, modern industrial economics implies a much more critical view and derives considerably more scope for anticompetitive arrangements and effects'.

[156] Joshua D. Wright, 'The Roberts Court and the Chicago School of Antitrust: The 2006 Term and Beyond', Competition Policy International, Vol. 3, No. 2, 2007, pp. 32–33.

[157] Wolfgang Kerber and Ulrich Schwalbe, 'Economic Principles of Competition Law', in Günther Hirsch, Frank Montag and Franz Jürgen Säcker (eds.), *Competition Law: European Community Practice and Procedure – Article-by-Article Commentary*, Sweet & Maxwell, London, 2008, p. 233.

[158] Oliver Budzinski, 'Monoculture versus Diversity in Competition Economics', Cambridge Journal of Economics, Vol. 32, No. 2, 2008, p. 301: 'Methodologically, post-Chicago industrial economics introduces advanced game theory, linear (and, more infrequently, non-linear) mathematical dynamics, theory-based empirical studies (modern econometrics), and (most recently) experimental economics'.

represent different parties in courts fairly pervasive. Svetiev, addressing in this respect the problem of conflicting expert testimonies, concludes that '[w]hatever the reason for the contest, in most cases courts do not have the tools to resolve it. Yet to deny access to such input altogether by invoking authority based on judicial "intuitions" and "ideologies" seems a peculiar response to this problem'.[159] Sullivan observes in this regard that 'in a post-Chicago world the answer will always depend on what the analyst does with the empirical details'.[160] Budzinski suggests that there is much empirical evidence showing that Post-Chicago economists disagree upon core antitrust issues and concludes that '[t]he claim that there is a broad consensus among industrial economists . . . which can serve as a basis for an objective "scientific competition policy", has to be rejected'.[161]

In contrast to the Chicago School, they see market freedom as one options among others, and not as *the* option. Therefore, Post-Chicago theorists can advocate different visions of the role of antitrust in economic life, perceiving competition either as an independent economic value, or as a means to achieve other economic goals. These goals may differ from deontological fairness and economic right to compete to purely utilitarian consumer welfare, federalist or industrialist interests. The solutions proposed by the Post-Chicagoans also significantly differ from each other, as long as their scientific testability is questionable in principle.[162]

A landmark case which highlights the end of the 'monopoly' of the Chicago-oriented rationale in front of the US Supreme Court is the *Eastman Kodak* decision.[163] However, the transition from the developed narrative to new methods and standards of argumentation was fairly slow. One of the reasons for this was 'the difficulty of developing operational

---

159 Yane Svetiev, 'Antitrust Governance: The New Wave of Antitrust', Loyola University Chicago Law Journal, Vol. 38, No.3, 2007, p. 612.

160 Lawrence A. Sullivan, 'Post-Chicago Economics: Economists, Lawyers, Judges and Enforcement Officials in a Less Determinate Theoretical World', Antitrust Law Journal, Vol. 63, No. 2, 1995, p. 674.

161 Oliver Budzinski, 'Monoculture versus Diversity in Competition Economics', Cambridge Journal of Economics, Vol. 32, No. 2, 2008, p. 304.

162 Herbert J. Hovenkamp, 'The Reckoning of Post-Chicago Antitrust', in Antonio Cucinotta, Roberto Pardolesi and Roger Van den Bergh (eds.), *Post-Chicago Developments in Antitrust Law*, Edward Elgar Publishing, Cheltenham, 2002, p. 5: '[P]ost-Chicago economic theories . . . are not testable in the conventional positivist sense. That is, often all that economists can do is produce data that are minimally consistent with the theory, but often they cannot rule our alternative explanations'.

163 *Eastman Kodak Co. v. Image Technical Services, Inc.*, 504 U.S. 451 (1992).

rules based on game-theoretic approaches'.[164] Furthermore, there are also many cases[165] in which the Court expressed explicit doubts about the reliability of economic expert evidence.[166] The *Kodak* case itself has been considered by some distinguished commentators to be controversial and it was suggested that it 'has done more harm than good and should be overruled'.[167] *Kodak* and *Hartford Fire*[168] were for over 16 years 'the last Supreme Court decision[s] favourable to plaintiffs in any sort of antitrust suit'.[169] The development of antitrust jurisprudence later on[170] may, however, serve an as indication of some changes in the position of the Supreme Court in this respect.

At the methodological level the Post-Chicago School is characterised by its reliance on inductive analysis,[171] basing its techniques on a rich Industrial Organisation methodology with its elaborated empirical research,[172] focusing 'on quantifiable, short-run welfare effects'[173] and its rejection of classical abstract economic presumptions.[174] This

---

164 Christopher M. Grengs, 'Verizon v. Trinko: From Post-Chicago Antitrust to Resource-Advantage Competition', Journal of Law, Economics and Policy, Vol. 2, No. 1, 2006, p. 127.

165 *Daubert v. Merrell Dow Pharm., Inc.*, 509 U.S. 579 (1993); *General Elec. Co. v. Joiner*, 522 U.S. 136 (1997); *Kumho Tire Co. v. Carmichael*, 526 U.S. 137 (1999).

166 Malcolm B. Coate and Jeffrey H. Fischer, 'Can Post-Chicago Economics Survive *Daubert*?', Akron Law Review, Vol. 34, No. 4, 2001, p. 795.

167 Herbert J. Hovenkamp, 'Post-Chicago Antitrust: A Review and Critique', Columbia Business Law Review, Vol. 16, No. 2, 2001, p. 282.

168 *Hartford Fire Ins. v. California* (91-1111), 509 U.S. 764 (1993).

169 Warren S. Grimes, 'Fifteen Years of Supreme Court Antitrust Jurisprudence: The Defendant Always Wins', in Roger Zäch, Andreas Heinemann and Andreas Kellerhals (eds.), *The Development of Competition Law – Global Perspectives*, Edward Elgar Publishing, Cheltenham, 2010, p. 29.

170 *American Needle, Inc. v. National Football League* 560 U. S. ____ - 08-661 (2010).

171 Malcolm B. Coate and Jeffrey H. Fischer, 'Can Post-Chicago Economics Survive *Daubert*?', Akron Law Review, Vol. 34, No. 4, 2001, p. 822: 'Chicago analysis represents an example of generalizing [i.e. "deductive" as the context of the paper reveals] theory, while Post-Chicago Economics defines various types of exemplifying [i.e. "inductive"] theories'.

172 Herbert J. Hovenkamp, 'The Antitrust Movement and the Rise of Industrial Organisation', Texas Law Review, Vol. 68, No. 1, 1989, p. 112: '[T]he early writers on industrial organization were concerned largely with policy problems. As the field of industrial organization matured, it became more technical and theoretical, and less concerned with policy'.

173 Oliver Budzinski, 'Monoculture versus Diversity In Competition Economics', Cambridge Journal of Economics, Vol. 32, No. 2, 2008, p. 301.

174 Lawrence A. Sullivan, 'Post-Chicago Economics: Economists, Lawyers, Judges and Enforcement Officials in a Less Determinate Theoretical World',

also distinguishes them from the Chicago School, which bases itself on a classical deductive, presumptions-oriented analytical reasoning and criticises its methodological opponents on account of the open-endedness and epistemological indeterminacy of empiricism.[175] This new 'expertise-based' antitrust economics transforms theoreticians into direct participants in the litigation process, who, following Sullivan, 'take on the roles of advocates, presenting and explaining the outcomes they reached to a court or agency by means of contextual analysis'.[176] The game-theoretic approach of the Post-Chicago School provides a good analysis of 'how strategic actions may generate more complex firm behaviour than a simple model would predict'.[177] The negative externality of this modelling is that it can envisage, predict and justify almost any reasonable conduct and outcome.[178] The economic rationale of the Industrial Organisation still requires putting the emphasis more on the welfare effects[179] than on any deontological aspect of competition.

Despite the fact that the 'Chicago School means many different things to different people in the antitrust community',[180] its main premises are identifiable. Conversely, the very term 'Post-Chicago' implies that the movement connects itself to the Chicago School, even if in a critical way, and that the better understanding of the main postulates of Post-Chicago

---

Antitrust Law Journal, Vol. 63, No.2, 1995, p. 678: '[P]ost-Chicagoans must persuade the Court or jury to accept their way of organising and evaluating myriad factual details to reach a judgment that is factual and particular, not normative and universal'.

[175] Some authors (e.g. John J. Flynn, 'Legal Reasoning, Antitrust Policy and the Social "Science" of Economics', Antitrust Bulletin, Vol. 33, No. 4, 1988) conversely suggest that the Chicago School's methodology is 'a simplistic form of deductive logic' (ibid., p. 724) providing detailed and elaborate arguments in this respect (ibid., pp. 724–727).

[176] Lawrence A. Sullivan, 'Post-Chicago Economics: Economists, Lawyers, Judges and Enforcement Officials in a Less Determinate Theoretical World', Antitrust Law Journal, Vol. 63, No. 2, 1995, p. 678.

[177] Malcolm B. Coate and Jeffrey H. Fischer, 'Can Post-Chicago Economics Survive *Daubert*?', Akron Law Review, Vol. 34, No. 4, 2001, p. 796.

[178] More radical critique suggests that 'the non-legal "barriers to entry" literature in industrial organization is hopelessly confused and the bulk of it must be ignored for antitrust purposes', Dominick T. Armentano, 'Time to Repeal Antitrust Regulation?', The Antitrust Bulletin, Vol. 35, No. 2, 1990, p. 314.

[179] Oliver Budzinski, 'Modern Industrial Economics and Competition Policy: Open Problems and Possible Limits', IME Working Paper, No. 93/09, 2009, p. 15.

[180] Joshua D. Wright, 'The Roberts Court and the Chicago School of Antitrust: The 2006 Term and Beyond', Competition Policy International, Vol. 3, No. 2, 2007, p. 26.

antitrust lies in its main points of disagreement with the Chicagoans. Royall[181] describes the five most common aspects of their opposition:[182] (i) the abstraction and simplicity of economic presumptions which imply that all market participants are driven exclusively by intentions of profit maximisation, which ultimately are always beneficial for total welfare; (ii) the reliance upon economic theory as opposed to empirical facts (it must be added that the Chicago School shows much greater flexibility when the issue of per se illegality is concerned – this shows that the new opponents of the Chicago School are *Post*-Chicagoans in relation to some questions and *neo*-Chicagoans for others); (iii) placing too much confidence in the market's self-discipline (though this aspect was never advocated straightforwardly by the Chicago School, Chicagoans were never orthodox libertarians and the financial crisis in 2008–2010 led some of them to reaffirm this stand more explicitly);[183] (iv) an overly narrow view of market power and conceptual toleration (sometimes the better term is 'justification') of market dominance; and (v) a limited view of efficiency, restricted to its allocative aspects and general hostility towards its 'proactively improved' elements.

Although the history of antitrust ideas cannot be drawn in clear and homogeneous periods, dominated by one or another vision of competition, the conflict between the evolutionary (laissez-faire) and the intentionalist (proactive, interventionalist) perceptions of the market process can be taken as a relevant epistemological guide to understand the shift from one antitrust set of criteria to the other. Both approaches have their strong theoretical roots in 19th-century economic thought. The former is based on the ideas of Darwin and to an even larger extent of Spencer;[184] the latter on the ideas developed by representatives of the Historical School and institutionalism. According to Page, 'the conflict . . . is part of a dialectic between two opposing, incommensurable ideologies that has persisted for

---

[181] Sean M. Royall, 'Editor's Note: Symposium Post-Chicago Economics', Antitrust Law Journal, Vol. 63, No. 2, 1995, pp. 445–447.

[182] For a more economic analysis of the main differences between the schools see Malcolm B. Coate and Jeffrey H. Fischer, 'Can Post-Chicago Economics Survive *Daubert*?', Akron Law Review, Vol. 34, No. 4, 2001, pp. 813–816.

[183] Richard A. Posner, *A Failure of Capitalism: The Crisis of '08 and the Descent into Depression*, Harvard University Press, Cambridge, Massachusetts, 2009.

[184] Mary S. Morgan, 'Competing Notions of "Competition" In Late Nineteenth-Century American Economics', History of Political Economy, Vol. 25, No. 4, 1993, p. 579: 'The evolutionary view of the world was made vivid for American social theorists of the late nineteenth century – not so much by Charles Darwin, but by Herbert Spencer's evolutionary sociology'.

centuries . . . [and it] is inherent in antitrust',[185] perceiving the Sherman Act as a compromise between them.[186] Wright, however, sees 'many problems with this pendulum narrative', suggesting among other things that it 'tempted commentators to adopt extreme and misleading descriptions of one camp or the other – but most frequently of the Chicago School'.[187] Acknowledging the relativity of such a historical modelling, this book still presumes that 'the pendulum narrative' permits the problem of switch in antitrust priorities to be addressed. Although the role of the main antitrust schools cannot be reduced to the question of their ideological conflicts,[188] doctrinal tensions between evolutionists and intentionalists played an important role in shaping the main antitrust concepts.[189] From this perspective, the emergence of the Post-Chicago School can be perceived as a reaction to the dominance of evolutionary premises in antitrust, under the influence of the Chicago School. These views were based on a presumption of the universal nature of economic laws, which do not depend on particularities and contexts. One of the paramount economic maxims advocated by the Chicagoans was that of market self-correcting forces.

The second dimension of the dichotomy between these schools can be seen in another perpetual 'natural' economic law: the conflict between universalists and historicists. It can be traced through whole history of Western economic thought, and received its conceptual description in the writings of Menger.[190] While universalists suggest that economic life

---

[185] William H. Page, 'Ideological Conflict and the Origins of Antitrust Policy', Tulane Law Review, Vol. 66, No. 1, 1991, p. 6.

[186] William H. Page, 'The Ideological Origins and Evolution of U.S. Antitrust Law', in Wayne D. Collins (ed.), *Issues in Competition Law and Policy*, American Bar Association Publishing, Chicago, 2008, p. 3.

[187] Joshua D. Wright, 'The Roberts Court and the Chicago School of Antitrust: The 2006 Term and Beyond', Competition Policy International, Vol. 3, No. 2, 2007, p. 32.

[188] Herbert J. Hovenkamp, 'The Reckoning of Post-Chicago Antitrust', in Antonio Cucinotta, Roberto Pardolesi and Roger Van den Bergh (eds.), *Post-Chicago Developments in Antitrust Law*, Edward Elgar Publishing, Cheltenham, 2002, p. 3.: '"Post-Chicago" antitrust policy represents little more than another swing in antitrust's ideological pendulum'.

[189] William H. Page, 'Legal Realism and the Shaping of Modern Antitrust', Emory Law Journal, Vol. 44, No. 1, 1995, pp. 47–49.

[190] Walter Eucken, *The Foundations of Economics: History and Theory in the Analysis of Economic Reality*, The University of Chicago Press, Chicago, 1951, pp. 55–56: 'Menger laid down the principle on which many economists carry on their work. A dualism has become widely established in economics. What the theoretical sciences aim at or seek to know is the *general* of phenomena, and for the historical sciences it is the *individual* or particular aspects and characteristics of the empiri-

is subject to general, organic principles of how the relations between the rational actors and their regulators are organised, historicists submit that there is not much use for general economic laws, unless they are adapted to a peculiar set of circumstances characteristic of any country at any moment in its historical development. The shift from one antitrust trend to the other is always predetermined by changes in the mainstream economic narrative. The establishment of the Harvard School with its S–C–P paradigm can be seen as a reaction of universalists to the development of the Empirical Institutional Organisation perspective.[191] From the very beginning of antitrust law American Industrial Organisation theory has been separated into two methodological parts: the neoclassical universalists, 'highly theoretical, ideologically conservative, suspicious of empirical research'[192] and the empirical historicists, who, conversely, were 'suspicious of theory, which [allegedly] could easily be manipulated for political ends'.[193] Being universalist by nature, the S–C–P paradigm absorbed the emerging trend of the context dependency of antitrust policy advocated by the Empirical Institutional Organisation approach, which by its nature is historical. The Harvard School, with its strong historical elements (the elements of the Empirical Institutional Organisation were absorbed and not eliminated) was eventually replaced by the Chicago School, which advocates a strongly universalist methodology with its common reliance on the invisible hand of the market and universal principles of wealth maximisation. The Chicago School has subsequently been replaced in turn by the more context-dependent and empirically based Post-Chicago School, which by its nature is historical. Despite some synthetic elements, the same pendulous switches can also be observed during earlier periods in economic history. These two elements are mutually dependent because '[w]ithout general-theoretical study there can be no scientific experience in . . . [economics], just as there cannot be without individual-historical study'.[194] Another possible criterion to distinguish

cal world. The two objectives are equally justified, particularly in economics' (emphasis in the original).

191 Wolfgang Kerber and Ulrich Schwalbe, 'Economic Principles of Competition Law', in Günther Hirsch, Frank Montag and Franz Jürgen Säcker (eds.), *Competition Law: European Community Practice and Procedure – Article-by-Article Commentary*, Sweet & Maxwell, London, 2008, p. 220.

192 Herbert J. Hovenkamp, 'The Antitrust Movement and the Rise of Industrial Organisation', Texas Law Review, Vol. 68, No. 1, 1989, p. 112.

193 ibid.

194 Walter Eucken, *The Foundations of Economics: History and Theory in the Analysis of Economic Reality*, The University of Chicago Press, Chicago, 1951, p. 42.

the Chicago and Post-Chicago Schools has been suggested by Hovenkamp in his seminal piece 'Antitrust Policy after Chicago'.[195] He refers to '[o]ne of the most significant debates in welfare economics',[196] namely that between the marginalist and ordinalist schools. The former emphasised the individual, subjective importance of value (basing the presumption on the principle of marginal utility), while the latter is purely 'objective' in this respect. The Chicago School may be perceived in this respect as having an ordinalist approach (measuring welfare with 'constant dollars'), with no or minimal concerns for the redistribution of wealth (with 'slicing up the pie fairly'),[197] whereas the Post-Chicago School is much more marginalist in this respect ('a sum of money given to a poor person might enable the poor person to educate herself or buy an automobile, while the same sum given to a wealthy person would have no measurable effect on the wealthy person's behavior').[198] This aspect of the taxonomy is correlated to the problem of in-/commensurability and is addressed in this book in relation to the philosophical foundations of competition and the question of balancing.

Finally, the third possible way of distinguishing the Chicago and Post-Chicago Schools is the conflict between economic positivists and normativists (these two parts can be classified further as well).[199] The separation is common in social sciences (and is addressed in a more theoretical way in Chapter 4; its practical implications are also relevant to the discussion of balancing). In law the positive analysis should not be confused with positivism. The former 'attempts to describe the phenomena of law not in propositions that state how men should behave under certain circumstances, but in propositions that tell how they

---

[195] Herbert J. Hovenkamp, 'Antitrust Policy after Chicago', Michigan Law Review, Vol. 84, No. 2, 1985.

[196] ibid, p. 236.

[197] Laurence H. Tribe, 'Constitutional Calculus: Equal Justice or Economic Efficiency?', Harvard Law Review, Vol. 98, No. 3, 1985, p. 593.

[198] Herbert J. Hovenkamp, 'Antitrust Policy after Chicago', Michigan Law Review, Vol. 84, No. 2, 1985, p. 237.

[199] Coleman (Jules L. Coleman, 'Efficiency, Exchange, and Auction: Philosophic Aspects of the Economic Approach to Law', California Law Review, Vol. 68, No. 2, 1980, pp. 221–222) separates law and economics into the normative and analytical, with the following separation of the latter upon the descriptive (providing the economic rationale for application of the existing legal rules) and positive (providing economic rationale for the legal system in general, giving economic models as an epistemic tool for understanding the law); Posner (Richard A. Posner, 'Law and Economics in Common-Law, Civil-Law, and Developing Nations', Ratio Juris, Vol. 17, No. 1, 2004, p. 67) talks about heuristic, descriptive and normative functions of economic analysis of law.

actually do behave'.[200] The latter suggests, on the contrary, that law should be applied regardless of its eventual efficiency. In other words, the former aspect relies on what has been *posited by the natural course of events* and the latter on what has been *posited by law*. The taxonomy became popular in economics after the publication of Friedman's essay 'The Methodology of Positive Economics',[201] but the very essence of the conflict has been present throughout the history of modern economic thought. Friedman himself attributes its articulation in the economic context to Keynes (John Neville, not John Maynard), who distinguishes between 'the conception of political economy as a positive, abstract and deductive science' and 'the conception of political economy as an ethical, realistic and inductive science'.[202] Friedman submits at the very outset that '[c]onfusion between positive and normative economics is to some extent inevitable',[203] setting up the important methodological premise that pure positive economics should be free of any ethical considerations. Keynes's research shows that because each method is a complex and relatively self-sufficient model of analysis, the protagonists of both methods often interpret the same classical texts in their own manner. Budzinski refers to the eloquent Carrollian 'mile-to-mile-map'-style[204] insight of Robertson[205] and suggests that '[t]he analytical dimension of the selection problem refers to the non-existence of one "right" model. Each model inevitably must simplify the underlying real case (complexity reduction) in order to create meaningful information'.[206] This leads to the situation where, for example '[i]t has been said of [Adam Smith] that he first raised political economy to the dignity of a deductive science. But he has also been regarded as the founder of the historical method

200 Hans Kelsen, 'The Pure Theory of Law and Analytical Jurisprudence', Harvard Law Review, Vol. 55, No. 1, 1941, p. 52.

201 Milton Friedman, 'The Methodology of Positive Economics' in Milton Friedman (ed.), *Essays in Positive Economics*, University of Chicago Press, 1953.

202 John N. Keynes, *The Scope and Method of Political Economy*, Macmillan and Co., London, 1897, p. ix.

203 Milton Friedman, 'The Methodology of Positive Economics' in Milton Friedman (ed.), *Essays in Positive Economics*, University of Chicago Press, 1953, p. 3.

204 Lewis Carroll, 'Sylvie and Bruno Concluded', in *The Complete Works of Lewis Carroll*, The Nonesuch Press, London, 1939, pp. 556–557: 'We actually made a map of the country, on the scale of *a mile to the mile!*'.

205 Joan Robinson, *Essays in the Theory of Economic Growth*, Macmillan, London, 1962, p. 33: 'A model which took account of all the variegation of reality would be of no more use than a map at the scale of one to one'.

206 Oliver Budzinski, 'Modern Industrial Economics and Competition Policy: Open Problems and Possible Limits', IME Working Paper, No. 93/09, 2009, p. 19.

in political economy.'[207] This is consonant with Eucken's suggestion that 'the theoretical scientist leaves the individual historical aspect to the historical economist, while the latter leaves the "general" aspect to the theorist'.[208] Further, Keynes submits that those who develop a positive economic analysis should not refer to the normative aspects of economics and the other way around, suggesting that '[r]egarding political economy as a positive science, it is of course clear that neither laissez faire nor any other maxim of conduct can form an integral portion of its teaching'.[209] Hovenkamp suggests that 'even free market economists . . . have recognized an important difference between theoretical economics and public policymaking, particularly if the policies are being made in a democratic State'.[210] While addressing analytically the positive aspects of economics, Katz observes its pragmatic usefulness in advancing professional expertise inasmuch as it 'helps economists to separate out professional arguments, which get classified as positive, from extraprofessional arguments, which get classified as normative'.[211] The Chicago School, with its emphasis on market self-corrective elements, can be perceived in this taxonomy as a clear example of normative economics, whereas the Post-Chicago approach comes closer to the positive aspects of economic analysis and depends less on value judgements and normative imperatives.[212] The outcomes of the positive analysis should, however, be considered as a hypothesis[213] rather than a prescription for antitrust enforcement. This reserved approach to the role of economic

---

[207] John N. Keynes, *The Scope and Method of Political Economy*, Macmillan and Co., London, 1897, p. 10.

[208] Walter Eucken, *The Foundations of Economics: History and Theory in the Analysis of Economic Reality*, The University of Chicago Press, Chicago, 1951, p. 56.

[209] John N. Keynes, *The Scope and Method of Political Economy*, Macmillan and Co., London, 1897, p. 71.

[210] Herbert J. Hovenkamp, 'Antitrust Policy after Chicago', Michigan Law Review, Vol. 84, No. 2, 1985, pp. 223–224.

[211] Avery W. Katz, 'Positivism and the Separation of Law and Economics', Michigan Law Review, Vol. 94, No. 7, 1996, p. 2246.

[212] William H. Page, 'The Chicago School and the Evolution of Antitrust: Characterization, Antitrust Injury, and Evidentiary Sufficiency', Virginia Law Review, Vol. 75, No. 7, 1989, p. 1237: 'Normative analysis seeks to incorporate the insights of positive theory into an administrable policy program. The Chicago normative approach purports to offer a relentless logic connecting the analysis of the effects of specific practices to the formulation of concrete substantive rules governing those practices, typically rules of per se legality'.

[213] Malcolm B. Coate and Jeffrey H. Fischer, 'Can Post-Chicago Economics Survive *Daubert*?', Akron Law Review, Vol. 34, No. 4, 2001, p. 821: 'Friedman

knowledge in antitrust prevents its generalisation and universalisation, which in turn may help to dodge the disillusionment that follows each economic recession.

The history of US competition policy and law can be explored from two perspectives: evolutionary and pendulous. According to the former, the development of competition theory has a linear character and changes from one dominant approach to the next, revealing thereby the progressive nature of antitrust policy. The latter vision suggests, on the contrary, that the antitrust doctrine is developing in a cyclical manner, rejecting the strict rationale of constant evolution of the theory of competition, and that some ideological postulates and methodological techniques receive priority over others depending on the political and social context. These priorities change over time, transforming cyclically from the mainstream to the heterodoxy. It would be misleading to support only one of these views, since both visions are backed by sound arguments reflected in the economic reality. It is equally necessary for epistemic purposes to give a methodological priority to one of the visions. This research tends to develop its arguments from the cyclical perspective.

3.2 EVOLUTION OF COMPETITION LAW FROM THE EU PERSPECTIVE

The development of the theory of antitrust in the US has influenced the evolution of competition law in other parts of the world, including Europe.[214] Although each jurisdiction produces its own context-specific solutions to various competition problems, from a historical perspective only the European aspects of antitrust theory can be modelled as an alternative to the mainstream narrative of the development of competition law as it evolved in the US. Furthermore, the evolution of the American antitrust scholarship was based to a large extent on the European economic and legal theoretical foundations and in particular on the comprehensive discussion of the methodology of economic analysis, developed among the deductive, universal approach of neoclassical economics and the

---

cautions that the validity of a hypothesis is not sufficient for scientific acceptance because many other hypotheses may also be valid'.

[214] Brigitte Leucht, 'How German Is It? The Emergence of European Union Competition Policy and the Ordo-Liberal Model', in Eric Bussière, Michel Dumoulin and Sylvain Schirmann (eds.), *Intégration Économique et Gouvernance Européenne Depuis les Années Cinquante*, L, Harmattan, Paris, 2014, pp. 15–18.

inductive, context-specific reasoning of the Historical School.[215] Some ideas about competition law were articulated in Austria in the 1890s.[216] The history of European competition is explored in this chapter from the theoretical perspective. Often the basic ideas which were discussed in Europe are consonant with relevant polemics in the US;[217] sometimes, however, European theorists and practitioners of antitrust tend to address similar problems from a different perspective, which creates a fruitful soil for comparative observations. Some of them are also relevant for the topic of this book.

3.2.1 The Ordoliberal Roots of European Antitrust

The evolution of the European competition policy is closely connected and deeply influenced by the Ordoliberal economic and legal tradition. Despite its visible German roots, the school bases its theoretical premises on the broader pan-European economic culture,[218] characterised by the strong heritage of two often incompatible and sometimes antagonistic trends: the importance of economic freedom and the significant role given to public authorities in the regulation of state–market relation-

---

215 Herbert J. Hovenkamp, 'The Antitrust Movement and the Rise of Industrial Organisation', Texas Law Review, Vol. 68, No. 1, 1989, pp. 112–115: 'By the mid 1880s, questions about methodology began to divide American economists into two groups: (1) the more traditional, English or American-trained neoclassicists and (2) the "new school", taught in the German historical approach'.

216 David J. Gerber, 'Constitutionalizing the Economy: German Neo-Liberalism, Competition Law and the "New" Europe', The American Journal of Comparative Law, Vol. 42, No. 1, 1994, p. 49.

217 Lawrence A. Sullivan and Wolfgang Fikentscher, 'On the Growth of the Antitrust Idea', Berkeley Journal of International Law, Vol. 16, No. 2, 1998, pp. 230–231: 'A striking point is the considerable similarity between the liberal constitutionalism that developed in America during the pre-New Deal years and the Freiburg school. . . . Both see the protection of the individual against powerful private economic interests as an analogue to the protection of the individual against undue state intrusion. Both value competition as instrumental to the attainment of a range of related political and economic objectives. Even the Freiburg concept "*Soziale Marktwirtschaf*" had analogues in both American constitutional and American antitrust law'.

218 Daniel Johnson, 'Exiles and Half-exiles: Wilhelm Röpke, Alexander Rüstow and Walter Eucken', in Alan Peacock and Hans Willgerodt (eds.), *German Neo-Liberals, and the Social Market Economy*, The Macmillan Press, London, 1989, p. 41: '[Walter Eucken's father, philosopher, Nobel laureate] Rudolf Eucken . . . counted among his pupils the very brilliant Max Scheler whose frequent use of the Augustinian concept of ordo may well have been the immediate source of the title of Walter Eucken's later journal'.

ships. Etymologically the term 'Ordoliberalism' embraces the origins of both: its *ordo* (order) part refers to state regulation and its *liberal* part refers to economic freedom, creating 'a synthesis of order and liberty'.[219] The phenomenon of competition and the essence of competition law both embrace this Ordoliberal dichotomy: on the one hand competition can be seen as the quintessence of economic freedom; on the other hand, 'freedom, human dignity, and justice, cannot be left to chance but must be consciously guided'.[220] The protection of these values and even their regulation limit freedom.[221] This dilemma is well known for freedom itself and is reflected in the notion of positive and negative liberty. The connection between the two concepts is even stronger if one takes into account the fact that Ordoliberalism was not exclusively developed as an economic theory, incorporating into the domain of competition theory significant elements of socio-political normative claims, which have some repercussions in legal theory, being reflected in the notion of economic rights. By *translating* political economic interests into the *language* of rights, the Ordoliberals articulated an independent discourse about competition, which is no longer considered solely within the pragmatic economic apparatus of cost–benefit analysis, but encapsulates also strong deontological elements as any other theory of right does. In spite of its support for strong state intervention in creating a proper regulatory environment for competition,[222] and its latent evolution in tragic times

---

219 Michael Wohlgemuth, 'A European Social Model of State-Market Relations – The Ethics of Competition from a "Neo-liberal" Perspective', Zeitschrift für Wirtschafts- und Unternehmensethik – Journal for Business, Economics & Ethics, Vol. 9, No. 1, 2008, p. 71.

220 Siegfried G. Karsten, 'Eucken's "Social Market Economy" and Its Test in Post-War West Germany: The Economist as Social Philosopher Developed Ideas That Paralleled Progressive Thought in America', American Journal of Economics and Sociology, Vol. 44, No. 2, 1985.

221 Viktor J. Vanberg, 'The Freiburg School: Walter Eucken and Ordoliberalism', Freiburg Discussion Papers on Constitutional Economics, 04/11, 2004, p. 17: 'That the noted dilemma exists is not the fault of the Freiburg research program, it lies in the nature of things. And it speaks to the intellectual honesty of the founders of this program that they did not pretend to be able to offer an easy answer'.

222 Wilhelm Röpke, *Civitas humana – Grundfragen der Gesellschafts- und Wirtschaftsreform*, Rentsch-Zürich, Erlenbach, 1949, p. 76, translated and quoted in Oliver Budzinski, 'Monoculture versus Diversity in Competition Economics', Cambridge Journal of Economics, Vol. 32, No. 2, 2008, p. 306: '[A] fair, just, and well-functioning competition order cannot exist without a deliberate legal–moral framework and without permanent supervision of those conditions under which competition must take place as genuine performance competition'.

leading to somehow ambivalent observations[223] and 'superficial similarities'[224] with what Ordoliberalism genuinely opposed (proposing the *socialisation* of the state as an alternative to the *étatisation* of society),[225] the classical Ordoliberal view is critical of instrumentalist public opportunism (doctrine of selective intervention),[226] which might support competition in some sectors, while sacrificing it for the benefits of some economic interests in others. This means that Ordoliberalism opposed state *dirigisme*, perceiving it as 'an unacceptable subordination of freedom in micro affairs to the macro prerogatives of central planners',[227] and a fortiori the Schmittian conception of the state.[228] Eucken 'himself was a firm believer in the self-regulating and self-correcting properties

---

[223] Jamie Peck, *Constructions of Neoliberal Reason*, Oxford University Press, Oxford, 2010, pp. 58–59: 'While some of the founding Ordoliberals had gone into exile (or "half-exile") during the Nazi era, others remained in Germany, joining the Akademie für Deutsches Recht, helping to "realize the national-socialist program" in the field of law and economics, and engaging in a high-risk struggle with advocates of centralized planning in the context of Hitler's evolving economic philosophy. . . . Along with Walter Eucken and Franz Böhm, Müller-Armack was a member of the Akademie, exhibiting a facility for compromise that would later find reward in the social market era, when he would become the "guardian of neoliberal beliefs within the machinery of government"'.

[224] Daniel Johnson, 'Exiles and Half-exiles: Wilhelm Röpke, Alexander Rüstow and Walter Eucken', in Alan Peacock and Hans Willgerodt (eds.), *German Neo-Liberals, and the Social Market Economy*, The Macmillan Press, London, 1989, pp. 47–48.

[225] Jan Tumlir, 'Franz Böhm and the Development of Economic-constitutional Analysis', in Alan Peacock and Hans Willgerodt (eds.), *German Neo-Liberals, and the Social Market Economy*, The Macmillan Press, London, 1989, p. 131.

[226] Wernhard Möschel, 'The Proper Scope of Government Viewed from an Ordoliberal Perspective: The Example of Competition Policy', Journal of Institutional and Theoretical Economics, Vol. 157, No. 1, 2001, p. 4: 'As examples, one may take the goal of: (a) equilibrium in foreign trade (export cartels); (b) structural policy . . .; (c) full-employment policy (permission for mergers to preserve jobs); (d) currency policy . . . [S]uch policies represent a kind of governmental management technique for the achievement of concrete goals. This differs clearly from the ordoliberal concept of competition'.

[227] Johannes R. B. Rittershausen, 'The Postwar West German Economic Transition: From Ordoliberalism to Keynesianism', Institut für Wirtschaftspolitik an der Universität zu Köln Working Paper, No. 07/1, 2007, p. 19.

[228] Christian Joerges and Florian Rödl, '"Social Market Economy" as Europe's Social Model?', European University Institute Working Paper, Law, No. 2004/8, 2004, p. 14: 'Schmitt's strong state claimed the political primacy of politics over economy, whereas the ordoliberals sought to impose a stable legal framework on the economy which the political system, for its part, was to respect'.

of the market'.[229] In fact, the very concept of protecting the competitive process challenges *dirigisme*.[230] Joerges and Rödl call this model 'liberal interventionism',[231] Hayek, 'restrained liberalism'[232] and Foucault, 'liberal governmentality':[233] other prima facie oxymoronic notions, which alongside such terms as 'social market economy' or 'libertarian paternalism'[234] reflect the perpetual dialectical controversy of the state–market relationship, internalising thereby the notion that freedom as a precondition for prosperity as well as freedom taken as the ultimate aim should not be reduced to freedom's self-glorification and autarchy.[235]

Although the theoretical premises of Ordoliberalism have their intellectual roots in the 18th, 19th and early 20th centuries' history of economic thought, and some political aspects of Ordoliberalism can be traced back to the German 19th-century National-Liberal movement,[236] the development of Ordoliberal theory was determined by the specificity of German and European pre- and post-war economies within 'neoliberal' theoretical framework (the term 'neoliberal' is taken as a generic term

229 Norman P. Barry, 'Political and Economic Thought of German Neo-Liberals', in Alan Peacock and Hans Willgerodt (eds.), *German Neo-Liberals, and the Social Market Economy*, The Macmillan Press, London, 1989, p. 106.

230 David J. Gerber, Richard Azarnia, 'Dirigisme and the Challenge of Competition Law in France', Cardozo Journal of International & Comparative Law, Vol. 9, No. 1, 1995, pp. 9–10.

231 Christian Joerges and Florian Rödl, '"Social Market Economy" as Europe's Social Model?', European University Institute Working Paper, Law, No. 2004/8, 2004, pp. 13–14.

232 John P. Bladel, 'Against Polanyi-Centrism: Hayek and the Re-Emergence of "Spontaneous Order"', The Quarterly Journal of Austrian Economics, Vol. 8, No. 4, 2005, p. 22.

233 Nils Goldschmidt and Hermann Rauchenschwandtner, 'The Philosophy of Social Market Economy: Michel Foucault's Analysis of Ordoliberalism', Freiburg Discussion Papers on Constitutional Economics, 07/04, 2007, p. 2.

234 Richard H. Thaler and Cass R. Sunstein, *Nudge: Improving Decisions about Health, Wealth, and Happiness*, Yale University Press, New Haven, 2008.

235 Isaiah Berlin, 'Two Concepts of Liberty', in Isaiah Berlin, *Liberty*, Oxford University Press, Oxford, 2002, p. 214: '[I]ndividual freedom is [by no means], even in the most liberal societies, the sole or even the dominant, criterion of social action'.

236 Edward N. Megay, 'Treitschke Reconsidered: The Hegelian Tradition of German Liberalism', Midwest Journal of Political Science, Vol. 2, No. 3, 1958, pp. 316–317: 'Especially the works of Alexander Rüstow, Wilhelm Röpke, and Walter Eucken . . . Liberalism, are decidedly in the tradition Treitschke's Hegelian Liberalism. There are some important differences, of course, but the ultimate ideal is the powerful community- state as an ordering force above the conflicting interests of society and as representing the public good (the universal)'.

for modern liberalism),[237] as a response to new economic and socio-political challenges, to which traditional liberal views were unable to respond.[238] It should be pointed out that, despite phonetic similarity and some methodological links,[239] the term *neoliberalism* significantly differs from neoclassical economics. As far as competition is concerned, the methods and premises of classical economics are at least as important for the neoliberals as for the neoclassicals. As Wohlgemuth indicates,[240] the program text for a reassessment of the liberal heritage was Lippmann's *The Good Society*,[241] which raised the discussion ('Colloque Lippmann') among the leading continental theorists in Paris in 1938. The main polemic was directed at finding a middle ground between 'the falsity of a too literal laissez faire'[242] and the public reaction that rejected the classical liberal premises moving towards different perverse forms of collectivism. In his book Lippmann develops a thesis which is consonant with the Ordoliberal premises on the state–market relationship. He argues that the concept of the free market should not be juxtaposed to that of state power,[243] concluding that state regulation does not necessarily imply state interventionism.

Ordoliberal views were developed in opposition to the alliance of public

237 Klaus Dieter John, 'The German Social Market Economy – (Still) a Model for the European Union?', Theoretical and Applied Economics, Vol. 3, No. 3, 2007, p. 5.

238 Carl J. Friedrich, 'The Political Thought of Neo-Liberalism', The American Political Science Review, Vol. 49, No. 2, 1955, p. 510: 'This strength of liberalism in Germany is rather paradoxical, considering the weakness of German liberalism in the past. The paradox can be at least partially explained by the fact that this past weakness lends to liberalism a certain aura of novelty'.

239 David Harvey, *A Brief History of Neoliberalism*, Oxford University Press, Oxford, 2009, pp. 20–21.

240 Michael Wohlgemuth, 'A European Social Model of State-Market Relations – The Ethics of Competition from a "Neo-liberal" Perspective', Zeitschrift für Wirtschafts- und Unternehmensethik – Journal for Business, Economics & Ethics, Vol. 9, No. 1, 2008, p. 70.

241 Walter Lippmann, *The Good Society*, Transaction Publishers, New Brunswick, 2005.

242 Frank H. Knight, 'Lippmann's The Good Society', The Journal of Political Economy, Vol. 46, No. 6, 1938, p. 864.

243 Walter Lippmann, *The Good Society*, Transaction Publishers, New Brunswick, 2005, p. 186: 'The whole effort to treat laissez-fare as a principle of public policy, and then to determine what should be governed by law and what should not be, was based on so obvious an error that it seems grotesque. The error was in thinking that any aspect of work or of property is ever unregulated by law. The notion that there are two fields of social activity, one of anarchy and one of law, is false'.

and private economic powers reflected in states' enhancement of cartels,[244] 'a process which originated in the 1870s'.[245] Two decades later cartels were recognised by the German judiciary.[246] After Bismarck the 'German economy increasingly implemented corporatist methods in the industrial relations',[247] perceiving corporations' integrative role in society. In 1907 some industries were cartelised up to 82 per cent.[248] As Tumlir reports, in Germany's industry, commerce and financial sectors there were officially registered up to 700 cartels, structured as roof organisations. He also illustrates the common attitude to cartels, by quoting a promotional pamphlet of a German cartel from the 1920s.[249] Therefore, 'by the turn of the century Germany had become known as "the Land of the Cartels"'.[250] After 1933 in some cases membership in cartels was mandated by law.[251] As Möschel explains, the strong culture of individual economic liberty, developed

---

244 David J. Gerber, 'Constitutionalizing the Economy: German Neo-Liberalism, Competition Law and the "New" Europe', The American Journal of Comparative Law, Vol. 42, No. 1, 1994, p. 82: 'For the ordoliberals, economic power was the problem of competition law'.

245 Oliver Budzinski, 'Monoculture versus Diversity in Competition Economics', Cambridge Journal of Economics, Vol. 32, No. 2, 2008, p. 305.

246 Wolfgang Kerber, Ulrich Schwalbe, 'Economic Principles of Competition Law', in Günther Hirsch, Frank Montag, Franz Jürgen Säcker (eds.), *Competition Law: European Community Practice and Procedure – Article-by-Article Commentary*, Sweet & Maxwell, London, 2008, p. 211: 'In 1897, the German Reichsgericht decided in the Sächsischen Holzstoff-Fabrikanten (Saxon Wood Pulp Manufacturers) case that cartel agreements were allowed under the principle of freedom of contract'.

247 Umut Devrim Özbideciler, 'Social Market Economy: An Inquiry into the Theoretical Bases of German Model of Capitalism', http://etd.lib.metu.edu.tr/upload/1041896/index.pdf, accessed on 4 April 2011, p. 8.

248 Wernhard Möschel, 'Competition Policy from an Ordo Point of View', in Alan Peacock and Hans Willgerodt (eds.), *German Neo-Liberals, and the Social Market Economy*, The Macmillan Press, London, 1989, p. 143.

249 Jan Tumlir, 'Franz Böhm and the Development of Economic-constitutional Analysis', in Alan Peacock and Hans Willgerodt (eds.), *German Neo-Liberals, and the Social Market Economy*, The Macmillan Press, London, 1989, p. 129: 'The Association of German Industry described its functions in a 1920s pamphlet as follows: (a) Research, consultation, archive service and interpretation of the decisions of the Cartel Court; (b) Defence of cartels in general and against unjustified attacks in particular; representation of industry's interests before the legislature; monitoring developments in the economy and opinions of the Cartel Court; (c) Implementation of officially approved cartel principles'.

250 David J. Gerber, *Law and Competition in Twentieth Century Europe: Protecting Prometheus*, Oxford University Press, Oxford, 2001, p. 75.

251 Wolfgang Kerber and Ulrich Schwalbe, 'Economic Principles of Competition Law', in Günther Hirsch, Frank Montag and Franz Jürgen Säcker

in Germany after the French Revolution, was oriented predominantly 'vis-à-vis governmental restraints, . . . but not vis-à-vis restraints among competitors'.[252] This was the reason for Böhm to insist on 'a decisive fight against both private and public power over the market'.[253]

Governmental support of cartelised industries was based on evidence that cartels can deliver more effectively the expected outcomes in terms of economic growth; these forms of cooperation can be more responsive to the public needs; they are easier to coordinate than more atomistic structures – all these elements were of particular significance for the countries preparing for and participating in military activities. Cartels were practical as a tool to fight hyperinflation.[254] In addition, cartels were considered as a powerful mercantilist instrument in terms of support of the domestic industries at the international level as well as due to their alleged economic efficiency.[255] Another important difficulty for the prohibition of cartels was related to the principles of individual freedom of contract, reflected in German private law.[256] All these facts show that at the time cartels were considered either beneficial or at least Janus-faced,[257] but by no means economically harmful. The later categorical criticism of cartels was

(eds.), *Competition Law: European Community Practice and Procedure – Article-by-Article Commentary*, Sweet & Maxwell, London, 2008, p. 211.

[252] Wernhard Möschel, 'Competition Policy from an Ordo Point of View', in Alan Peacock and Hans Willgerodt (eds.), *German Neo-Liberals, and the Social Market Economy*, The Macmillan Press, London, 1989, p. 143.

[253] Franz Böhm, *Wirtschaftsordnung und Staatsverfassung*, Mohr Siebeck, Tübingen, 1950, p. 69, translated and quoted in Carl J. Friedrich, 'The Political Thought of Neo-Liberalism', The American Political Science Review, Vol. 49, No. 2, 1955, p. 511.

[254] Wernhard Möschel, 'Competition Policy from an Ordo Point of View', in Alan Peacock and Hans Willgerodt (eds.), *German Neo-Liberals, and the Social Market Economy*, The Macmillan Press, London, 1989, p. 143: 'The Cartel Ordinance of 1923, which was enacted at the zenith of hyper-inflation, stabilized this development by generally sanctioning cartels'.

[255] Herbert J. Hovenkamp, 'The Antitrust Movement and the Rise of Industrial Organisation', Texas Law Review, Vol. 68, No. 1, 1989, p. 123: 'The economists believed that breaking the giant trusts into smaller firms would deprive modern business of the benefits of economies of scale'.

[256] Ernst-Joachim Mestmäcker, 'The Development of German and European Competition Law with special Reference to the EU Commission's Article 82 Guidance of 2008', Max Planck Private Law Research Paper No. 10/1, 2010, p. 13: 'German courts treated cartels as valid private law contracts. . . . [T]he "prohibition principle" for cartels was criticised as unconstitutional because it infringed freedom of contract'.

[257] David J. Gerber, *Law and Competition in Twentieth Century Europe: Protecting Prometheus*, Oxford University Press, Oxford, 2001, p. 88.

to some extent the result of the influence of the US antitrust experience,[258] which (despite the early modest successes of the rule of reason rationale) was still dominated by the pre-Chicago per se prohibition approach. The influence of the US antitrust doctrine should not overshadow the paramount role of Ordoliberalism.[259] Wigger, referring to the conceptual differences between Ordoliberalism and the US antitrust model, observes that Ordoliberals 'strongly opposed the US antitrust enforcement practice that relied so heavily on courts and on private enforcement'.[260] Böhm, a leading legal figure of Ordoliberalism, acknowledged the paramount nature of the individual freedom of contract but emphasised that it should be restricted by the principles of private law in general and the principle of the voluntary nature of transactions in particular.[261] Property rights were no longer perceived as 'entitlements for their own sake that provide their owners with an unlimited assignment of power. Their justification and strength depend on competition'.[262] This view is based on Hayek's concerns about 'a mechanical extension of the property concept',[263] leading to the extension of harmful privileges.

3.2.1.1 Ordoliberalism and the Historical School

The Ordoliberal reliance on economic analysis was always limited by broader theoretical and constitutional factors.[264] This feature distinguishes

---

258 Imelda Maher, 'Re-imagining the Story of European Competition Law', Oxford Journal of Legal Studies, Vol. 20, No. 1, 2000, p. 155: 'In the aftermath of the Second World War, the Americans set as one of the conditions of their withdrawal from Germany the introduction of a competition law'.

259 David J. Gerber, 'Constitutionalizing the Economy: German Neo-Liberalism, Competition Law and the "New" Europe', The American Journal of Comparative Law, Vol. 42, No. 1, 1994, p. 63: 'The ordoliberals created the intellectual framework for competition law long before the end of the Second World War and with minimal reference to U.S. antitrust experience'.

260 Angela Wigger, 'Competition for Competitiveness: The Politics of the Transformation of the EU Competition Regime', dare.ubvu.vu.nl/bitstream/1871/15601/5/8237.pdf, accessed on 23 April 2011, p. 128.

261 Jan Tumlir, 'Franz Böhm and the Development of Economic-constitutional Analysis', in Alan Peacock and Hans Willgerodt (eds.), *German Neo-Liberals, and the Social Market Economy*, The Macmillan Press, London, 1989, p. 136.

262 Lawrence A. Sullivan and Wolfgang Fikentscher, 'On the Growth of the Antitrust Idea', Berkeley Journal of International Law, Vol. 16, No. 2, 1998, p. 214.

263 Friedrich A. von Hayek, '"Free" Enterprise and Competitive Order', in Friedrich A. von Hayek, *Individualism and Economic Order*, The University of Chicago Press, Chicago, 1958, p. 114.

264 Franz Böhm, Walter Eucken and Hans Grossmann-Doerth, 'The Ordo Manifesto of 1936', in Alan T. Peacock and Hans Willgerodt (eds.), *Germany's*

the Ordoliberal School from its intellectual predecessor and methodological opponent, the German Historical School. The latter's premises enabled 'unprincipled relativism'[265] or 'a fatalist-relativist attitude'[266] by relying on the historical context and rejecting any theoretical generalisation, which in addition created intellectual barriers between theorists from different countries,[267] and was often castigated for its incapability to predict the historical turmoil in post-Weimar Germany. The Historical School was the dominant discourse at the time, and many Ordoliberal ideas evolved from it.[268] Despite his strong opposition to the Historical School, Eucken, one of the founders of Ordoliberalism, admitted that '[e]conomic life is to be understood against the background of the current historical situation: . . . the English economy of the seventeenth century in the context of that century, and the economy of today in the context of today'.[269] However, he rejected the claim that economic policy should be limited to a distilled experience of the past which often delivered nothing more than 'a chaos of details', suggesting that reality cannot be understood, unless taken 'in a general form, and therefore [made] accessible to theoretical investigation'.[270] Streit points out that when Eucken started his academic work the economic discourse was dominated by the Historical School, which explains the impact of the historicist methodology on Eucken's research, but his opposition to the main principles of the Historical School

Social Market Economy: Origins and Evolution, Macmillan, London, 1989, p. 24: 'The problems of the economic system can be comprehended and brought to a solution, if realism and fundamental thought are combined, difficult though that might be'.

[265] Viktor J. Vanberg, 'The Freiburg School: Walter Eucken and Ordoliberalism', Freiburg Discussion Papers on Constitutional Economics, 04/11, 2004, p. 1.

[266] Franz Böhm, Walter Eucken and Hans Grossmann-Doerth, 'The Ordo Manifesto of 1936', in Alan T. Peacock and Hans Willgerodt (eds.), *Germany's Social Market Economy: Origins and Evolution*, Macmillan, London, 1989, p. 18.

[267] David J. Gerber, 'Constitutionalizing the Economy: German Neo-Liberalism, Competition Law and the "New" Europe', The American Journal of Comparative Law, Vol. 42, No. 1, 1994, p. 34.

[268] Friedrich A. Lutz, 'Introduction', in Walter Eucken, *The Foundations of Economics: History and Theory in the Analysis of Economic Reality*, The University of Chicago Press, Chicago, 1951, p. 5: '[A]t the beginning of [Eucken's] career, he did some work along the lines of the Historical School. . . . [But later on he] became, among German economists, the foremost opponent of the Historical School'.

[269] Walter Eucken, *The Foundations of Economics: History and Theory in the Analysis of Economic Reality*, The University of Chicago Press, Chicago, 1951, p. 36.

[270] ibid, p. 41.

was already visible in his early writings.[271] Eucken does not reject the historical method, but suggests that it should be dialectically complemented by a more theoretical analysis.[272] Only in this dialectical tension can a solution be found.

The Ordoliberal emphasis on generalised economic principles is difficult to reconcile with its severe criticism of legal positivism.[273] Legal positivism limits its theoretical ambits to pure generalisation, leaving aside the historical and contextual specificities of legal systems. It is genuinely agnostic to the content of law and holds that it is beyond the cognitive capacity of jurisprudence to predict the political future, let alone to promote any ideology. Deviations from this perception reject the deductive principles upon which a legal system is based, reverting back to historical empiricism and context-dependency. The discrepancy between the emphasis made by Ordoliberalism on universal *economic* principles and its interest in a specific good *law* shows that the actual intellectual relations between the Historical and Ordoliberal thoughts should be seen rather as a gradual shift from one paradigm to another than a clear-cut critical discontinuity. While claiming the necessity of general theoretic models, Eucken expressed reservations against an uncritical axiomatic perception of economic principles.[274] Arguably the German post-war economic miracle cannot be reduced to the design of a proper balance between the *ordo*-,

---

271 Manfred E. Streit, 'The Freiburg School of Law and Economics', in Peter J. Boettke (ed.), *The Elgar Companion to Austrian Economics*, Edward Elgar Publishing, Cheltenham, 1994, p. 508.

272 Walter Eucken, *The Foundations of Economics: History and Theory in the Analysis of Economic Reality*, The University of Chicago Press, Chicago, 1951, p. 43: 'A superficial compromise between theoretical and historical investigation or mere methodological reflections about their cooperation are pointless. The sharpness and tension of this antinomy must be fully understood. This historical aspect of the problem requires perception, intuition, synthesis, understanding, and a feeling for living individual experience. The general theoretical aspect calls for reasoning, analysis, and the elaboration of analytical models'.

273 Franz Böhm, *Die Ordnung der Wirtschaft als geschichtliche Aufgabe und rechtsschöpferische Leistung*, W. Kohlhammer, Stuttgart, 1937, pp. ix–xi, quoted and analysed in David J. Gerber, 'Constitutionalizing the Economy: German Neo-Liberalism, Competition Law and the "New" Europe', The American Journal of Comparative Law, Vol. 42, No. 1, 1994, p. 35.

274 Walter Eucken, 'Die Wettbewerbsordnung und ihre Verwirklichung', *Jahrbuch für die Ordnung von Wirtschaft und Gesellschaft*, Vol. 2, 1949, cited in Christian Ahlborn, Carsten Grave (trans.), Walter Eucken, 'The Competitive Order and its Implementation', Competition Policy International, Vol. 2, No. 2, 2006, p. 229: '[A] science that establishes certain models axiomatically, failing to seek and find forms that exist in the real world is unsuitable for this purpose'.

social- and *liberal* wings of the market process. The mere reliance on the rule of law and the economic constitution are hardly sufficient conditions for sustainable prosperity.[275] The institutional framework, the cultural principles and the uniqueness of the historical context also played a pivotal role in this process.[276] The latter components were always emphasised by the Historical School.[277] In addition, as Ebner argues, the concept of social market economy, while fitting basic Ordoliberal propositions, also contains significant elements of the Historical School and 'needs to be assessed in the context of that historist tradition',[278] particularly as far as the specificity of particular historical periods is concerned.[279]

Another significant Ordoliberal criterion for the adequacy of the state–market relationship is the concept of rule of law, perceived as a commitment of public authorities to the principles of democratic governance, which implies the subordination of the state to the law and the elimination of arbitrary political manipulation with legal principles, allowing prevention of abuses of power by public authorities. Mestmäcker distinguishes three aspects of this principle: (i) to control the discretionary power of antitrust authorities; (ii) to fine-tune dominant undertakings' market power; (iii) to protect legitimate interests of competitors, suppli-

---

275 Carol Harlow, 'Voices of Difference in a Plural Community', The American Journal of Comparative Law, Vol. 50, No. 2, 2002, p. 342: 'The rule of law clearly forms an essential element of liberal democracy and plays its part in providing the theoretical basis for an independent judiciary, but it forms only one side of a balanced constitution or debate about a balanced constitution'.

276 David J. Gerber, 'Convergence in the Treatment of Dominant Firm Conduct: The United States, the European Union, and the Institutional Embeddedness of Economics', Vol. 76, No. 3, 2010, p. 953: 'When institutions apply economics, the scientific and thus abstract methods of economics become embedded in the rules and procedures of the institution that uses them'.

277 Helge Peukert, 'Walter Eucken (1891–1950) and the Historical School', in Peter Koslowski (ed.), *The Theory of Capitalism in the German Economic Tradition: Historism, Ordo-liberalism, Critical Theory, Solidarism*, Springer, Hannover, 2000, p. 94: 'One of the main postulates of the Historical School is that individuals are influenced by motives that cannot be quantitatively measured'.

278 Alexander Ebner, 'The Intellectual Foundations of the Social Market Economy: Theory, Policy, and Implications for European Integration', Journal of Economic Studies, Vol. 33, No. 3, 2006, p. 207.

279 Nils Goldschmidt, Michael Wohlgemuth, 'Social Market Economy: Origins, Meanings, Interpretations', Constitutional Political Economy, Vol. 19, No. 3, 2008, p. 271: '[F]or Müller-Armack, the Social Market Economy was more an economic, social and cultural style – a concept first developed by the younger Historical School to describe the understanding of the individuality of different economic periods and combining it with an analysis of the "laws" of historical development'.

ers and customers.[280] As for the former two criteria the concept of rule of law depends on the legal and political culture of the society to which it is applied. The concept of rule of law is ambivalent in this respect; it is often misleading and tautological.[281] It has two different meanings. In the *substantive* sense it is often used as a political optimum of democratic states, where all public decisions are transparent, legal rules correspond with accountability standards, the authorities are subject to the strict public control of society and its institutions, and law is not applied retroactively and not interpreted arbitrarily in a way which would place the state above the law. The state is seen as a diligent agent acting in the interest of the people, who delegate their political will to public institutions while remaining the real sovereigns and the ultimate goals of any public activity. Such a view can be juxtaposed to the *procedural* approach to the rule of law, which mirrors to a large extent the principles of legal positivism, implying that law should be obeyed regardless of the internal evaluation of those who apply it or its substantive content. The former notion was advocated by Hayek (though he accepted some importance of the latter as well), the latter by Kelsen,[282] which is closely related to the notion of legal certainty.[283] This implies that '[t]he rule of law is a political ideal which a legal system may lack or may possess to a greater or less degree'.[284]

---

[280] Ernst-Joachim Mestmäcker, 'The Development of German and European Competition Law with Special Reference to the EU Commission's Article 82 Guidance of 2008', Max Planck Private Law Research Paper No. 10/1, 2010, pp. 15–16.

[281] Joseph Raz, 'The Rule of Law and Its Virtue', in Joseph Raz, *The Authority of Law, Essays on Law and Morality*, Oxford University Press, Oxford, 2009, p. 212: 'It is said that the rule of law means that all government action must have foundation in law, must be authorised by law. But is not that a tautology? Actions not authorised by law cannot be the actions of the government as a government. They would be without legal effect and often unlawful'.

[282] Richard A. Posner, 'Kelsen versus Hayek: Pragmatism, Economics, and Democracy', in Richard A. Posner, *Law, Pragmatism and Democracy*, Harvard University Press, Cambridge, Massachusetts, 2003, p. 289: 'Kelsen's theory of law is content-neutral; Hayek is interested only in content'.

[283] Torben Spaak, 'Moral Relativism and the *Rechtsstaat*', ssrn.com/abstract=923435, accessed on 19 September 2010, pp. 2–3: 'Whereas European writers speak of the *Rechtsstaat*, . . . English-speaking writers speak of the *rule of law*. . . . Hans Kelsen explains that a *Rechtsstaat* is commonly understood to be a democratic state with independent courts whose decisions can be predicted and in which certain fundamental rights are respected. . . . [However] Kelsen maintains that the principle of the *Rechtsstaat* is really nothing more than the principle of *legal certainty*' (emphasis in the original).

[284] Joseph Raz, 'The Rule of Law and Its Virtue', in Joseph Raz, *The Authority of Law, Essays on Law and Morality*, Oxford University Press, Oxford, 2009, p. 211.

Zywicki and Sanders explain that the former is a positivist perception of the rule of law, while the latter reflects the idea of law as a spontaneous order.[285] While the two approaches are present in different proportions in any democratic legal system, this co-existence does not eliminate significant discrepancies between the two models. The former is value oriented and depends on the context,[286] while the latter is formalistic and universal in its value-neutral rationale. The political and economic success of the substantive principles of the rule of law, developed and promoted by the Ordoliberal School, largely depended upon the real historical and cultural context in which these principles were applied. These principles are inductive imperatives rather than abstract universal premises.[287] Mere reliance on the *substantive* rule of law cannot guarantee economic prosperity and political democracy in all situations. It is not sufficient and cannot be successful in the absence of some institutional preconditions, its proper understanding in society, reflected in a common political culture. Although the Ordoliberal School tries to promote universal principles of economic constitution, developed upon 'the idea of constitutional liberty that inspired the European and Scottish enlightenment',[288] in 'the intellectual traditions of idealist German philosophy, particularly that of Immanuel Kant'[289] and conceptualised 'in the closing decades of the nineteenth century',[290] the real political success of such powerful ideas

---

[285] Todd J. Zywicki and Anthony B. Sanders, 'Posner, Hayek & the Economic Analysis of Law', George Mason University Law and Economics Research Paper Series, 07-05, 2007, p. 47.

[286] Walter Eucken, 'Die Wettbewerbsordnung und ihre Verwirklichung', *Jahrbuch für die Ordnung von Wirtschaft und Gesellschaft*, Vol. 2, 1949, cited in Christian Ahlborn, Carsten Grave (trans.), Walter Eucken, 'The Competitive Order and its Implementation', Competition Policy International, Vol. 2, No. 2, 2006, p. 228: 'So, for example, the competitive order in Germany will look entirely different to that in Belgium or in the United States'.

[287] Wernhard Möschel, 'The Proper Scope of Government Viewed from an Ordoliberal Perspective: The Example of Competition Policy', Journal of Institutional and Theoretical Economics, Vol. 157, No. 1, 2001, pp. 3–4.

[288] Ernst-Joachim Mestmäcker, 'The Development of German and European Competition Law with Special Reference to the EU Commission's Article 82 Guidance of 2008', Max Planck Private Law Research Paper No. 10/1, 2010, pp. 12–13.

[289] Wernhard Möschel, 'Competition Policy from an Ordo Point of View', in Alan Peacock and Hans Willgerodt (eds.), *German Neo-Liberals, and the Social Market Economy*, The Macmillan Press, London, 1989, pp. 148–149.

[290] Jan Tumlir, 'Franz Böhm and the Development of Economic-constitutional Analysis', in Alan Peacock, Hans Willgerodt (eds.), *German Neo-Liberals, and the Social Market Economy*, The Macmillan Press, London, 1989, p. 136.

is subject to the unique socio-cultural context, in which the principles are applied – which is essentially the argument, articulated and promoted by the Historical School.[291] This also explains the intellectual connections between Ordoliberalism and New Institutional Economics.[292]

The deep connections between the Ordoliberal and Historical Schools are captured in the notion of 'the great antinomy'.[293] The antinomy was perceived as a deep conceptual discrepancy between the two main sources of economic knowledge: historical empiricism and theoretical universalisation. While the former was dominant in German pre-war economic theory, the latter was popular in the Anglo-American literature. Ordoliberals acknowledged the significance of both epistemological tools, recognising the inevitability of their constant clash. The economic constitution was meant to integrate elements of both, not to reject their main components, but to relinquish the dominance or exclusivity of either. The proposed methodology could be perceived as a happy middle point between two orthodoxies, but the proposal was more nuanced. Since the intellectual roots of Ordoliberalism are grounded in idealist Kantian philosophy,[294] the concept of antinomy should be taken as a dialectical conflict (dialectics of the abstract and the concrete).[295] Accordingly, the conflict cannot be resolved or mitigated by a simple acceptance of the positive aspects that both approaches hold. The antinomies are irresolvable. They can only be operationalised. In the context of the regulation of competition this implies that both empirical and theoretical methods could be used, without eliminating the discrepancies between them. They are actualised by the decision-makers, depending on the institutional preconditions of the decision-making process.[296] A similar 'symbiotic

---

291 Nils Goldschmidt and Michael Wohlgemuth, 'Social Market Economy: Origins, Meanings, Interpretations', Constitutional Political Economy, Vol. 19, No. 3, 2008, p. 267: 'Eucken's theory can be seen as the combination of the traditions of the German Historical School, Neo-Kantism and Phenomenology'.

292 Manfred E. Streit and Michael Wohlgemuth, 'The Market Economy and the State: Hayekian and Ordoliberal Conceptions', Max-Planck-Institut zur Erforschung von Wirtschaftssystemen, Discussion paper, 06/97, 1997, p. 14.

293 David J. Gerber, 'Constitutionalizing the Economy: German Neo-Liberalism, Competition Law and the "New" Europe', The American Journal of Comparative Law, Vol. 42, No. 1, 1994, p. 40.

294 Wernhard Möschel, 'The Proper Scope of Government Viewed from an Ordoliberal Perspective: The Example of Competition Policy', Journal of Institutional and Theoretical Economics, Vol. 157, No. 1, 2001, pp. 6–7.

295 Evald V. Ilyenkov, *The Dialectics of the Abstract and the Concrete in Marx's Capital*, Progress, Moscow, 1982.

296 Walter Eucken, *The Foundations of Economics: History and Theory in the Analysis of Economic Reality*, The University of Chicago Press, Chicago, 1951,

character'[297] is envisaged for the relationship between the legal and economic discourses. In spite of the similarities between the schools (which are visible, in particular, when both are contrasted to the neoclassical economic analysis),[298] Ordoliberalism, with its emphasis on the competitive process and universal ex ante political economic principles, significantly differs from the historicist intellectual tradition. However, it encompasses its premises and by combining them in 'the great antinomy'[299] with theoretical generalisations perceives the economic reality dialectically.

3.2.1.2 The Ordoliberal perception of competition

The conceptual foundations of the Ordoliberal School were developed 'as a result of the spontaneous cooperation of economists and jurists'[300] at the University of Freiburg in the 1930s, which was at that time a fruitful place for generating legal and economic approaches to competition,[301] creating 'the matrix of a new brand of liberal thought'.[302] The main task of Ordoliberalism has been to implement the ideas of economic freedom

---

pp. 145–147: 'The borderline for *competition* . . . is not to be drawn by fixing a number of suppliers or demanders. This is impossible. But whether a supplier or demander is in competition or oligopoly can be ascertained in any concrete case from what each one in the market takes as given in his economic plan' (emphasis in the original).

297 David J. Gerber, 'Constitutionalizing the Economy: German Neo-Liberalism, Competition Law and the "New" Europe', The American Journal of Comparative Law, Vol. 42, No. 1, 1994, p. 56.

298 Herbert J. Hovenkamp, 'The Antitrust Movement and the Rise of Industrial Organisation', Texas Law Review, Vol. 68, No. 1, 1989, p. 115: 'Under the neoclassical system, morals, psychology, and sociology played little or no role in explaining the behavior of the economic individual or firm. The historical approach, on the other hand, was far more holistic – more inclined to account for everyday phenomenon, even if no rational "economic" explanation was available'.

299 Walter Eucken, *The Foundations of Economics: History and Theory in the Analysis of Economic Reality*, The University of Chicago Press, Chicago, 1951, pp. 41–44.

300 Manfred E. Streit, 'The Freiburg School of Law and Economics', in Peter J. Boettke (ed.), *The Elgar Companion to Austrian Economics*, Edward Elgar Publishing, Cheltenham, 1994, p. 508.

301 Viktor J. Vanberg, 'The Freiburg School: Walter Eucken and Ordoliberalism', Freiburg Discussion Papers on Constitutional Economics, 04/11, 2004, p. 1: 'Freiburg University's "Fakultät für Rechts- und Staatswissenschaften" that included law as well as economics provided a conducive framework for the combination of legal and economic perspectives that is characteristic of the Freiburg School and of the Ordo-liberal tradition'.

302 David J. Gerber, 'Constitutionalizing the Economy: German Neo-Liberalism, Competition Law and the "New" Europe', The American Journal of Comparative Law, Vol. 42, No. 1, 1994, p. 25.

into a broader constitutional framework. This political dimension of Ordoliberalism distinguishes it from other approaches to competition perceived primarily from the economic perspective.[303] In this respect Ordoliberalism is similar to the early American antitrust jurisprudence, which also treated competition as a prerequisite for liberal democracy rather than tying it exclusively to economic rationalism. Here one can also find an explanation for the communicative difficulties between different visions of the role of the competitive process in the economy. From a purely economic perspective, competition can be seen either as an important methodological component of perfect equilibrium, or – in its applied sense – as an instrument through which such important societal interests as industrial growth, innovations, social stability, market integration, and consumer or total welfare are generated. In both cases real competition in the markets is not of paramount importance. From the methodological angle it is a mere indicator that markets are functioning optimally. Competition in this respect is a criterion to assess whether demand meets supply.[304] Competition policy is then taken as a tool for striking a balance between lowering prices and maintaining minimum incentives to invest/compete. The ideal situation would be one where suppliers could recoup their investments and receive extra benefits, sufficient for sustainable growth. From an applied perspective, competition is not taken as an evaluative criterion of market optimality, but as a regulatory tool by which market players are encouraged to generate growth, wealth or welfare, or to perform other public economic goals.

Ordoliberals perceive the main theoretical approach to competition differently. For them competition is also an important economic precondition for a democratic political system. They transferred its centre of gravity from economic to politics. Such a transition shows that the

---

[303] David J. Gerber, *Law and Competition in Twentieth Century Europe: Protecting Prometheus*, Oxford University Press, Oxford, 2001, p. 17: '[Law] *created* freedom by constraining power. The transfer of this basic idea from political thought to the economic sphere was a key conceptual move in the development of European competition law' (emphasis in the original).

[304] Paul J. McNulty, 'Economic Theory and the Meaning of Competition', The Quarterly Journal of Economics, Vol. 82, No. 4, 1968, p. 644: 'The "perfection" of the concept of competition, that is, the emergence of the idea of competition as itself a market structure, was a distinguishing contribution of neoclassical economics. The groundwork for this development was laid by Cournot . . . According to him, the effects of competition had reached their limit when the output of each firm was "inappreciable" with respect to total industry output, and could be subtracted from the total output "without any appreciable variation resulting in the price of the commodity"'.

competitive process is not only a technical component of equilibrium-based abstract modelling and not merely a means to generating welfare or growth. Competition itself deserves to be protected inasmuch as its existence predetermines the constitutional structure of the market economy. The concept of economic competition evolved from 'a mere aphorism [to] a principle [attaining] the quality of an ordering concept'.[305] In a broader methodological perspective this shift implies that competition has become the object of two developed disciplines – legal theory and political philosophy. Both operate to a large degree within the language of *rights*, while economic thinking is a more *rational*, *efficiency*- and *interests*-oriented area.[306] One of the main specificities of the rights-oriented argumentation lies in its deontology-based narrative. Rights are *often* perceived in absolute terms, and *usually* they are divorced from the pragmatism of economics, concentrated mainly on 'the game of utilitarian calculus'.[307] In other words, rights are protected not due to their capability to contribute to economic development. Quite the contrary, they are considered as something which should be protected in spite of (and due to) its inefficiency. Hence, they are not seen as a tool to promote efficiency.[308] On the normative side this means that competition is not considered any longer only as a means, but in some cases it is also treated as an end,[309] as a value in itself.[310] The constitutionalisation of competition implies its perception

---

305 Knut Wolfgang Nörr, 'On the Concept of "Economic Constitution" and the Importance of Franz Böhm from the Viewpoint of Legal History', European Journal of Law and Economics, Vol. 3, No. 4, 1996, p. 350.

306 Manuel C. Branco, *Economics Versus Human Rights*, Routledge, London, 2009, pp. 17–19.

307 Michael Wohlgemuth, 'A European Social Model of State-Market Relations – The Ethics of Competition from a "Neo-liberal" Perspective', Zeitschrift für Wirtschafts- und Unternehmensethik – Journal for Business, Economics & Ethics, Vol. 9, No. 1, 2008, p. 75.

308 Ronald M. Dworkin, *Taking Rights Seriously*, Harvard University Press, Cambridge, Massachusetts, 1978, p. 333: 'There would be no point in the boast that we respect individual rights unless that involved some sacrifice, and the sacrifice in question must be that we give up whatever marginal benefits our country would receive from overriding these rights when they prove inconvenient'.

309 Franz Böhm, Walter Eucken and Hans Grossmann-Doerth, 'The Ordo Manifesto of 1936', in Alan T. Peacock and Hans Willgerodt (eds.), *Germany's Social Market Economy: Origins and Evolution*, Macmillan, London, 1989, p. 24: 'Free competition must not be stopped on the erroneous grounds of alleged unfair practice. On the other hand, it must not be allowed to degenerate into truly unfair competition either'.

310 Wernhard Möschel, 'Competition Policy from an Ordo Point of View', in Alan Peacock and Hans Willgerodt (eds.), *German Neo-Liberals, and the Social Market Economy*, The Macmillan Press, London, 1989, p. 147: 'Ordo-liberal

as an important right, grounded in the broader prerequisite of economic freedom,[311] implying 'an adaptation and transfer of ideas from liberal political theory to the economy'.[312] According to the Ordoliberal visions of the role of the competitive process, 'not only should the endeavours of competition be given free rein, but more importantly, competition should be created and produced'.[313]

This approach disentangles competition from the economic outcomes which it eventually generates,[314] transforming agent–principal subordinated relations between economic goals and competition to their societal parity, while at the same time not claiming the primacy of competition, as '[l]iberty is not the only goal of men',[315] but merely raising the possibility for freedom-oriented values to trump utilitarian interests.[316] Competition thereby cannot be measured solely via its beneficial effects on society, but rather competition itself becomes a societal benefit. This vision does not reject the quintessential role of the economic analysis of competition,[317]

---

policy does not rely exclusively on the long-term process of self-healing of the overall society, but protects the individual's economic freedom of action as a value in itself against any impairment of excessive economic power'.

311 Walter Eucken, 'What Kind of Economic and Social System?', in Alan T. Peacock and Hans Willgerodt (eds.), *Germany's Social Market Economy: Origins and Evolution*, Macmillan, London, 1989, p. 34: 'Properly understood, freedom, humanitarianism and legal rights belong together and are indivisibly tied to one another'.

312 David J. Gerber, 'Constitutionalizing the Economy: German Neo-Liberalism, Competition Law and the "New" Europe', The American Journal of Comparative Law, Vol. 42, No. 1, 1994, p. 47.

313 Nils Goldschmidt and Hermann Rauchenschwandtner, 'The Philosophy of Social Market Economy: Michel Foucault's Analysis of Ordoliberalism', Freiburg Discussion Papers on Constitutional Economics, 07/04, 2007, p. 23.

314 Pinar Akman, 'Searching for the Long-Lost Soul of Article 82EC', Oxford Journal of Legal Studies, Vol. 29, No. 2, 2009, p. 275: '[E]fficiency was not an *aim*, but rather an expected *result* of competition for ordoliberals' (emphases in the original).

315 Isaiah Berlin, 'Two Concepts of Liberty', in Isaiah Berlin, *Liberty*, Oxford University Press, Oxford, 2002, p. 172.

316 Norman P. Barry, *Welfare*, Open University Press, Buckingham, 1999, p. 6: 'The disentangling of welfare from other values should not be seen merely as some sanitizing process, a necessary cleansing exercise whereby out political language is purified so that value disagreements can be more easily identified. It also has a more substantive implication. This is that the assimilation of other values to the welfare ideal imposes upon a society an agreement about values, an hierarchy of ends and purposes which is unlikely to exist'.

317 Franz Böhm, Walter Eucken and Hans Grossmann-Doerth, 'The Ordo Manifesto of 1936', in Alan T. Peacock and Hans Willgerodt (eds.), *Germany's Social Market Economy: Origins and Evolution*, Macmillan, London, 1989,

which by its nature is result oriented.[318] However the economic investigation of the phenomenon of *competition* is not equal to the more economic approach to competition *law*.[319] Because competition law was *always* influenced by economic theory, the more economic approach entails 'having a common economics basis for all antitrust decisions, i.e. a single economic competition theory'.[320] Its emphasis on the constitutional importance of economic freedom reveals that Ordoliberalism is not only an economic theory, but also a 'social philosophy',[321] which puts competition at the centre of its conceptual gravity.

The economic virtue of competition can be jeopardised not only by governmental interventionist policy, but also by private powers.[322] The danger of cartels and other anticompetitive practices of private market participants was constantly emphasised by the Ordoliberal School,[323] via

pp. 24–25: 'How the line is to be drawn between unfair and permissible competition, whether there is free competition or not, whether competition is restricted, whether competition is efficient or obstructive, whether or not price-cutting contradicts the principle of the system – all these issues can only be decided by investigations conducted by economists into the various states of the market'.

318 Amartya Sen, 'Freedom of Choice: Concept and Content', European Economic Review, Vol. 32, No. 2–3, 1988, p. 271: 'It is fair to say that in the general tradition of economics the instrumental role of freedom is much more prominent than its intrinsic relevance'.

319 Franz Böhm, Walter Eucken and Hans Grossmann-Doerth, 'The Ordo Manifesto of 1936', in Alan T. Peacock and Hans Willgerodt (eds.), *Germany's Social Market Economy: Origins and Evolution*, Macmillan, London, 1989, p. 25: 'The *collaboration* of the two sciences [economics and law] is clearly essential' (emphasis added).

320 Oliver Budzinski, 'Monoculture versus Diversity in Competition Economics', Cambridge Journal of Economics, Vol. 32, No. 2, 2008, p. 296.

321 Wernhard Möschel, 'The Proper Scope of Government Viewed from an Ordoliberal Perspective: The Example of Competition Policy', Journal of Institutional and Theoretical Economics, Vol. 157, No. 1, 2001, p. 3.

322 Manfred E. Streit, 'Economic Order, Private Law and Public Policy: the Freiburg School of Law and Economics in Perspective', Journal of Institutional and Theoretical Economics, Vol. 148, No. 4, 1992, p. 69: '[Traditionally, p]rivate attempts to close markets by formation of cartels were considered legitimate applications of the freedom to contract, disregarding the corresponding reduction of freedom to compete of third parties'.

323 Wilhelm Röpke, 'Wirtschaftlicher Liberalismus und Staatsgedank', in Wilhelm Röpke, *Gegen die Brandung*, Rentsch-Zürich, Erlenbach, 1959, pp. 44–45, translated and quoted in Edward N. Megay, 'Anti-Pluralist Liberalism: The German Neoliberals', Political Science Quarterly, Vol. 85, No. 3, 1970, p. 425: '[Liberals must work] for the idea of the state and against the lack of freedom in which private economic monopolies – supported by a government leading a shadow existence – keep the economy captive'.

the broader concept of freedom.[324] The concept of competition is thus synthetically divided into *competition on the merits*,[325] which is concentrated on a firm's internal capacity for better performance and *handicap competition*, which reflects a firm's interests in trying 'to absolutely deteriorate the performance of the competitors',[326] increasing thereby its own position on the market. It must be noted that such a division can be achieved only analytically and ex post. Any attempt to envisage a clear-cut dividing line between them tends to create false negatives which would undermine both the essence and the effect of competition. In practice the two aspects are deeply connected. On the normative side, the reduction of the concept of competition to its desirable parts could distort the meaning of competition. Arguably, competition should be protected as a whole. Sometimes handicap competition reflects creative techniques which can eventually improve market performances. In addition, from a pure deontological perspective the individual freedom to compete should not be constantly subordinated to its positive, beneficial aspects.[327] Freedom and utility are incommensurable. Aspects which lead to a significant infringement of other economic goals or are self-defeating for competition itself should be addressed only externally by balancing pro-competitive and harmful effects in each particular case. Criticism of such reduction is developed in Section 3.2.2, which analyses the Austrian approach to competition with an attempt to synthesise the premises of both deontological antitrust schools.

---

324 Franz Böhm, 'Die vier Saulen der Freiheit', in 'Was muss die freie Welt tun?', Aktionsgemeinschaft Soziale Marktwirtschaft Tagung, Protokoll No. 13, 1959, pp. 55–56, translated and quoted in Edward N. Megay, 'Anti-Pluralist Liberalism: The German Neoliberals', Political Science Quarterly, Vol. 85, No. 3, 1970, p. 430: 'Freedom . . . consists in the latitude of activity which accrues to me by the fact that neither the government nor any fellow-citizens have power of command over me'.

325 Wolfgang Kerber, 'Should Competition Law Promote Efficiency? Some Reflections of an Economist on the Normative Foundations of Competition Law', Marburg Papers on Economics, No. 09, 2007, p. 15: 'The central tenet of this concept of "Leistungswettbewerb" ("competition on the merits") was that the rules for this market game should be shaped so that only the overall quality of performance (merit) should determine market success'.

326 Oliver Budzinski, 'Monoculture versus Diversity in Competition Economics', Cambridge Journal of Economics, Vol. 32, No. 2, 2008, p. 308.

327 Isaiah Berlin, 'Two Concepts of Liberty', in Isaiah Berlin, *Liberty*, Oxford University Press, Oxford, 2002, p. 174: 'Every plea for civil liberties and individual rights, every protest against exploitation and humiliation, against the encroachment of public authority, or the mass hypnosis of custom or organised propaganda, springs from this individualistic, and much disputed, conception of man'.

The constitutional pattern of competition should not be reduced to its descriptive aspects (i.e. to constitutional rules which regulate economic activities).[328] Mestmäcker warns against a perception of the concept of economic constitution, as a direct transposition of the principles of political constitutions in economics. His argument that '[t]he province and purpose of political constitutions were traditionally the empowerment of government to intervene in the market and to suspend economic liberties'[329] would be a clear overstatement if it were not taken from a historical perspective. In any event, it articulates that the concept of economic constitution should not be taken mechanistically. It is an indicator of the strong conceptual connections that exist between the regulatory power of law, ideological aspects of political theory and functional features of economic analysis.[330] The term is connected to the notion of *Ordnungspolitik*, which embraces the transparent application of economic regulation, subordinating the markets to 'a state-administered framework [of] "ordered competition"',[331] based on the principles of workable competition,[332] and implies a necessary 'explicit or implicit . . . constitutional choice',[333] limited, however, within the framework of the *rules* of the economic *game*.[334] The welfare-centred approach '– in contrast to the

---

[328] Manfred E. Streit and Werner Mussier, 'The Economic Constitution of the European Community', Constitutional Political Economy, Vol. 5, No. 3, 1994, p. 320.

[329] Ernst-Joachim Mestmäcker, 'The Development of German and European Competition Law with Special Reference to the EU Commission's Article 82 Guidance of 2008', Max Planck Private Law Research Paper No. 10/1, 2010, p. 12.

[330] Wernhard Möschel, 'Competition Policy from an Ordo Point of View', in Alan Peacock and Hans Willgerodt (eds.), *German Neo-Liberals, and the Social Market Economy*, The Macmillan Press, London, 1989, p. 151: 'Just as it is the first task of a political constitution to tie governmental power to the law, so it is the first task of an economic constitution to solve the problem of private economic power'.

[331] Brigitte Leucht, 'How German Is It? The Emergence of European Union Competition Policy and the Ordo-Liberal Model', in Eric Bussière, Michel Dumoulin, Sylvain Schirmann, *Intégration Économique et Gouvernance Européenne Depuis les Années Cinquante*, L'Harmattan, Paris, 2014, p. 11.

[332] Lawrence A. Sullivan and Wolfgang Fikentscher, 'On the Growth of the Antitrust Idea', Berkeley Journal of International Law, Vol. 16, No. 2, 1998, p. 220: 'The workable competition concept was used in three alternative theoretical forms: As the model of "intensive competition" (*intensiver Wettbewerb*), . . . as a concept of "effective competition" (*wirksamer Wettbewerb*), . . . and as a concept of "pragmatic competition" (*praktischer Wettbewerbsbegriff*)' (emphasis in the original).

[333] Alberto Pera, 'Changing Views of Competition, Economic Analysis and EC Antitrust Law', European Competition Journal, Vol. 4, No. 1, 2008, p. 145.

[334] Walter Eucken, 'Die Wettbewerbsordnung und ihre Verwirklichung', *Jahrbuch für die Ordnung von Wirtschaft und Gesellschaft*, Vol. 2, 1949, cited in

traditional paradigm – is no longer thought to consist of . . . formulating certain "rules of play"',[335] but focuses on the effects which the conduct has either on consumer or total welfare.

Rights-based reasoning is particularly visible in the core of the Ordoliberal School as represented by its Freiburg part. The Cologne brand of Ordoliberalism was more oriented towards the social function of markets.[336] Due to its major political influence, Ordoliberalism became an umbrella term for a broader vision of the development of the market economy predetermined by distributive elements. Although the role of Ordoliberalism in elaborating and implementing the concept of social market economy was significant, the latter cannot be reduced to the former as it encompasses broader political goals and is, as Vanberg shows, result driven (though with significant deontological elements).[337] The Freiburg vision of Ordoliberalism, on the other hand, is considered as 'a strictly *procedural and rule-oriented* liberalism'.[338] It is more concerned with the 'devising of rules which determine the role of the state by approximating to market exchanges as closely as possible'.[339] The procedural vision of Ordoliberalism emphasises the role of freedom 'whatever the outcome of that process'.[340] Müller-Armack, the founder of the concept

---

Christian Ahlborn, Carsten Grave (trans.), Walter Eucken, 'The Competitive Order and its Implementation', Competition Policy International, Vol. 2, No. 2, 2006, p. 227: 'Freedom of the consumer exists, but not the freedom to choose how to define the rules of the game or the forms which the economic process takes'.

335 Roger Zäch and Adrian Künzler, 'Freedom to Compete or Consumer Welfare: The Goal of Competition Law According to Constitutional Law' in Roger Zäch, Andreas Heinemann and Andreas Kellerhals (eds.), *The Development of Competition Law – Global Perspectives*, Edward Elgar Publishing, Cheltenham, 2010, p. 63.

336 Manfred E. Streit and Michael Wohlgemuth, 'The Market Economy and the State: Hayekian and Ordoliberal Conceptions', Max-Planck-Institut zur Erforschung von Wirtschaftssystemen, Discussion paper, 06/97, 1997, p. 3.

337 Alfred Müller-Armack, 'The Meaning of the Social Market Economy', in Alan T. Peacock and Hans Willgerodt (eds.), *Germany's Social Market Economy: Origins and Evolution*, Macmillan, London, 1989, p. 82: 'The idea behind the social market economy is that market freedom is combined with social balance'.

338 Viktor J. Vanberg, 'The Freiburg School: Walter Eucken and Ordoliberalism', Freiburg Discussion Papers on Constitutional Economics, 04/11, 2004, p. 2.

339 Alan Peacock and Hans Willgerodt, 'Overall View of the German Liberal Movement', in Alan Peacock and Hans Willgerodt (eds.), *German Neo-Liberals, and the Social Market Economy*, The Macmillan Press, London, 1989, p. 3.

340 Norman P. Barry, 'Political and Economic Thought of German Neo-Liberals', in Alan Peacock and Hans Willgerodt (eds.), *German Neo-Liberals, and the Social Market Economy*, The Macmillan Press, London, 1989, p. 111.

of social market economy, '[i]n contrast to Eucken and Böhm . . . saw the principle of free market competition and the idea of social balance as potentially antagonistic ideals',[341] considering that a set of economic rules should be supplemented by active socially oriented policies. Such an 'end-state liberalism' presupposes 'some ultimate aims which characterize a "good society"'.[342] The Ordoliberal School (both its Freiburg and Cologne versions) can then be seen as a deontological approach to competition, which consequently – as Willgerodt and Peacock show[343] – has often been criticised for being formalist,[344] while the concept of social market economy includes significant utilitarian elements,[345] related to the 'social adjustment'[346] of the economic system. However, the distinction is neither absolute nor clear cut, since both branches advocated a constitutional approach to competition and the incorporation of the ethos of the competitive process 'into a total life style'[347] and neither was agnostic to the social components of market economy.

The deontological understanding of competition played a pivotal role in the following conceptualisation of the ethical, humanistic foundations of the competitive process – a view which does not restrict the notion of competition to its eventual positive effects for the economy but rather perceives it as a fundamental prerequisite for freedom and humanism.[348]

---

341 Nils Goldschmidt, Michael Wohlgemuth, 'Social Market Economy: Origins, Meanings, Interpretations', Constitutional Political Economy, Vol. 19, No. 3, 2008, p. 270.

342 Alan Peacock and Hans Willgerodt, 'Overall View of the German Liberal Movement', in Alan Peacock and Hans Willgerodt (eds.), *German Neo-Liberals, and the Social Market Economy*, The Macmillan Press, London, 1989, p. 3.

343 Hans Willgerodt and Alan T. Peacock, 'German Liberalism and Economic Revival', in Alan T. Peacock and Hans Willgerodt (eds.), *Germany's Social Market Economy: Origins and Evolution*, Macmillan, London, 1989, p. 6.

344 Egon Edgar Nawroth, *Die Sozial- und Wirtschaftsphilosophie des Neoliberalismus*, Heidelberg and Löwen, Kerle, 1961, p. 380.

345 Manfred E. Streit and Michael Wohlgemuth, 'The Market Economy and the State: Hayekian and Ordoliberal Conceptions', Max-Planck-Institut zur Erforschung von Wirtschaftssystemen, Discussion paper, 06/97, 1997, p. 3.

346 Hans Otto Lenel, 'Evolution of the Social Market Economy', in Alan Peacock and Hans Willgerodt (eds.), *German Neo-Liberals, and the Social Market Economy*, The Macmillan Press, London, 1989, p. 27.

347 Alfred Müller-Armack, *Stabilität in Europa: Strategien und Institutionen für eine europäische Stabilitätsgemeinschaft*, Econ Verlag, Düsseldorf, 1971, p. 328, translated and quoted in Werner Bonefeld, 'Free Economy and the Strong State: Some Notes on the State', Capital & Class, Vol. 34, No. 1, 2010, p. 19.

348 Reinhard Behlke, *Der Neoliberalismus und die Gestaltung der Wirtschaftsverfassung in der Bundesrepublik Deutschland*, Duncker & Humblot, Berlin, 1961, p. 38, translated and quoted in David J. Gerber, 'Constitutionalizing

The constitutional dimension of competition and its disentanglement from economic performance sets Ordoliberalism apart from economic utilitarianism.[349] In its analysis of the conceptual theses of Ordoliberalism, Budzinski explores Eucken's main premises,[350] dividing them into constitutional principles (price level stability; the absence of public and private market barriers; respect for private property; consistency of economic policy; freedom of contract; corporate liability; and predictability) and regulatory principles (proactive battling against monopolies; regulating income policy; internalisation of external effects; and mitigation of anomalies of labour supply).[351] These principles correspond to the catalogue theses, developed by the founders of Ordoliberalism.[352] Maher summarises them, reducing the Ordoliberal perception of competition to four key issues: (i) the protection of individual freedom with efficiency as a by-product; (ii) a strong governmental role in the protection of this freedom; (iii) the subordination of the government and all market players to the substantive requirements of the rule of law; and (iv) the perception of competition as the socio-cultural neoliberal product of an open society.[353] Competition becomes part of a broader regulatory set of constitutional requirements. This does not mean that the competitive process is designed in a way to facilitate the achievement of other economic goals, but it shows that competition belongs to the main economic priorities of public policy.

---

the Economy: German Neo-Liberalism, Competition Law and the "New" Europe', The American Journal of Comparative Law, Vol. 42, No. 1, 1994, p. 36: 'Neoliberalism is not to be viewed as a direction in economics or economic policy, but as a humanistically-based intellectual orientation, in which philosophers, socialists, historians, legal and economic scholars have combined, even on the international level'.

349 Roger Zäch and Adrian Künzler, 'Freedom to Compete or Consumer Welfare: The Goal of Competition Law according to Constitutional Law' in Roger Zäch, Andreas Heinemann and Andreas Kellerhals (eds.), *The Development of Competition Law – Global Perspectives*, Edward Elgar Publishing, Cheltenham, 2010, p. 64: '[I]n the USA, the EU and Switzerland the freedom of individuals to compete is protected by constitutional law and . . . the goal of competition law is not to promote consumer welfare directly by this legislation'.

350 Walter Eucken, *Grundsätze der Wirtschaftspolitik*, Rohwolt Verlag, Hamburg, 1959, pp. 160–177.

351 Oliver Budzinski, 'Monoculture versus Diversity in Competition Economics', Cambridge Journal of Economics, Vol. 32, No. 2, 2008, p. 307.

352 Heinz G. Grossekettler, 'On Designing an Institutional Infrastructure for Economies', Journal of Economic Studies, Vol. 21, No. 4, 1994, pp. 17–18.

353 Imelda Maher, 'Re-imagining the Story of European Competition Law', Oxford Journal of Legal Studies, Vol. 20, No. 1, 2000, p. 164.

3.2.2 Competition from the Perspective of the Austrian School

The economic ideas of the Austrian School originated in the 19th century. Though the Austrian School of economics has its origins in Europe, its theoretical development and intellectual influence played a bigger role in the US than in Europe. Although the origins of the European competition model are rooted in Austria[354] and were developed as a response to the cartelisation of major industries, the Austrian School has not contributed to the formation of European antitrust. In fact, its strong adherence to laissez-faire and its emphasis on entrepreneurship and individualism were difficult to reconcile with the significant regulatory role that states traditionally play in Europe, even if the intellectual influence of the Austrian School on the role of the competitive process remains significant.[355] As in the case of Ordoliberalism, the Austrian approach to competition in general, and its reliance on the spontaneous order in particular, is based upon the ideas articulated by Scottish Enlightenment philosophers[356] and developed by other liberal philosophers. While describing Mill's conception of freedom, Berlin suggests that it generates 'spontaneity, originality, genius, . . . mental energy, . . . moral courage. . . . [Otherwise s]ociety will be crushed by the weight of "collective mediocrity"'.[357] The Austrian reference to the act of entrepreneurial discovery resembles the philosophical concept of creativity, developed by Berdyaev,[358] which emphasises the irrational aspects of incentives to discover new ways to pursue commercial interests, and Foucault's 'valorisation of struggle'.[359]

---

354 David J. Gerber, 'The Origins of European Competition Law in Fin-de-Siècle Austria', The American Journal of Legal History, Vol. 36, No. 4, 1992, p. 405: 'The central features of this European model of competition law were first articulated in Austria during the last decade of the nineteenth century'.

355 Maher M. Dabbah, *The Internationalisation of Antitrust Policy*, Cambridge University Press, Cambridge, 2003, p. 29: 'The ideas which emerged from the Austrian antitrust law experience during the nineteenth century were crucial in supporting the creation of antitrust law culture in Europe as a whole'.

356 John P. Bladel, 'Against Polanyi-Centrism: Hayek and the Re-Emergence of "Spontaneous Order"', The Quarterly Journal of Austrian Economics, Vol. 8, No. 4, 2005, p. 15.

357 Isaiah Berlin, 'Two Concepts of Liberty', in Isaiah Berlin, *Liberty*, Oxford University Press, Oxford, 2002, p. 174.

358 Nicolas Berdyaev, *The Meaning of the Creative Act*, Victor Gollancz Ltd, London, 1955, p. 225: 'The essential in artistic creativity is victory over the burden of necessity. . . . Every creative artistic act is a partial transfiguration of life'.

359 Leslie P. Thiele, 'The Agony of Politics: The Nietzschean Roots of Foucault's Thought', The American Political Science Review, Vol. 84, No. 3, 1990, p. 919: '[A political struggle may be seen as] a struggle for the establishing of condi-

The dynamism of entrepreneurial discovery embraces the rationale of Clark[360] and Schumpeter's vision of the market process. Although some differences exist between Schumpeter and the Austrian School in this regard,[361] they are primarily related to the role of the entrepreneur in the economic market modelling[362] and do not render the two visions mutually exclusive.

The primary relevance of the Austrian School in respect with competition is twofold: positive and normative. On the positive side it developed the dynamic aspect of the market process, competition being contemplated as a discovery procedure,[363] 'a never-ending interplay of creative and adaptive modes of behaviour',[364] disentangling the competitive process from the neoclassical concept of perfect competition. The normative aspects of the Austrian scholarship are related to the perception of competition as an important economic right. Both elements were also articulated by Ordoliberalism, notwithstanding different regulatory priorities and different methodological principles. In some sense both schools

---

tions in which self-creation in made possible, in which the assertion of individuality and otherness is viable'.

360 John B. Clark, 'The Limits of Competition', Political Science Quarterly, Vol. 2, No. 1, 1887, pp. 56–57.

361 Israel M. Kirzner, 'Creativity and/or Alertness: A Reconsideration of the Schumpeterian Entrepreneur', Review of Austrian Economics, Vol. 11, No. 1, 1999, pp. 15–17.

362 Ulrich Witt, 'Evolutionary Economics', in Peter J. Boettke (ed.), *The Elgar Companion to Austrian Economics*, Edward Elgar Publishing, Cheltenham, 1994, pp. 541–542: 'Being entrepreneur is, according to Schumpeter, not an occupation or a profession, but rather a unique, and rarely found, capacity to carry out new combination of resources; that is, innovations. The basis of this capacity is held to be a peculiar personality and motivation . . ., an interpretation with obvious elitist connotations. In this respect, Schumpeter clearly contrasts with Mises and Kirzner who interpret the entrepreneurial element as a basic human capacity, an alertness that everyone possesses more or less'.

363 Friedrich A. von Hayek, 'Competition as a Discovery Procedure', The Quarterly Journal of Austrian Economics, Vol. 5, No. 3, 2002, p. 9: 'In sporting events, examinations, the awarding of government contracts, or the bestowal of prizes for poems, not to mention science, it would be patently absurd to sponsor a contest if we knew in advance who the winner would be. Therefore, . . . I wish now to consider competition systematically as a procedure for discovering facts which, if the procedure did not exist, would remain unknown or at least would not be used'.

364 Oliver Budzinski, 'An Evolutionary Theory of Competition', University of Southern Denmark – Department of Environmental and Business Economics Working Paper, 2004, http://papers.ssrn.com/sol3/papers.cfm?abstract_id=534862, accessed on 25 February 2011, p. 13.

can be perceived as ideological allies,[365] as both perceive the right to compete as a deontological value. However, while the Ordoliberal School supports the regulatory model of competition and puts some emphasis on the prohibition of anticompetitive practices, the Austrians defend a non-interventionist approach and consider competition as an evolutionary model in constant change. For them antitrust laws necessarily *restrict* competition more than they *protect* it. In contrast, the market's invisible hand is considered as the key remedy against ineffective competitors.

The natural spirit of competition impels firms to invent new strategies of promotion for their products and services in the markets, and any regulatory barriers are seen as artificial obstacles in the way of the evolutionary market process. It would be a mistake, however, to reduce the Ordoliberal vision to its constitutionalist dimension, while perceiving the Austrian approach as that of rent-seekers.[366] The Austrian School also refers to constitutional principles and does not merely represent the opportunistic interests of the economically fittest. Whereas the Austrian laissez-faire ideology can be operationalised by beneficiaries of the market games, Austrianism itself is rather agnostic to its eventual application rent-seekers: it advocates competitive freedom without promoting the particular preferences and interests of industrial champions, develops its core ideas within the constitutional framework, and requires the government to support competition by abstaining from intervention in the market process. The Austrian School emphasises the dynamism and unpredictability of market interactions, placing entrepreneurial discovery at the centre of their research.[367] Since the notion is grounded in the principles of creativity and free economic action, '[t]he combination is the meaning of liberalism'.[368]

---

365 William H. Page, 'Ideological Conflict and the Origins of Antitrust Policy', Tulane Law Review, Vol. 66, No. 1, 1991, pp. 9–10: 'The term ideology is normally used pejoratively to suggest that an opposing belief is illusion, myth, dogma, or false consciousness. . . . [But ideology n]ot only . . . permits subjectively coherent perception, it serves a pragmatic, normative role in the organisation of a polity'.

366 James M. Buchanan, 'Post-Reagan Political Economy', in James M. Buchanan, *Constitutional Economics*, Basil Blackwell, Oxford, 1991, p. 2: '[I]t is useful to think of politics . . . as a struggle between the rent-seekers, who try to secure private profits or rents through the authority of government, and the constitutionalists, who seek to constrain this authority. And it is important to recognise that all of us, or almost all, are likely to play on both sides of this super game simultaneously'.

367 Israel M. Kirzner, *How Markets Work: Disequilibrium, Entrepreneurship and Discovery*, Institute of Economic Affairs, London, 2000, p. 31.

368 Frank H. Knight, 'The Sickness of Liberal Society', Ethics, Vol. 56, No. 2, 1946, p. 95.

Both schools are constitutional in this respect; both support methodologically a conceptual separation of the competitive process from its eventual welfare effects; and both are categorised in this research as deontological, by opposition to the utilitarian perception of antitrust, which perceives competition *solely* or *generally* as a means to achieving other important public economic goals.

The Austrian School is a generic term which refers to the ideological dimension of the school rather than to its geographical origins, although the historical context of the development of competition by the Austrians was significant as well. Conditionally and schematically, it can be separated into four generations. The main ideas of the Austrian School were developed in the late nineteenth century by Menger,[369] Böhm-Bawerk[370] and Wieser.[371] The second, inter-war generation was represented by Hayek[372] and Mises,[373] followed by Kirzner[374] and Lachmann.[375] The fourth generation covers contemporary research in the Austrian School tradition. The doctrine as a whole is intellectually and philosophically rooted in classical economics and developed the principles of the invisible hand of the market and the spontaneous order in particular.[376] Historically, the Austrian methodology can be perceived in opposition to the dominant approach in the German-speaking countries, that is the Historical School. While the former supports a universal subjectivist approach to economics (the methodology of 'Austrian Aristotelianism'),[377] based on libertarian

---

369 Carl Menger, *Principles of Economics*, Ludwig von Mises Institute, Auburn, Alabama, 2007.

370 Eugen von Böhm-Bawerk, *The Positive Theory of Capital*, Macmillan and Co., London, 1888.

371 Friedrich von Wieser, *Social Economics*, Adelphi Company, New York, 1927.

372 Friedrich A. von Hayek, *Monetary Theory and the Trade Cycle*, Sentry Press, New York, 1933.

373 Ludwig von Mises, *Human Action – A Treatise on Economics*, William Hodge and Co., 1949.

374 Israel M. Kirzner, *The Economics Point of View*, Van Nostrand, the Institute for Humane Studies, Menlo Park, California,1960.

375 Ludwig Lachmann, *Capital and Its Structure*, Universal Press, Kansas, 1978.

376 Evelyn L. Forget, 'Jean-Baptiste Say and Spontaneous Order', History of Political Economy, Vol. 33, No. 2, 2001, p. 194: 'During the eighteenth century, a set of profoundly new ideas that would later be identified as "spontaneous order" began to emerge in British social theory'.

377 Barry Smith, 'Aristotelianism, Apriorism, Essentialism', in Peter J. Boettke (ed.), *The Elgar Companion to Austrian Economics*, Edward Elgar Publishing, Cheltenham, 1994, p. 33.

laissez-faire principles, the latter is considered to be regulatory and pro-interventionist.[378] Unlike Historical empiricism, the Austrian approach is deductive and emphasises the general principles of economics rather than the particularities of each economic system. It rejects the experimental method of economic analysis, is sceptical of the reliability and comprehensiveness of experimental economics' results, as well as the verifiability of science, and claims that subjectivist elements lead to reliable conclusions, derived from the collected economic data bias. The reliance upon universal abstract knowledge is a feature shared by Ordoliberalism and Austrianism. Similar to the Ordoliberal School,[379] Austrians base their philosophical premises on Husserl's phenomenology (Husserl's method of *phenomenological reduction* was reflected in Eucken's method of *isolating abstraction*),[380] arguing that methodologically 'the "objective" methods of the natural sciences are not appropriate to the human science',[381] which explains the scepticism of both schools towards empiricism and statistical attempts to explain economic phenomena by mathematics. The rejection of the rationale of the Historical School is essentially methodological. Mises acknowledges the importance of the historical economic knowledge, but he rejects the necessity to interpret economics through the lens of history.[382] Although it is considered a heterodox economic school and opposes mathematical and statistical analysis in economics, the Austrian approach contributed to the development of neoclassical economics, in particular to the theory of value, and has played an important role in the *marginalist revolution*.

Austrians perceive competition as a natural cause of economic life.

---

[378] Ludwig von Mises, 'Planning for Freedom', in Ludwig von Mises, *Planning for Freedom and Twelve Other Essays and Addresses*, Libertarian Press, Illinois, 1974, p. 4: 'All the essential ideas of present-day interventionist progressivism were neatly expounded by the supreme brain-trusters of imperial Germany, Professors Schmoller and Wagner [the leading figures of the Historical School]'.

[379] Nils Goldschmidt and Hermann Rauchenschwandtner, 'The Philosophy of Social Market Economy: Michel Foucault's Analysis of Ordoliberalism', Freiburg Discussion Papers on Constitutional Economics, 07/04, 2007, p. 2.

[380] Manfred E. Streit, 'The Freiburg School of Law and Economics', in Peter J. Boettke (ed.), *The Elgar Companion to Austrian Economics*, Edward Elgar, Cheltenham, 1994, p. 510.

[381] Gary B. Madison, 'Phenomenology and Economics', in Peter J. Boettke (ed.), *The Elgar Companion to Austrian Economics*, Edward Elgar, Cheltenham, 1994, p. 39.

[382] Ludwig von Mises, *Human Action – A Treatise on Economics*, William Hodge and Co., 1949, p. 66: 'There are no such things as a historical method of economics or a discipline of institutional economics. There is economics and there is economic history'.

They underline the innovative elements which competition brings for society, reject regulatory interventions even in the presence of natural monopolies, and suggest that the entrepreneurial spirit will always find a way to improve performances and to obtain one's share even in closed markets.[383] Monopoly does not undermine competition, as is the case for neoclassical equilibrium economics, but constitutes, on the contrary, the ultimate (if hypothetical) consequence thereof. Both phenomena 'serve to guard entrepreneurial rewards for innovation or other discoveries that promote social cooperation'.[384] On the other hand, Austrians persistently oppose state planning, suggesting that this type of absolute regulatory monopoly deprives the competitive process of the possibility to develop, based on the unpredictability of the conduct of market agents. These two views are not necessarily consistent with each other. Aside from significant economic, ethical and ideological differences between the regulatory monopoly of the state (e.g. economic planning) and complete economic monopoly (e.g. essential facility), they share some relevant similarities, illustrated by the Ordoliberal concerns of the transformation of economic strength into political power. Hayek, whose position belongs in between the Austrian and Ordoliberal Schools,[385] acknowledges the inevitability of economic planning, but emphasises its decentralised nature, performed by individuals via the mechanism of competition.[386] In addition he accepts that 'in certain circumstances it is true that even the power over prices, etc. may confer upon a monopolist the power of influencing the market behaviour of others in a manner which protects him against unwelcome competition'.[387] He concludes that the regulatory limitation of such practices should be allowed despite its prima facie intrusion into the individual freedom of contract, stigmatising 'the popular prejudice against bigness as such'.[388]

---

[383] ibid, p. 276: '[C]ompetition does not mean that anybody can prosper by simply imitating what other people do. . . . What a newcomer . . . needs most is brains and ideas'.

[384] Sanford Ikeda, 'Market Process', in Peter J. Boettke (ed.), *The Elgar Companion to Austrian Economics*, Edward Elgar Publishing, Cheltenham, 1994, p. 26.

[385] Stefan Kolev, 'F. A. Hayek as an Ordo-Liberal', Hamburg Institute of International Economics Research Paper, 5-11, 2010.

[386] Friedrich A. von Hayek, 'The Use of Knowledge in Society', in Friedrich A. von Hayek, *Individualism and Economic Order*, The University of Chicago Press, Chicago, 1958, p. 79.

[387] Friedrich A. von Hayek, *Law, Legislation and Liberty*, Vol. 3, 'The Political Order of a Free People', Routledge & Kegan Paul, London, 1976, pp. 72–73.

[388] ibid, p. 77.

On the other hand, he considers that intervention should not expand to all monopolies ipso facto, admitting their desirability for competition. Economic monopolies only superficially support non-interventionism. Their expanding economic interests use pressure groups to obtain the most favourable regulatory treatment, so laissez-faire is in this respect only a subtle transitory stage towards the instrumentalisation of political power for the interests of industrial champions. The problem can be treated either preventively or proactively. Austrians favour the former, Ordoliberals the latter. Preventive treatment entails public control over monopolies, not allowing them to cross the imaginary line delimiting economic and political powers, and is usually limited to the problem of barriers to entry.[389] The proactive approach leads to the creation of methodical rules of economic games and gives a strong role to competition law, establishing the behavioural and structural thresholds, applicable automatically or at least systematically to all market players in certain situations. The notion of proactive antitrust is similar in this respect to the term 'managed competition'.[390]

3.2.3 The Brussels and the Neo-Brussels Schools of Antitrust

The Ordoliberal roots of EU antitrust law and policy have their theoretical and practical explanations. The first one is related to the ideological belief in economic freedom and liberal democracy, upon which the whole integration project is based. The latter can be explained by the significant role played by Germany in the first decades of European integration. The influence of Ordoliberal ideas was not only present within the German political economic and legal discourses, but also in countries like Italy[391] and France,[392] as well as in the Community in general,[393] and

---

389 Israel M. Kirzner, 'How Markets Work: Disequilibrium, Entrepreneurship and Discovery', Institute of Economic Affairs, London, 2000, p. 6: '[F]reedom of entry is the only requirement for a competitive market to exist and, in general, it is only governments which can erect genuine barriers to entry'.

390 Rudolf J. Peritz, 'Three Visions of Managed Competition, 1920–1950', The Antitrust Bulletin, Vol. 39, No. 1, 1994, p. 273.

391 Luigi Einaudi, *Selected Economic Essays*, Palgrave Macmillan, New York, 2006.

392 Agnès Labrousse and Jean-Daniel Weisz (eds.), *Institutional Economics in France and Germany: German Ordoliberalism versus the French Regulation School*, Springer, Berlin, 2001.

393 Brussels Report on the General Common Market (Spaak Report), Intergovernmental Committee on European Integration, 21 April, 1956, http://www.ena.lu, accessed on 3 April 2011.

in its Competition Directorate in particular.[394] As Joerges argues, the task of European integration 'matched ordo-liberal conceptions of the framework conditions for a market economic system'.[395] The idea of competition has been significantly conceptualised within the discourse of European integration. The role of competition law in the European Union is central at least from three perspectives: (i) competition as a driving force for integration of different European markets; (ii) competition as a tool to enhance innovations and benefit consumers; (iii) competition as an important economic freedom. The last dimension has strong Ordoliberal roots. Although these three aspects can coexist, they often clash with each other. Their relative importance varied in time.

Initially the European integration project was based on Ordoliberal premises,[396] embedded in the principles of social market economy[397] and reflected in particular in the structure of Article 101(1) TFEU[398] and Regulation 17/62[399] and (to a lesser extent) in Article 102 TFEU.[400] By applying the intentional method of interpretation, while analysing the *travaux préparatoires* of the Community Treaties, it was argued that at least the part related to the abuse of dominance has been primarily determined by the argument of efficiency rather than the idea of economic freedom.[401] This fact alone does not necessarily conflict with the fact that '[m]ost of the leading German representatives in the founding of the European Communities were closely associated with ordoliberalism or at

---

394 Stephen Martin, 'The Goals of Antitrust Policy', in Wayne D. Collins (ed.), *Issues in Competition Law and Policy*, American Bar Association Publishing, Chicago, 2008, p. 67: 'The place given to maintaining freedom of action, by Commissioner von der Groeben and by the Commission, shows the impact of Ordoliberal thinking on EC competition policy'.

395 Christian Joerges, 'The Law in the Process of Constitutionalizing Europe', European University Institute Working Paper, No. 2002/4, 2002, p. 11.

396 David J. Gerber, 'Constitutionalizing the Economy: German Neo-Liberalism, Competition Law and the "New" Europe', The American Journal of Comparative Law, Vol. 42, No. 1, 1994, pp. 71–73.

397 Alexander Ebner, 'The Intellectual Foundations of the Social Market Economy: Theory, Policy, and Implications for European Integration', Journal of Economic Studies, Vol. 33, No. 3, 2006, p. 217.

398 Alberto Pera, 'Changing Views of Competition, Economic Analysis and EC Antitrust Law', European Competition Journal, Vol. 4, No. 1, 2008, p. 147.

399 Nicola Giocoli, 'Competition versus Property Rights: American Antitrust Law, the Freiburg School, and the Early Years of European Competition Policy', Journal of Competition Law and Economics, Vol. 5, No. 4, 2009, pp. 778–779.

400 Pinar Akman, 'Searching for the Long-Lost Soul of Article 82EC', Oxford Journal of Legal Studies, Vol. 29, No. 2, 2009, pp. 290–291.

401 ibid, p. 269.

least shared an appreciation of it',[402] as the Ordoliberal conception of competition cannot be reduced solely to economic freedom.[403] The efficiency component is ipso facto implied in any mainstream economic theory.[404] In addition, 'it becomes necessary to give up the image of a unitary ordoliberal school'.[405] Ordoliberalism applies a differentiated approach to different antitrust problems. At least from the perspective of the process-oriented part of Ordoliberalism, 'the presence of monopoly . . . does not automatically license state intervention'.[406] Mestmäcker points out that '[e]fficiency . . . does not define the right of undertakings to participate in transborder commerce and competition';[407] the rights which are protected by Article 102 TFEU are granted equally to the dominant undertaking and its rivals. On the practical side, Drexl[408] refers to the fact that the provisions of the Treaty are applied by European courts systematically,[409] which implies that Article 102 TFEU should be interpreted in the same

---

[402] David J. Gerber, 'Constitutionalizing the Economy: German Neo-Liberalism, Competition Law and the "New" Europe', The American Journal of Comparative Law, Vol. 42, No. 1, 1994, p. 71.

[403] Jack Wiseman, 'Social Policy and the Social Market Economy', in Alan Peacock and Hans Willgerodt (eds.), *German Neo-Liberals, and the Social Market Economy*, The Macmillan Press, London, 1989, p. 162: 'In grossly simplified form, the position of the Ordo-liberals may be described by reference to the three objectives of freedom, *efficiency* and equity' (emphasis added).

[404] Lawrence A. Sullivan and Wolfgang Fikentscher, 'On the Growth of the Antitrust Idea', Berkeley Journal of International Law, Vol. 16, No. 2, 1998, p. 230: 'Efficiency is just one legislative goal among others. Other legislative goals for German antitrust are to maximise the number of competitors; to promote the freedom of market entry; to protect small business against unfair inroads made by big industry trade; to increase the plurality of publicised opinions in press merger cases; to protect environment; to increase employment; and to achieve international competitiveness'.

[405] Ernst-Joachim Mestmäcker, 'The Development of German and European Competition Law with Special Reference to the EU Commission's Article 82 Guidance of 2008', Max Planck Private Law Research Paper No. 10/1, 2010, p. 13.

[406] Norman P. Barry, 'Political and Economic Thought of German Neo-Liberals', in Alan Peacock and Hans Willgerodt (eds.), *German Neo-Liberals, and the Social Market Economy*, The Macmillan Press, London, 1989, p. 112.

[407] Ernst-Joachim Mestmäcker, 'The Development of German and European Competition Law with special Reference to the EU Commission's Article 82 Guidance of 2008', Max Planck Private Law Research Paper No. 10/1, 2010, p. 17.

[408] Josef Drexl, 'Competition Law as Part of the European Constitution', in Armin von Bogdandy and Jürgen Bast (eds.), *Principles of European Constitutional Law*, Hart Publishing, Oxford, Verlag CH Beck, Munich, 2010, pp. 664–665.

[409] Case 6/72, *Europeemballage and Continental Can v. Commission* ECR 1973, p. 215, para. 25: 'In any case Articles [101] and [102] cannot be interpreted in such a way that they contradict each other, because they serve to achieve the same aim'.

vein as Article 101 TFEU. Schweitzer points out in this respect that, since the main concern of Ordoliberalism was the problem of cartels, '[n]o fully developed ordoliberal position on the treatment of market dominance existed at the time'[410] and that many Ordoliberals opposed the outright prohibition of monopolisation as proposed in the Spaak Report. In any event, '[t]he influence of the Freiburg School can . . . clearly be felt in the Article 82 case law'.[411]

As Akman persuasively shows, from an historical perspective 'the abuse prohibition was actually more pro-business and less restrictive of freedom than the only other alternative, namely the outright prohibition of dominant positions'.[412] It must, however, be pointed out that the Ordoliberal perception of competition does not embrace the concept of absolute economic freedom, and its outright hostility to cartels and monopolies does not entail the absolute prohibition, but rather the internalisation of the problem as another aspect of antinomy (ordo vs. liberal; social vs. market). The absolute reference to economic freedom is rhetoric which is conceptually closer to the Austrian School, even though the latter would emphasise freedom of contract and the freedom of a monopolist to utilise its dominant position, and not the freedom/ability of competitors to participate in the market process.

The critical argument of Akman is helpful at another level: it shows that the European integration project was merely *influenced* by Ordoliberalism, but did not espouse either its premises or its principles. This is the reason why the concept of the common market, developed primarily by French political elites, played such a paramount role in EU integration. This partially explains why the primary political task of European competition law was to create an internal market.[413] Antitrust was used as an instrument to homogenise divergent European markets, reducing them to the common *Community* denominator. While the narratives of Ordoliberalism were

---

410 Heike Schweitzer, 'Parallels and Differences in the Attitudes towards Single-Firm Conduct: What Are the Reasons? The History, Interpretation and Underlying Principles of Sec. 2 Sherman Act and Art. 82 EC', EUI Working Paper, Law, 2007/32, 2007, pp. 15–17.

411 Roger J. Van den Bergh and Peter D. Camesasca, *European Competition Law and Economics: A Comparative Perspective*, Sweet & Maxwell, London, 2006, p. 48.

412 Pinar Akman, 'Searching for the Long-Lost Soul of Article 82EC', Oxford Journal of Legal Studies, Vol. 29, No. 2, 2009, p. 291.

413 Renato Nazzini, 'Article 81 EC between Time Present and Time Past: A Normative Critique of "Restriction of Competition" in EU Law', Common Market Law Review, Vol. 43, No. 2, 2006, p. 498: 'The objective of market integration lies at the heart of the Article 81(1) prohibition'.

always visible in the decisions of the Commission and European courts, the main distinction between the Ordoliberal School and the Brussels School lies in the dominance of the market integration narrative above the competition-centric vision of Ordoliberalism. According to Gerber, 'Ordoliberal ideas were particularly well suited to the pursuit of European unification through creation of a common market'[414] and the objective of a *common market* itself does not reveal the ideological principles upon which the markets should be integrated.[415] The *commonality* of the markets does not necessarily lead to their *liberalisation.* The history of European integration shows that both concepts were developing to a large degree harmoniously. This similarity, however, makes the difference between them even more blurred. The ideas of economic freedom were used in the context of European integration *primarily* as a tool to eliminate *inter-state* barriers and *inter-state* anticompetitive practices. Such a federalist policy is often supported by relying on economic freedom, even though the notion belongs to another ideological paradigm, which can be achieved by different methods, including *dirigisme* at the beginning of EU integration.[416] It is technically possible to have *heterogeneous* European markets, each of which would maintain and promote (in their own way) neoliberal principles of economic freedom; it is also possible to have a *homogeneous* European market, where the principles of economic freedom are not protected. Fortunately, the historical development of the European Union reveals that both concepts are developing in parallel and that European competition law has both substantive and instrumental application. This harmony, however, does not eliminate the conceptual differences between the European Union as *primarily* an integration project and the concept of economic competition as *primarily* a liberal constitutional project.

Aside from the instrumental application of competition rules, another feature of the Brussels School of antitrust is its legal formalism. The doctrinal support of formalism was also associated with Ordoliberalism,[417]

---

[414] David J. Gerber, 'Constitutionalizing the Economy: German Neo-Liberalism, Competition Law and the "New" Europe', The American Journal of Comparative Law, Vol. 42, No. 1, 1994, p. 72.

[415] For a more nuanced view see Pablo I. Colomo, 'Article 101 TFEU and Market Integration', Journal of Competition Law and Economics, Vol. 12, No. 4, 2016.

[416] Heike Schweitzer, 'Parallels and Differences in the Attitudes towards Single-Firm Conduct: What Are the Reasons? The History, Interpretation and Underlying Principles of Sec. 2 Sherman Act and Art. 82 EC', EUI Working Paper, Law, 2007/32, 2007, pp. 10–11.

[417] Christian Ahlborn and Carsten Grave, 'Walter Eucken and Ordoliberalism:

and it is often considered as a tool to protect the procedural rights of competitors.[418] Yet, as Pera argues, 'it was not the attention to the competitive process which led to the excessive formalism in the application of Article [101 TFEU]',[419] but rather the purposive interpretation by the Commission and the Courts of the competition provisions of the Treaty and their primary concern that vertical agreements can portion out the internal market, as evidenced in *Consten & Grundig*,[420] as well as other early cases. The federalist perception of EU antitrust rules assumes that the primary task of European competition law is to integrate and homogenise the markets. Instrumentalism and formalism are indeed connected here: if the meta-goal of EU law is the establishment of an internal market (Article 3(3) TEU), then some antitrust rules could be applied formalistically (from the competition-centred rationale), serving as an excuse for their pro-internal market instrumental application.[421] Similarly, a literal reading of Article 101 TFEU may also reveal the subordination of the EU antitrust rule to the integration imperative. Such a reading would show that anticompetitive agreements are not prohibited because of their detrimental effects for consumers or competition in itself, but 'as incompatible with the internal market'. The *internal* in this respect is superior to the *market*, being not necessarily related to *market economy*, but rather to the process of homogenisation of the domestic markets in EU Member States. The internal market can potentially be established with or without competition: the normative requirements of Article 127 TFEU, referring to the guarantee of an *open market economy with free competition* is one among many arguments against this hypothetical claim, which does not reject, however, the fact that the phonetically similar concepts of the *internal market* and *open market* are in fact two different objectives – which can

---

An Introduction from a Consumer Welfare Perspective', Competition Policy International, Vol. 2, No. 2, 2006, p. 208.

[418] Christopher Bright, 'EU Competition Policy: Rules, Objectives and Deregulation', Oxford Journal of Legal Studies, Vol. 16, No. 4, 1996, p. 546.

[419] Alberto Pera, 'Changing Views of Competition, Economic Analysis and EC Antitrust Law', European Competition Journal, Vol. 4, No. 1, 2008, p. 157.

[420] Case C–56/64 *Consten & Grundig v. Commission* ECR 1966 p. 429.

[421] Josef Drexl, 'Competition Law as Part of the European Constitution', in Armin von Bogdandy and Jürgen Bast (eds.), *Principles of European Constitutional Law*, Hart Publishing, Oxford, Verlag CH Beck, Munich, 2010, p. 664: 'According to the understanding of the ECJ [Case 6/72, *Europeemballage and Continental Can v. Commission* ECR 1973 p. 215, para. 24], the provisions of European competition law serve to implement a system of undistorted competition in the internal market. However, this objective does not constitute an end in itself but an instrument to promote the objectives of Article 2 EC'.

coincide, but can also collide. Drexl points to indirect evidence thereof,[422] showing in his analysis of the legal status of competition in the Lisbon Treaty that the federalist perception of competition taken as a tool of integration was among the dominant approaches in European antitrust. Finally, formalism is an indispensable (though not sufficient) attribute of any legal system and jurisprudence as a discipline. The axiomatic way of reasoning (formalism in economics) constitutes also an important part of neoclassical economic analysis,[423] which is often perceived as a remedy for legal formalism.

The process of European integration is in a permanent *statu nascendi*; the limits of harmonisation of the EU markets can be characterised by their horizon-effect. Nowadays, however, the level of integration is incomparably higher than in the first decades. Many significant areas of economic and political life have been transferred/delegated by Member States to the European authorities. Alongside the formerly dominant *negative* integration, concentrating on the *elimination of economic differences* between Member States, the mechanisms of *positive* integration, addressing the task of *creating economic similarities*, have become dominant in the European political discourse. This conceptual shift has inevitably led to a change of priorities in the main regulatory policies. Market integration alone does not serve as a significant justification for a *creative* interpretation of competition law.[424] The Brussels School's ethos of market integration is being gradually replaced (though without it being abandoned) by the Neo-Brussels ethos of consumer welfare as a common denominator for EU policies and objectives, leading to an interpretation of competition rules through the prism of consumers' interests,[425] perceived inter alia

---

[422] Josef Drexl, 'Competition Law as Part of the European Constitution', in Armin von Bogdandy and Jürgen Bast (eds.), *Principles of European Constitutional Law*, Hart Publishing, Oxford, Verlag CH Beck, Munich, 2010, p. 662: 'The guarantee of such a system that protects undistorted competition within the internal market has been omitted [in the Lisbon Treaty]'.

[423] Arjo Klamer, 'Formalism in Twentieth-Century Economics', in Peter J. Boettke (ed.), *The Elgar Companion to Austrian Economics*, Edward Elgar Publishing, Cheltenham, 1994, p. 49: 'Like grammar, a formal general equilibrium system represents the basic economic structure. . . . [T]he form of the system is separated from its content'.

[424] Case T-41/96 *Bayer AG v. Commission* ECR 2000 II-3383, paras. 158–167.

[425] Heike Schweitzer, 'Competition Law and Public Policy: Reconsidering an Uneasy Relationship: The Example of Art. 81', EUI Working Paper, Law, 2007/30, 2007, pp. 1–2: '[A]ccording to the Commission, . . . [t]he formerly strong inter-linkage between competition rules and the market integration goal should be softened, . . . if not abandoned, . . . and the accompanying concept of freedom to compete should be given up'.

through the lens of industrial policy as developed in the Lisbon Agenda.[426] Then again, the decline of the dominance of the market integration narrative may also be perceived as the impetus to develop a more competition-centred interpretation of Article 101 TFEU.

A phonetically similar shift has also occurred in the US antitrust regime, though the powerful consumer-centred rhetoric has been used by the Chicago School for ideological purposes, as a proxy for justification of formally anticompetitive conduct. What has happened in the EU, however, could be called consumer welfare metamorphosis, an ideological reincarnation of the concept of consumer welfare and its transformation from the rule of reason argument into a proactive regulatory yardstick, meant to evaluate the whole antitrust policy. The instrumental standard of consumer welfare has been transformed into a technical one (with a more precise term 'consumer surplus'),[427] which is used by authorities for normative purposes to design competition policy, impose sanctions, evaluate behaviours and conceptualise the phenomenon of competition. The *metamorphosis* takes place in that the initial purpose of consumer welfare was to limit regulatory intervention, whereas nowadays it is often used as a justification for additional intervention – the Chicago School thereby opened a Pandora's box,[428] by developing a concept which could easily be turned against its own ideological principles.

As far as the proactive role of antitrust authorities is concerned (visible in particular in merger and liberalisation policies), the Neo-Brussels approach is influenced by its Ordoliberal roots, stemming from the notion of the 'strong state' as 'a narrowly limited means used to achieve a functioning and humane economic order'.[429] However, it deviates from Ordoliberalism as far as the normative aspects of competition are concerned. The last important characteristic of the Neo-Brussels School is its intensive use of sophisticated economic analysis, based primarily on the techniques of Industrial Organisation and application

---

426 Heike Schweitzer, 'The Role of Consumer Welfare in EU Competition Law', in Josef Drexl, Reto M. Hilty, Laurence Boy, Christine Godt and Bernard Remiche (eds.), *Technology and Competition: Contributions in Honour of Hanns Ullrich*, Larcier, Brussels, 2009, p. 539.

427 Barak Y. Orbach, 'The Antitrust Consumer Welfare Paradox', Journal of Competition Law and Economics, Vol. 7, No. 1, 2011.

428 Oles Andriychuk, 'Dialectical Antitrust: An Alternative Insight into the Methodology of the EC Competition Law Analysis in a Period of Economic Downturn', European Competition Law Review, Vol. 31, No. 4, 2010, pp. 169–171.

429 Nils Goldschmidt and Hermann Rauchenschwandtner, 'The Philosophy of Social Market Economy: Michel Foucault's Analysis of Ordoliberalism', Freiburg Discussion Papers on Constitutional Economics, 07/04, 2007, p. 9.

of game-theoretic methods,[430] which in general is in line with the Post-Chicago approach. Alongside the EU shift from the market integration narrative towards internal economic policies and together with a changed standard for the evaluation of competition from the perspective of consumer welfare, the use of advanced economic methods constitutes the third defining element of this European regulatory trend as a new school of antitrust.

3.3 CONCLUSIONS

The task of this chapter was to describe the evolution and conceptual foundations of competition laws in the US and EU. In legal theoretical terms the first wave of antitrust legislation in the US as well as S–C–P-oriented aspects of the Harvard and Ordoliberal Schools can be associated with the development of pre-modern legal formalism[431] and the categorical denial of anticompetitive practices. The pre-modern legal theoretical, categorical nature of these schools was mitigated by the strong influence of the economic analysis of competition and the perception of antitrust not only from the perspective of formal rules, but also in a broader socio-economic and political perspective. These features can be seen in the context of the dominance of legal realism which *opened* the self-referential essence of law to economic, political and socio-cultural expertise. The origins of the US and EU antitrust laws therefore embrace both the pre-modern categorical nature of per se rules while being embedded in legal formalism and *rationalisation* of law, reflected in the broader societal goals of competition as developed in the modernist legal theory by legal realism. The *ordo* categorical nature nowadays is considered as too formalistic, to the extent that legal realism continues to be the main analytical discourse of antitrust.[432] The pendulum, however, will eventually switch in another direction, since legal certainty cannot be fully sac-

---

430 Oliver Budzinski, 'Modern Industrial Economics and Competition Policy: Open Problems and Possible Limits', IME Working Paper, No. 93/09, 2009, p. 9.

431 Aleksander Peczenik, 'Scientia Juris: Legal Doctrine as Knowledge of Law and as a Source of Law', *Treatise of Legal Philosophy and General Jurisprudence*: Vol. 4, Springer, New York, 2007, p. 65: 'Legal doctrine is a product of pre-modern evolution, for it developed in a line that spans from Greek philosophy and Roman law to medieval *jus commune* and the reaction against natural law effected in the spirit of Hegel and Savigny' (emphasis in the original).

432 David J. Gerber, 'Constitutionalizing the Economy: German Neo-Liberalism, Competition Law and the "New" Europe', The American Journal of Comparative Law, Vol. 42, No. 1, 1994, p. 76: 'Particularly in the legal realism-

rificed for the benefits of ad hoc economic efficiency. Arguably, this shift will take place within the framework of post-modern jurisprudence, with its emphasis on the problems of legal indeterminacy and interpretation. The more economic approach alone could not suffice insofar as economic analysis is also the object of different interpretations and conclusions. As will be argued in the following chapters, the virtue of legal certainty should be able to *compete* with the virtue of economic efficiency within the pluralistic socio-legal tradition, embraced inter alia by the Post-Chicago School of antitrust. This implies some re-reading of the main concerns of Ordoliberalism, mitigating thereby its severe hostility to any kind of lobbying.[433] Competition cannot dominate the constitutional agenda. However, if underestimated, it inevitably becomes instrumental to such societal interests as consumer welfare or market integration, thereby reducing its normative independence. The consequentialist perception of deontological values can endanger the principles of liberal democracy,[434] transforming market economy into command planning.[435] The same negative aspect of the exclusivity of the efficiency-argumentation has been also addressed in legal[436] and economic[437] theory. Competition should

---

dominated legal world of the United States, many reject the proposition that articulated legal norms can generally be relied on as effective guidelines for conduct'.

433 Carl J. Friedrich, 'The Political Thought of Neo-Liberalism', The American Political Science Review, Vol. 49, No. 2, 1955, p. 525: 'Likewise rejected by these liberals is the democratic quietism which accepts the pluralism of competing interests and pressure groups as somehow issuing in a parallelogram of forces from which the public interest emerges in adequate doses'.

434 Hans Willgerodt and Alan T. Peacock, 'German Liberalism and Economic Revival', in Alan T. Peacock and Hans Willgerodt (eds.), *Germany's Social Market Economy: Origins and Evolution*, Macmillan, London, 1989, p. 7.

435 Roger Zäch and Adrian Künzler, 'Freedom to Compete or Consumer Welfare: The Goal of Competition Law according to Constitutional Law' in Roger Zäch, Andreas Heinemann and Andreas Kellerhals (eds.), *The Development of Competition Law – Global Perspectives*, Edward Elgar Publishing, Cheltenham, 2010, pp. 76–77: 'Instances of the instrumentalisation of fundamental basic rights tend to be found in societies organised on socialist principles and/or in centrally planned economies where governmental agencies have to decide which economic behaviour will in the future have positive results for society (result-oriented approach)'.

436 Avery W. Katz, 'Positivism and the Separation of Law and Economics', Michigan Law Review, Vol. 94, No. 7, 1996, p. 2246: '[E]fficiency easily can be put in the service of affirmatively evil ends. . . . [E]fficiency can appear to be value-free, because whether it is desirable depends upon whether the ends it serves are desirable'.

437 Friedrich A. von Hayek, 'Competition as a Discovery Procedure', The Quarterly Journal of Austrian Economics, Vol. 5, No. 3, 2002, p. 14: '[A]ll

pluralistically coexist with other constitutional values. It also requires some conceptual lobbying. These statements constitute the main topics of the following two chapters.

socialism has no other aim than to transform catallaxy (as I am pleased to call market order, to avoid using the expression "economy") into a true economy in which a uniform scale of values determines which needs are satisfied and which are not'.

4. The normative value of competition

This chapter explores the nature of the competitive process, assuming that 'competition is a permanent feature of human society'.[1] Its main purpose is to address the phenomenon of competition from a broader theoretical perspective.[2] By comparing the normative status and regulatory approach to competition in political and cultural public contexts, it emphasises similarities between these two aspects of competition and antitrust.[3] It is argued that the regulation of economic competition should implement some normative premises and methodological tools, developed in political theory, in order to articulate properly the peculiar economic nature of the competitive process and to reallocate its normative place in the set of public values.[4] This transposition can be explained by the fact that the 'political roots of the policy of competition are deeper and older than its economic roots',[5] and to the extent that the '[a]doption of competition law is a political act . . ., [d]ebate on objectives cannot be limited

---

[1] Richard T. Ely, 'Competition: Its Nature, Its Permanency, and Its Beneficence', Publications of the American Economic Association, 3rd Series, Vol. 2, No. 1, 1901, p. 67.

[2] Lawrence A. Sullivan, 'Economics and More Humanistic Disciplines: What Are the Sources of Wisdom for Antitrust?', University of Pennsylvania Law Review, Vol. 125, No. 6, 1977, p. 1214: '[A]ntitrust scholarship could usefully explore the styles of analysis and some of the material from the humanistic disciplines of history and philosophy, and . . . it might be useful to draw upon social sciences other than economics, particularly on sociology and political science'.

[3] Robert H. Bork, Ward S. Bowman, Jr., 'The Crisis in Antitrust', Columbia Law Review, Vol. 65, No. 3, 1965, p. 364: '[Apart from economic prescriptions, antitrust] is also an expression of a social philosophy, and educative force, and a political symbol of extraordinary potency'.

[4] Maher M. Dabbah, *The Internationalisation of Antitrust Policy*, Cambridge University Press, Cambridge, 2003, p. 57: 'An adequate understanding of antitrust law and policy . . . requires insights from political science and public administration to complement the legal and the economic perspectives. It is regretted that this "third intellectual strand" . . . remains little systematically analysed'.

[5] Corwin D. Edwards, *Big Business and the Policy of Competition*, The Press of Western Reserve University, Cleveland, 1956, p. 5.

to economic arguments'.[6] The chapter begins by analysing competition from the philosophical perspective, showing that the competitive process constitutes an important attribute of human reasoning. The competitive process is analysed mainly through the prism of dialectics, with the purpose of articulating the dynamism, mutual influence and general similarities of both areas. The chapter continues by exploring the role of competition in liberal democracy, observing their mutual dependence,[7] and making a comparative analysis of its different elements, concluding that non-utilitarian characteristics are typical for all aspects of competition. It implies that its normative protection goes beyond the positive influence of competition on society and is considered instead as a fundamental ideological (and not an indispensable or organic) component of societies which share certain historical experience and cultural values. The chapter also addresses the dilemmatic nature of the competitive process, which apart from its positive aspects, tends to jeopardise other significant societal values, as well as competition itself. The self-destructive elements of competition[8] are explored in philosophy and political science more intensively than in the domain of antitrust. An attempt has been made to transfer the existing discussion to the area of economic competition. Due to the structural similarities of the phenomena as such, the regulatory remedies existing in one area may be considered as useful for other areas as well, recognising at the same time the potential danger of the mechanical transposition of these techniques from one regulatory area to the other. The self-destructive aspects of competition were the reason behind the introduction of competition law, which protects competition by limiting some of its elements. After describing the main normative attributes of competition, it reverts to the discussion on the goals of economic competition, as developed in the economic, political and legal theory of antitrust. It supports the view that the competitive process should be perceived as a methodologically independent constitutional value,[9] the significance

---

[6] Alexander Schaub, 'Competition Policy Objectives', Working Paper, in Claus-Dieter Ehlermann and Laraine L. Laudati (eds.), *The Objectives of Competition Policy*, European Competition Law Annual 1997, Hart Publishing, Oxford, 1998, p. 125.

[7] David W. Barnes, 'Antitrust, the Rule of Reason, and Democracy', Review of Industrial Organization, Vol. 14, No. 2, 1999, p. 121.

[8] Nicolas Berdyaev, 'The Metaphysical Problem of Freedom', Put, Vol. 9, No. 1, 1928, http://www.berdyaev.com/berdiaev/berd_lib/1928_329.html, accessed on 25 April, 2011: 'The dynamics of freedom leads to the tragedy of its self-destruction'.

[9] Roger Zäch and Adrian Künzler, 'Freedom to Compete or Consumer Welfare: The Goal of Competition Law According to Constitutional Law' in Roger Zäch, Andreas Heinemann and Andreas Kellerhals (eds.), *The Development*

of which should not be reduced to its eventual welfare effects.[10] The constitutionality of competition apart from the normative aspects also reflects the very structure of legal reasoning.[11] This normative claim is not new,[12] though it is often considered to be outdated. Describing the main differences between regulation of political aspects of competition and the economic ones, it explains why the competitive process is perceived solely as an instrumental, non-essential means to achieve other important economic values. It makes an attempt to recalibrate the main premises of the two deontological antitrust traditions – the Austrian and Ordoliberal traditions – in a symbiotic theory, which emphasises the normative importance of competition, while recognising the regulatory limits of its protection. The analysis of regulatory restraints of free competition reveals that, in addition to its internal dangers, the competitive process can often violate other significant societal interests and is therefore subject to limitations and restrictions. However, these regulatory limits do not influence the nature of competition, but only address the issues of its application and protection.[13] The internal significance of each value goes beyond the

of Competition Law – Global Perspectives, Edward Elgar Publishing, Cheltenham, 2010, pp. 67–68: 'It is enough for restraint on competition to be intended or effected. . . . Rules with the direct purpose of maximising consumer welfare do not exist in the EC Treaty'.

[10] Walter Adams and James W. Brock, 'Antitrust and Efficiency: A Comment', New York University Law Review, Vol. 62, No. 5, 1987, p. 1116: 'The primary purpose of antitrust is to perpetuate and preserve a system of governance for a competitive, free enterprise economy. Efficiency and consumer welfare constitute ancillary benefits that are expected to flow from a system of economic freedom'.

[11] Christian Kirchner, 'Goals of Antitrust and Competition Law Revisited' in Dieter Schmidtchen, Max Albert and Stefan Voigt (eds.), *The More Economic Approach to European Competition Law*, Mohr Siebeck, Tübingen, 2007, p. 8: 'Economic and legal approaches are structurally different. Economic approaches are often using formal models which are to demonstrate welfare effects of different goals of competition law . . . Legal approaches may – from a constitutional perspective – view goals of competition law as sub-goals. They have to be defined in a manner that they best fit into the constitutional set of goals'.

[12] Lawrence A. Sullivan, *Handbook of the Law of Antitrust*, West Publishing, St. Paul, 1977, p. 20: 'As legislative history . . . and case law . . . both disclose, the general objective of the antitrust laws is the maintenance of competition. . . . Competition per se thus becomes a goal of the legal order'.

[13] Corwin D. Edwards, *Big Business and the Policy of Competition*, The Press of Western Reserve, University Cleveland, 1956, p. 5: '[F]or today the anti-trust laws . . . are often discussed as though the sole basis for evaluating them were their bearing upon the attainment of strictly economic goals. Undoubtedly the economic impact of the policy of competition must be fully considered. But our interest in abundance of goods and services, full employment of resources,

regulatory preferences and should be explored regardless of its actual status on the political agenda. This methodological premise opens a set of epistemological problems of balancing, revealing situations where different incompatible values are equally legitimate and should be protected by the decision-maker. The analysis of the balancing and the role of the competitive process in the hierarchy of public values is offered in the next chapter.

4.1 THE PHENOMENON OF COMPETITION FROM THE PHILOSOPHICAL PERSPECTIVE

Competition plays a central role in developing the political and cultural background of the intellectual premises upon which contemporary democracies are based. It may be perceived 'as organising principle of the cultural market'.[14] The analysis of the philosophical roots of competition may be helpful in the proper articulation of its economic dimension.[15] The competitive process has been articulated, explored and appraised since antiquity. Ancient Greek philosophy and mythology addressed the issue of competition, perceiving it as an important condition for physical, psychic and societal existence. Competition is an ambivalent category. It is often related to deficiency, aggression and violence. These two areas are closely related indeed. No act of competition is fully deprived of elements of rivalry, but it also reflects the higher-ranked values of accomplishment, progress and improvement. The concept of competition – *eris* (Ἔρις) – was used in Greek philosophy not only as a reflection of strife or discord, but in a broader sense, as a human desire for achievement. The observation of this Janus-faced essence of competition can be traced back at least to Hesiod's writings in the 7th century BCE.[16] Thalmann points out that

---

stability, technological progress, and similar economic objectives cannot justify us in disregarding the political foundations of our free society'.

[14] Maurizio Lazzarato, 'Neoliberalism in Action: Inequality, Insecurity and the Reconstruction of the Social', Theory Culture Society, Vol. 26, No. 6, 2009, p. 115.

[15] Alexander Schaub, 'Competition Policy Objectives', Working Paper, in Claus-Dieter Ehlermann and Laraine L. Laudati (eds.), *The Objectives of Competition Policy*, European Competition Law Annual 1997, Hart Publishing, Oxford, 1998, 119: 'The subject is, indeed, much older than the first modern competition law. Moreover, it has not been the "exclusive territory" of economics or law, but also has philosophical and political elements'.

[16] Robert Lamberton, *Hesiod*, Yale University Press, New Haven, 1988, pp. 105–133.

Hesiod's poem 'Works and Days' explicitly refers to the two closely connected, but different meanings of competition.[17] The one is praised, another is blamed. These two are hardly separable, but still distinct. In addition he points out that both have the same genealogy, are derived from the same natural force and even share the same name, though only beneficial competition is praised. Thalmann provides another illustration in Greek mythology in the analogy with the divinity of the sea, which is simultaneously monstrous and benign.[18] This common heritage of the *good* and *bad* competition shows their natural ontological unity and inseparability.[19] The elaboration of the notion of inseparability of the two-faced nature of competition was considered by Nietzsche as 'one of the most remarkable of Hellenic ideas';[20] he claimed that both personal talents and societal virtues must be developed through a struggle. Nietzsche also argued that the eristic contest should exist as a process which prevents the emergence of domination, even if developed in the process of competition.[21] For Heraclitus 'eris is justice'.

This essential closeness of the positive and negative aspects of natural phenomena can be addressed instrumentally and cognitively. The former would concentrate on the intentional interventions into the natural causes of events, aiming at eliminating or limiting the negative aspects, while enhancing the positive ones; the latter, on the other hand, would be interested in the phenomenon as a whole, trying to capture the dialectical

---

17 Hesiod, 'Works and Days', 11–19, translated and quoted in William G. Thalmann, '"The Most Divinely Approved and Political Discord": Thinking about Conflict in the Developing Polis', Classical Antiquity, Vol. 23, No. 2, 2004, p. 362: 'It turns out that the lineage of the Strifes [*Erides*] is not single, but upon the earth / there are two. The one a person would praise on understanding her, / but the other deserves blame. Their spirits are distinct. / For the one promotes war and conflict. / the wretch! No mortal loves this one, but out of necessity, / the intentions of the gods, they honour the eris that weighs heavily upon them / To the other dark Night gave birth earlier, / the son of Kronos seated on high, dwelling in the *aether*, / placed her in the roots of the earth; she is much better for mortals' (emphasis in the original).

18 ibid, p. 363.

19 Joseph Farrell, 'Complexity, Diversity and Antitrust', Antitrust Bulletin, Vol. 51, No. 1, 2006, p. 171: '[T]here sometimes seems to be an increasing demand for convincing and detailed proof that competition is good for consumers in each case. The antitrust laws protect "competition" – not just "good competition"'.

20 Friedrich Nietzsche, 'Homer's Contest', in Friedrich Nietzsche, *On the Genealogy of Morality*, Cambridge University Press, Cambridge, 2007, p. 176.

21 Bonnie Honig, 'The Politics of Agonism: A Critical Response to "Beyond Good and Evil: Arendt, Nietzsche, and the Aestheticization of Political Action" by Dana R. Villa', Political Theory, Vol. 21, No. 3, 1993, p. 530.

tensions, 'the rhythm of motion'[22] within it, implying that the artificial isolation of the object solely to its positive parts will diminish its ontological essence. Both approaches are not incompatible, and often are mutually beneficial. While the former addresses the usefulness of a phenomenon, the latter concentrates on its comprehensive understanding. If taken critically, the latter approach is often perceived as a redundant, extensive and useless exercise, while the former, on the other hand, is often accused of reductionist simplicity. The regulatory discourse of competition policy is characterised by the dominance of the instrumental approach. A methodological mistake is often made, reducing the phenomenon of competition solely to its positive parts and blaming externalities. However, this would be correct only at the level of policy choices. At the cognitive level the positive and negative aspects of competition are inseparable in principle.[23] When for epistemological purposes the phenomenon of competition is reduced only to its positive, beneficial sides, investigation lacks completeness.

The double nature of competition, simultaneously harmful and beneficial, is the object of constant *melioration*, but even the most skilfully drawn separation line between good and bad competition cannot embrace the phenomenon without including elements of both. Fully beneficial, synthetically designed *competition* would cease to have meaning. A similar problem exists with respect to freedom. In fact the relations between freedom and competition are very complex. While they are distinguishable,[24] the latter notion is an important part of the former. This approach guides this research. Both freedom and competition by their nature go beyond the utilitarian optimisation benchmark; their essence

---

22 Herbert Spencer, *First Principles*, D. Appleton and Co., New York, 1914, pp. 228–233.

23 Frank H. Knight, 'Human Nature and World Democracy', The American Journal of Sociology, Vol. 49, No. 5, 1944, p. 410: '[N]o clear separation can be made between "freedom from" coercion – of custom or authority – and "freedom to" act, which presupposes power'.

24 Wulf-Henning Roth, 'Strategic Competition Policy: A Comment on EU Competition Policy' in Hanns Ullrich (ed.), *The Evolution of European Competition Law: Whose Regulation, Which Competition*, Edward Elgar Publishing, Cheltenham, 2006, p. 45: 'It is obvious from the case law that, in the application of Article 81(1) EC, there is an important difference between the notion of a restriction of economic freedom and a "restraint of competition". It is simply not *sufficient* to show that individual parties . . . are restricted in their economic freedom. Nor is a restriction of commercial freedom a necessary prerequisite for a restraint of competition, as may be inferred from the case law concerning information exchange' (emphasis in the original).

embraces elements of subjectivity and irrationality, and any attempt to cultivate productive freedom or beneficial competition should include at least some elements of harmfulness and undesirability. This does not mean that competition should not be improved. On the contrary, its constant improvement is the essence of any rational society. The emphasis on the elements of harmfulness is there to point out that such an improvement process has a perpetual dialectical nature. This 'perpetuity of contest [taken] . . . to identify the affirmative dimensions of contestation'[25] is the process with no final destination, which diminishes neither the importance of the intention to improve nor the improvement itself, but should always recognise this double-edged essence of competition, at least as a method of enquiry.

4.1.1 Competition *qua* Dialectics

Competition in its eristic sense is closely related to the notion of dialectics. In fact dialectics can be considered as the philosophical embodiment of competition. By analysing the concept of dialectics, the phenomenon of competition can be understood properly. Dialectical reasoning is based on the analysis of conflicting theses, without denying their correctness. It reflects the constant articulation of the syntheses – conclusions, derived from the theses – implying that none of the theses can be absolutely correct. The truth is only presumptive; it reveals itself in the synthesis. After being created, the synthesis becomes subject to another claim, transforming thereby into a new thesis and ad infinitum. Such dynamism explains the mechanics of thinking as well as the mechanics of the universe. The former refers to the epistemological problems of cognition, the latter to ontological ones. Dialectics itself is agnostic to the normative or any other ethical premises, being confined to the problem of *understanding* of a process rather than to its gradual improvement. The tasks of improvement concern those who develop and defend the theses, not those who observe the process as such. Dialectics therefore can be seen as an *engine*, generating *energy*, and not as a *steering wheel*, which transmits this *energy* in one or another direction.

Adler distinguishes three types of dialectics:[26] (i) noetic dialectics; (ii) regulative dialectics; and (iii) reflective dialectics. All three are relevant

---

25 Bonnie Honig, *Political Theory and the Displacement of Politics*, Cornell University Press, Ithaca, 1993, p. 15.

26 Mortimer J. Adler, 'The Idea of Dialectic', in Mortimer J. Adler, Robert M. Hutchins and John Van Doren (eds.), *The Great Ideas Today*, Encyclopaedia Britannica, Chicago, 1986, p. 167.

for defining its connections with competition. The first refers to Plato's *The Republic* vision of dialectics 'as knowledge of the ultimate realities',[27] implying the process of philosophical analysis itself. The second type *explains* the physical reality (including the extrapolations of dialectical principles of constant contradictions to the historical processes – which this research disagrees with); it can also be named dialectics of ontology. The third explains the process of thinking and how the objects are perceived by the thinker, addressing the act of reasoning (including both – traditional dialogue as well as the internal *dialogue* of the person with himself); it can be named dialectics of epistemology. The first and the third types are very similar, and both are also very closely connected with the second, so the classification serves rather analytical purposes, not creating clear demarcation lines between the types.

The most obvious visual explication of dialectics is present in the *taijitu* symbol, composed of two semicircles – black and white, and divided in the middle by an S-shaped line (as present in the South Korean flag). Both semicircles contain in the middle a small circle of another colour, demonstrating thereby the mutual transformation of one into the other. The symbol was present in the early Chinese, Celtic, Roman and Etruscan cultures, and is most explicitly articulated in Taoism, reflecting the Yin-and-Yang ontological and epistemological foundations of the human mind and the natural world.[28] Without the internal struggle no synthesis can be created, which implies that all human knowledge is based on accumulated and synthesised conflicts. The notion of conflict primarily reflects the cognitive way of reasoning and not the aims or intentions of those who undertake the action. The idea of Yin-and-Yang shows the dialectical essence of any communication and any act of thinking in general. The principle is universal and is applicable to any theoretical problem, including the dialectics of qualitative and quantitative methods of research,[29] or balancing the tradition with innovation.[30]

---

[27] ibid.

[28] Zhou Dunyi, 'Explanation of the Diagram of the Supreme Ultimate', quoted and translated in Joseph A. Adler, 'Zhou Dunyi: The Metaphysics and Practice of Sagehood', in William Theodore De Bary and Irene Bloom (eds.), *Sources of Chinese Tradition*, Vol. 1, Columbia University Press, New York, 1999, pp. 673–674: 'The alternation and combination of yang and yin generate water, fire, wood, metal, and earth'.

[29] Roger Clark and Angela Lang, 'Balancing Yin and Yang: Teaching and Learning Qualitative Data Analysis within an Undergraduate Quantitative Data Analysis Course', Teaching Sociology, Vol. 30, No. 3, 2002, p. 358.

[30] James R. Brandon, 'Kabuki and Shakespeare: Balancing Yin and Yang', TDR, Vol. 43, No. 2, 1999, p. 15.

In the Western world the origins of dialectics go back to the pre-Socratic Greek philosophy. Heraclitus claimed that 'everything was one and many, one thing now and many things before or hereafter'.[31] With his famous 'all is in a state of flux', Heraclitus emphasised the dynamic nature of the universe, evolving by its constant changes. His notion of the unity of opposites represents one of the central claims of dialectics. The dialectical principles are also present in the dilemmas, aporias and paradoxes, articulated inter alia by Zeno. This way of reasoning shows the ultimate arbitrariness of any decision or choice, implying that true harmony is impossible to capture in a static world without contradiction. Any notion is contestable ipso facto, inasmuch as for any statement there is always a possibility to develop a meaningful opposition. Zeno's as well as other Greek philosophers' paradoxes contain the universal dialectical laws, developed in a laconic aphoristic form. The dialectical principles were not used as a cognitive method, but as an instrument for rhetorical argumentation. Such *externality* of dialectics,[32] however, does not negate its epistemic importance. In the Socratic and post-Socratic periods the ideas of dialectics were conceptualised and polished by Plato and Aristotle. The peripatetic tradition in general is based upon a fruitful confrontation, cross-examining and dialectical argumentation, rejecting dogmatism and hard hierarchies. The Socratic, dialogue-based dialectics emphasises the dynamic nature of cognitive discovery as well, though the concept of dialectics should not be reduced to the dialogue. The former is more specific and implies the elements of conflict and competition, while the latter sometimes contains the elements of contest only sporadically and can proceed in a quasi-consensual line of reasoning. Though even in such situations the presence of conflict cannot be negated, the term 'dialogue' is broader and should not be treated as a synonym or as a variety of dialectics. There are also logical links between the dialectical reasoning, which dominated European intellectual discourse and the development of such political values as freedom of speech and thought.[33] Inasmuch as dialectics internalises conflicts and disagreements, the dialectical approach by definition tolerates freedom

---

31 Harold Cherniss, 'The Characteristics and Effects of Presocratic Philosophy', Journal of the History of Ideas, Vol. 12, No. 3, 1951, p. 331.

32 Edward G. Ballard, 'On the Nature and Use of Dialectic', Philosophy of Science, Vol. 22, No. 3, 1955, p. 205: 'Dialectic, like love, has a good and a bad reputation. This ambivalence may be illustrated in different ways in almost every period of philosophical history'.

33 Enrico Berti, 'Ancient Greek Dialectic as Expression of Freedom of Thought and Speech', Journal of the History of Ideas, Vol. 39, No. 3, 1978, p. 350.

of speech regardless of its eventual *ineffectiveness* or the potential harm that it might cause.

Following its development in antiquity and wide use in medieval philosophy (when alongside rhetoric and grammar it was part of the trivium), dialectics has been reconceptualised by such philosophers as Kant, Fichte, Schelling and Hegel. Kant disentangled dialectics from the notion of universal logical truth, demonstrating the futility of ultimate answers to philosophical questions. For him dialectics was 'a sophisticated art of giving to ignorance, and indeed to intentional sophistries, the appearance of truth, by the device of . . . imitating the methodological thoroughness which logic prescribes'.[34] Regrettably, this vision of dialectics as an instrument of argumentation that claims universal applicability dominates the contemporary philosophical discourse. The real meaning of dialectics is not in its substitution of formal logic. It is a different domain. It operates a different language, proceeding 'not by logical progression from premise to conclusion but in an associative fashion . . . It is full of play and paradox, and has the structure less of formal argument . . . than of a poem or drama'.[35] And every time this prima facie repetition has in fact a different meaning since the thesis is constantly modifying itself, being influenced by the external antitheses. Despite Kant's severe criticism of dialectics, he developed a sophisticated model of antinomies, which contributed significantly to the understanding of dialectics as an ontological, epistemological and normative phenomenon – as opposed to the common post-Kantian understanding of dialectics as an illusion. An antinomy is 'a pair of contradictory positions that seem equally necessitated by reasoning'.[36] The Hegelian approach to dialectics internalises Kant's criticism, submitting that the antinomic nature of dialectics does not have to *solve* the equally plausible contradictions, explaining them self-referentially as dialectical. These different visions of the phenomenon mandate a clarification of how the term dialectics is *not* used in this book.

---

[34] Immanuel Kant, *Critique of Pure Reason*, Palgrave Macmillan, London, 2007, p. 99.

[35] James Boyd White, 'The Ethics of Argument: Plato's *Gorgias* and the Modern Lawyer', University of Chicago Law Review, Vol. 50, No. 3, 1983, p. 863.

[36] Jeanne L. Schroeder, 'The Laconomics of Apples and Oranges: A Speculative Analysis of the Economic Concept of Commensurability', Yale Journal of Law and Humanities, Vol. 15, No. 2, 2003, p. 356.

4.1.2 Dialectics and Value Pluralism

Dialectics and the competitive process may be perceived as 'the animating force that breathes life into the invisible hand and guarantees its functioning'.[37] Many theories may address or use it, but none can fully describe it. Otherwise the scientifically verifiable *visibility* of the *in*visible hand would be a *contradictio in terminis*.[38] The invisibility implies some non-rational elements, which cannot be fully covered by any scientific empirical explanation.[39] The alternative, holistic, approach implies rationalisation, quantification and the availability of the ultimate solution to any societal problem. The dialectical vision, on the contrary, reserves the epistemic place for the conflicting interpretations without making the right choice. The dialectical approach implies a plurality of solutions; it does not reduce all societal interests to a common denominator, acknowledging the inevitability of conflicts.

Value pluralism is accepted by democratic societies as an important precondition to governance, but also as a normative value. The discrepancies are considered not only inevitable, but also important. The differences and clashes of opinions are not only *acknowledged*, but also *encouraged*. In this second sense dialectics is dogmatic. It does not require justification. It is taken as a societal choice. Instead of looking for ultimate consistency and a complete hierarchical system of values, which may prima facie avoid the conflicts, the dialectical vision proposes a value-pluralistic model. Such a system implies that different values dialectically compete with each other, trying to prove their primacy over other values by developing different argumentative strategies within the framework of the balancing act – the mechanism, by which public decision-makers make an ad hoc constellation of the priorities of each particular value in each particular case which

---

[37] Peter Dietsch, 'The Market, Competition, and Equality', Politics Philosophy Economics, Vol. 9, No. 2, 2010, p. 214.

[38] Nicolas Berdyaev, *The Meaning of the Creative Act*, Victor Gollancz Ltd, London, 1955, p. 145: 'Creativity is something which proceeds from within, out of immeasurable and inexplicable depths, not from without, not from the world's necessity. The very desire to make the creative act understandable, to find a basis for it, is failure to comprehend it. To comprehend the creative act means to recognize that it is inexplicable and without foundation'.

[39] Chantal Mouffe, *On the Political*, Routledge, London, 2005, p. 10: '[T]he dominant tendency in liberal thought is characterised by a rationalist and individualist approach which forecloses acknowledging the nature of collective identities. This kind of liberalism is unable to adequately grasp the pluralistic nature of the social world, with the conflicts that pluralism entails; conflicts for which no rational solution could ever exist'.

requires public regulation. This constant dynamism of the system *can* be empirically justified by arguing that the competition of ideas, goods and services is the most efficient way to enhance public welfare and human dignity. Yet, its main premise is not empirically utilitarian, but deontologically normative. It is taken as a societal choice, as an ideological principle, upon which a certain community is interested to exist.

The humanistic principles of governance, developed and enhanced by liberal democracy, are based upon the principles of value pluralism, the rationale of which is dialectical and dynamic. The humanness claims invigorate the freedom claim.[40] The term liberal democracy is used in its broadest philosophical sense and should not be understood as any particular political ideology. It covers all political systems, ideologies, cultures and mentalities that acknowledge the humanistic primacy of individual over society, while subordinating at the same time this normative primacy to the functional sovereignty of public authority.[41] It acknowledges the primacy of freedom over necessity, while subordinating the normative value of freedom to the functional sovereignty of the collective interests. The relationships between the individual and society and between freedom and necessity are also dialectical, and they cannot be systematised under a holistic principle of a full non-conflicting coherency.

The algorithm of their dialectical coexistence has the following form: (– i) every society subordinates individuals; (– ii) society cannot exist without such subordination; (– iii) the Hobbesian state of nature, the war of all against all, should not be taken historically, but hypothetically – it covers the situation where the individual does not subordinate his will to society. This is the universal formula espoused by all societies in all historical and cultural contexts. Liberal democracies are also based upon these principles, with one reservation: (= iv) instead of placing the collective interests on the top of their hierarchy of values, they put on the top the humanistic principles of individuality and freedom, creating thereby *the dialectical spiral*. The latter does not negate the fundamental natural

---

40 Alexander Rüstow, 'Weltpolitische Folgerunge', in *Hat der Westen eine Idee?*, Aktionsgemeinschaft Soziale Marktwirtschaft Tagung, Protokoll No. 7, 1957, p. 87, translated and quoted in Edward N. Megay, 'Anti-Pluralist Liberalism: The German Neoliberals', Political Science Quarterly, Vol. 85, No. 3, 1970, p. 429: '[F]reedom to what purpose? . . . [F]reedom is needed for being a man, for the actualization of humanness'.

41 Viktor J. Vanberg, 'Liberal Constitutionalism, Constitutional Liberalism and Democracy', Freiburg Discussion Papers on Constitutional Economics, 09/04, 2009, p. 3: '[B]y extending its ideal of individual autonomy to the level of constitutional choice liberalism can be reconciled with the "basic ideal of democracy"'.

principles of organisation of the societal order (+ i), it simultaneously acknowledges most values that, if taken in the absence of the principle of the subordination of individuals to society, would be self-destructive for this society (+ ii), since the sum of all unregulated individual freedoms would lead to the collapse of society and, thereby to the collapse of individuals, as individuals can neither comprehend nor actualise their individuality without society (+ iii).

The same dialectical spiral is reflected in the notion of liberal democracy, as perceived in this research.[42] It encompasses any system of governance that, while strongly articulating its legitimate force over the *private* individual and *public* polity alike, without unnecessary rhetoric, directs its collective aims towards the achievement of individual benefits, conceived in the humanistic philosophical, cultural, aesthetic, artistic and consumptive traditions of liberty, free will and welfare.[43] This is the only distinctive feature of liberal democracy, and any political system – regardless of the ways in which it governs[44] – could in principle conform to the term liberal democracy.[45] Conversely, the fact that a political system is governed by majority rule and that its citizens are actively participating in the public life of the polity does not automatically mean that it is interested in pursuing the aims of humanism and individual liberty.[46] The rule of the majority and the principles of deliberative democracy reflect best the positions of the people; it is the easiest and maybe the most reliable way to adjust public power to the intentions of the people, but at the same time it is the

---

42 Friedrich A. von Hayek, *Law, Legislation and Liberty*, Vol. 3, 'The Political Order of a Free People', Routledge & Kegan Paul, London, 1976, p. 163: '*Man has not developed in freedom.* The member of the little band to which he had had to stick to survive was anything but free. . . . Freedom was made possible by the gradual evolution of *the discipline of civilization which is at the same time the discipline of freedom*' (emphasis in the original).

43 Frank H. Knight, 'Human Nature and World Democracy', The American Journal of Sociology, Vol. 49, No. 5, 1944, p. 410: 'The existence of man as a free individual is a function of free society, which is the product of biological evolution and human culture history'.

44 György Márkus, 'On Freedom: Positive and Negative', Constellations, Vol. 6, No. 3, 1999, p. 273.

45 Isaiah Berlin, 'Two Concepts of Liberty', in Isaiah Berlin, *Liberty*, Oxford University Press, Oxford, 2002, p. 177: '[T]here is no necessary connection between individual liberty and democratic rule'.

46 Carl Schmitt, *The Crisis of Parliamentary Democracy*, MIT University Press, Cambridge, Massachusetts, 1985, p. 16: 'The unanimous opinion of one hundred million private persons is neither the will of the people nor public opinion. . . . The stronger the power of democratic feeling, the more certain is the awareness that democracy is something other than a registration system for secret ballots'.

easiest way to ochlocracy or mob rule;[47] it does not necessarily reflect the political values of liberal democracy.[48]

4.1.3 Dialectics and the Necessity of (Tragic) Choices

The dialectics of conflicts between different values is reflected in Hegel's notion of *the tragic*. This concept is central for dialectics and is relevant to understanding the phenomenon of freedom and competition.[49] The tragic implies the impossibility of an ultimate resolution for any conflict.[50] The concept itself is value neutral. Unlike the phonetically similar notion of *tragedy*, it does not address the aesthetic or emotional part of the conflict.[51] The tragic is not a situation, but an objective condition of mind, which constantly faces the necessity to make choices. Schroeder distinguishes in this respect two genres of antique art and two approaches to dialectics respectively: tragedy and comedy. The former is characterised by the irreconcilability of the different plots, characters and situations, while in the latter 'conflicts are resolved in a happy ending'.[52] This view could be extrapolated also to the relations between monism and pluralism, where the former seeks the ultimate reconciliation of controversies, while the latter internalises the conflict into its methodology and axiology. Schroeder classifies Hegel's dialectics as

---

47 Harold J. Laski, *Liberty in the Modern State*, Faber & Faber, London, 1930, p. 36: '[D]emocracy, of itself, is no guarantee of freedom'.

48 Chantal Mouffe, *On the Political*, Routledge, London, 2005, p. 6: 'The mistake of liberal rationalism is to ignore the affective dimension mobilised by collective identifications and to imagine that those supposedly archaic "passions" are bound to disappear with the advance of individualism and the progress of rationality. This is why democratic theory is so badly prepared to grasp the nature of "mass" political movements as well as phenomena such as nationalism'.

49 Nicolas Berdyaev, *Freedom and the Spirit*, The Centenary Press, London, 1935, p. 131: '[Freedom] has its own destiny and cannot be understood except by those who have entered into its tragic dialectic'.

50 Joseph Raz, 'Free Expression and Personal Identification', Oxford Journal of Legal Studies, Vol. 11, No. 3, 1991, pp. 322–323: 'The attempt by some thinkers (most notably Rawls) to find as extra, or meta-position from which to reconcile the conflicting views does not seem to hold much promise'.

51 James G. Finlayson, 'Conflict and Reconciliation in Hegel's Theory of the Tragic', Journal of the History of Philosophy, Vol. 37, No. 3, 1999, p. 494: 'A theory of tragedy would be genre-specific, a theory about tragedies . . . Aristotle's *Poetics* is a theory of tragedy. . . . By contrast, a theory of the tragic is not a theory about tragedies. It is not genre specific, for not only tragedies are tragic' (emphasis in the original).

52 Jeanne L. Schroeder, 'The End of the Market: A Psychoanalysis of Law and Economics', Harvard Law Review, Vol. 112, No. 2, 1998, p. 499.

the *comic* side of dialectics, and this perception of Hegel's philosophy, perhaps the most plausible from the point of view of the extrapolation of his dialectical method to social history and his emphasis on the national spirit as the ultimate reconciliatory force of all human interactions, but not for his dialectics of nature and dialectics of reasoning. The comic side of dialectics is also present in the Marxist dictatorship of the proletariat. Although both are associated with dialectics, none represent it in the sense taken in this book. The possibility of reconciliation and active contribution to reconciliation is both legitimate and desirable, but these options go beyond dialectics and cannot be considered dialectical.

The ultimate essence of the tragic reveals the impossibility of final harmony – a final state which conversely is emphasised by the holistic thinking, which believes that conflicts not only *must* be but *can* actually be resolved.[53] The omnipotence of reason, collective will and governance can in theory – if not in practice – create a harmonious conflict-free existence. The dialectical approach rejects both – the *possibility* of solving the conflicts (on the positive side) and the *necessity* thereof (on the normative side).[54] The notion of harmony requires conflicts and competition, harmony is a dynamic flux, encompassing elements of indeterminacy and vagueness rather than a fully definable state of affairs akin to heaven or communism. As Finlayson argues, the 'Hegelian reconciliation refers to a resolution of conflict through the continuance of conflict',[55] which leads to the perpetual nature of any decision-making process. The Hegelian vision of the dynamism of freedom shows that 'freedom . . . is not an easy thing, it is a difficult thing, it proceeds through tragic contradiction'.[56] Dialectics negates neither the necessity of reconciliation nor the willingness therefor, but merely extends the process ad infinitum. Dialectics addresses and

---

[53] John Gray, *Isaiah Berlin*, Harper Collins, London, 1995, p. 1: 'Political life, like moral life, abounds in radical choices between rival goods and evils, where reason leaves us in the lurch and whatever is done involves loss and sometimes tragedy'.

[54] Isaiah Berlin, 'Two Concepts of Liberty', in Isaiah Berlin, *Liberty*, Oxford University Press, Oxford, 2002, p. 214: 'If, as I believe, the ends of men are many, and not all of them are in principle compatible with each other, then the possibility of conflict – and of tragedy – can never wholly be eliminated from human life, either personal or social. The necessity of choosing between absolute claims is then an inescapable characteristic of the human condition'.

[55] James G. Finlayson, 'Conflict and Reconciliation in Hegel's Theory of the Tragic', Journal of the History of Philosophy, Vol. 37, No. 3, 1999, p. 503.

[56] Nicolas Berdyaev, *Slavery and Freedom*, The Centenary Press, London, 1943, p. 30.

internalises the plurality of values, their incommensurability and their incompatibility.[57]

Any decision holds elements of arbitrariness, inasmuch as no decision can fully solve the conflict. Trivial cases are prima facia free from contradictions, though in fact contradictions in such trivial cases are also trivial and therefore virtually invisible. But the more difficult the case becomes, the more articulated the contradictions appear. In this sense, dialectics fundamentally differs from logic. The latter, provided the premises of a syllogism are true, achieves the correct answer, while the former does not even attempt it. The tragic in the Hegelian sense does not refer to the amount of suffering which any chosen option would lead to. The concept of tragic is not emotional; it refers to the dilemmatic nature of the choice itself rather than to the substantive content of the chosen. In the context of economics, the inevitability of choices mitigates the neoclassical methodological concern with indeterminacy. Full determinacy can be present in mathematical modelling, but it is impossible in antitrust regulation. Economic indeterminacy itself constitutes a fruitful area for research.[58]

4.1.4 The Concept of Positive and Negative Freedom and Competition Policy

Freedom, and economic freedom in particular, is composed of two inseparable polar components. These two components constitute the positive and negative aspects of the phenomenon. Although the history of this philosophical problem goes back to antiquity and was significantly developed by Kant in his antinomies, in contemporary times it was most strongly articulated by Berlin. This research partly shares Berlin's approach to the notion of positive and negative freedom, but perceives them in a dialectical interplay. It should be noted that for Berlin: '[t]he "positive" sense of the word "liberty" derives from the wish

---

[57] John Kekes, *The Morality of Pluralism*, Princeton University Press, Princeton, 1993, p. 21: '[C]onflicts among reasonable conceptions of a good life and reasonable values must be recognized as unavoidable features of an adequate understanding of morality and politics'.

[58] Oliver Budzinski, 'Modern Industrial Economics and Competition Policy: Open Problems and Possible Limits', IME Working Paper, No. 93/09, 2009, p. 18: 'Dealing with uncertainty and principle limits to predictability have always been the core of market process-oriented competition economics . . . and connecting their insights more strongly with antitrust-focused modern industrial economics might represent an interesting – but to my knowledge not yet existing – research programme'.

on the part of the individual to be his own master'.[59] At the *individual* level positive freedom can be seen as articulated, rational, conscious execution of the individual's own will, or as Laski puts it, '[w]e desire freedom . . . in order to that we may be ourselves at our best',[60] or as Nelson explains it, 'the status of a fully self-realized human being . . . the actual achievement of a particular condition of life'.[61] The notion of negative freedom is understood by Berlin as being free from coercion, as 'warding off interference'.[62] In other words, at the individual level he appreciates positive freedom more, merely considering negative freedom as a *conditio sine qua non*, which does not have significance or merit in itself. It has been acknowledged in the literature that both aspects of freedom are inseparably connected.[63] At the collective level Berlin acknowledged that some aspects of positive (posited) liberty may be developed by authoritarian methods. Subsequently, even if he considers positive freedom genuinely more important than negative freedom, Berlin criticised the literalist extrapolation of this taxonomy from the realm of the individual to that of the collective.[64] This point is also observed by Laski.[65] A similar shift from individualism towards collectivism has happened in relation to Darwinian ideas on evolution and natural selection. Initially these views were considered as a justification for the laissez-faire approach to individual actions, while later in the 19th century the theory was operationalised for the sake of collectivist goals, even including eugenics.[66] Berlin was cautious in respect to the rationality of *collective* positive freedom, while being sympathetic to *individual* positive freedom. Whereas he saw the latter as the actualised, fulfilled act of genuine freedom, he stigmatised the former as a potential legitimisation of the

[59] Isaiah Berlin, 'Two Concepts of Liberty', in Isaiah Berlin, *Liberty*, Oxford University Press, Oxford, 2002, p. 178.

[60] Harold J. Laski, *Liberty in the Modern State*, Faber & Faber, London, 1930, p. 23.

[61] Eric Nelson, 'Liberty: One Concept Too Many?', Political Theory, Vol. 33, No. 1, 2005, p. 60.

[62] Isaiah Berlin, 'Two Concepts of Liberty', in Isaiah Berlin, *Liberty*, Oxford University Press, Oxford, 2002, p. 174.

[63] Gerald C. MacCallum, 'Negative and Positive Freedom', The Philosophical Review, Vol. 76, No. 3, 1967, p. 312.

[64] Isaiah Berlin, *Four Essays on Liberty*, Oxford University Press, Oxford, 1990, pp. xlii–xliii.

[65] Harold J. Laski, *Liberty in the Modern State*, Faber & Faber, London, 1930, pp. 28–31.

[66] Richard Weikart, 'The Origins of Social Darwinism in Germany, 1859–1895', Journal of the History of Ideas, Vol. 54, No. 3, 1993, p. 469.

authoritarian actions of a community. Gray observes in this respect that '[w]hereas choice presupposes genuine rivalry among conflicting goods, rational will [of the collective positive freedom] points to one, and only one course of action'.[67] This holistic view of the rational will implies the ultimate compatibility and commensurability of all values, which is not the case for the dialectical, pluralistic perspective.[68] The application of the pluralistic approach, however, is not a negation of rational will, as '[w]e owe our freedom to restraints of freedom',[69] and '[n]othing could be more false historically than the notion that men are naturally free and equal',[70] but the negation of the will as *the ultimate answer* to the repercussions of freedom. Other authors introduce a moral dimension into the notion of freedom,[71] an approach which is not supported in this research, inasmuch as freedom and its utility are taken separately.

A *negative* may also mean a purely cognitive approach to freedom. This implies that it is the *absence* of freedom that often helps to reveal its necessity, which explains why freedom can be appreciated more in societies where it is severely suppressed. Two remarks should be made in this respect: one is substantive and the other methodological. As to the substance, the concept of negative freedom should not be reduced to mere freedom from constraints, as expressed in Mill's famous liberty principle whereby the freedom of one person ends at the point where the freedom of another begins. This perception is incorrect from both the ontological and methodological perspectives. The first implies that freedom is not a zero-sum concept – it *may* be stopped from being applied at that imaginary point, but it cannot cease to be *freedom* – though *the-freedom-restrained* for the benefit of the other. The second aspect means that such a view

---

67 John Gray, *Isaiah Berlin*, Harper Collins, London, 1995, p. 21.

68 Isaiah Berlin, *Four Essays on Liberty*, Oxford University Press, Oxford, 1990, p. x: 'It seems to me that the unfavourable contrast sometimes drawn between "negative" liberty and other, more obviously positive, social and political ends sought my men . . . has its roots . . . in an ancient doctrine according to which all truly good things are linked to one another in a single, perfect whole; or, at the very least, cannot be incompatible with one another'.

69 Friedrich A. von Hayek, *Law, Legislation and Liberty*, Vol. 3, 'The Political Order of a Free People', Routledge & Kegan Paul, London, 1976, p. 163.

70 Frank H. Knight, 'Human Nature and World Democracy', The American Journal of Sociology, Vol. 49, No. 5, 1944, p. 410.

71 Maria Dimova-Cookson, 'A New Scheme of Positive and Negative Freedom – Reconstructing T. H. Green on Freedom', Political Theory, Vol. 31, No. 4, 2003, p. 509: 'Positive freedom is gained by producing goods for others, by engaging in moral action, whereas negative freedom is gained by receiving goods coming from someone else's moral action'.

can easily be instrumentalised to oppress freedom.[72] Negative freedom is taken in this research rather as an irrational, spontaneous action or willingness to act, and not as a mere precondition for positive freedom. Both aspects therefore have some significance, and both require the other in order to develop into *complete* freedom, where the *completeness* refers not to the absoluteness of freedom, but to freedom being completed by the union of its two parts – the negative and the positive, 'determined by some primordial condition to action'.[73] This approach acknowledges that in order to be properly defined such phenomena as freedom and competition should not be synthetically disentangled from their undesirable, negative aspects. The analysis of the spirit of entrepreneurial discovery or the spirit of competition would be significantly reduced if perceived exclusively in terms of its improved, cultivated form. As Berdyaev claims, the 'spirit emanates not only from the Deity but also from the primal pre-existential freedom, from the *Ungrund*',[74] revealing thereby the dialectical dynamism of freedom, composed of two antagonistic elements, which constantly collide. The *Ungrund* or the abyss 'is prior to and indeed the source of being'.[75] Freedom thereby is perceived as a partly created and partly spontaneous phenomenon.[76]

Both polarities of freedom dialectically coexist, and neither can exist without the other. They simultaneously negate and enhance each other. While for Berlin, positive freedom is an advanced stage of freedom, the freedom which is self-realised and articulated, this research does not give primacy to either, relying on the perception of complete freedom articulated by Berdyaev.[77] Both authors acknowledge that in a commonsense

---

72 Michael Polanyi, 'The Growth of Thought in Society', Economica, New Series, Vol. 8, No. 32, 1941, p 430: 'The desire for personal freedom is the desire to be left alone; it does not define its purpose, because that would limit the freedom which is wanted. The demand is entirely irresponsible, and is put forward as a personal right of the individual. . . . The totalitarian view . . . may tolerate personal freedom, but only so far as this does in no way affect the collective interests of the community'.

73 Herbert Spencer, *First Principles*, D. Appleton and Co., New York, 1914, p. 245.

74 Nicolas Berdyaev, *Spirit and Reality*, The Centenary Press, London, 1939, p. 33 (emphasis in the original).

75 Lewis Owens, '"Does This One Exist"? The Unveiled Abyss of Nikos Kazantzakis', Journal of Modern Greek Studies, Vol. 16, No. 2, 1998, p. 335.

76 Frank H. Knight, 'The Sickness of Liberal Society', Ethics, Vol. 56, No. 2, 1946, p. 92: 'An element of curiosity and surprise is equally essential to interest in any activity'.

77 Nicolas Berdyaev, *The Meaning of the Creative Act*, Victor Gollancz Ltd, London, 1955, p. 145: 'Freedom is the ultimate: it cannot be derived from

perception positive freedom is the only aspect of freedom which deserves to be taken as virtue, while at the same time recognising that such a view is incapable of understanding the phenomenon of freedom as such. Complete freedom is thus the composition of the natural, spontaneous irrational reflections of negative freedom, dialectically combined with the rationality of positive freedom. Ontologically none of the two aspects are better or hierarchically more important than the other,[78] and epistemologically the line between them is impossible to draw.[79] It may well be that for an individual the positive aspects of freedom are more important than its negative aspects, which shows his intellectual and emotional maturity. Yet, it does not imply that these aspects are more important for defining the phenomenon of freedom itself, which inevitably should contain elements of irrationality and spontaneity. The extent to which this complete characteristic of freedom does not correspond to the interests of the individual simply reflects the significance of freedom in his life, his consent to mitigate his freedom with other – more rational and less controversial – virtues which provide him with higher intellectual and mental security than freedom does.

As to the second, methodological remark, it should be noted that the concept of negative and positive freedom is mainly used in this book to illustrate its repercussions in the economic sphere. Unlike the former context, it refers, therefore, more to collective freedom than to individual freedom. This changes the meaning of the terms positive and negative. It does consider that both aspects of freedom are at the same regulatory level of importance, and that they are in a dialectical relation, but it does not perceive the former as irrational and the latter as rational, inasmuch

anything: it cannot be made the equivalent of anything. Freedom is the baseless foundation of being: it is deeper than all being'.

[78] Lawrence Crocker, *Positive Liberty: An Essay in Normative Political Philosophy*, Martinus Nijhoff Publishers, The Hague, 1980, p. 5: '[T]here are not two fundamentally different kinds of freedom. . . . [There is] the continuity between the positive and negative accounts. . . . [T]he line between positive and negative liberty is, in many important respects, so insubstantial and arbitrary that there is no good moral reason to insist upon it'.

[79] Michel Rosenfeld, 'Hate Speech In Constitutional Jurisprudence: A Comparative Analysis', Cardozo Law Review, Vol. 24, No. 4, 2003, p. 1523: 'Hate speech – that is, speech designed to promote hatred on the basis of race, religion, ethnicity or national origin – poses vexing and complex problems for contemporary constitutional rights to freedom of expression. . . . The constitutional treatment of these problems, moreover, has been far from uniform as the boundaries between impermissible propagation of hatred and protected speech vary from one setting to the next'.

as these concepts are hardly applicable to collective entities – negative freedom in respect to economic competition implies competition policy, directed to *protection* of competition, policies which *eliminate the obstacles* to free competition, while the concept of positive freedom is reflected in policies which *promote* competition, *creating the conditions* for free competition. While it may appear that only positive freedom *forces men to be free*, it is in fact the task of both positive and negative collective freedoms. Both presuppose each other, while remaining in dialectical polarities. Both imply some level of regulatory intervention, inasmuch as neither negative (preventive) nor positive (proactive) antitrust policy can be performed without the active involvement of a regulatory authority. Although traditionally antitrust law performed mostly a preventive role,[80] it can be neither reduced to nor fully understood from this negative perspective only. The dialectical dependence of positive and negative competition policies is similar to the evolution of the concept of European integration. The whole project started under the principles of *elimination of the differences* between the markets in the Member States. Soon it was proven that by eliminating the barriers between the national economies the EU project required also the *creation of similarities*, which implies the development of joint proactive initiatives, directed at the harmonisation of the internal market. Both negative and positive aspects of integration are inseparable, although historically the former preceded the latter. In the area of competition law, a similar process can be observed: its primary aim was the *protection* of competition; in due course this goal has been progressively supplemented by its *promotion* (through liberalisation and partly merger policies). In spite of the temporal distance between the emergences of these two aspects of antitrust policy, both are indispensable components of the notion, and they are in the dialectical interplay. As for the concept of positive and negative freedom, the notions of preventive and proactive antitrust policies supplement each other, and neither is more important at the level of the substance – though from a purely legal perspective, the ex post mechanisms by which negative (preventive) antitrust policy is predominantly conducted may appear more reliable (in respect to legal certainty in particular) than ex post proactive antitrust. The ex ante–ex post difference is not, however, absolute: negative (preventive) antitrust

[80] Maher M. Dabbah, *The Internationalisation of Antitrust Policy*, Cambridge University Press, Cambridge, 2003, pp. 46–47: 'Antitrust law . . . is generally negative and prohibitory in both nature and wording. . . . This is obvious since antitrust law does not directly encourage competition, but rather seeks . . . to prevent any form of anti-competitive behaviour in the market'.

policy may well be performed ex ante, while positive (proactive) competition measures may be taken ex post.[81]

Finally, freedom is not a concept which should be *evaluated* against something. Internally it is an ultimate value, self-reflective and self-evaluative. In this respect it is necessary to distinguish the *phenomenon* of freedom from the *right* to freedom. The former is value free. Although it exists within a context, the context neither defines nor subordinates the phenomenon of freedom. The latter, on the contrary, is always taken in context; it is always defined by the context, and can never be taken as an absolute, to the extent that rights conflict with each other and none can be *fully* protected at the regulatory level. The separation of the *phenomenon* of freedom (competition) from freedom (competition) as a *right* plays an important role in the regulatory process. Competition as a phenomenon does not have to be limited or circumscribed by other related phenomena in order to be limited at the level of rights. These two aspects of competition will never coincide. The rights aspect is always more narrow than the phenomenon aspect. The relation between phenomenon and right is similar to the relation between right and interest. Both imply an opposition between the deontological and utilitarian positions, but while in the former case rights are taken from the utilitarian point of view, as less abstract and more context dependent than phenomena, in the latter case rights are deontological, as they are more independent on the context than interests. There is no need, therefore, to define competition at the level of the phenomenon as something which leads to welfare, growth or any other utilitarian consequence. Competition as a phenomenon is value neutral; it inevitably contains elements of irrationality; and its genuine meaning would be distorted, if reduced to its positive societal aspects only.

4.2 THE NORMATIVE ROLE OF COMPETITION IN LIBERAL DEMOCRACY

Competition is the central distinctive feature of liberal democracy.[82] It is present in many areas of public and private relationships.[83] The main

[81] Pablo I. Colomo, 'On the Application of Competition Law as Regulation: Elements for a Theory', Yearbook of European Law, Vol. 29, No. 1, 2010, pp. 264–266.

[82] Giuliano Amato, *Antitrust and the Bounds of Power: The Dilemma of Liberal Democracy in the History of the Market*, Hart Publishing, Oxford, 1997, pp. 2–4.

[83] Maher M. Dabbah, *The Internationalisation of Antitrust Policy*, Cambridge University Press, Cambridge, 2003, p. 58.

aspects of competition in the public domain touch upon the political, cultural and economic spheres.[84] The relevance of the analogy has been accepted both in politics in the notion of the 'marketplace of ideas'[85] and in economics,[86] particularly by the representatives of the 'civil rights approach to antitrust'.[87] It has been argued that 'whoever desires political freedom must also allow economic freedom and vice versa since the freedom of economic activity is a vital constituent of the basic rights of personal and political freedom'.[88] It is normatively and methodologically possible to explore competition as a multidimensional phenomenon.[89] This can be explained by the deep historical penetration of ethical values into the discourse of economics,[90] and the importance of economic competition as a cultural phenomenon,[91] and as a condition of pluralism.[92]

---

[84] James M. Buchanan, Richard E. Wagner and John Burton, 'The Consequences of Mr Keynes', in James M. Buchanan, *Constitutional Economics*, Basil Blackwell, Oxford, 1991, p. 96: 'In a democracy, political competition bears certain resemblances to market competition. Private firms compete among themselves in numerous, complex way to secure the patronage of customers. Politicians compete among themselves for the support of the electorate by offing promising policies and programmes which they hope will get them elected or re-elected'.

[85] *Abrams v. United States*, 250 U.S. 616 (1919).

[86] George J. Stigler, 'Economic Competition and Political Competition', Public Choice, Vol. 13, No. 1, 1972.

[87] Paul H. Brietzke, 'The Constitutionalisation of Antitrust: Jefferson, Madison, Hamilton and Thomas C. Arthur', Valparaiso University Law Review, Vol. 22, No. 2, 1988, p. 298.

[88] Dieter Wolf, 'Competition Policy Objectives', Working Paper, in Claus-Dieter Ehlermann and Laraine L. Laudati (eds.), *The Objectives of Competition Policy*, European Competition Law Annual 1997, Hart Publishing, Oxford, 1998, p. 129.

[89] Harold Demsetz, 'Economic, Legal and Political Dimensions of Competition', University of California, Los Angeles Discussion Paper, No. 209, 1981, p. 15.

[90] David J. Gerber, 'Prometheus Born: Shaping the Relationship Between Law and Economic Conduct', St. Louis University Law Journal, Vol. 38, No. 3, 1994, pp. 674–675: 'In the Western political tradition ... the regulation of economic conduct has been heavily influenced ... by the languages of religion, philosophy and ethics rather than being exclusively an issue of wealth and power'.

[91] Spencer S. Waller, 'Market Talk: Competition Policy in America', Law & Social Inquiry, Vol. 22, No. 2, 1997, p. 438: '[One of the explanations of antitrust law is associated] with deep spiritual and cultural values regarding the importance of competition and individual entrepreneurship in the American psyche'.

[92] Hideaki Kobayashi, 'Competition Policy Objectives', Panel Discussion, in Claus-Dieter Ehlermann and Laraine L. Laudati (eds.), *The Objectives of Competition Policy*, European Competition Law Annual 1997, Hart Publishing, Oxford, 1998, p. 6: 'In some countries "pluralism" mainly signifies cultural or

Jenny suggests that '[i]f economic democracy will help promote political democracy, this constitutes a political goal which is beyond the scope of microeconomic theory'.[93]

Competition plays an important role in art,[94] as well as in any creative human activity in general. As Knight suggests, 'whenever people are free to do what they want to do, they organize a contest of some sort or participate in, or support, one already organized'.[95] In politics competition is performed by political parties, movements and interest groups, which promote their ideas, constantly competing with each other for the support of the citizens.[96] Not denying Buchanan's argument on the differences between market and political competition,[97] it is worth noting that although the quintessence of political competition is reflected in elections, it should not be reduced to the process of voting as such. The clear analogy between voters and consumers[98] alone does not exhaust the whole spectrum of similarities. Politics implies a constant competition for the constituency. This is a continuous process which cannot be reduced to elections or all-or-nothing outcomes. This implies that, not unlike markets, politics is a form of perpetual competition and elections only perform a function of external assessment of its outcomes.

---

ethic pluralism. In Japan and several other countries, however, it [also] signifies the need to preserve a variety of sizes or types of enterprises, which is basically an economic concern'.

[93] Frederic Jenny, 'Competition Policy Objectives', Panel Discussion, in Claus-Dieter Ehlermann and Laraine L. Laudati (eds.), *The Objectives of Competition Policy*, European Competition Law Annual 1997, Hart Publishing, Oxford, 1998, p. 3.

[94] Roland Vaubel, 'The Role of Competition in the Rise of Baroque and Renaissance Music', Journal of Cultural Economics, Vol. 29, No. 4, 2005, p. 277.

[95] Frank H. Knight, 'Economists on Economic Ethics', International Journal of Ethics, Vol. 48, No. 1, 1937, p. 106.

[96] Harold J. Laski, *Liberty in the Modern State*, Faber & Faber, London, 1930, p. 39: 'Responsible government in a democracy lives always in the shadow of coming defeat'.

[97] James M. Buchanan, Richard E. Wagner and John Burton, 'The Consequences of Mr Keynes', in James M. Buchanan, *Constitutional Economics*, Basil Blackwell, Oxford, 1991, p. 96: 'There are also, it is worth noting, important differences between market and political competition. Market competition is continuous . . .. Political competition is intermittent. . . . Market competition allows several competitors to survive simultaneously. . . . Political competition leads to an all-or-nothing outcome. . . . [Also p]oliticians are simply not held liable for their promises'.

[98] Franz Jürgen Säcker, 'Legal Foundations of Competition', in Günther Hirsch, Frank Montag and Franz Jürgen Säcker (eds.), *Competition Law: European Community Practice and Procedure – Article-by-Article Commentary*, Sweet & Maxwell, London, 2008, p. 6.

In addition, political competition exists *within* the parties, between the adherents of their different ideological, cultural, geographical and strategic programmes or platforms, and between the supporters of different potential leaders. These aspects of competition are mostly visible at the level of primaries, where different candidates from the same party fiercely compete to be nominated for general elections. This mode of political competition, as exists for example in the US voting system, shows that although the real political power shifts between the two main parties, this duopoly does not preclude political debates within the two rival factions. In fact, parties are not monolithic, but composed of many fragmented and often conflicting groups of influence. This type of competition exists even in systems ruled by one official party, but its presence is limited to non-transparent back-stage tensions between members of the politburo or any other ideological political monopoly. The difference between the two is not in the level of competition, but in the public awareness of its importance. The former shows common support for the principles of political competition, considering it as an indispensable component of public life; the latter treats it as an externality, which endangers the coherence and harmony that supposedly exist in such societies. Strong public support for political competition does not increase the degree of confidence in the outcomes that it generates, but rather reflects a collective adherence to the principles of competition as free circulation of political ideas. Finally, the notion of political competition can be traced to the very principle of the separation of powers.[99]

In cultural life competition also plays a pivotal role. It exists in the form of free speech, which is considered to be one of the paramount values of liberal democracy. Free speech enables fruitful interactions between members of a community; it tolerates pluralities of views, differences in beliefs and values, and the possibility to express marginal aspects of one's personal identity without being subject to oppression or humiliation. Free speech goes far beyond the political realm, providing a fruitful soil for cultural interaction, where different ideas compete with each other independently of their benefits for the majority. Societies with a developed culture of public and private competition are not necessarily wealthier or stronger than those where free speech is not considered very important and where its protection is tied to international commitments

[99] Aharon Barak, *The Judge in a Democracy*, Princeton University Press, Princeton, 2006, p. 216: 'Tension between the courts and the other branches is natural and, in my opinion, also desirable. . . . Indeed, the constant tension between the judicial branch and the other branches stems from their distinct roles'.

or rhetorical slogans instead of a genuine appreciation of the value of freedom of expression.

The common feature that should unite competition in its political, cultural and economic context is its conceptual disentanglement from its societal outcomes. Neither political nor cultural competition is directed to the selection of the *best* party or the *best* idea. Competition is not the *best* way to deliver prosperity, growth and welfare. Its outcomes are not necessarily optimal or even beneficial for society in general. Often competition can lead to harmful outcomes and it is not immunised from flows and fallacies. These negative aspects of competition cannot be eliminated from the phenomenon without depriving it of its original meaning. The reduction of competition to its *good* components is an aim, external to competition as such. This aim should preoccupy those who perform an ad hoc reconciliation of the conflicting values and principles, and it should not have an impact on the definition of the phenomenon of competition as such. This deontological approach to competition differs from the empirical view, embraced in the famous saying that *democracy is the best of the worst*, which contends that despite its externalities, freedom is supported due to the lack of any reliable alternative; as well as from purely empirical observations, which claim support for freedom because *it does work well*, thus circumscribing freedom to its performance.[100] These aspects are important indeed, but the deontological support for competition goes beyond well-being. Arguably, the more authoritarian way of governance could in principle lead to *better* outcomes in political, cultural and economic terms. This premise would be difficult but not impossible to prove. Yet, if proven, it could mean that freedom and competition should be replaced by a *better* approach to public administration. Competition is often redundant and unpredictable, while reliance on economic rationality is aimed at optimisation. This is the reason why in art utilitarianism is a synonym of minimalism: architectural aesthetic extravagances are not *needed* – the simpler the better in terms of resource allocation. Hence, regulators often try to reduce competition to its positive effects, establishing both theoretical and legislative yardsticks.[101] History shows that in some

---

100 Harold J. Laski, *Liberty in the Modern State*, Faber & Faber, London, 1930, pp. 80–81: '[A]ll restrictions upon freedom of expression upon the ground that they are seditious or blasphemous are contrary to the well-being of society'.

101 Oliver Budzinski, 'Monoculture versus Diversity in Competition Economics', Cambridge Journal of Economics, Vol. 32, No. 2, 2008, p. 313: 'As such, the question of whether or not pluralism in competition economics represents a "case of wasteful competition" can be discussed. . . . According to this view, a monoculture focusing on the right theory would avoid waste and yield beneficial

situations free elections could be replaced by a more stable, reliable and effective form of governance. Cultural competition as well can generate unnecessary tensions within the community and its limitation or elimination could increase social cohesion. However, these features are irrelevant for the deontological perception of freedom, which is protected, promoted and enhanced for its own sake as a distinctive attribute of human beings rather than a way to reach prosperity and solidarity. Free competition in politics does not necessarily lead to the election of the best party; free speech includes hateful or offensive speech; free market is not necessarily better economically than central planning. There are many examples where the limitation of competition increases prosperity as well as other measurable values. Freedom is not a *conditio sine qua non* for welfare. Freedom is a non-utilitarian category. It is protected independently of its societal benefits.

The beneficial consequences of freedom are not easily measured and calculated.[102] Its benefits are often *qualitative* and not *quantitative*. Freedom and competition intrinsically contain the possibility of mistake. Freedom does not provide immunity from failure and its outcomes are not always positive. This is the reason why freedom can be seen as a *luxury product* of liberal democracy: a product which can be afforded only by those societies which are aware of its danger and can *enjoy it responsibly*; a *luxury* which refers to intangible long-term benefits, it is the *luxury* of politeness or the *luxury* of organic food rather than *luxury* in its nouveau riche sense – though, here again, both aspects are present in the phenomenon of freedom. A society which accepts freedom and competition does it intentionally, being aware of their potential danger, having '[t]he courage to take meaninglessness into itself'.[103] The *ethos* of freedom is not transferable from one polity to the other as easily as the *idea* of freedom. It develops within a community, reflecting its tragic as well as heroic past, its cultural, political and historical specificity, its collective fears, stereotypes, memory and expectations, shared values and interests. Accordingly, while freedom belongs to the most universal human features, it remains context

---

outcomes. . . . However, it remains unclear how the right theory can be identified and whether the mere existence of concurring paradigms represents a sign of their deficiencies, leading to a call for a scientific revolution in the field'.

102 Norman P. Barry, 'Unanimity, Agreement, and Liberalism: A Critique of James Buchanan's Social Philosophy', Political Theory, Vol. 12, No. 4, 1984, p. 579: '[I]t is clearly apparent that a purely calculative approach to the justification of liberalism is internally inadequate'.

103 Paul Tillich, *The Courage to Be*, Yale University Press, New Haven, 1952, p. 172.

specific and predetermined by the peculiarities of the community within which it exists. The emergence of the *economic* freedom to compete coincides with its long *political* and *cultural* evolution in societies with articulated preference for humanistic values. The concept of economic freedom in general, and the concept of economic competition in particular, have close natural links with its political and cultural *counterparts*, and should be perceived and analysed through the lens of their mutual influence.

The similarities between the different aspects of competition are related to the fact that they all belong to the same societal aspect of freedom. While the functioning of the competitive process in politics and cultural life has its direct reflection in the public sphere – to the extent that politics are also a part of free speech, whereas free speech is a part of the political agenda – the links between them and economic competition are not highly visible. In addition, the specification of antitrust, which is based on technical economic expertise and complicated jurisprudence, also hinders the perception of the market process from a broader constitutional perspective. The necessity of a broader constitutional perception of competition in economics is only acknowledged by the minority.[104] This situation often leads to a sectoral, fragmented approach to different areas of competition, although their conceptual similarities may be a fruitful field for comparative analysis. One of the main discrepancies between the regulation of political and cultural competition on the one hand and its economic counterpart on the other lies in the opposition between the deontological approach that dominates the former and the consequentialist utilitarianism that rules over the latter.[105] The deontological view disentangles the phenomenon of competition from the eventual positive outcomes which it could generate, while the utilitarian vision perceives competition through the lens of its positive societal impact. Since in the political and cultural life the deontological vision is balanced with other, more pragmatic and less ideological outcomes, such approach has not been taken as an absolute. In the economic sphere, however, a similar deterrent balance is nowhere

---

104 John J. Flynn, 'Antitrust Policy and the Concept of A Competitive Process', New York Law School Law Review, Vol. 35, No. 4, 1990, p. 896: '[I]t is essential to antitrust policy that the concept of "competition" be understood as "competition as a process", that its meaning be derived from a multiplicity of disciplines, including economics, . . . and that the deeper normative meaning of the concept be properly understood and inductively employed'.

105 Robert H. Bork, Ward S. Bowman, Jr., 'The Crisis in Antitrust', Columbia Law Review, Vol. 65, No. 3, 1965, p. 365: 'Competition is desirable . . . because it assists in achieving a prosperous society and permits individual consumers to determine by their actions what goods and services they want most'.

to be found.[106] This leads to a situation where only the beneficial part of competition is protected and to a definition of the very phenomenon of competition from the perspective of welfare. In such a view, economic practices which contribute to consumer or total welfare are considered pro-competitive, while those which harm consumers are deemed anti-competitive. This mainstream *economic* rationale has been extrapolated to the domain of law.[107] This dominant trend in the theory of antitrust reduces the meaning and significance of the competitive process, which is often considered merely as a negative externality in the welfare-generating economic process.

The idea of competition as an essential element of the liberal democratic political culture should not be treated as a universal remedy or as an absolute imperative. The competitive process is only one of many political virtues, and it should not automatically prevail over others. The fallacy is not the limited application of the principles of competition, but the interpretation of the phenomenon through a perspective that a priori includes in the definition of competition values to which it allegedly should be subordinated.[108] The conceptual reduction of competition to its *beneficial* impact on consumer welfare leads to a logical mistake, reducing the essence of competition to its desirable components, and distorting thereby the semantics of the term. Subsequently, '"competition" in economics has become a term of art that has broken away from ordinary

---

[106] Wolfgang Kerber, 'Should Competition Law Promote Efficiency? Some Reflections of an Economist on the Normative Foundations of Competition Law', Marburg Papers on Economics, No. 09, 2007, p. 16: 'The problem is that economics has not yet developed normative concepts that integrate the idea of protected rights for individual persons or firms into their normative approach'.

[107] Christian Ahlborn and A. Jorge Padilla, '*From* Fairness *To* Welfare: Implications for the Assessment of Unilateral Conduct under EC Competition Law', in Claus-Dieter Ehlermann and Mel Marquis (eds.), *European Competition Law Annual 2007: A Reformed Approach to Article 82 EC*, Hart Publishing, Oxford, 2008, pp. 55–56: '[L]egal rules and institutions should be assessed taking *exclusively* into consideration their impact on the well being of individuals. Thus, a legal rule will be regarded superior to another if the aggregate impact of the former on the welfare of individuals exceeds the aggregate welfare impact of the latter. Under this normative approach, therefore, a fairness-based antitrust rule will necessarily be pronounced inferior to a welfare-driven rule, unless both coincide' (emphasis in the original).

[108] Harold J. Laski, *Liberty in the Modern State*, Faber & Faber, London, 1930, p. 13: '[T]he pressure of numbers and the diversity of desires make necessary both rules and compulsions. Each of these are limitations upon freedom. Some of them are essential to happiness, but that does not make them for a moment less emphatically limitations'.

usage'.[109] The fact that the value of the competitive process is much better articulated and protected in the political and cultural spheres can be explained by the specificity of the economic apparatus, which intentionally reduces the whole spectrum of public values to a set of calculable data. Economics is aware of its limits, and always tries to expand it, including the incorporation into its modelling of more nuanced variables, using inter alia game-theoretic methods.[110] This does, however, diminish the predictability of the models.[111] The theoretical algorithms which help preserving the deontological features of competition, while enabling its balancing for the purposes of welfare or security, would be of use in the area of economic competition. At the same time some empirical balancing techniques are better developed in antitrust than in politics and culture.

4.2.1 The Concept of the Adversary in Politics

The role of the adversary constitutes one of the distinct features of liberal democracy. Although it has been articulated more explicitly in political theory than in antitrust, economic competition is also perceived from this perspective.[112] This system of thought implies both normative and positive aspects. On the positive side it emphasises the importance of conflicts

---

[109] Oliver Black, *Conceptual Foundations of Antitrust*, Cambridge University Press, Cambridge, 2005, p. 8.

[110] Wolfgang Kerber and Ulrich Schwalbe, 'Economic Principles of Competition Law', in Günther Hirsch, Frank Montag and Franz Jürgen Säcker (eds.), *Competition Law: European Community Practice and Procedure – Article-by-Article Commentary*, Sweet & Maxwell, London, 2008, p. 231: 'These models can analyse problems in which firms interact repeatedly and decide sequentially or simultaneously on their action parameters, while taking into account the reactions of their competitors'.

[111] Herbert J. Hovenkamp, 'Antitrust Policy after Chicago', Michigan Law Review, Vol. 84, No. 2, 1985, p. 284: 'Under more complex models information becomes more ambiguous and more difficult to interpret. When that happens, the value of economic models begins to diminish in relative importance. In short, once the model becomes more complex, the policymaker necessarily relies on values that lie outside the model. The result is an antitrust policy that will always have a noneconomic, or political, content'.

[112] Michel Foucault, *Geschichte der Gouvernementalität II: Die Geburt der Biopolitik*, Suhrkamp, Frankfurt, 2004, p. 208, quoted and translated in Nils Goldschmidt and Hermann Rauchenschwandtner, 'The Philosophy of Social Market Economy: Michel Foucault's Analysis of Ordoliberalism', Freiburg Discussion Papers on Constitutional Economics, 07/04, 2007, p. 23: 'Not a society made up of supermarkets, but a society made up of entrepreneurs. The *homo oeconomicus* that some want to recreate is not the man of trade, not the man of consumption, but the man of entrepreneurship and production' (emphasis in the original).

between equally significant political values, considering as inevitable the necessity to make choices without denying the significance of downgraded values and not decreasing them formally in the axiological taxonomy of society. On the normative side it claims that the conflict between values should not only be tolerated as inevitable, but also internalised and protected as an important condition for a free society and fruitful theoretical discussion,[113] where different – sometimes incompatible – ideas, interests and beliefs are allowed to be freely circulated. Liberal democracies, in this sense, do not promote the anarchistic chaos of self-interests; the issues of security, social cohesion, tolerance and other elements of the societal *immune system* necessary for the protection of public interests are just as important as liberal values themselves.[114] The idea behind such a vision presumes that values should compete with each other for the attention of decision-makers.[115] It appreciates more the real availability of free choices than the formal possibility to participate collectively in the decision-making process,[116] although it acknowledges that these two distinct aspects of democracy are often mutually enhancing. This vision of society has been called 'agonistic liberalism'[117] and embraces the plurality of values taken in their dynamic, interactive coexistence.[118] This formula

---

113 Oliver Budzinski, 'Monoculture versus Diversity in Competition Economics', Cambridge Journal of Economics, Vol. 32, No. 2, 2008, p. 315: 'Diversity of competition theories can be regarded as a sustainable imperative of science instead of a temporary phenomenon or an evidence of incapacity'.

114 David W. Barnes, 'Antitrust Dialogue on Social Science, Cultural Values, and Merger Law', Antitrust Bulletin, Vol. 33, No. 4, 1988, p. 625: '[There are many] threats to . . . democracy that might arise if we do not control the competitive process'.

115 Chantal Mouffe, 'Introduction: Schmitt's Challenge', in Chantal Mouffe (ed.), *The Challenge of Carl Schmitt*, Verso, London, 1999, p. 4: 'Democratic debate is not a deliberation aimed at reaching *the one* rational solution . . ., but a confrontation among adversaries' (emphasis in the original).

116 Amartya Sen, 'Freedom of Choice: Concept and Content', European Economic Review, Vol. 32, No. 2–3, 1988, p. 270: 'That freedom must have *instrumental* importance as a means to other ends is obvious enough. . . . But the existence of *instrumental* relevance . . . does not entail a denial of *intrinsic* importance as well' (emphasis in the original).

117 John Gray, *Isaiah Berlin*, Harper Collins, London, 1995, p. 1: '[U]ltimate human values are objective but irreducibly diverse, . . . they are conflicting and often uncombinable. . . . I call the political outlook which this idea inspires in Berlin's work *agonistic liberalism*, taking the expression from the Greek word *agon*, whose meaning covers both competition or rivalry and the conflicts of characters in tragic drama' (emphasis in the original).

118 Isaiah Berlin, *Four Essays on Liberty*, Oxford University Press, Oxford, 1990, p. 1: 'If the claims of two (or more than two) types of liberty prove

implies that 'not only must one's own desire be articulated on the market, but the agonal character of the market itself is to be desired'.[119]

Even though it is considered one of the highest values, freedom itself is not taken as an absolute, because from the perspective of agonistic liberalism, it also should *compete* with other values and interests.[120] Furthermore, the indeterminacy which naturally conditions any choice makes the establishment of any ex ante algorithm of the eventual trade-offs and compromises impossible. This approach significantly differs from the purely deontological perceptions of freedom (of a Kantian, Rawlsian or Habermasian nature), which claim ultimate importance and hierarchical dominance, eliminating thereby the necessity for pluralism, in which freedom itself is a party to the contest.[121] The claim of liberal monists is that freedom cannot be balanced against other interests or, as Hart comments in relation to Rawls' position, that 'liberty may only be limited for the sake of liberty and not for the sake of other social and economic advantages'.[122] However attractive this approach may appear from the ideological standpoint, it contains both normative and positive weaknesses. The former include situations where the overemphasised value of freedom would lead to *open* opposition from the advocates of competing values, eventually downgrading the hierarchical position of freedom, or to the *hidden* misinterpretation of the concept of freedom, whenever clashing values interpret freedom in their own terms, claiming that freedom should be *responsible*, *inclusive* or *reasonable* – the more attributes qualify the concept, the less *freedom* remains in it, which is what the distributive justice approach of Rawls leads to. From the positive perspective this approach is unrealistic, as the phenomenon of freedom cannot cover the whole spectrum of vital societal interests unless protected by authoritarian methods – which again would be impossible, since the oppression from

---

incompatible in a particular case, and if this is an instance of the clash of values at once absolute and incommensurable, it is better to face this intellectually uncomfortable fact than to ignore it, or automatically attribute it to some deficiency on our part which could be eliminated by an increase in skill or knowledge'.

[119] Nils Goldschmidt and Hermann Rauchenschwandtner, 'The Philosophy of Social Market Economy: Michel Foucault's Analysis of Ordoliberalism', Freiburg Discussion Papers on Constitutional Economics, 07/04, 2007, p. 22.

[120] John Gray, *Isaiah Berlin*, Harper Collins, London, 1995, p. 27.

[121] Chantal Mouffe, 'Carl Schmitt and the Paradox of Liberal Democracy', in Chantal Mouffe (ed.), *The Challenge of Carl Schmitt*, Verso, London, 1999, pp. 46–47: '[I]n both Rawls and Habermas . . . the very condition for the creation of consensus is the elimination of pluralism from the public sphere'.

[122] Herbert L. A. Hart, 'Rawls on Liberty and Its Priority', The University of Chicago Law Review, Vol. 40, No. 3, 1973, p. 534.

freedom of other values to promote their dominance over freedom as a *value* is a *contradictio in terminis*.

Therefore, the notion of pluralistic liberalism is used as an alternative to monistic liberalism. This dialectical vision of values is taken both for positive and normative purposes. The former means that the alternative monistic approach to values, which implies the possibility to find the *right* answer, by a systematic hierarchy of different societal interests into a coherent corpus, is impossible to achieve in pluralistic societies. It entails the inevitability of balancing and the necessity of its constant presence in political life. The competition of values is considered as a representation of the competitive process at the meta-political level of the decision-making process. On the *substance* the arguments of liberal value-monists appear very attractive[123] and may be shared by the pluralists, but from a *methodological* point of view the prescriptive style of their rhetoric fits better for convincing activists than impartial analysts.

The pluralistic vision of democracy, embraced in the notion of agonistic liberalism emphasises the importance of the adversary in any public process of interaction, be it politics, economics or culture. As Mouffe argues, '[t]he adversary is in a certain sense an enemy, but a legitimate enemy with whom there exists a common ground'.[124] The existence of such common ground is of fundamental importance. It is the precondition for a *normal* conflict, not a fight at any cost. Values constantly compete with each other, but the *normality* of this situation often eliminates and always mitigates or trivialises the conflict as such. Instead of being perceived in its ethical sense, as direct confrontation, it becomes a pragmatic, natural state of affairs, which does not involve emotions or bad intentions. In the philosophical sense the existence of common ground is a *sine qua non* condition for any contestation and any conflict. Only the existence of the *shared* enables the existence of the *contested*. This feature of conflicts is most visible in sporting contests, which contain the stylised topology of all main attributes of conflicts. This element distinguishes liberal democracies

---

123 Laurent B. Frantz, 'The First Amendment in the Balance', The Yale Law Journal, Vol. 71, No. 8, 1962, p. 1443: 'If the first amendment is subject to *ad hoc* balancing, it is inherently incapable of any . . . assurances. Under it, the right to speak and publish is never clear, since it is never defined. Whether one had a right to speak or publish cannot be known until after the event and depends on the unpredictable weight which a court may someday give to "competing interests". No doubt the boldest will speak anyway, but many others will be deterred merely by the pervasive and ineradicable uncertainty' (emphasis in the original).

124 Chantal Mouffe, 'Introduction: Schmitt's Challenge', in Chantal Mouffe (ed.), *The Challenge of Carl Schmitt*, Verso, London, 1999, p. 4.

embedded in the principle of *agonism* from the holistic visions of democracy, which seek full static harmony and attempt to eliminate features that cannot be matched with their principles (*antagonism*).[125] Ironically, antagonistic attempts to erase conflicts lead to some unarticulated oppression from the antagonists, generating the same heat, but not remaining that productive, often being fatal, always dangerous for the system itself. This type of conflict is always a vertical argument, an argument *against* the rules, whereas in the agonistic democracy this argument is made horizontally, *within* the rules.

4.2.2 The Concept of the Adversary in Jurisprudence

Competition plays an important role in jurisprudence. The competitive rivalry constitutes the core of the adversarial judicial process. It encompasses the dynamism of legal argumentation, and the dialectical connection between the arguments of the parties and the judicial decision.[126] The role of dynamism in legal argumentation has been emphasised by the legal process jurisprudence.[127] Sebok refers in this respect to 'the valorisation of adjudication'.[128] It encompasses the importance of conflicting reasoning in the process of discovering the essence of a legal rule, embracing 'a dynamic relationship that prevents either side from claiming victory or being collapsed into the other'.[129] The adversarial tradition can be juxtaposed with the inquisitorial, canonical approach to legal reasoning, which implies the existence of the ultimate truth in each case, relying either on legal rules (dogmatism) or common sense (realism) as the instruments for finding the right answer. The legal process jurisprudence assumes the

---

[125] ibid.

[126] Eveline T. Feteris, 'Recent Developments in Legal Argumentation Theory: Dialectical Approaches to Legal Argumentation', International Journal for the Semiotics of Law, Vol. 7, No. 20, 1994, p. 133: 'From 1970, a new approach to legal argumentation has been developed in which legal argumentation is considered from the perspective of a discussion procedure in which a legal standpoint is defended according to certain rules for rational discussion. In approaches to legal argumentation which can be called dialectical, legal argumentation is considered as part of a dialogue about the acceptability of a legal standpoint'.

[127] Neil Duxbury, 'Faith in Reason: The Process Tradition in American Jurisprudence', Cardozo Law Review, Vol. 15, No. 3, 1993, p. 602.

[128] Anthony J. Sebok, *Legal Positivism in American Jurisprudence*, Cambridge University Press, Cambridge, 1998, p. 143.

[129] Philip Soper, 'Critical Notice: Legal Systems, Normative Systems, and the Paradoxes of Positivism', Canadian Journal of Law and Jurisprudence, Vol. 8, No. 2, 1995, p. 363.

presence of elements of subjectivity, relativity and indeterminacy in law, arguing that any legal norm and any judicial fact can lead to competing interpretations, and that opposite decisions are often equally justifiable. The adversarial judicial process is usually addressed descriptively. Its redundancies, cost-ineffectiveness and rhetorical nature are among the common disadvantages of this approach. In this respect it is similar to the concepts of political, cultural and economic competition, which are often characterised by these features. Another aspect of the system which should be addressed critically is the fact that the decision-maker usually 'knows nothing of the litigation until the trial'.[130]

Legal process jurisprudence is not limited solely to the descriptive elements of the adversarial process. The dynamism of competitive rivalry also contains normative attributes. It addresses 'contradictory principles and determines the proper balance between competing social interests'.[131] Apart from being an *effective* tool for stimulating the inventiveness and diligence of the parties, it also encompasses important elements of procedural democracy. None of the aspects of freedom can be limited to its beneficial *outcomes*. Freedom is not necessarily the most effective way for humans to coexist. It is supported and encouraged for its own sake. The dynamism of the legal process constitutes in this respect the jurisprudential part of competition, which is also intentionally enhanced by liberal democracies despite its obvious disadvantages. This argument is developed not as an outright justification of the adversarial process as a system where 'party-controlled courts receive more information than judge-centred courts',[132] but primarily to demonstrate that the eventual ineffectiveness of the system cannot be considered a sufficient reason for its negation, hence emphasising the normative elements of the competitive process rather than the normative correctness of the system as a whole. It is important to connect these competition-centred elements of the adversarial model with the general democratic value of competition,[133] as well as with other repercussions of competition, related inter alia to cross-cultural

---

[130] Ellen E. Sward, 'Values, Ideology, and the Evolution of the Adversary System', Indiana Law Journal, Vol. 64, No. 2, 1989, p. 312.

[131] Joseph W. Singer, 'Legal Realism Now', California Law Review, Vol. 76, No. 2, 1988, p. 508.

[132] Jona Goldschmidt, 'The Pro Se Litigant's Struggle for Access to Justice: Meeting the Challenge of Bench and Bar Resistance', Family Court Review, Vol. 40, No. 1, 2002, p. 41.

[133] Ellen E. Sward, 'Values, Ideology, and the Evolution of the Adversary System', Indiana Law Journal, Vol. 64, No. 2, 1989, p. 301: 'The virtues of the adversary system, are so deeply engrained in the American legal psyche that most lawyers do not question it'.

relations,[134] free speech,[135] individual freedom,[136] and sport contests.[137] It underlines the fundamental significance of the competitive process.[138] Elements of the competitive process are present in both adversarial and inquisitorial systems, and these elements are more important for the argument than the procedural rules.

While the pure legal process jurisprudence is determined in discovering the reason of rules 'which is embodied in the fabric of the law itself',[139] the role of the adversarial in jurisprudence is broader. Competition is not limited in this respect solely to the domain of law, but is expanded to different theoretical approaches and practical strategies of the parties, which operate with different empirical evidence and economic models in order to convince the court. These extralegal elements are intrinsically linked to legal argumentation. The link is particularly visible in antitrust.[140] The importance of legal process jurisprudence in antitrust is not only visible in the inclusion of expert evidence into the domain of judicial analysis,[141] but also in its scepticism of dogmatism. Dogmatism is not the exclusive domain of law. Economics is often dogmatic as well, insisting that the outcomes of theoretical models or empirical facts may guide either legal decision-making or at least legal interpretation. The method of legal process accepts these claims alongside the parallel claims of legal

---

134 Allan Lind, John Thibaut and Laurens Walker, 'A Cross-Cultural Comparison of the Effect of Adversary and Inquisitorial Processes on Bias in Legal Decision Making', Virginia Law Review, Vol. 62, No. 2, 1976, pp. 274–275.

135 Geoffrey C. Hazard, *Ethics in the Practice of Law*, Yale University Press, New Haven, 1978, p. 123.

136 Monroe H. Freedman, 'Our Constitutionalized Adversary System', Chapman Law Review, Vol. 1, No. 1, 1998, p. 57.

137 Ronald J. Krotoszynski, 'The New Legal Process: Games Peoples Play and the Quest for Legitimate Judicial Decision Making', Washington University Law Quarterly, Vol. 77, No. 4, p. 1999, p. 1010 et seq.

138 Rudolph J. R. Peritz, *Competition Policy in America: History, Rhetoric, Law*, Oxford University Press, Oxford, 1996, p. 3: 'Competition policy has been one of twentieth-century America's most durable goods. Whether in business, politics, sports or speech, a vision of robust rivalry – of free competition – has inspired our social theories, directed our practices, and informed our public discourse'.

139 Neil Duxbury, 'Faith in Reason: The Process Tradition in American Jurisprudence', Cardozo Law Review, Vol. 15, No. 3, 1993, p. 602.

140 William H. Page, 'Legal Realism and the Shaping of Modern Antitrust', Emory Law Journal, Vol. 44, No. 1, 1995, pp. 49–50.

141 Yane Svetiev, 'Antitrust Governance: The New Wave of Antitrust', Loyola University Chicago Law Journal, Vol. 38, No. 3, 2007, p. 612: '[E]ven with both proper reasoning and methodology, the economists may arrive at a genuine disagreement about the competitive significance of the case, particularly if the outcomes of interest extend to the medium to longer term'.

formalism, although it does not treat them as absolutes, but rather with some understanding of the peculiarities of each discipline, which due to its methodological boundaries often operates with a conception of ultimate truth, not being able to internalise competing perceptions of the truth, as developed by other disciplines or methods. This distinguishes the jurisprudence of legal process from the law and economics movement, which *internalises* the law into the domain of economics, explaining (positively) and justifying it (normatively) in terms of the economic rationale.[142]

4.2.3 The Concept of *Libido* and Psychological Aspects of Competition

Adversarial dynamism is present in every aspect of public and private life, as well as in natural events. The phenomenon of economic competition shares these features, peculiar to all aspects of competition, and can benefit from and contribute to other areas of human knowledge which address similar problems. These links were partially explored by behavioural and evolutionary economics,[143] the branches of economic theory interested in the psychological and biological aspects of the decision-making process in general and competition in particular,[144] but also by their predecessors in the instinct theory of institutional economics,[145] developed in the late nineteenth century in the US. During this period, American economists created the foundations for all major contemporary schools of competition.[146] Alongside the traditional definition of

[142] Joseph W. Singer, 'Legal Realism Now', California Law Review, Vol. 76, No. 2, 1988, p. 504.

[143] David J. Gerber, *Law and Competition in Twentieth Century Europe. Protecting Prometheus*, Clarendon Press, Oxford, 2001, p. 28: 'The late nineteenth century was in some ways a halcyon period for the general idea of competition. The Darwinian image of human history that was restructuring social thought gave the process of competition the central role in the story. Competition became . . . a central device for interpreting human actions'.

[144] Richard R. Nelson, 'Recent Evolutionary Theorizing About Economic Change', Journal of Economic Literature, Vol. 33, No. 1, 1995, p. 54.

[145] Pier F. Asso and Luca Fiorito, 'Human Nature and Economic Institutions: Instinct Psychology, Behaviorism, and the Development of American Institutionalism', Journal of the History of Economic Thought, Vol. 26, No. 4, 2004, pp. 445–446.

[146] Mary S. Morgan, 'Competing Notions of "Competition" in Late Nineteenth-Century American Economics', History of Political Economy, Vol. 25, No. 4, 1993, pp. 564–565: 'Their literature reveals a variety of ideas: competition could be an activity, a process, a game, an economic institution, an agency of natural laws, or even a fundamental law of nature. The perceived outcomes

efficiencies,[147] evolutionary economists introduce the notion of 'adaptive efficiency', which perceives competition 'as a genuine evolutionary process',[148] aiming at maintaining diversity in the market, emphasising the elements of creativity and adaptability of market participants,[149] and structurally very similar to sports contests,[150] though economics as a part of moral philosophy was always interested in the biological laws of nature.[151] These approaches are still overshadowed by the mainstream neoclassical analysis,[152] which is based on the principles of 19th-century physics[153] rather than on the dynamism of rivalry. Mestmäcker explains this by the absence of a mechanism 'to deduce from welfare effects standards to judge the positive or negative contribution of individual competitive conduct to the resultant complex and dynamic economic process'.[154]

For the proper articulation of the meaning and the role of the competitive process in regulatory policy it may be also useful to highlight its similarity with the concepts of *libido* and sublimation, as developed in psychoanalysis. The comparison of competition with a 'type of energy' has

were equally diverse. Competition was admired as the regulator of the economy, or as the generator of growth and progress, but feared as the selector that judged between the fit and the unfit in the struggle for existence'.

147 Herbert J. Hovenkamp, 'Antitrust Policy after Chicago', Michigan Law Review, Vol. 84, No. 2, 1985, pp. 237–240.

148 Oliver Budzinski, 'Monoculture versus Diversity in Competition Economics', Cambridge Journal of Economics, Vol. 32, No. 2, 2008, p. 311.

149 Westel W. Willoughby, 'The Ethics of the Competitive Process', The American Journal of Sociology, Vol. 6, No. 2, 1900, pp. 149–151.

150 Stan Metcalfe, Ronald Ramlogan and Elvira Uyarra, 'Economic Development and the Competitive Process', Centre on Regulation and Competition Working Paper Series, No. 36, 2002, p. 13.

151 Friedrich A. von Hayek, 'Freedom, Reason and Tradition', Ethics, Vol. 68, No. 4, 1958, p. 232: 'Since the emphasis we shall have to place on the role which selection plays in this process of social evolution today is likely to create the impression that we are borrowing the idea from biology, it is worth stressing that it was in fact the other way round: there can be little doubt that it was from the theories of social evolution that Darwin and his contemporaries derived the suggestion for their theories'.

152 Wolfgang Kerber, 'Should Competition Law Promote Efficiency? Some Reflections of an Economist on the Normative Foundations of Competition Law', Marburg Papers on Economics, No. 09, 2007, p. 16: 'From . . . [the] welfare-theoretic perspective, freedom of contract or entrepreneurial freedom have no particular value of their own'.

153 Geoffrey M. Hodgson, 'Thorstein Veblen and Post-Darwinian Economics', Cambridge Journal of Economics, Vol. 16, No. 3, 1992, p. 285.

154 Ernst-Joachim Mestmäcker, 'The Development of German and European Competition Law with Special Reference to the EU Commission's Article 82 Guidance of 2008', Max Planck Private Law Research Paper No. 10/1, 2010, p. 16.

been used at the very beginning of the development of antitrust theory;[155] it is also relevant in the jurisprudential analysis of dialectics and can be encompassed in the notion of 'the eroticism of market relations'.[156] The notion of *libido* is equal to the philosophical *entelechy*, based primarily on the Platonic notion of *eros*,[157] encompassing the condition of full self-realisation and self-fulfilment of a thing. This *vital impetus*[158] is perceived as a non-articulated spontaneous desire, as a vital force which drives and pre-determines human behaviour. In terms of its regulation, its nature is similar to the notion of *Ungrund*, as developed in idealist philosophical tradition: '[t]he void (the *Ungrund* of Böhme) . . . is the source of every kind of life . . .. It conceals within itself the possibility both of evil and of good'.[159] This hidden energy of individuality constitutes in this sense the *creative nothingness*,[160] the potential for all human actions, which at the same time remains irrational, incomprehensible and destructive. This implies that 'the powers of creation and the powers of destruction are united in such a way that it is impossible to separate them unambiguously'.[161] The notion of *libido* has been developed within the vitalist tradition of psychology, which rejected the rationalist neurological explanation of the mind. The latter approach perceives the problem of evolution of human psychology in purely scientific explanations, while the former does not reduce it to the empirically verifiable apparatus, submitting that the issues of desire and motivation are predetermined by the elements of spontaneity, which by definition are indefinable by the mechanism. These two approaches should not be perceived as antagonists; often they supplement each other, and neither exclusive scientism nor pure irrational explanations of the complex phenomena of human behaviour are adequate.[162] By showing

---

155 Herbert J. Hovenkamp, 'The Antitrust Movement and the Rise of Industrial Organisation', Texas Law Review, Vol. 68, No. 1, 1989, p. 144.

156 Jeanne L. Schroeder, 'The End of the Market: A Psychoanalysis of Law and Economics', Harvard Law Review, Vol. 112, No. 2, 1998, p. 493.

157 Boris Vysheslavtsev, *Etika Preobrazhennogo Erosa (The Ethics of Transformed Eros)*, Republic, Moscow, 1994, pp. 45–47.

158 Henri Bergson, *Creative Evolution*, Hern Hold, New York, 1911, p. 87.

159 Nicolas Berdyaev, *Freedom and the Spirit*, The Centenary Press, London, 1935, p. 165 (emphasis in the original).

160 Hans Waldenfels, 'Absolute Nothingness. Preliminary Considerations on a Central Notion in the Philosophy of Nishida Kitaro and the Kyoto School', Monumenta Nipponica, Vol. 21, No. 3/4, 1966, p. 364.

161 Lasse Halme, *The Polarity of Dynamics and Form: The Basic Tension in Paul Tillich's Thinking*, Lit Verlag, Helsinki, 2003, p. 79.

162 Hilde Hein, 'Molecular Biology vs. Organicism: The Enduring Dispute between Mechanism and Vitalism', Synthese, Vol. 20, No. 2, 1969, p. 249.

that everything *may well have* a scientific explanation, a typical scientific approach makes the mistake of implying that everything *indeed has* such an explanation. Leaving aside the issues of transcendental beliefs, an empirical objection can be raised in respect to the limits of available knowledge.[163] This objection is relevant to the regulation of both political and economic freedom.[164] However, the empirical objection is less important than the ontological one. Things may always be addressed empirically, but the empirical analysis should be aware of the existence of elements that go beyond the scientific calculus. A similar clash occurs in economics between those who claim that competition should be rationalised in order to deliver positive economic outcomes for society and those for whom the phenomenon of competition goes beyond reductionism.

Libido in the psycho-philosophical sense is comparable to negative individual freedom. *Libido* inevitably contains both creative and destructive elements (*destrudo*).[165] The *destrudo*, as well as negative freedom, is inseparable from its positive, behavioural, self-disciplining parts. These elements of *destrudo* are present in every act of competition, in every expression of freedom; they are a component of the emotional polyphony and cannot be singled out and eliminated. For Mill these elements of *destrudo* are present in any natural expression of envy, hatred and uncharitableness.[166] He associated it with competition, but such accusation could be made also to any other expression of freedom, if perceived from the utilitarian or virtue ethicist position. Wolff interprets Mill's point, claiming that competition is wrong from a deontological perspective, and it can only be justified on very limited consequentialist grounds, in cases where it is really capable of delivering better economic performance.[167] It should be noted

---

[163] Friedrich A. von Hayek, 'The Use of Knowledge in Society', The American Economic Review, Vol. 35, No. 4, 1945, p. 519: 'The peculiar character of the problem of a rational economic order is determined precisely by the fact that the knowledge of the circumstances of which we must make use never exists in concentrated or integrated form, but solely as the dispersed bits of incomplete and frequently contradictory knowledge which all the separate individuals possess'.

[164] Lawrence A. Sullivan, 'The Viability of the Current Law on Horizontal Restraints', California Law Review, Vol. 75, No. 3, 1987, p. 865: 'Efficiency issues require an eclectic approach. Their presence may be confirmed or refuted by engineering evidence, by conventional price theory, by strategic analysis, by transaction costs, or by evolutionary economics'.

[165] Edoardo Weiss, *Principles of Psychodynamics*, Grune & Stratton, New York, 1950.

[166] John S. Mill, *Principles of Political Economy*, Oxford University Press, Oxford, 1998, p. 385.

[167] Jonathan Wolff, 'The Ethics of Competition', in Geraint Parry, Asif

in this respect that neither competition nor *libido* are guiding principles for human behaviour or social norms. They are only important parts of these guiding principles.

The phenomenon of self-discipline is comparable to the public regulation of competition. Neither self-discipline nor public regulation is capable of fully comprehending or actualising the spontaneity of the individual development or creative market process respectively. At the same time, if left unregulated, these reflections of negative individual or economic freedom will lead to harmful consequences for the external environment as well as to their own self-destruction. Regulation therefore always *limits* the spontaneity of competition and creativity, but such limitation is not always oppressive. Whereas limitation is to some extent properly oppressive, it is also partly done for the interests of competition. The view which perceives limitation *only* as restrictions *against* competition[168] does not take into account this second aspect. The main regulatory task is then to find the proper dynamic balance between the creative and destructive natures of spontaneous self-realisation. The difficulty of such a task lies in the illusionary temptation to oppress the irrationality of *libido*, limiting it solely to its positive creative outcomes. The negative aspects of the spontaneous process are perceived in this context not as inevitable and inseparable elements of *libido*, but as negative externalities, as some flaws which *can* and *should* be eliminated from the *contaminated* expression of freedom. This approach fully dominates rational economic analysis, which is ready to tolerate the positive consequences of the spontaneous market process, while fully eliminating its negativity by a limitation of the freedom of economic activity and the regulation of market failures. The concept of market failure is ambivalent in itself. *Externally*, in a dynamic economic model what appears to be a market failure may generate possibilities for future innovative improvements.[169] *Internally*, market failure is the consequence of an expression of individual economic freedom, and the latter should be always included into the

---

Qureshi, and Hillel Steiner (eds.), *The Legal and Moral Aspects of International Trade: Freedom and Trade*, Vol. 3, Routledge, London, 1998, p. 84.

168 Frank H. Easterbrook, 'Antitrust and the Economics of Federalism', Journal of Law and Economics, Vol. 26, No. 1, 1983, p. 23: 'Regulation displaces competition. Displacement is the purpose, indeed the definition, of regulation'.

169 Jean-Luc Gaffard, Michel Quéré, 'What's the Aim for Competition Policy: Optimizing Market Structure or Encouraging Innovative Behaviours?', Journal of Evolutionary Economics, Vol. 16, No. 1, 2006, p. 176: 'Once market imperfection appears as a means for making viable any innovative choice, it is no longer acceptable to reduce it to market failure or to oppose it to market success'.

test. The proportion of the importance of each value is context dependent and impossible to define ex ante. However, the balancing act should not be reduced to a simple evaluation of the positive and negative impact which different values can generate in each particular case, but should also take into account their respective specificities. Utilitarian values can convince the decision-maker of their usefulness for society more easily than deontological values, which refer to absolute and not relative categories, and do not fit well into the balancing process. This specificity of deontological values should be considered in the form of an extra awareness-bonus, which each decision-maker should provide while balancing them. Besides, the regulation of freedom should not be taken only as its limitation, but also as its improvement. The decision-maker should not be interested only in protecting other values *from* freedom, but also in *promoting* freedom, while remaining aware that its promotion cannot be achieved if he intends to eliminate the spontaneous unpredictable elements of freedom, inasmuch as these negative elements of irrationality constitute the indispensable core of freedom, without which the phenomenon would be meaningless. No individual can develop himself into a mature *normal* human being without the creative energy of *libido*, and no individual can maintain his maturity unless this internal energy is limited, or sublimated, transcended at a higher, more articulated level.[174] The dialectical cycle of *eros–nomos–agape*,[175] – where the first is a creative motif of freedom (in both its positive and negative origins); the second is limitation (both internal and external); and the third is a harmony – is in a constant *statu nascendi*. It is a dynamic movement, where the synthesis of harmony immediately becomes a new thesis, calling for another antithesis. This dialectics is present both in individual psychology as well as at the collective level. In the former the driving creative force is reflected in the notion of *libido/eros*, in the latter it is based on the principles of perpetual entrepreneurial discovery.

4.3 SELF-DESTRUCTIVE NATURE OF COMPETITION

Economic competition shares another characteristic with its political and cultural counterparts – it is not absolute and is often the object of

---

[174] Westel W. Willoughby, 'The Ethics of the Competitive Process', The American Journal of Sociology, Vol. 6, No. 2, 1900, p. 158.

[175] Anders Nygren, *Agape and Eros*, The University of Chicago Press, Chicago, 1982, pp. 247 et seq.

limitations.[176] As Eucken argues, '[t]he spirit of freedom has helped to bring about industrialisation yet this industrialisation has become a serious threat to freedom'.[177] It means that the regulator is supposed 'to prevent this freedom from destroying its own prerequisites',[178] by protecting 'competition from its self-destructing forces'.[179] The limitation of freedom is necessary as no value and no right can be protected in pluralistic democracy without taking into account other societal interests. The resemblance of the different aspects of competition is, however, only partial; which significantly distinguishes antitrust from other aspects of competition. This distinction leads to a one-sided view of economic competition, as if its only task were the promotion of other public values. To remedy this situation it is necessary to clarify where the difference lies. The limitation of freedom has two rationales, an internal and an external one. The former relates to a situation where freedom is protected from its self-destructive elements and coercion is directed to the achievement of a *better, greater, more articulated* freedom, the positive individual freedom in Berlin's sense. Under these conditions some aspects of freedom are limited for its own sake, for the achievement of the freedom's own improvement; in Laski's terms, 'a sacrifice of some liberty [is made] to a greater freedom'.[180] In contrast, the external limitation is not established *for* freedom, but for the protection of other values *from* freedom. In these situations freedom is balanced against other important societal values. These values are countless, and include inter alia the issues of security, privacy, wealth, growth, cohesion, and consumer or total welfare.[181] In a word, the internal limitation of competition ensures the *protection* (preventive antitrust policy)

---

[176] Jonathan Wolff, 'Libertarianism, Utility and Economic Competition', Virginia Law Review, Vol. 92, No. 7, 2006, p. 1611: 'The right to liberty is never a right to act in all the ways one might wish'.

[177] Walter Eucken, 'What Kind of Economic and Social System?', in Alan T. Peacock and Hans Willgerodt (eds.), *Germany's Social Market Economy: Origins and Evolution*, Macmillan, London, 1989, p. 34.

[178] Wernhard Möschel, 'Competition Policy from an Ordo Point of View', in Alan Peacock and Hans Willgerodt (eds.), *German Neo-Liberals, and the Social Market Economy*, The Macmillan Press, London, 1989, p. 148.

[179] Oliver Budzinski, 'Monoculture versus Diversity in Competition Economics', Cambridge Journal of Economics, Vol. 32, No. 2, 2008, p. 305.

[180] Harold J. Laski, *Liberty in the Modern State*, Faber & Faber, London, 1930, p. 15.

[181] Albert A. Foer, 'The Political-Economic Nature of Antitrust', Saint Louis University Law Journal, Vol. 27, No. 2, 1983, p. 340: 'To speak of antitrust as if it can be reduced to a set of extrapolations from price theory is to miss the richness of the interactions, throughout our history, which have necessitated the somewhat roiling coexistence of multiple goals'.

and *promotion* (proactive antitrust policy) of competition itself, while the external limitation protects other values from the competitive process, which is not a universal ultimate remedy for all economic situations. Both modes of limitation are performed under the balancing act, when different values *compete* for the regulator's attention and support in each particular instance. The task of a decision-maker in these cases is not to *calculate* the best option, but to *mitigate* all available ones.[182]

4.3.1 Three Regulatory Circles

The three-circled regulatory model in Figure 4.1 is introduced in order to clarify the differences between the regulation of competition in the political and cultural spheres, on the one hand, and in antitrust, on the other. The three regulatory circles mirror the different stages in the public regulation of competition. The first – *big* – circle encompasses the fundamental democratic principle that all expressions of the freedom to compete are recognised, promoted and protected, since the fundamental goal of liberal governance is the enhancement of freedom. At this stage no assessment of the legitimacy of the competitive conduct is made and all actions are authorised by default, as a matter of principle. The second – *middle* – circle situated inside the big one covers only part of these authorised actions and prohibits those that significantly endanger other values. Endangered values may be either internal or external; the former violate the principles of freedom itself, while the latter violate other public values. Thus any expression of freedom, which substantially discriminates against other individuals, is prohibited, to the extent that freedom is not absolute and should be balanced with other values.[183] The outright prohibition expressed in the middle circle would run counter to the balancing principle, as it would entail the absolute dominance of non-discrimination principles over the principles of freedom. Therefore the third – *small* – circle, which is situated in the centre of the three-circled diagram as well as at the core of this analysis, re-authorises the prohibited actions, which while being expressions of freedom (covered by the

---

[182] Lawrence A. Sullivan, 'The Viability of the Current Law on Horizontal Restraints', California Law Review, Vol. 75, No. 3, 1987, p. 865: '[A] judge, having determined what economic goals are reflected in the statute and the case law, must select manageable ways to mediate between those [antitrust] goals and the evidence before him'.

[183] *Schenck v. United States*, 249 U.S. 47 (1919): 'The most stringent protection of free speech would not protect a man in falsely shouting fire in a theatre and causing a panic'.

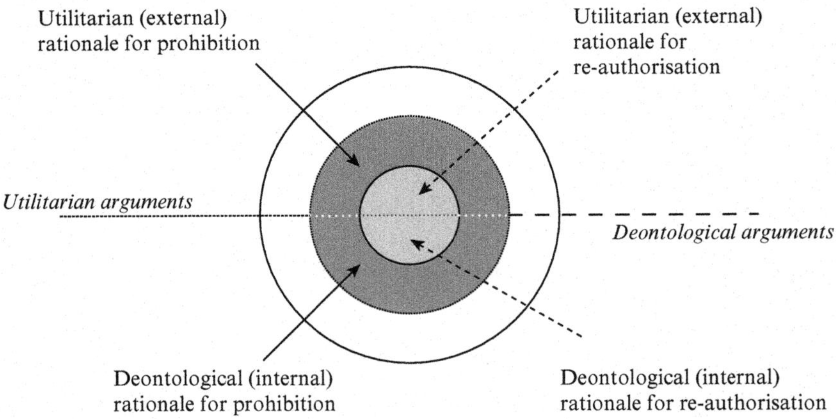

Figure 4.1 Two rationales for prohibition and re-authorisation

big circle) prohibited due to their violation of other values (covered by the middle circle) can still be allowed under the balancing test. In addition, the three-circled diagram is horizontally separated into two equal parts. This separation shows the two major grounds for the regulation of freedom – internal and external, or deontological and utilitarian. The former implies that the reason for (i) authorisation, (ii) prohibition and subsequent (iii) re-authorisation is freedom itself; while the latter covers justifications which lie outside the sphere of freedom and represent the influence of other values. The model can be explained by a demonstration in the three relevant areas under analysis: politics; cultural life; and antitrust (Figure 4.1).[184]

In politics at the first level – the big regulatory circle – the assumption is that all expressions of political ideas are allowed in liberal democracies since they enhance freedom itself (the internal justification) and indirectly promote utilitarian values such as better regulation, accountability, representation, vivid discussion and other important aspects of public life (the external justification). However, in the political competition not *all* parties are allowed to participate in public life – the condition reflected in the middle circle. Those who promote ideas that endanger the principles of democracy by declaring racial, immoral, xenophobic or other aggressive goals, are prohibited. This is an *external* protection, the protection *from*

[184] Oles Andriychuk, 'Rediscovering the Spirit of Competition: On the Normative Value of the Competitive Process', Competition Law Journal, Vol. 6, No. 3, 2010.

political freedom. Political parties are not allowed to pursue objectives which significantly obstruct or violate the political process itself, whenever the achievement of these goals leads to the elimination of competition in politics. History knows many instances, hypothetical or real, where a party came to power by free democratic elections, monopolised the political life, oppressed opposition and eliminated the mere possibility of political competition in the future.[185] Parties which have such intentions or methods are not allowed to participate in elections or are prohibited outright. These cases constitute limitations of the political freedom *for* freedom itself. It is done as a matter of principle, even if the prohibited parties may in fact increase wealth, growth or social cohesion. Those outcomes can be deemed irrelevant when freedom is jeopardised. Finally, at the level of the third, small regulatory circle, conditionally prohibited parties, which endanger freedom or other important public values, may be readmitted to participate in the democratic competitive process. In other words, not *all* political parties or movements whose programmes contain aspects harmful for freedom or other public goods are prohibited. Some parties are re-authorised, at the end of the (real or simulated) balancing act – if the endangered values are outweighed by positive utilitarian outcomes for society – for example, when the harm caused is compensated by a better articulation of real societal problems, which need to be addressed at the public level. This is an external justification. Similarly, some parties may be re-authorised if the political system considers that the value of the free competitive process itself outweighs the real or potential dangers which these parties can cause or are causing. This is the internal, deontological justification of freedom for its own sake. Be it in politics or cultural life, justification is not limited to the utilitarian, measurable, tangible effects which these parties may generate. Since freedom is difficult to measure, some elements of indeterminacy that cannot be verified by a purely empirical analysis are accepted in the interests of freedom.[186] While diligent governance should address both immediate and long-term problems, the

---

[185] Oliver Budzinski, 'Monoculture versus Diversity in Competition Economics', Cambridge Journal of Economics, Vol. 32, No. 2, 2008, p. 305: 'The notion of the limits of freedom where the freedom of others is restricted was particularly important for the original ordoliberalists since prewar Germany had experienced how both the democracy (political freedom) and the market economy (economic freedom) had been eroded because participants had been allowed to use their freedom to discard freedom as such'.

[186] Klaus Günther, 'The Pragmatic and Functional Indeterminacy of Law', German Law Journal, Vol. 12, No. 1, 2011, p. 407: 'It is assumed that the addressees of indeterminate norms can make use of their autonomy instead of merely exhibiting mechanical obedience'.

temporal aspect further militates for the impossibility to find the right and ultimate answer, based only on one of these temporal criteria.[187]

This algorithm similarly applies in relation to the *cultural life* of the community. At the first regulatory level – the big circle – it is assumed that any aspect of the cultural competitive process, reflected in freedom of speech, should be protected by default. The utilitarian justification of this principle is provided by the fact that free speech enhances discussion, facilitates understanding between different cultures, helps to reveal hidden societal problems and difficulties between its different groups, promotes the principles of openness and provides a fruitful circulation of ideas, which enhance cultural life in general.[188] The deontological justification is given by the fact that freedom belongs to the paramount values of humanism, and the ability to express individual ideas, thoughts, actions or beliefs deserves to be promoted for its own sake, as a matter of principle.[189] Again, not all forms of free expression are beneficial. Some can endanger social well-being, by promoting thoughts and expressing views which are incompatible with the principles of tolerance, privacy, security, public morality and other utilitarian values. Others can infringe the principles of freedom itself. The expression of extreme views, primitive emotional superstitions or appeals to violence not only violates the utilitarian values of society, it can also endanger freedom itself, by diminishing its significance or reputation, and restricting the spheres where it can be used afterwards. Therefore at the level of the middle circle some parts of freedom of speech are prohibited. It is important to point out that those actions prohibited in the middle circle remain expressions of freedom (i.e. still belong to the big circle). They belong simultaneously to both circles. This situation can be called the Ouroboros paradox, which refers to the similar problem of Bork's antitrust paradox,[190] but addresses

---

[187] Joseph Raz, 'Free Expression and Personal Identification', Oxford Journal of Legal Studies, Vol. 11, No. 3, 1991, p. 324: 'There is reason to favour legal arrangements which provide institutional recognition for the distinction between everyday short term politics, and those aspects of our political life which protect the basic features of our culture. Freedom of expression belongs to the latter, and should receive the kind of institutional protection given to the fundamentals of our culture'.

[188] Michel Rosenfeld, 'Hate Speech In Constitutional Jurisprudence: A Comparative Analysis', Cardozo Law Review, Vol. 24, No. 4, 2003, p. 1523.

[189] Carol Harlow, 'Voices of Difference in a Plural Community', The American Journal of Comparative Law, Vol. 50, No. 2, 2002, p. 340: 'Cultural diversity is valuable in its own right and is a basic strength of the European enterprise, providing a valuable genetic store of cultural experience'.

[190] Robert H. Bork, *The Antitrust Paradox – A Policy at War with Itself*, Basic Books, New York, 1978.

it from a different angle.[191] The ancient symbol of the snake eating its own tail shows both how fragile freedom is and how easily it can destroy itself,[192] hence requiring a thorough protection by those societies which sufficiently understand and appreciate its virtue. At the same time it shows that this self-destructive characteristic is an indispensable component of freedom, revealing its dialectical nature, which must contain elements of an irrational suicidal character. The self-destruction of freedom cannot be eliminated. It is inherent in the tragic dialectics of freedom – it constantly recreates itself by an act of self-destruction. Following Gerber's aesthetics of the metaphorical comparison of competition with Prometheus,[193] it could be said that competition contains the elements of the mythical firebird phoenix, cyclically destroying and resurrecting itself (the metaphor has been applied to antitrust, though in a different context).[194] Following Liefmann, '[c]ompetition leads to monopoly; monopoly leads to competition',[195] both forces have similar origins. Pure freedom consists of positive, cultivated elements, as well as of negative, irrational aspects. Society should always try to cultivate freedom, improving it, but this cannot be done by the elimination of the negative parts – they are in a polar dependency on each other. Freedom may be limited for the sake of other values, but it should not be defined in terms of these values. The virtue, to which freedom owes its protection at the first regulatory level (big circle), does not disappear due to its eventual harmfulness as reflected

---

191 Lawrence A. Sullivan and Wolfgang Fikentscher, 'On the Growth of the Antitrust Idea', Berkeley Journal of International Law, Vol. 16, No. 2, 1998, p. 225: 'In reality, Bork's paradox is a misunderstanding, because the real paradox in economic law is that economic liberty tends to abolish economic liberty (Plato's and Popper's freedom paradox). . . . [T]he paradox does not concern antitrust, rather liberty'.

192 Christian Ahlborn and A. Jorge Padilla, '*From* Fairness *To* Welfare: Implications for the Assessment of Unilateral Conduct under EC Competition Law', in Claus-Dieter Ehlermann and Mel Marquis (eds.), *European Competition Law Annual 2007: A Reformed Approach to Article 82 EC*, Hart Publishing, Oxford, 2008, pp. 55–56: 'Somewhat paradoxically, EC competition law is meant to protect economic freedom by constraining in a non-discretionary fashion the decision-making freedom of dominant firms'.

193 David J. Gerber, *Law and Competition in Twentieth Century Europe: Protecting Prometheus*, Oxford University Press, Oxford, 2001, p. 16.

194 Stephen Martin, 'The Goals of Antitrust and Competition Policy', in Wayne D. Collins (ed.), *Issues in Competition Law and Policy*, Vol. 1, American Bar Association Publishing, Chicago, 2008, p. 20.

195 Robert Liefmann, 'Monopoly and Competition as the Basis of a Government Trust Policy', Quarterly Journal of Economics, Vol. 29, No. 2, 1915, p. 323.

at the second regulatory level (middle circle). Freedom inevitably contains the elements of both the rational and irrational, the positive and negative, the harmful and beneficial. The reason for its protection by default can be found in the evolutionary choice which a society makes. Neither freedom nor any other deontological value can find a justification in a purely rational economic way of reasoning.[196] This reasoning can indeed be helpful, but its methods describe only part of the phenomenon, reducing freedom to its purely utilitarian calculus, and distorting thereby the concept of freedom as such. Freedom and rights are protected not *because* they are beneficial for society and deliver better empirically verifiable outcomes, but exactly due to their eventual inefficiency.[197] As Hayek explains, '[f]reedom granted only when it is known beforehand that its effects will be beneficial is not freedom'.[198] This implies that 'there would be no point in arranging a competition if the winner were known in advance',[199] and that 'the justification of competition as a discovery procedure creates empirical questions which by definition cannot be tested'.[200] For Knight, 'there is always an element of luck; there are games of pure chance, but a game of pure skill is a self-contradictory idea'.[201] The reduction of the competitive process to its welfare-generating elements negates the very principles of competition – which is the case in sports, where the outcome of a game would be defined by the probability of the stronger team winning, as well as in economic life in general. Peritz argues for 'freeing antitrust argument from the prison of price theory, and for reconstituting antitrust as public interest law',[202] which means that '[s]ocial policy . . . should not eliminate

---

196 Laurence H. Tribe, 'Constitutional Calculus: Equal Justice or Economic Efficiency?', Harvard Law Review, Vol. 98, No. 3, 1985, p. 592: 'The Constitution cannot be cabined in any calculus of costs and benefits'.

197 Herbert J. Hovenkamp, 'Distributive Justice and the Antitrust Laws', George Washington Law Review, Vol. 51, No. 1, 1982, p. 2: 'Many areas of the law protect individual rights, despite the inefficiency of their recognition'.

198 Friedrich A. von Hayek, *The Constitution of Liberty*, Routledge & Kegan Paul, London, 1960, p. 31.

199 Roger Zäch and Adrian Künzler, 'Freedom to Compete or Consumer Welfare: The Goal of Competition Law according to Constitutional Law' in Roger Zäch, Andreas Heinemann and Andreas Kellerhals (eds.), *The Development of Competition Law – Global Perspectives*, Edward Elgar Publishing, Cheltenham, 2010, pp. 77–78.

200 Adrian Vermeule, 'The Invisible Hand in Legal Theory', Harvard Public Law Working Paper, No. 09-43, 2009, p. 6.

201 Frank H. Knight, 'The Sickness of Liberal Society', Ethics, Vol. 56, No. 2, 1946, p. 92.

202 Rudolph J. Peritz, 'A Counter-History of Antitrust Law', Duke Law Journal, Vol. 39, No. 2, 1990, p. 269.

the anti-social effects of competition, but the mechanisms that work against competition'.[203]

Once they have been selected as important values by a certain political community, freedom and rights do not have to prove their effectiveness when contested.[204] They must be allowed to be ineffective and their importance for society should not be defined by the measurable yardstick of welfare. The fact that 'only quantitative (econometric) tests may provide hard evidence'[205] should not imply that only *hard evidence* may serve as a sufficient legal reason for regulation. If freedom and rights were *efficient* there would be no need for their protection – they would be self-executable. This is the reason why those aspects of freedom which are considered harmful are allowed to be re-authorised at the third regulatory level (small circle), if their eventual harmfulness for freedom itself or other values is outweighed by their potential benefits. These benefits again are either *external* to freedom itself – when the harmful speech provisionally prohibited also enhances public awareness of the existing problem, contributes to the broader discussion or serves as a test-case for major societal problems; or *internal* – when no such justification is available, but the act is still allowed, if it has been proven to the decision-maker during the balancing analysis that such an act deserves to be protected as a matter of freedom. Freedom of expression does not necessarily have to be tolerant. Often it offends. The offensiveness of freedom does not rob it of its value as freedom.[206] Being free does not provide immunisation from the prohibition of such expression, inasmuch as no value can be fully protected in pluralistic societies, but such prohibition should not attempt to *redefine* the meaning of freedom, restricting it to its non-conflicting parts, or the meanings which are consensually recognised as unequivocally beneficial. Those societies where free speech constitutes an important public value face many instances where no utilitarian justification whatsoever could

---

[203] Michel Foucault, *Geschichte der Gouvernementalität II: Die Geburt der Biopolitik*, Suhrkamp, Frankfurt, 2004, p. 226, quoted and translated in Nils Goldschmidt and Hermann Rauchenschwandtner, 'The Philosophy of Social Market Economy: Michel Foucault's Analysis of Ordoliberalism', Freiburg Discussion Papers on Constitutional Economics, 07/04, 2007, p. 23.

[204] *Faretta v. California* 422 U.S. 806 (1975): 'Personal liberties are not rooted in the law of averages'.

[205] Roger J. Van den Bergh and Peter D. Camesasca, *European Competition Law and Economics: A Comparative Perspective*, Sweet & Maxwell, London, 2006, p. 9.

[206] *Kingsley In'l Pictures Corp. v. Regents*, 360, 688–689 U.S. 684 (1959): '[The First Amendment] protects expression which is eloquent no less than that which is unconvincing'.

be provided for free hate speech: when speech is used to promote neo-Nazi[207] or racist[208] perversions, or significantly hinders individual privacy without any *utilitarian* public justification.[209] Yet, these acts have still been tolerated because the free circulation of ideas does not necessarily have to be constantly cross-checked by the yardstick of welfare or common good. In the area of cultural competition the ambivalent essence of free speech can be traced back to the fairness doctrine, in the US broadcasting market in the middle of the nineteenth century. According to its premises, every party concerned had an equal opportunity to discuss controversial issues on the same media platform. Its constitutionality was originally supported[210] but later rejected,[211] which shows how difficult it is to find the proper balance between the self-enhancing and self-destructive deontological elements of freedom. The intensity of the debates around the nature of free speech demonstrates how highly the deontological aspects of the competitive process are valued in the political and cultural areas.[212] This is not the case in antitrust.

4.3.2 The Flaw in Antitrust Regulation of the Competitive Process

The significant similarities in the regulation of competition in politics and culture also cover antitrust.[213] As the analysis of the structure of EU competition law reveals, these similarities are only partial. Discrepancies between the re-authorisation mechanism as applied to politics and culture on the one hand, and antitrust on the other, constitute the major problem for the regulation of competition in economics. The elimination of this inconsistency is the main function of the normative proposal elaborated in this book.

At the first regulatory level (the big circle) competition in economics is protected like its political and cultural counterparts. The principle of open market economy with free competition has always been a constitutional value of the EU. Similarly, at the second level (the middle circle) competi-

---

207 *National Socialist Party of America v. Village of Skokie*, 432 U.S. 43 (1977).

208 *Brandenburg v. Ohio*, 395 U.S. 444 (1969).

209 *Mosley v. the United Kingdom*, ECHR, Application no. 48009/08, 10.5.2011.

210 *Red Lion Broadcasting Co. v. FCC*, 395 U.S. 367 (1969).

211 *Miami Herald Publishing Co. v. Tornillo*, 418 U.S. 241 (1974).

212 *Citizens United v. Federal Election Commission* 558 U.S. 310 (2010) (Docket No. 08-205).

213 Oliver Budzinski, 'Monoculture versus Diversity In Competition Economics', Cambridge Journal of Economics, Vol. 32, No. 2, 2008, p. 306: 'A market economy requires a thoroughly designed and continuously policed competition order because market competition inheres a tendency towards self-termination'.

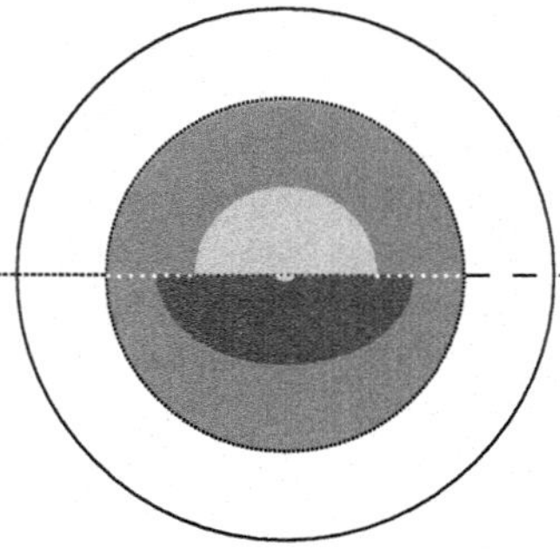

Figure 4.2 Utilitarian ground for re-authorisation

tion can be limited if it significantly encroaches upon other values. The structure of Article 101(1) TFEU jointly with other provisions of the Treaty provides protection for utilitarian (external) societal interests as well as for competition itself. The main divergence takes place at the third level (the small circle), embedded in Article 101(3) TFEU, which enables the re-authorisation of otherwise prohibited practices only if these practices simultaneously distort competition (remaining within the limits of Article 101(1) TFEU) and contribute to external utilitarian values: (i) help in 'improving the production or distribution of goods' – i.e. industrial growth; (ii) promote 'technical or economic progress' – i.e. innovations; and (iii) allow 'consumers a fair share of the resulting benefit' – i.e. consumer welfare. These three external societal values may lead to the re-authorisation of practices that infringe competition (Figure 4.2).[214]

The EU case law also introduced some other public interests into the list, but all of them are external to competition, and therefore belong to the upper part of the small circle. These exceptions have taken two different legal forms. On the one hand, Article 101(3) TFEU has been interpreted broadly, expanding the actual scope for re-authorisation of anticompetitive practices due to their positive impact on the environment, culture, public health, employment or regional and industrial development,[215] or even outright interpretation of the whole Article 101 TFEU from the

---

214 Oles Andriychuk, 'Rediscovering the Spirit of Competition: On the Normative Value of the Competitive Process', Competition Law Journal, Vol. 6, No. 3, 2010.

215 Heike Schweitzer, 'Competition Law and Public Policy: Reconsidering an Uneasy Relationship: The Example of Art. 81', EUI Working Paper, Law, 2007/30, 2007, pp. 6–7.

perspective of welfare.[216] On the other hand, Article 101(1) TFEU may become the object of the same trade-off, suggesting that some public policy concerns – mostly including[217] (i) self-regulation practices by collective bodies[218] and (ii) collective bargaining agreements[219] – sanction certain apparently anticompetitive practices' infringement of EU competition rules. From a methodological perspective these two approaches are similar and fit into the upper part of the small circle. The difference between them is purely procedural and related to the burden of proof.[220] None of these values has 'a place in the interpretation of Article [101 TFEU], unless they are compatible with the competition rules';[221] yet, it does not mean that they do not conflict with the principles of competitive process. The conflict is inevitable. Any alternative to the pluralistic vision of values encompassed in the holistic approach would lead to either the subordination of these values to competition or the reduction of the term competition to its welfare-enhancing elements. In this respect, Monti observes that from a neoclassical economic point of view the very logic of Article 101(3) is senseless and explains that 'if an agreement's anticompetitive harms are outweighed by its pro-competitive benefits, then the agreement does not restrict competition at all'.[222] A similar difficulty emerges with the con-

---

216 Alberto Heimler, 'Competition Policy Objectives', Panel Discussion, in Claus-Dieter Ehlermann and Laraine L. Laudati (eds.), *The Objectives of Competition Policy*, European Competition Law Annual 1997, Hart Publishing, Oxford, 1998, pp. 18–19: 'I believe that maximising consumer welfare is generally the objective of our laws. This is the case with respect to Art. [101] in its entirety. We should not distinguish results under Art. [101(1)] and [101(3)]; rather, we should see the whole as one system. This allows us to see that Art. [101] as a whole must be interpreted under the constraint of maximisation of consumer welfare'.

217 Heike Schweitzer, 'Competition Law and Public Policy: Reconsidering an Uneasy Relationship: The Example of Art. 81', EUI Working Paper, Law, 2007/30, 2007, pp. 3–4.

218 Case C-309/99, *J. C. J. Wouters, J. W. Savelbergh and Price Waterhouse Belastingadviseurs BV v. Algemene Raad van de Nederlandse Orde van Advocaten,* intervener: Raad van de Balies van de Europese Gemeenschap, ECR 2002 p. I-01577; Case C-519/04 P, *David Meca-Medina and Igor Majcen v. Commission*, ECR 2006 p. I-06991.

219 Case C-67/96, *Albany International BV v. Stichting Bedrijfspensioenfonds Textielindustrie* ECR 1999 p. I-05751.

220 Article 2 of Council Regulation (EC) No 1/2003 of 16 December 2002, OJ L 1, 4.1.2003, p. 1.

221 Constanze Semmelmann, 'The Future Role of the Non-Competition Goals in the Interpretation of Article 81 EC', Global Antitrust Review, Vol. 1, No. 1, 2008, p. 46.

222 Giorgio Monti, 'Article 81 EC and Public Policy', Common Market Law Review, Vol. 39, No. 5, 2002, p. 1060.

sensually accepted view that restrictions that can be objectively necessary to achieve some legitimate goals automatically fall outside Article 101(1) TFEU.[223] This view is logically inconsistent inasmuch as one phenomenon cannot define the other. The suggested solution sorts this conceptual fallacy out.

Re-authorised agreements remain anticompetitive, because 'the assessment of restraints on competition must be made exclusively on the basis of competition-based criteria'.[224] Their harm for competition at the second level does not become less on account of the (eventual) improvement of other important public life domains. Article 101(3) TFEU also mentions competition as a reason for re-authorisation. However this criterion is not fully dissociated from the above-mentioned values and serves only as a *precondition* for the authorisation. In order to be re-authorised, agreements should not 'afford such undertakings the possibility of eliminating competition in respect of a substantial part of the products in question'. In spite of the arguments, explored by Molle and Säcker,[225] from both the wording and the monistic structure of Article 101 TFEU, the promotion of competition in the sense of Article 101(3) TFEU is not considered as an additional criterion for authorisation. It can only be adopted jointly with welfare-based values. It is not perceived as a separate reason, independently from other values. In other words, this provision merely states that competition in these cases should be *limited* as little as possible. It addresses the same aspects of competition as Article 101(1) TFEU. It does not account for situations where an agreement can correspond to the conditions of Article 101(1) TFEU, while at the same time contributing to the *improvement* of competition in the relevant market, from the perspective of economic assessment, or to the *establishment* of competition in another equally relevant market. In truth, such circumstances might be rare and demonstrating their existence would impose a heavy burden of proof – that the agreement while restricting competition in some sense,

---

223 E.g. Case 56/65, *Société Technique Minière v. Maschinenbau Ulm GmbH*, ECLI: EU: C: 1966 38.

224 Roger Zäch and Adrian Künzler, 'Freedom to Compete or Consumer Welfare: The Goal of Competition Law according to Constitutional Law' in Roger Zäch, Andreas Heinemann and Andreas Kellerhals (eds.), *The Development of Competition Law – Global Perspectives*, Edward Elgar Publishing, Cheltenham, 2010, pp. 68–69.

225 Alexander Molle and Franz Jürgen Säcker, 'Anti-Competitive and Pro-Competitive Elements of an Agreement', in Günther Hirsch, Frank Montag and Franz Jürgen Säcker (eds.), *Competition Law: European Community Practice and Procedure – Article-by-Article Commentary*, Sweet & Maxwell, London, 2008, p. 613.

simultaneously improves it in the other – on the undertakings involved. However, the mere fact that this possibility has been *entirely* and unequivocally negated does matter. This situation represents the pivotal difference between the regulation of competition in political and cultural areas on the one hand, and antitrust policy and law on the other. In the former areas the possibility that limiting the political freedom to compete or restricting free speech can contribute to other important aspects of the competitive process is not excluded a priori. These deontological options are not exclusive; the utilitarian grounds for re-authorisation remain unchanged. Hence, the eventual inclusion of these conditions would not be done at the cost of utilitarian justifications. However, the current wording of Article 101(3) TFEU *exclusively* envisages utilitarian reasons and does not even enable a hypothetical option for re-authorisation on deontological grounds. This aspect of antitrust rules is not limited to the EU and other jurisdictions have a similar approach to the issue. The explanation for this holistic perception of antitrust can be found in the doctrinal analysis of the goals of competition policy and law.

4.4 CONCLUSIONS

The task of this chapter was to explore the phenomenon of competition from a normative perspective.[226] The role of the competitive process is of paramount importance in liberal democracy.[227] It is not limited to economics, but covers all major areas of public and private life. The meaning of competition would be significantly diminished if perceived *solely* as a means to the general welfare, as the economic approach suggests.[228] This would entail a one-dimensional perception of antitrust

---

[226] Ulrich Immenga, 'Future Competition Law', Working Paper, in Claus-Dieter Ehlermann and Laraine L. Laudati (eds.), *The Objectives of Competition Policy*, European Competition Law Annual 1997, Hart Publishing, Oxford, 1998, p. 184: 'A competition system corresponds not only with free markets, but also with individualism, freedom of expression, free flow of information and non-intervention by governments in the market process. This is a liberal view of state and man, driven by self-interest as the supreme motivation force'.

[227] Paul J. McNulty, 'Economic Theory and the Meaning of Competition', The Quarterly Journal of Economics, Vol. 82, No. 4, 1968, p. 639: '[C]ompetition is, in our system, a political and social desideratum no less than an economic one' (emphasis in the original).

[228] Massimo Motta, *Competition Policy: Theory and Practice*, Cambridge University Press, Cambridge, 2004, p. xvii: '[Competition policy is] the set of policies and laws which ensure that competition in the marketplace is not restricted

reality.[229] The competitive process in economics, politics and cultural life contributes significantly to the improvement of societal well-being. Yet, this feature is neither an exclusive nor even the best attribute of competition. It is proposed to distinguish between the *goals* and *benefits* of antitrust,[230] so that welfare is a consequence, a societal benefit of the competitive process, which does not replace or redefine it.[231] History knows many cases where competition served as an obstacle to utilitarian public goals. Some societies are aware of this *externality* and consciously reject this method; others accept these flaws, because competition is decisive for the functioning of a healthy democratic system. The difficulty with this acceptance lies in its justification, and is most noticeable in the area of economic competition. Instead of recognising the inevitability of the externalities of competition and mitigating them under the balancing test, those externalities are combated and condemned as anticompetitive, which implies that genuine competition is harmless, and all the negative elements should be eliminated as non-decisive for the definition of the phenomenon. As the analysis of the philosophical concept of freedom reveals, the negative aspects of competition are inseparably linked with its positive aspects. This dialectical connection should be tolerated and enhanced. The role of competition policy is not welfare generating, but competition generating. This role cannot be contemplated or performed without balancing competition against other significant values.

---

in such a way as to reduce economic welfare . . . [which is] a standard concept for economists . . . is the objective that competition policies should pursue'.

229 Harlan M. Blake, William K. Jones, 'Toward a Three-Dimensional Antitrust Policy', Columbia Law Review, Vol. 65, No. 3, 1965, p. 422: 'Trying to measure a three-dimensional world with a one-dimensional yardstick must be terribly frustrating. . . . [One cannot] measure [one's] way across the antitrust terrain with a rigid ruler of economic efficiency'.

230 Claus-Dieter Ehlermann, 'Introduction, Objectives of Competition Policy in General', in Claus-Dieter Ehlermann and Laraine L. Laudati (eds.), *The Objectives of Competition Policy*, European Competition Law Annual 1997, Hart Publishing, Oxford, 1998, p. ix.

231 Frank H. Knight, 'The Rôle of Principles in Economics and Politics', The American Economic Review, Vol. 41, No. 1, 1951, p. 9.

5. The mechanics of balancing

This chapter explores situations in which two or more equally important values conflict with each other. It analyses different theoretical approaches to the eventual reconciliation of these conflicts and it applies their answers to the value of the competitive process. The problem of balancing is intensively discussed in economics, political theory and jurisprudence.[1] It is also of particular relevance in antitrust.[2] Some balancing techniques are applied universally; others are more context specific and are relevant only for a particular discipline. None, however, can be envisaged in a form of the universal rule, since 'there is no algorithm for weighing in legal doctrine'.[3] In a pluralist society balancing is inevitable.[4] On a practical level, balancing is widely used in competition law and most explicitly present in the broader notion of rule of reason.[5] The task of this chapter,

---

[1] Norbert Kloten, 'Role of the Public Sector in the Social Market Economy', in Alan Peacock and Hans Willgerodt (eds.), *German Neo-Liberals, and the Social Market Economy*, The Macmillan Press, London, 1989, p. 77: 'It is very difficult to determine to what extent interdependent sub-systems are in conformity with one another. For example, how much "state" can market economy tolerate?'

[2] Donald Dewey, 'The Economic Theory of Antitrust: Science or Religion?', Virginia Law Review, Vol. 50, No. 3, 1964, p. 421: 'The necessity of making this choice [between decentralised decision-making and efficiency] has largely prevented the development of per se rules . . .. So long as federal judges are reasonable men par excellence, it will continue to do so'.

[3] Aleksander Peczenik, 'Scientia Juris: Legal Doctrine as Knowledge of Law and as a Source of Law', *Treatise of Legal Philosophy and General Jurisprudence*: Vol. 4, Springer, New York, 2007, p. 118.

[4] Carl Schmitt, *The Crisis of Parliamentary Democracy*, MIT Press, Cambridge, Massachusetts, 1985, p. 40: '[Balancing act] can be found in every aspect of intellectual life [. . .] a balance of trade in international economics, the European balance of power in foreign politics, the cosmic [balance] of attraction and repulsion, the balance of the passions in the works of Malebranche and Shaftesbury, even a balanced diet is recommended'.

[5] According to Fikentscher (Wolfgang Fikentscher, *Wirtschaftsrecht*, C.H. Beck, Munich, 1983, translated and quoted in Jan Peeters, 'The Rule of Reason Revisited: Prohibition on Restraints of Competition in the Sherman Act and the EEC Treaty', The American Journal of Comparative Law, Vol. 37, No. 3, 1989, p. 522) there are four types of rule of reason: '(a) wirtschaftspolitische (economic policy) rule of reason: the restraint of trade is upheld for economic

therefore, is to provide some operational models which describe how the constitutionally recognised value of competition can coexist with other important societal interests. The normative statement on the constitutional importance of competition, as developed in the previous chapter (Section 4.2) should not be perceived as an absolute.[6] Constitutionalisation does not guarantee full protection, but merely enables the respective value to use constitutional trump argument in adjudicative process. While the task of the previous chapter was primarily prescriptive, the following chapter mostly resorts to positive analysis, without making normative statements. Different approaches to and techniques of balancing are explored with the primary purpose of analysing both intra- and inter-value communications, as well as the interactions of values with the decision-makers. Therefore, the main task is not to *design* any special model of balancing, but *to articulate properly* the existing algorithms of communication, which should demonstrate the operational aspect of the normative argument that the book puts forward.

On the terminological side, the following two issues should be clarified. First, the terms *values*, *interests, goals* and *rights* are used in this chapter as synonyms unless otherwise specified, as shorthand for individual or societal goods which deserve to be either protected or enhanced at the public level. Whereas differences of meaning between these terms exist and have been widely acknowledged, they are irrelevant to the methodology of this part of the research.[7] Indeed courts often use these terms interchangeably.

---

reasons; (b) rechtspolitische (legal policy): the restraint of trade is upheld on legal grounds, such as unfair competition laws, ancillary restraints considerations and opportunistic grounds (so-called de minimis concept: the minor importance of the restraint does not justify the expenditure of legal efforts to analyze it); (c) sozialpolitische (socio-political) rule of reason: the restraint is upheld by taking into account such factors as the protection of small businesses, consumers, and other societal interests; (d) allgemeinpolitische (political) rule of reason: the restraint of trade will be upheld on pure political grounds'.

[6] Calvin Goldman, 'Competition Policy Objectives', Panel Discussion, in Claus-Dieter Ehlermann and Laraine L. Laudati (eds.), *The Objectives of Competition Policy*, European Competition Law Annual 1997, Hart Publishing, Oxford, 1998, p. 327: '[W]e must consider how to deal with conflicting competition law objectives. Objectives are often not compatible. . . . The key to dealing with this problem is the balancing process. Comparing harms from anticompetitive acts to efficiency gains is like comparing apples with oranges'.

[7] Robert Alexy, *A Theory of Constitutional Rights*, Oxford University Press, Oxford, 2002, p. 51: '[T]he differences are only terminological. The judgement does not refer to "competition" but to "tension" and "conflict", and that which competes and is to be balanced is not called "principle" but "duty", "requirement", "constitutional right", "claim" and "interest"'.

The distinction between exchangeable and utility values, as developed by classical economics is acknowledged but does not impinge upon the purposes of this research. The distinction between a right defined as 'an individuated political aim [and] a goal [defined as] a nonindividuated political aim'[8] is not internalised here either, to the extent that rights and goals are both considered at some point (a) as relative and (b) as collective. Besides *rights* are only protected in their quality of society's political *goals*. Secondly, the definition of constitutionality is taken here in its broader sense. This implies that (a) 'a constitution is a conceptual necessity of every legal system',[9] and that (b) each public value is explicitly or indirectly acknowledged at the highest societal level in the political system of liberal democracies.

5.1 AUTOPOIESIS OF VALUES

From the perspective of the philosophy of science, there are two conceptual approaches to address an issue of research: universal and particular. The former implies an instrumental, applied inquiry, aiming to utilise the scientific discoveries; the latter is interested in the discovery itself.[10] Such a distinction is operational only – in *reality* both coexist, constantly fertilising each other; in *theory* they should be taken separately. The separation is analytical and it is always followed by reunification, but conceptually it is an independent step of any research. The first methodological premise therefore is that every value requires a separate treatment.

The process of decision-making is analytically separated into two stages, namely internal and external. At the internal level every value is considered as a self-sufficient autopoietic system. At the end of the internal analysis that helps to perform a deep context-independent exploration of the specificity of each value, they can be compared with each other.

---

8 Ronald M. Dworkin, 'Hard Cases', Harvard Law Review, Vol. 88, No. 6, 1975, p. 1068.

9 John Gardner, 'Can There Be a Written Constitution?', University of Oxford Legal Research Paper Series, Paper No. 17, 2009, p. 1.

10 Daniel M. Hausman, 'Introduction', in Daniel M. Hausman (ed.), *The Philosophy of Economics – An Anthology*, Cambridge University Press, Cambridge, 2008, pp. 5–6, (emphasis in the original): 'There are two main schools of thought. *Scientific realists* hold that . . . science should . . . discover new truths . . . and explain phenomena. . . . *Antirealists* . . . regard the goals of science as exclusively practical. . . . [They] do not repudiate theorising [b]ut they locate [the importance of theories] in their role in helping people to anticipate and control phenomena'.

balancing test, while analysing positive and negative impacts of economic behaviours.[170]

While prima facie the alternative proposal has very similar practical outcomes, it derives from a different methodological premise. First, it abandons the intention to fully subordinate the irrationality of the spontaneous market actions to the clear and predictable yardstick of equilibrium economics, not denying its methodological inevitability for understanding 'the functioning of the price system in a decentralised economy'.[171] As Mason explains, the antithesis of the social perception of monopoly is *free* competition, 'understood to be a situation in which the freedom of any individual or firm to engage in legitimate economic activity is not restrained by the state, by agreements between competitors or by the predatory practices of a rival',[172] whereas the antithesis of monopoly perceived from the economic rationale is *pure* and not *free* competition, which is a hypothetical situation, taken for the sake of the purity of the economic thinking rather than as a normative claim.[173] These two perceptions do not coincide.

Second, the alternative proposal acknowledges that freedom is a non-utilitarian category that is not assessed or supported only by the positive outcomes which it can bring to society. Freedom, creativity and the egoistic desire of power are not perceived as instruments of welfare, but as independent societal values. Third, these values are not absolute, and they must be balanced against other values. They can significantly encroach on societal interests, harming and destroying by their spontaneity the very framework of the system which protects them. The encroachment alone does not constitute a sufficient reason for repressing freedom. In order to be limited, the interests of freedom should be outweighed in the balancing

---

170 Oles Andriychuk, 'Economic Freedom as Political Virtue: An Insight from the Perspective of Value Pluralism', European Journal of Legal Studies, Vol. 3, No. 1, 2010, pp. 130–132.

171 Harold Demsetz, 'Economic, Legal and Political Dimensions of Competition", University of California, Los Angeles Discussion Paper, No. 209, 1981, p. 6.

172 Edward S. Mason, 'Monopoly in Law and Economics', The Yale Law Journal, Vol. 47, No. 1, 1937, p. 36.

173 Daniel Zimmer, 'Protection of Competition v. Maximizing (Consumer) Welfare', in Jürgen Basedow and Wolfgang Wurmnest (eds.), *Structure and Effects in EU Competition Law: Studies on Exclusionary Conduct and State Aid*, Kluwer, Alphen aan den Rijn, 2011, p. 31: 'Economics as a positive discipline, can provide no answer to policy questions. Economists can, of course, make propositions to rule makers and rule makers may decide for or against the adoption of such a proposition'.

As explained by Sartor,[11] in each argumentation case a decision-maker evaluates both the positive and negative aspects of the argument, presuming that no universal absolute truth can be discovered. Therefore, the two-step analytical process requires some *de*-construction (not to be confused with Heidegger's and Derrida's deconstruction), or dissembling of the imaginary coherence of all public interests followed by their *re*-construction. The first step embraces the rationale of modernism (systemic coherence, clarity, consistency); conversely, the second step is postmodern (indeterminacy, ambivalence, context-dependency).[12] Such a two-step approach is opposed to the syncretising holism which holds that every interdisciplinary or inter-value interaction 'reveals' something new and beneficial for all participants.[13] Every regulatory case could be split into its particular components, before deciding upon the values it affects. Each value is perceived separately. It is seen as a centre of gravity, around which all other values turn. The dialectical analysis at this stage is performed only for the sake of a comprehensive understanding of the essence of this public value. Since no regulator is an expert on the internal nature of *all* societal values, and because these values are subjected to balancing acts, their internal structure is constantly analysed by the experts and interest groups who strive to promote this value on the higher regulatory level of priority. The first stage is predominantly based on self-sufficiency, while the second usually refers to economic rationality. The two stages are separated analytically[14] – while in reality they constitute a mutually dependent continuum.

The analytical two-step separation can be subdivided in several steps. The first, value-centric step delves into (but is not limited to) the analysis

---

[11] Giovanni Sartor, 'A Formal Model of Legal Argumentation', Ratio Juris, Vol. 7, No. 2, 1994, p. 177.

[12] Edwin Fruehwald, 'Postmodern Legal Thought and Cognitive Science', Hofstra University School of Law Legal Studies Research Paper Series, Research Paper No. 06-31, 2006, pp. 2–3.

[13] Avery W. Katz, 'Positivism and the Separation of Law and Economics', Michigan Law Review, Vol. 94, No. 7, 1996, p. 2261: 'One must consider the foreign discipline's practices on its own terms, and only then consider whether and how those terms and practices shed light on one's own. It will not do to borrow superficially the practices of another discipline or culture, such as efficiency analysis or formal modelling, without understanding the larger terms in which those practices are understood'.

[14] Daniel M. Hausman, Michael S. McPherson, 'Taking Ethics Seriously: Economics and Contemporary Moral Philosophy', Journal of Economic Literature, Vol. 31, No. 2, 1993, p. 672. 'The simple picture of the economist who provides value-free technical information to the decision maker is at best a useful caricature'.

of the following components of values: their origins; their main features and attributes; their importance for society; the role they play; the means to protect them from other values/decision-makers (direct protection); their enhancement by other values/decision-makers (direct promotion); the threats and dangers they pose for other values (indirect protection of themselves); their promotion of other values (indirect promotion of themselves); the communicative strategies available to achieve a higher position in a regulatory hierarchy of values; the main competing values; whether they can be considered as 'allies' and under which conditions; the dominant regulatory paradigm and the aspects of the value to emphasise in a given context; the dominant regulatory *currency* and how to get the most advantageous *exchange rate* (how to sell itself to the decision-maker).

The second step is also subdivided into many steps, including the analysis of: the main societal interests and priorities; the peripheral societal interests; the most efficient way to reconcile conflicting values; compensatory mechanisms of those de-prioritised; developing regulatory currency which reflects different components of the system and optimises the choices; communicative strategies with other values. The difference between the two steps is the following: during the first step values are separates *egos*; while during the second step they are coherent *components* of regulatory mechanism. At the first stage they are non-dividable and incommensurable, while at the second stage they are subjected to constant trade-offs. No value can be diminished at the first stage and no value can be fully protected at the second one. This two-step model is not normative, but it reflects the positive dialectical law of a whole and its parts, which implies that any object is simultaneously a coherent whole, and a part of another object, which again is a whole and a part of another one and so on, ad infinitum.

Therefore, on the first level all values are conceptually autopoietic. Autopoiesis (from the Greek: αυτό – 'self'; and ποίησις – creation) reflects the principle of self-sufficiency and self-maintenance of a system. The term itself has been coined by Maturana and Varela[15] and initially applied to biological systems only. Later on it expanded to social sciences, in particular in the context of Luhmann's[16] systems theory. The principle of autopoiesis of values is not sufficient in and of itself. It should be followed by some inter-system communication and ad hoc decision-making, which

---

[15] Humberto Maturana and Francisco Varela, *Autopoiesis and Cognition: The Realization of the Living*, Kluwer, Dordrecht, 1972.

[16] Niklas Luhmann, *Law as a Social System*, Oxford University Press, Oxford, 2003.

implies that the regulatory scale 'is empty until the court decides what to put into it'.[17] This two-step approach reflects the principles of systems theory.[18] Hence, the autopoiesis of values is not a normative statement, but a positive one. Its primary task is epistemological. Autopoiesis reflects the notion of pure science, which is self-sufficient if perceived from the methodological perspective. This approach was attacked from different angles,[19] mostly due to the fact that it can be misinterpreted as the normative self-sufficiency of science or the societal religion of progress.[20]

In consequence, the first-step analysis of values should remain epistemologically free from moral judgement.[21] Thus any research question which has an internal rationale can be posed without taking into account its eventual harmfulness for society. It is only at the next (external) stage that the normative evaluation of the question takes place. The legitimate decision-maker can then conclude if the question deserves societal promotion, should be left on its own, or needs to be prohibited altogether due to its harmfulness for fundamental societal interests. This would be the case, for example, for eugenic research on human embryos, which is prohibited at the external level, because it creates significant dangers to the moral,

---

17 Laurent B. Frantz, 'The First Amendment in the Balance', The Yale Law Journal, Vol. 71, No. 8, 1962, p. 1435.

18 Günther Teubner, 'Autopoiesis in Law and Society: A Rejoinder to Blankenburg', Law & Society Review, Vol. 18, No. 2, 1984, p. 292: 'While classical notions of system concentrated on the internal relations of the elements and searched for emerging properties of the system ("the whole is more than the sum of the parts"), modern open systems theories stress the exchange relations between system and environment'.

19 Friedrich A. von Hayek, 'Individualism and Economic Order', The University of Chicago Press, Chicago, 1948, p. 1: 'To advocate any clear-cut principles of social order is today an almost certain way to incur the stigma of being an unpractical doctrinaire. It has come to be regarded as the sign of the judicious mind that in social matters one does not adhere to fixed principles but decides each question "on its merits"; that one is generally guided by expediency and is ready to compromise between opposed views'.

20 The history of the doctrinal fight against pure science has been analysed by Polanyi (Michael Polanyi, 'The Growth of Thought in Society', Economica, New Series, Vol. 8, No. 32, 1941, pp. 428–429) who showed inter alia that contrary to the common perception, pure science was considered as a big threat by both European totalitarian regimes at that time.

21 Friedrich A. von Hayek, 'Competition as a Discovery Procedure', The Quarterly Journal of Austrian Economics, Vol. 5 No. 3, 2002, pp. 11–12: 'The notion that we must formulate our theories so that they can be immediately applied to observable statistical or other measurable quantities seems to me to be a methodological error which, had the natural sciences followed it, would have greatly obstructed their progress'.

ethical or humanistic dimension of life in society. On the other hand, at the internal level such research does have its intrinsic autopoietic value, and presents some interest for science. Actually, it is even very attractive from the purely scientific perspective. Whereas in spite of all the controversy it raises, eugenics may find significant public support due to its eventual positive outcomes for medical patients, more drastically unacceptable scientific practices also exist. Yet, all of them contain this internal positive element. The less acceptable these practices are for society, the smaller the chances are for their internal features to be placed into the broader, external, public context. However, these internal positive features still exist and cannot be ignored, at least for the theoretical premises of the balancing act.

The suggested two-step model is more coherent than its one-step alternative. Yet, because the two-step test is seldom performed in the decision-making process, harmful activities or values tend to be declared internally invalid. In this perspective, research on human embryos would often be called scientifically unsound, rather than internally interesting but externally harmful. The normative neutrality of autopoietic systems implies that, internally, all of them are philosophical ends in themselves. Their only raison d'être is to 'maintain their autopoietic organisation of self-reproduction as long as it is possible to do so'.[22] They are directed to self-observation, perceiving the external environment only in terms relevant to their own epistemological *box*. This is also the case for each scientific discipline that limits itself to its internal apparatus, observing the environment from its peculiar perspective, without reference to any moral aspects, which are external for positive science itself.[23]

It has been argued that the full closeness of autopoietic systems prevents them from interacting with the external world (environment) and that this feature makes them useless self-referential exercises.[24] Arguably an autopoietic law would be protected from the influence of the doctrine, legal culture, economic facts or social necessities. There are several conceptual ways to clarify the fact that autopoiesis does not constitute

---

22 Niklas Luhmann, 'Deconstruction as Second-Order Observing', New Literary History, Vol. 24, No. 4, 1993, p. 771.

23 Milton Friedman, 'The Methodology of Positive Economics' in Milton Friedman (ed.), *Essays in Positive Economics*, University of Chicago Press, 1953, p. 4: 'Positive economics is in principle independent of any particular ethical position or normative judgements. . . . [I]t deals with "what is", and not with "what ought to be"'.

24 Jeanne L. Schroeder, 'Fear of Freedom: A Polemic Against Policy Scholarship', Cardozo Law School, Jacob Burns Institute for Advanced Legal Studies, Working Paper Series No. 35, 2001, p. 7: '[M]any professors assume that normative policy recommendations is the *only* valid goal of scholarship' (emphasis in the original).

isolation. According to Teubner, autopoietic systems are characterised by their ability to selectively absorb some relevant parts of other systems.[25] According to Lange the autopoietic legal model should not be treated as 'a completely closed system'[26] to the extent that the environment is capable of influencing the communicative processes within the system itself. Neves suggests that 'self-referential closure, that is, normativity for the legal system, does not serve as the system's end in itself but rather as a condition for openness'.[27] Lianos agrees with Luhmann and suggests that although 'a situation of incommensurability between the two discourses should not be excluded, autopoietic social systems are cognitively open to their environment, despite being normatively closed'.[28] All these views may be considered in this respect as neo-Kantian, which implies, as Ebenstein explains it, that every act of scientific cognition is a pure theoretical exercise, which is undertaken due to the fact that every 'thing in itself' in unknowable and therefore 'the object of cognition is logically "created" by the knowing subject. This creation has a purely epistemological character'.[29] This approach to the law, as will be shown in the next chapter on legal theory, is one of the main characteristics of legal positivism. This helps avoiding a vulgarised perception of positivism as narrow-minded black-letter legalism or 'mechanical jurisprudence'. If this were not the case, the author who coined that very phrase,[30] would not claim that 'now that Stammler has retired, [Kelsen] is unquestionably the leading jurist of the time'.[31] Indeed, legal positivism derives its origins from scientific positivism, a modernist attempt to conceptualise all areas of human knowledge. Yet it should not be perceived as a mere extension of logical positivism. It is also misleading, as Sebok shows, to associate legal positivism with sociological

---

25 Günther Teubner, *Autopoietic Law: a New Approach to Law and Society*, Walter de Gruyter & Co., Berlin, 1987.

26 Bettina Lange, 'Understanding Regulatory Law: Empirical versus Systems-Theoretical Approaches?', Oxford Journal of Legal Studies, Vol. 18, No. 3, 1998, p. 455.

27 Marcelo Neves, 'From the Autopoiesis to the Allopoiesis of Law', Journal of Law and Society, Vol. 28, No. 2, 2001, p. 251.

28 Ioannis Lianos, 'Lost In Translation? Towards a Theory of Economic Transplants', Current Legal Problems, Vol. 62, No. 1, 2009, pp. 358–359.

29 William Ebenstein, 'The Pure Theory of Law: Demythologizing Legal Thought', California Law Review, Vol. 59, No. 3, 1971, p. 621.

30 Roscoe Pound, 'Mechanical Jurisprudence', Columbia Law Review, Vol. 8, No. 8, 1908, pp. 620–621: 'The nadir of mechanical jurisprudence is reached when conceptions are used, not as premises from which to reason, but as ultimate solutions. So used, they cease to be conceptions and become empty words'.

31 Roscoe Pound, 'Law and the Science of Law in Recent Theories', The Yale Law Journal, Vol. 43, No. 4, 1934, p. 532.

positivism of Comte or positive economic analysis, which both claim that 'social life could be analyzed and reformed through the careful use of the mathematical techniques of measurement and analysis'.[32] On the other hand, legal indeterminacy creates a major challenge to law. However, this challenge can be addressed within the framework of autopoiesis without having to appeal to morality, economics or any other system of social norms. Effectively, the methodological autopoiesis that is concerned with the *internal* perception of a phenomenon, emphasising its absoluteness, cannot be fully dissociated from the *external* stage in which different autopoietic values communicate with each other.[33] This is the essence of the dialectics of balancing.[34] Another way of explaining the communicative process would be a reference to a notion of ideal law (as explored in the Chapter 6.3 on legal theory) as one of the dialectical dimensions of law. The ideal law (ideal not in a sense of 'imaginary' or 'best', but as an immanent part of material law) could then serve as a proxy through which formal law can absorb ideas from the external environment.

5.2 BALANCING AND THE INTERPRETATION OF VALUES

Balancing is an unavoidable part of any decision-making process, be it in law,[35] economics,[36] or any other human activity. In spite of the technical

---

32 Anthony J. Sebok, *Legal Positivism in American Jurisprudence*, Cambridge University Press, Cambridge, 1998, p. 33.

33 Michael Polanyi, *The Logic of Liberty*, Routledge, London, 1951, p. 3: 'Until fairly recently it used to be commonly assumed that . . . [pure sciences] served their own purpose, the discovery of knowledge for the love of truth. Do we still accept that view?'

34 Max Weber, 'Science as a Vocation', Daedalus, Vol. 87, No. 1, 1958, pp. 112–113: 'Only by strict specialization can the scientific worker become fully conscious, for once and perhaps never again in his lifetime, that he has achieved something that will endure. . . . [But only both], enthusiasm and work, and above all both of them jointly, can entice the idea'.

35 John J. Flynn, 'Legal Reasoning, Antitrust Policy and the Social "Science" of Economics', Antitrust Bulletin, Vol. 33, No. 4, 1988, pp. 721–722: 'The legal process is constantly confronted with reconciling competing and conflicting moral values underlying its rules in light of the specific realities of individual disputes, role definitions, and the consequences of the decision. Indeed, this function is central to the legal process, and the art with which it is carried out distinguishes the great jurists from the mediocre'.

36 According to one of the founders of the early Chicago School, Viner (Jacob Viner, 'The Short View and the Long in Economic Policy', The American

differences between the terms balancing and proportionality,[37] they are used in this research as synonyms,[38] as the conditions for proportionality (suitability, necessity and proportionality *sensu stricto*)[39] and balancing (ontological prerequisite to reconcile the conflicts within a system) are both covered by the requirements analysed in this chapter. As shown by Alexy, one can be deduced from the other.[40] Alternatively, the balancing act may be juxtaposed with the principle of proportionality, which would imply that the former is a colloquial perception of indispensability of weighing the arguments that occurs in 'any form of reasoning or argumentation about the values in question',[41] while the latter is 'a specific judicial test that pretends to balance values while avoiding any moral reasoning, bypassing any discourse on priorities, [that] pretends to resolve value conflicts by assessing the degree of their relative coexistence'.[42] Other authors suggest that in constitutional jurisprudence the term balancing has a 'narrower and more specific import, referring to explicit judicial weighing',[43] considering both balancing and weighing as the third step of the principle of proportionality.[44]

Economic Review, Vol. 30, No. 1, 1940, p. 2.), '[t]here are always a number of different values to be considered, moreover, and satisfaction of one often involves disregard of the other. This makes necessary a sort of weighing process'.

[37] Madhav Khosla, 'Proportionality: An Assault on Human Rights?: A Reply', International Journal of Constitutional Law, Vol. 8, No. 2, 2010, pp. 229–231.

[38] Moshe Cohen-Eliya and Iddo Porat, 'American Balancing and German Proportionality: The Historical Origins', International Journal of Constitutional Law, Vol. 8, No. 2, 2010, p. 265: '[T]he analytical differences between the two concepts are not substantial enough to account for the differences in attitudes toward them'.

[39] Frederick Schauer, 'Balancing, Subsumption, and the Constraining Role of Legal Text', Symposium on Rights, Law, and Morality: Themes from the Legal Philosophy of Robert Alexy, New College, Oxford University, 10–11 September 2008, http://papers.ssrn.com/sol3/papers.cfm?abstract_id=1403343, accessed on 16 April 2010, p. 9: 'Indeed, it is slightly misleading even to refer to proportionality reasoning as "balancing," for the language of balancing suggests either that the opposing interests must be compared on their own merits, without being subject to rules of weight, . . . presumptions, burdens of proof, or various other devices that influence the outcome in one way or another'.

[40] Robert Alexy, 'On the Structure of Legal Principles', Ratio Juris, Vol. 13, No. 3, 2000, p. 297.

[41] Jeremy Waldron, 'Fake Incommensurability: A Response to Professor Schauer', Hastings Law Journal, Vol. 45, No. 4, 1994, p. 819.

[42] Stavros Tsakyrakis, 'Proportionality: An Assault on Human Rights?', International Journal of Constitutional Law, Vol. 7, No. 3, 2009, p. 474.

[43] Louis Henkin, 'Infallibility under Law: Constitutional Balancing', Columbia Law Review, Vol. 78, No. 5, 1978, p. 1024.

[44] Virgílio Afonso da Silva, 'Comparing the Incommensurable: Constitutional Principles, Balancing and Rational Decision', Oxford Journal of Legal Studies, Vol. 31, No. 2, 2011, p. 274.

The inevitability of balancing can be explained by the following factors: (1) the polysemy of values; (2) the in-/commensurability of values; (3) the homonymy of values; (4) conflicts of values; (5) the scarcity of regulatory choices. (1) The polysemy of values is understood here primarily in an epistemological sense, which deals with the phenomenon of interpretation, and in a systemic sense, which addresses the issues of composition of normative models. Epistemologically it is based on the premises of value pluralism and relativises any absolute appraisal of values. On a systemic level polysemy refutes a monolithic hierarchy of values, which constitutes the only conceptual alternative to balancing. (2) The in-/commensurability of values addresses the problem of value assessment from a dialectical perspective by applying to this situation a dialectical law of the quantity–quality continuum. It explores the two end-of-the-spectrum positions, which sequentially uphold *quantification* of values and their *qualification*. The former standpoint claims that every value is (ought to be) quantifiable, suggesting different criteria for this purpose. According to the latter approach, each value is peculiar and incommensurable. After exploring the strengths and weaknesses of both positions, they are operationalised following the dialectical method, which encompasses the static polarity of these views, but reconciles them in a dynamic interplay. (3) The homonymy of values is a situation where different actors or conceptions have their own specific perception of the same phenomenon, wrongly attributing the same understanding to actors, who have conflicting understandings of the same value. This situation is very common in *inter*- and in particular in *cross*-disciplinary studies, where the meaning of a certain value as defined in one discipline is implicitly transferred to the phonetically identical term, which has a different meaning in the other discipline. The main emphasis is put on the problems encountered in the homonymy of the term 'competition', the understanding of which differs in political, legal, economic and cultural studies. (4) Conflicts of values are a natural situation in which different values irreconcilably collide. Unlike the former three situations, which explore mainly the epistemological, *subjective* aspects of the understanding of the meaning of different values, conflicts of values are analysed from an *objective* perspective. This requires taking an external approach to each value, not addressing the issues of peculiarity of their meanings, presuming the existence of an objective, common, consensually agreed perception of each of them. The main task is to analyse the *mechanics* of conflict, highlighting the structure of the communicative process between them. The main attention in substantive terms is paid to the conflict between the competitive process and welfare-centric interests. (5) The task of the fifth subsection is to explore the conditions that influence regulatory choices. Its main premise is that each decision-making process is predetermined by a scarcity of available options, which implies that no conflict can be reconciled without sacrificing some aspects of certain values or some values altogether. Unlike the former part of the analysis, which addresses the issues of natural conflicts between certain values and implies that certain values often contradict each other (e.g. free speech vs. privacy; security vs. freedom; spending vs. saving), this subsection explores more context-dependent situations, predetermined by a scarcity of the resources necessary to satisfy the claims made by different values and the objective inability of regulators to protect sufficiently each and every value in every case.

5.2.1 Polysemy of Values and Negation of Hierarchies

The *polysemy* (multiple meaning) of values[45] constitutes the main precondition of balancing. If all rights, values and interests had a single, *objective*[46] meaning which did not change depending on the perspective they were assessed from or the context they were set in, the problem of their reconciliation would be difficult but not theoretically impossible. There are two conceptual ways to address conflicting interests: hierarchical central planning[47] or pluralistic (with many nuanced versions in practice).[48] A rule-setter in the first case would be able to rely on his authority and priorities to establish a hierarchy between the different values, which could then be

[45] Friedrich Waismann, 'Language Strata', in Antony G. N. Flew (ed.), *Logic and Language* (Second Series), Basil Blackwell, Oxford 1953 (Alonzo Church, 'Review', The Journal of Symbolic Logic, Vol. 38, No. 4, 1973, p. 663): 'Statements may be *true* in different senses, *verifiable* in different senses, *meaningful* in different senses. Therefore the attempts at defining "truth", or at drawing a sharp line between the meaningful and the meaningless, etc., are doomed to fail'.

[46] The notions of *objective* and *subjective* are not used in this context as a reflection of ontological primacy, in which the first encompasses the Aristotelian idea that value is encoded in the object, while the second perceives the value as volatile utility being assessed and evaluated by each individual inductively as suggested by Spinoza. This research is concentrated more on the societal rather than the philosophical aspect of the value.

[47] John Gray, *Isaiah Berlin*, Harper Collins, London, 1995, p. 1: '[T]he idea of perfect society in which all genuine ideals and goods are achieved is not merely utopian; it is incoherent'.

[48] Walter Eucken, 'Die Wettbewerbsordnung und ihre Verwirklichung', Jahrbuch für die Ordnung von Wirtschaft und Gesellschaft, Vol. 2, 1949, cited in Christian Ahlborn, Carsten Grave (trans.), Walter Eucken, 'The Competitive Order and its Implementation', Competition Policy International, Vol. 2, No. 2, 2006, p. 226: '[U]ltimately there is only a choice between a centrally administered control of essential parts of the economic process and the competitive order'.

modified if the meaning of the values or the set of the priorities changed, in accordance with a formal procedure. The decisions in these hierarchies are based on subsumption.[49] This imperative-based, monistic model has many advantages, like homogeneity, certainty and predictability. Therefore, in spite of the danger of falling into 'a tyranny of values'[50] many social systems are inclined to follow it.[51] The rationale of this argument is similar to the economic notion of 'voluntary simplicity', as described by Schwartz in *The Paradox of Choice*,[52] which implies that the more options are available, the harder the choices and the outcomes of these choices can be. These *mono*semic (having a single-meaning) models presuppose the unconditionality of the authority, since any questioning of the established hierarchy endangers the functioning of the system. Some judges also share this view, and while recognising the natural inevitability of conflicts, shift the decision from the courts to the legislator.[53] Therefore, the hierarchical models of rules are mostly to be found in the systems in which the authority of the rule-setter and the validity of values are not questioned: religious beliefs, authoritarian political regimes or moral dogmas.[54] The efficiency of these models is contestable from the perspective of liberal democracy.[55] This research does not explore empirical arguments about the inefficiencies of hierarchical structures. For methodological purposes

---

49 Robert Alexy, 'On Balancing and Subsumption: A Structural Comparison', Ratio Juris, Vol. 16, No. 4, 2003, pp. 433–435.

50 Lorenzo Zucca, *Constitutional Dilemmas – Conflicts of Fundamental Rights in Europe and the USA*, Oxford University Press, Oxford, 2007, p. 22.

51 Gareth Davies, 'Constitutional Disagreement in Europe and the Search for Pluralism', Eric Stein Working Paper No 1/2010, 2010, p. 1: 'Where there are multiple sources of apparently constitutional law one always takes precedence and the other is then no longer constitutional. Dialogue may help the legal sources reconcile, but it does not change the normative hierarchy between them'.

52 Barry Schwartz, *The Paradox of Choice: Why More is Less*, HarperCollins, London, 2005.

53 Robert H. Bork, *The Antitrust Paradox: A Policy At War With Itself*, Simon & Schuster, 1993, p. 429: 'Many statutory policies conflict to some degree with other statutory policies. Whether or not they should do so, and to what degree, is a subject for legislation rather than adjudication'.

54 Sleat (Matt Sleat, 'Liberalism, Fundamentalism and Truth', Journal of Applied Philosophy, Vol. 23, No. 4, 2006, p. 405), while being sceptical of such a perception, provides a clear definition of it: 'One way in which we may be tempted to understand the distinction we make in practice between liberals and fundamentalists is via the issue of truth. Liberals are generally more sceptical about truth while fundamentalists tend to be more objectivist, believing not only that objective truth exists but also that they know it'.

55 Henry M. Oliver, 'German Neoliberalism', The Quarterly Journal of Economics, Vol. 74, No. 1, 1960, p. 124: '[The neoliberals'] economic critique

it is assumed that these models *can* be efficient. This presumption has been taken by the authors, who while accepting the instrumental importance of the polysemy, claim that its primary importance is deontological rather than utilitarian.[56] The monosemy is criticised *despite* its eventual efficiency rather than *due to* its alleged inefficiency. Barak correctly observes that even a *mono*semic categorisation of values is basically another sort of balancing, made ex ante, in which evaluation of all values is made on an all-or-nothing basis, and adds that 'the technique of balancing is generally preferable to that of categorisation'.[57] Yet this does not change the hypothesis that *mono*semic models significantly reduce, even if they do not eliminate altogether, both the necessity of balancing and the many negative externalities of the balancing act.

The day-to-day functionality of such imperative-based systems also has its weaknesses, however, and is usually criticised from three perspectives: normative, empirical and systemic. The *normative* criticism is made from within the hierarchical system and its main concern is not related to the functioning of the system itself, but rather to the place which certain values have within the model. A member of the group can disagree, for instance, that religious norms condemn divorce more severely than abortion and therefore propose their hierarchical swapping. The proposed changes do not challenge either the validity or the legitimacy of the system as such but merely suggest a rearrangement of the hierarchy of values. It changes the content of the hierarchy without changing its structure.

The *empirical* criticism, on the contrary, is made from an external perspective of the hierarchical system by those who are questioning its very effectiveness. It refers mainly to the problem of the asymmetry of knowledge and claims that the certainty and predictability of rigid rules are detrimental to flexibility, reasonability and responsiveness, which are the main attributes of the *adversarial*, balanced systems.[58] The empirical facts are used to support the claim that authoritative hierarchical systems do not work as effectively as proportional models, which are much

---

of interventionism stresses malallocation and disequilibria, both political and international'.

56 James M. Buchanan, *Liberty, Market and the State*, Wheatsheaf Books, Brighton, 1986, p. 250: 'My argument stems from the conviction that there is no generalizable *instrumental* defence of democratic political procedures' (emphasis in the original).

57 Aharon Barak, *The Judge in a Democracy*, Princeton University Press, Princeton, 2006, pp. 166–167.

58 Günther Teubner, '"And God Laughed . . ." Indeterminacy, Self-Reference and Paradox in Law', German Law Journal, Vol. 12, No. 1, 2011, p. 405: '[F]unctional differentiation of society means lateral interdependence, not hierarchical order'.

more considered, take into account different interests, never pretend to be entirely coherent, but reconcile conflicting interests in a harmonious manner. Sweet and Mathews observe that 'most judges are loath to build *intra*-constitutional hierarchies of norms',[59] preferring to assume that no right can be protected in an absolute manner. The balancing act plays a key role in such models. The empirical criticism is result oriented. It does not emphasise the *substantive* weaknesses or *normative* ambiguity of the hierarchical models, but focuses instead on its *functional, operational* flaws. For the tenant of this position, the hierarchical models are *bad* and *weak* rather than *wrong* or *dangerous*.

The final, *systemic*, mode of criticism is directed at the methodological weaknesses of monosemy, suggesting that both the meaning of values and their hierarchical importance is so volatile, ambivalent and context dependent that any attempt to set up a coherent taxonomy of values is both superficial and illusionary. Striving for coherence is a necessary condition for any regulatory model,[60] but it should only be treated as an aim, and not as a state of affairs. Indeed, '[t]he multitude of the visions of Value has generated a multitude of definitions'.[61] Unlike the *normative* criticism, this type of criticism does not refer to the validity of the hierarchy nor questions its existing classification; unlike the *empirical* criticism, it does not rely on the effectiveness of either model. Its primary concern is observational rather than prescriptive. The main argument put forward by this approach is that all the values, regardless of the intentions of the rule-setters, are in one way or another mutually collusive. The internal nature of values is irreconcilable and should be recognised and tolerated irrespective of regulatory priorities. As Marmor observes, 'rights [and in this respect also interests, values, goods] properly conceived, are both inherently limited and inherently controversial'.[62] Evidently, a broad recognition of different values, rights and interests creates problems at the level of their coexistence. The situation of permanent conflicts between them cannot be

---

[59] Alec S. Sweet and Jud Mathews, 'Proportionality Balancing and Global Constitutionalism', Columbia Journal of Transnational Law, Vol. 47, No. 1, 2008, p. 88.

[60] Jacob Viner, 'The Short View and the Long in Economic Policy', The American Economic Review, Vol. 30, No. 1, 1940, p. 2: '[Hard] choices are largely left implicit in . . . [the] selection of premises, and are rarely, and then usually apologetically, expressly avowed'.

[61] Walid Ben Ahmed and Bernard Yannou, 'Polysemy of Values or Conflict of Interests: A Multi-Disciplinary Analysis', International Journal of Value-Based Management, Vol. 16, No. 2, 2003, p. 170.

[62] Andrei Marmor, 'On the Limits of Rights', Law and Philosophy, Vol. 16, No. 1, 1997, p. 1.

prevented or even limited.[63] What the systemic approach, being primarily a positive theory, proposes instead is the *operationalisation* of the conflicts with the purpose of analysing the communicative strategies within the values and between them, as well as their interactions with rule-setters and decision-makers. The systemic analysis of the balancing act does not question the validity of rules, the legality of rights or the legitimacy of values; it focuses, instead, on the internal functioning of the balancing process, considering it as unavoidable (though less explicitly so) even in the monosemic imperative-based hierarchies. As Luhmann observes, the principle of internal epistemological conflict has been used by Greek Roman and then sixteenth-century thinkers who granted paradoxes 'the function of stimulating further thought',[64] where the conventional 'doxa' is contested by 'para-doxa'. He juxtaposes this principle with the medieval techniques which rely on authority to solve 'points of disputation', which entails some arbitrariness. This research conceptually reconciles these elements, attributing a key role to dialectical balancing while recognising the inevitability of arbitrariness.

It is more appropriate to use a *systemic* approach to balancing, with the purpose of developing stylised models of balancing and articulating the role which the value of the competitive process should play in this respect. The *constitutional* significance of the competitive process refers primarily to its *internal* characteristics. It does not provide or claim its absolute priority over other values at the *external* level. Adhering to the opposite view would paralyse the balancing exercise altogether and would represent nothing more than an expanded version of the imperative-based hierarchical system, placing the *absolute* democratic values on the top of the regulatory hierarchy.

By addressing the problem of the meaning of values from a *polysemic* methodological perspective, the systemic, positive analysis of balancing does not reject the principles of hierarchy as such. It merely questions the rigidity and categorical character of an absolute hierarchical order, addressing primarily the *hard cases* (leaving aside the trivial ones), and suggesting that each value can outweigh another one depending on the circumstances, which are unpredictable and volatile. According to Alexy, legal principles 'represent reasons which can be displaced by

---

63 Stavros Tsakyrakis, 'Proportionality: An Assault on Human Rights?', International Journal of Constitutional Law, Vol. 7, No. 3, 2009, p. 469: '[E]very choice we make can be depicted as the resolution of a divergence among countless alternatives'.

64 Niklas Luhmann, 'Deconstruction as Second-Order Observing', New Literary History, Vol. 24, No. 4, 1993, p. 770.

other reasons',[65] and it is for decision-makers and not for the principle itself to decide the relevance and importance of each reason in each case as principles 'lack the resources to determine their own extent'.[66] This pluralistic approach should not be understood as a form of nihilism, complete indeterminism or agnosticism. The *relativity* of each hierarchy of values is not absolute, but is *relative* itself. Each classification is developed and influenced by multiple institutional factors. The methodology of value pluralism is taken here as a critical cognitive counter-argument to the monistic perception of values with the primary task of articulating the *existing* models of balancing rather than *disproving* the alternative approach. Value pluralism also has its important *normative* significance (competition of ideas) though this chapter does not deal with it.

5.2.2 The Balancing Act and In-Commensurability of Values

The inevitability of balancing is predetermined by the dialectical relations between the *qualitative* and *quantitative* attributes that each value possesses. The former aspect of the values reflects primarily its uniqueness and incommensurability with other values.[67] Any public good or societal interest contains certain elements of exclusivity, individuality and peculiarity, which cannot be substituted or replaced by another. The very etymology of the term 'in-dividuality' suggests that it is something which cannot be divided, calculated or correlated with something else.[68] This implies the absence of rationally defined measures for the ultimate *quality*. A radical perception of the quality of value undermines the mere possibility of *quantification*.[69] It has been illustrated by US Supreme Court Justice Scalia, who suggests that 'the scale analogy is not really appropriate, since the interests on both sides are incommensurate. It is more like judging

---

65 Robert Alexy, *A Theory of Constitutional Rights*, Oxford University Press, Oxford, 2002, p. 57.

66 ibid.

67 Although the notion of commensurability is inherently present in the dialectical philosophy, the term itself has been transposed from mathematics by Feyerabend and Kuhn, Thomas S. Kuhn, 'Commensurability, Comparability, Communicability', PSA: Proceedings of the Biennial Meeting of the Philosophy of Science Association, Vol. 2, 1982, p. 669.

68 Harold J. Laski, *Liberty in the Modern State*, Faber & Faber, London, 1930, p. 31.

69 John M. Finnis, 'Natural Law and Legal Reasoning', Cleveland State Law Review, Vol. 38, No. 1, 1990, p. 9: 'The problem of incommensurability – the problem that there is no rationally calibrated scale for "weighing"'.

whether a particular line is longer than a particular rock is heavy'.[70] On the other hand, the quantifiable character of values shows that any individual or collective good can be eventually reduced to a common denominator, and hence calculated and provided with its *objective* evaluation.[71] This *price* of value enables quantification of different interests and provides an estimated criterion for their commensuration. In its radical form this approach, which essentially reflects Jevons' *perfect* 'law of indifference',[72] eliminates any qualitative discrepancies between values and refers only to the established 'price list', disabling thereby any *qualification* of separate components in the calculus.

These two attributes are inherently present in any value and they constitute the respective polar ends of the appraisal spectrum. *Quantification* refers to the external, applied, instrumental dimension of value, while *qualification* encompasses its internal, essential, subjective characteristics; in this perspective, the term *qualification* is not used either in its usual 'ability to perform' or 'restriction, limitation' meanings. The paramount epistemological importance of the issue has been revealed and conceptualised within the philosophical tradition of dialectics. The dialectical vision concentrates on the essence of the quality–quantity polarisation, perceiving their relation along a dynamic continuum.

The quality–quantity continuum is often interpreted as a linear evolutionary model, in which quantity gradually transforms into quality. Luhmann is sceptical about this conventional perception of dialectics and caricatures it in the following way: '[t]he different is the same, the same is different. So what?'[73] If vulgarised, this interpretation relies on the commonsensical perception that the more quantitative efforts are invested into something, the higher the qualitative outcome is, transforming this dialectical principle into a kind of 'diligence law': *the harder the work the better the results*, the method of trial and error. This misleading

---

70 *Bendix Autolite v. Midwesco Enterprises*, 486 U.S. 888, 897 (1988) (Scalia, J., concurring).

71 Catherine Valcke, 'Comparative Law as Comparative Jurisprudence: The Comparability of Legal Systems', The American Journal of Comparative Law, Vol. 52, No. 3, 2004, p. 720: 'Comparison is possible only among objects that are, simultaneously and without contradiction, unified and plural'.

72 William S. Jevons, *The Theory of Political Economy*, Macmillan and Co., London, 1888, p. 77: 'When a commodity is perfectly uniform or homogeneous in quality, any portion may be indifferently used in place of an equal portion: hence, in the same market, and at the same moment, all portions must be exchanged at the same ratio'.

73 Niklas Luhmann, 'Deconstruction as Second-Order Observing', New Literary History, Vol. 24, No. 4, 1993, p. 769.

interpretation is based on observations made from the development of natural phenomena and the evolution of human beings. Some politically instrumentalised forms of dialectics – dialectical materialism in particular – expanded the principle further to social relations,[74] suggesting that quantitative changes lead to qualitative modifications, where revolutions are perceived as bifurcation points for changing quantity into quality, importing the model into the historical relations of classes. These instrumentalist perceptions neglect the permanent presence of both qualitative and quantitative elements in the phenomena, simplifying the law of dialectics and making it attractive to political authoritarianism. Luhmann, reflecting on the dialectical law on correlation between the unity and its parts, observes a similar tendency to search for a common denominator in Hegel, submitting that the attempt of final reconciliation 'ends with the "absolute spirit" that itself is nothing but a paradox'.[75] Kelsen observes in this respect that Hegel's dialectics of history as a progressive realisation of Reason is futile and harmful.[76] The extrapolation of the dialectical principles to the metaphysical historical domain is disputable,[77] and is rejected in this research. Although these evolutionary aspects of the gradual transformation of quantities into qualities actually contain some dialectical reasoning as well, they do not constitute the core or the substantial part of the dialectics of quality and quantity. On the contrary, this linear perception can be often misleading, because its commonsense rationale perceives the law of dialectics as a fairly trivial intuition.

The central claim of the quantity–quality continuum is different. It is concentrated on the perpetual and instantaneous interactions of

---

[74] Joseph Stalin, 'Dialectical and Historical Materialism', 1938, http://www.marxists.org/reference/archive/stalin/works/1938/09.htm, accessed on 23 December 2010, p. 2: 'The dialectical method . . . holds that the process of development should be understood not as movement in a circle, not as a simple repetition of what has already occurred, but as an onward and upward movement, as a transition from an old qualitative state to a new qualitative state, as a development from the simple to the complex, from the lower to the higher'.

[75] Niklas Luhmann, 'Deconstruction as Second-Order Observing', New Literary History, Vol. 24, No. 4, 1993, p. 770.

[76] Hans Kelsen, 'The Natural-Law Doctrine before the Tribunal of Science', The Western Political Quarterly, Vol. 2, No. 4, 1949, p. 511.

[77] James G. Finlayson, 'Conflict and Reconciliation in Hegel's Theory of the Tragic', Journal of the History of Philosophy, Vol. 37, No. 3, 1999, p. 507: 'The problem is that it is not clear how the dialectic of tragic conflict can lead to a *metaphysical* reconciliation, although Hegel claims that it does' (emphasis in the original).

quantitative–qualitative elements of a phenomenon.[78] Each object and each value is simultaneously *qualifiable* and *quantifiable*. As Schroeder persuasively argues, 'although logically incompatible, every choice necessarily reflects a moment of both commensuration (the recognition of quantitative difference) and incommensuration (the recognition of qualitative difference)'.[79] These two attributes of values are inherent in all values and cannot be either separated or eliminated. Money as a common standard of the *quantifiable* and human life as a quintessence of the *qualifiable* still contain some latent elements of the opposite attributes, especially when they are taken out of abstraction into a context. Thus, one penny may be ranked higher than the other penny of the same pound objectively (for numismatic purposes) or subjectively (the first earned money; the coin, given by celebrity; the coin with which personal memories are connected etc.). A human life, conversely, holds some quantifiable elements. Even societies that affirm unequivocally Protagoras' standard that 'man is the measure of all things' sometimes have to quantify human life in situations of necessity (military service), for pragmatic reasons (life insurance) or as a matter of principle (no negotiation with terrorists).

The relations between quality and quantity are of capital importance for dialectics. It perceives them as mutually enhancing polarities.[80] If taken linearly, the transitions from quantity to quality may be observed at bifurcation points – the ultimate quantity of one quality which in the same time is the initial quantity of another quality (transformation of water into ice; age of legal capacity; borders between countries). From the dialectical perspective all these thresholds are rather conditional and relative and they are characterised by discontinuous *jump* or *change* when it is impossible to define the exact moment of quantitative transformation of one quality

---

78 Jacob Viner, 'The Short View and the Long in Economic Policy', The American Economic Review, Vol. 30, No. 1, 1940, p. 2: '[T]he decision is . . . made partly on the strength of quantitative information . . . and partly on the basis of a qualitative ranking of values'.

79 Jeanne L. Schroeder, 'The Laconomics of Apples and Oranges: A Speculative Analysis of the Economic Concept of Commensurability', Yale Journal of Law and Humanities, Vol. 15, No. 2, 2003, p. 350.

80 Helge Peukert, 'Walter Eucken (1891–1950) and the Historical School', in Peter Koslowski (ed.), *The Theory of Capitalism in the German Economic Tradition: Historism, Ordo-liberalism, Critical Theory, Solidarism*, Springer, Hannover, 2000, p. 94: 'Formalists develop the idea of relatively closed systems in which . . . mathematics being the language of science and "nature". . . . "Empiricists" argue that many kinds of order cannot be put in numbers. . . . In our view these are two great, equally valid but irreconcilable ontologies in the social sciences, especially in economics'.

in another, this moment 'is constantly slipping through our fingers'.[81] The jump itself is incomprehensible for consciousness as incomprehensible is the jump from the reality to the sleep or indeed from one thought to another. The quantity–quality aspect of dialectics is applicable to the classification of values as a principle of in-/commensurability. This approach negates the test proposed by Schauer, who suggests that '[t]he existence (or not) of incommensurable values can . . . be either the product or the proof of the truth (or not) of anticonsequentialism'.[82] Every value is absolute, unique and unquantifiable, but at the same time relative, comparable and quantifiable. The absolute elements of each value reflect its autopoietic characteristics of self-sufficiency; its relative attributes encompass the mechanical calculus of reconciliation and optimisation. These irreconcilable features are embedded in all values and create a perpetual communicative spiral. Depending on the context one of the dimensions is more relevant than the other, but their cross-dependency cannot be eliminated or neglected altogether.

The conditions of in-/commensurability determine the balancing of the competitive process with other important societal values. The decision-makers constantly face the dilemma of balancing.[83] The fact that one value outweighs another reveals (i) that its internal *qualities* are given higher *quantitative* priorities than the qualities of other values and (ii) that the opposite decision could have obtained if the internal qualities of its counterparts were ranked higher. This hierarchy is not absolute and it does not reflect the internal qualities of the values, but merely their external quantifiable usefulness. It also shows that even those values which are not supported on the decision-making level inherently maintain the qualitative attributes, and that those values which were priorities or considered as the absolute standard can be downgraded under a different act of evaluation. Essentially the in-/commensurability situation is of a dilemmatic nature and cannot therefore be abandoned, but only operationalised.[84]

---

81 Robert C. Post, 'Community and the First Amendment', Arizona State Law Journal, Vol. 29, No. 3, 1997, p. 473.

82 Frederick Schauer, 'Commensurability and Its Constitutional Consequences', Hastings Law Journal, Vol. 45, No. 4, 1994, p. 790.

83 Laurent B. Frantz, 'Is The First Amendment Law? A Reply to Professor Mendelson', California Law Review, Vol. 51, No. 4, 1963, p. 748: 'As soon as he finishes measuring the unmeasurable, the judge's next job is to compare the incomparable'.

84 Isaiah Berlin, *Four Essays on Liberty*, Oxford University Press, Oxford, 1990, p. 1: 'When such dilemmas arise it is one thing to say that every effort must be made to resolve them, and another that it is certain a priori that a correct, con-

5.2.3 Homonymy of Values and Interdisciplinarity

The homonymy of values is a situation where phonetically identical phenomena have a different definition or interpretation.[85] The broader the term is the bigger the scope for the homonymy to arise.[86] The seriousness of the problem of the homonymy of values in the theory of competition has been emphasised by Hayek.[87] The relevance is particularly visible due to the fact that 'competition policy inherently represents a multidisciplinary issue'.[88] Often the difference depends on the context, then the homonymy does not constitute a big difficulty.[89] However when this difference is nuanced, the interpretation of the terms may become problematic. This is particularly the case when the same values are explored by different disciplines, and in particular when these disciplines strive to expand their natural limits to other relevant domains. This is an objective process, since every discipline seeks coherence, and coherence 'is inherently expansive:

---

clusive solution must always in principle be discoverable – something that the older rationalist metaphysics appear to guarantee'.

[85] Some interdisciplinary studies address the meaning of the term 'value' as it is perceived by different areas of knowledge: e.g. Walid Ben Ahmed, Bernard Yannou, 'Polysemy of Values or Conflict of Interests: A Multi-Disciplinary Analysis', International Journal of Value-Based Management, Vol. 16, No. 2, 2003.

[86] Hans Kelsen, *General Theory of Law and State*, Russell & Russell, New York, 1973, p. 8: 'Since humanity is divided into many nations, classes, religions, professions and so on, often at variance with one another, there are a great many very different ideas of justice; too many for one to be able to speak simply of "justice"'.

[87] Friedrich A. von Hayek, *Individualism and Economic Order*, University of Chicago Press, 1948, 1949, p. 2: 'The difficulty which we encounter is not merely the familiar fact that the current political terms are notoriously ambiguous or even that the same term means nearly the opposite to different groups. There is the much more serious fact that the same word frequently appears to unite people who in fact believe in contradictory and irreconcilable ideas'.

[88] Oliver Budzinski, 'Modern Industrial Economics and Competition Policy: Open Problems and Possible Limits', IME Working Paper, No. 93/09, 2009, p. 7.

[89] Jeremy Waldron, 'Can There Be a Democratic Jurisprudence?', New York University School of Law Public Law & Legal Theory Research Paper Series, Working Paper No. 08-35, 2008, p. 1: 'There are lots of books written about football, by which I mean the game played in American high schools and colleges and organized at a professional level by the NFL. . . . There are also lots of books written about football, by which I mean the game Americans call "soccer", played all over the world by teams like Manchester United and Dynamo Kiev. . . . The general theory of football would look like the most esoteric and scholastic curiosity by contrast. Might something similar be said about general jurisprudence, the study of *law as such*?' (emphasis in the original).

It resists compartmentalization and seeks to encompass as much as possible.'[90] Every discipline has its established apparatus (its 'language', its 'silos'), which is predetermined by the main subject matter and prevailing methodology,[91] 'disciplines . . . [compete] for limited space . . ., have "interest" in their own reproduction and spread'.[92] The more established the discipline the less reflective it is in respect to alternative perceptions of the phenomena, given by other disciplines. The dominant *intra*disciplinary discourse tends to become thereby a *reine Sprache*, it abandons the limits of *intra*disciplinarity and universalises itself by attempting to interpret the same phenomenon as it is explored by other disciplines (the effect of *agglutination of power*).[93] The longer the distance between the expanded area of the discipline and its organic centre of gravity, the higher the possibility of misinterpretation is. Music *can* communicate feelings and it *can* communicate theories. The former is closer to its centre of gravity; the latter is very remote from it and can be related to music rather as a hypothetical postmodern entertainment. But both options are possible.[94] Law can address financial transactions and human dreams: the former are much closer to its natural centre of gravity than the latter, but both scenarios are hypothetically possible. Then again, when a music masterpiece is performed, the process is actualised as a *musical* performance. Many other real *sub*-acts are taking place simultaneously (physics – resonance of musical instruments; economics – musicians are paid for their performance; public safety – fire alarm in the hall is working; law – the piece is an object of intellectual property; subjective rivalry – between different violinists and ad infinitum). Yet all these simultaneous processes are subordinated to the main actual narrative of music – be it spiritual, aesthetic, mechanical, entertaining – and their objective existence and moral legitimacy do not

---

90 Ernest J. Weinrib, 'Legal Formalism: On the Immanent Rationality of Law', The Yale Law Journal, Vol. 97, No. 6, 1988, p. 972.

91 Avery W. Katz, 'Positivism and the Separation of Law and Economics', Michigan Law Review, Vol. 94, No. 7, 1996, p. 2236: '[E]conomists and lawyers get into trouble applying ordinary economic methodology to law without understanding its contextual presuppositions'.

92 Jack M. Balkin, 'Interdisciplinarity as Colonisation', Washington and Lee Law Review, Vol. 53, No. 3, 1995, p. 960.

93 Harold D. Lasswell and Abraham Kaplan, *Power and Society: A Framework for Political Inquiry*, Yale University Press, New Haven, 1950, p. 97.

94 Peter J. Hammer, 'Free Speech and the "Acid Bath": An Evaluation and Critique of Judge Richard Posner's Economic Interpretation of the First Amendment', Michigan Law Review, Vol. 87, No. 2, 1988, p.499: '[T]here are few significant legal issues that have not been subject to economic interpretation. Now, even the "free-speech icon" has been subjected to the "acid bath of economics"'.

entail their primacy, since the centre of gravity of the event is musical. One of the central questions of the theory of antitrust is how close or remote is the centre of gravity of economics in its attempts to explain the nature of social relationships.[95] Although the *quantifiability* element is not considered as an absolute by all economists,[96] the natural trend in economics shifts the discipline towards quantifiable elements.

The natural trend of the epistemic expansion of economics to the cognitive area of law can be compared with the place of mathematical analysis in economics itself,[97] which gradually substituted the philosophical narrative that dominated in the classical economics.[98] These processes are natural and they are encoded in every discipline. The ability of economics to assist legal reasoning rather than govern it has been recognised by many lawyers.[99] Certain epistemic concerns about the external application of economics to other social disciplines were expressed, however, by some economists even before the start of the law and economics movement.[100] The opposite influence of law as a discipline on economics

---

95 Rudolph J. Peritz, 'A Counter-History of Antitrust Law', Duke Law Journal, Vol. 39, No. 2, 1990, p. 265: '[B]ecause the economic logic of price theory has persuaded many of us to accept its claims of unrivalled precision and logical structure, we presume (or fear) that arguments founded in social values but not reflected in the current antitrust discourse of economics . . . simply cannot be adjudicated in a structured way'.

96 Oliver Budzinski, 'Modern Industrial Economics and Competition Policy: Open Problems and Possible Limits', IME Working Paper, No. 93/09, 2009, p. 17: '[L]acking ability to make a phenomenon mathematically feasible or to quantify the respective variables does not mean that these effects carry less importance for real-world welfare'.

97 Ioannis Lianos, 'Lost In Translation? Towards a Theory of Economic Transplants', Current Legal Problems, Vol. 62, No. 1, 2009, p. 353: 'Mathematics becomes the *reine Sprache* of economics . . . [It] ensures precision and openness to scrutiny for logical errors. It is *par essence* a universalistic language. . . . It is allegedly ideology free'.

98 Peter J. Boettke, 'The Use and Abuse of the History of Economic Thought within the Austrian School of Economics', History of Political Economy, Vol. 34, No. 2, 2002, p. 338.

99 Lawrence A. Sullivan, *Handbook of the Law of Antitrust*, West Publishing, St. Paul, 1977, p. 9: 'The great thing is to understand the power of economics and its potential, but also its limits – to draw upon it not as one who borrows, or imposes, but as one possessing a tool; to use it selectively, both wisely and well'.

100 John N. Keynes, *The Scope and Method of Political Economy*, Macmillan and Co., London, 1897, p. 6: '[E]conomic science deals with phenomena that are more complex and less uniform than those with which the natural sciences are concerned; and its conclusions, except in their most abstract form, lack both the certainty and the universality that pertain to physical laws'.

has been rather marginal. Balkin explains this by the fact that law in some sense 'is less academic discipline than a professional discipline . . ., skill oriented profession . . . [lacking] robust academic methodology'.[101] This is partially true if compared with history or, to a lesser extent, political science, with their rich apparatus and methodological scrutiny. It is not so obvious though in the case of economics, which is not only a theoretical, but also an applied discipline. Another reason for this disproportion may be related to the fact that, for a long time, law held a decision-making 'monopoly' in areas like antitrust and did not therefore need to expand its disciplinary boundaries. Balkin's (and Levinson's) more moderate view in this respect appears to be perhaps more accurate.[102] Nowadays the dominance of law in the sphere of competition has been successfully challenged by economics and these disciplines start *competing* for the position of main methodological narrative on antitrust.

A similar situation may occur also *within* a discipline when (i) one dominant perception substitutes another (a paradigm shift),[103] replacing the old meaning of the phenomenon by a novel understanding of it; (ii) between different subsystems of the same discipline[104] legal theoretical aspects of which are explored by Teubner as a phenomenon of 'relative autonomy of legal fields';[105] or (iii) even when different concepts use identical terms.[106] The continuity of the scientific knowledge in this case does

---

101 Jack M. Balkin, 'Interdisciplinarity as Colonisation', Washington and Lee Law Review, Vol. 53, No. 3, 1995, p. 964.

102 Jack M. Balkin and Sanford V. Levinson, 'Law and the Humanities: An Uneasy Relationship', Yale Journal of Law & the Humanities, Vol. 18, No. 2, 2006, p. 173: 'Although it is impossible to understand contemporary legal theory without recognizing its strongly interdisciplinary character, law has a most curious relationship to interdisciplinarity. Law seems endlessly to poach upon other disciplines and absorb many of their insights while still remaining law. Conversely, many disciplines have tried to invade and colonize law over the years, yet the legal academy still continues to produce legal scholarship that asks recognizably traditional sorts of legal questions'.

103 Thomas S. Kuhn, *The Structure of Scientific Revolution*, University of Chicago Press, 1962.

104 Duncan Kennedy, 'Legal Formality', The Journal of Legal Studies, Vol. 2, No. 2, 1973, p. 356: '[T]heories tend to try to expand their scope to cover as much of reality as possible. . . . [T]he theory assimilates each of the concepts without any revision of the fundamental postulate'.

105 Günther Teubner, '"And God Laughed . . ." Indeterminacy, Self-Reference and Paradox in Law', German Law Journal, Vol. 12, No. 1, 2011, p. 400.

106 Roscoe Pound, 'The Theory of Judicial Decision I. The Materials of Judicial Decision', Harvard Law Review, Vol. 36, No. 6, 1923, p. 643: 'As one reads the voluminous literature upon . . . [a legal] subject he soon feels that the disputants are speaking of different things, although calling them by one name. . . .

not allow the overthrown concepts to be completely eliminated, creating a situation of terminological homonymy, where different interpretations of the same phenomenon coexist and influence each other. The *intra*disciplinary awareness of such coexistence is significantly higher than in the *inter*disciplinary context, since all changes inside the discipline tend to be evolutionary and gradual, which is not always the case in *inter*disciplinary research. The enthusiasm and the natural inclination to dominate it counterparts that every discipline implicitly contains are often supplemented by the lack of awareness of genuinely useful elements which these counterparts possess. The dominant modernist trend towards specification and pragmatism leads to the deepening of the disciplinary silos, which contributes to the ignorance of how the neighbouring disciplines address a set of similar problems with very relevant potential implications for each other. The trend of expansion and the trend of ignorance are not mutually exclusive: the former reflects the deductive approach, while the latter is inductive. Whereas the former leads to big universalised theories, the latter is often ignored as unimportant, though it is the latter which brings the most fruitful elements to the interdisciplinary research.

The generic term 'interdisciplinarity' encompasses different but closely related sorts of communications between the disciplines, which, from a dynamic perspective, can be seen as stages. The situation where the disciplines do not abandon their apparatus, but merely cooperate on an equal footing, is known as *multidisciplinarity*. It is characterised by the complementarity of both disciplines. If, on the methodological level, different disciplines can maintain their self-referential nature, in practice the elements of multidisciplinarity are ubiquitously present, as pure *intra*-disciplinarity in the applied sense of the term can be safeguarded only hypothetically. Closer connection (*interdisciplinarity sensu stricto*) occurs when the disciplines share some apparatus, but are concentrated on the subject matter, revealing new components that are hardly possible to discover or explore *intra*disciplinarily. The next stage (*cross-disciplinarity*) reflects the situation where different disciplines share significant parts of their methodology, address the same area of knowledge, and influence each other's epistemology. The process is usually characterised by shared competences between the disciplines, where the substantive issues of one discipline are addressed by the methodology of the other (e.g. the economics of climate change or the economics of law; commonly known as law

---

All take for granted that they are talking about the same thing; that there is a single definite something called "the law" to be reached and apprehended by some one absolute method'.

and economics, while in fact the area is an evaluation of law from the perspective of economic reasoning). The last integrative stage of the process is *transdisciplinarity*, where the subjects of different related disciplines abandon their limits and can be treated beyond the apparatus of each. In spite of the obvious vagueness and relativity of the above definitions, they can be used sporadically to reflect the relations between the disciplines. More broadly, all these scenarios can be covered by the generic term *interdisciplinarity*.

The methodological epistemic differences between the disciplines should receive proper theoretical treatment. Otherwise homonymy can cause misunderstandings[107] and unnecessary tensions between different systems of knowledge. Often this situation leads to the *transplants* of some significant concepts peculiar to a dominant discipline into another, which allegedly *has to* be interpreted.[108] One of the main externalities of such *inter*disciplinarity is an intuitive perception of generated knowledge as being by definition superior and more advanced than *intra*disciplinary results. This vision perceives interdisciplinarity as an evolutionary step in science which negates the purism of old traditional disciplines. Another approach is to consider the relationships between the disciplines in zero-sum game terms and perceive the interdisciplinary scholar as 'no longer simply a person seeking after the truth . . .. Rather she is part of the vanguard of disciplinary colonisation'.[109] Interdisciplinarity may be very fruitful in a limited field, but it should not negate the narratives of traditional disciplines, which remain autopoietic, as music and poetry did when the art of singing was developed. On the one hand law stays fully autopoietic, and remains, following Luhmann, the product of its own operation, holding 'dynamic stability and operational closure'.[110] On the other hand, '[o]nly under the conditions of cognitive openness to the environment . . . can the legal system take measures to deparadoxicalize its self-reference and,

---

[107] John J. Flynn, 'The Misuse of Economic Analysis in Antitrust Litigation', Southwestern University Law Review, Vol. 12, No. 2, 1980, pp. 341–342: 'Economic theorising, unaware of its own assumptions and prejudices, is fraught with grave dangers for the law. . . . Operating with that school's hypothesis in a deductive fashion . . . carries with it the school's prejudices. . . . It outlaws competing value choices that are involved in the dispute but are not in conformity with the premises of the model'.

[108] Ioannis Lianos, 'Lost In Translation? Towards a Theory of Economic Transplants', Current Legal Problems, Vol. 62, No. 1, 2009, p. 349.

[109] Jack M. Balkin, 'Interdisciplinarity as Colonisation', Washington and Lee Law Review, Vol. 53, No. 3, 1995, p. 961.

[110] Niklas Luhmann, 'Deconstruction as Second-Order Observing', New Literary History, Vol. 24, No. 4, 1993, p. 771.

therefore, ensure connectivity for further operations'.[111] The dilemmatic nature of interdisciplinarity in law reveals its simultaneous benefits and dangers. This controversy has been captured in 'The Ordo Manifesto': on the one hand, '[c]omplaints about the specialisation of the individual sciences are levelled at the sciences of yesteryear . . .; sciences no longer stand apart from one another . . . and [t]he division of the humanities into political, economic, intellectual, ecclesiastical and art history has proved to be untenable',[112] while on the other hand the authors warn against the conceptual *merger* of different disciplines, suggesting that each 'must preserve its individuality if it is to achieve anything'.[113]

The homonymy of values, caused inter alia by their interdisciplinary analysis, plays an important role in the balancing process. Homonymy is a common situation for different systems. For example, legislation has different connotations in legal and political discourses.[114] Similarly, the phenomenon of competition has several meanings, some of which are mutually exclusive. The notion of competition in theoretical equilibrium economics reflects the purely hypothetical situation of final stability and coherence between supply and demand. This stage should be neither achieved nor protected; it is considered as a mere analytical instrument and not as a social goal. In the more applied aspects of the same discipline, competition is considered as an instrumental value which can be protected if it contributes to the increase of other important values. Welfare economics, for instance, perceives competition as a means and consumer welfare as *the* end.[115] Other economic approaches have different definitions of competition; they either consider it as a redundant and harmful

---

[111] Marcelo Neves, 'From the Autopoiesis to the Allopoiesis of Law', Journal of Law and Society, Vol. 28, No. 2, 2001, p. 251.

[112] Franz Böhm, Walter Eucken and Hans Grossmann-Doerth, 'The Ordo Manifesto of 1936', in Alan T. Peacock and Hans Willgerodt (eds.), *Germany's Social Market Economy: Origins and Evolution*, Macmillan, London, 1989, p. 25.

[113] ibid.

[114] Richard Nobles and David Schiff, 'Introduction' in Niklas Luhmann, *Law as Social System*, Oxford University Press, Oxford, 2004, pp. 8–9: 'Law will recognise a statute, and will conceptualise the meaning of that statute by reference to interpretative practices which it calls "the intention of parliament". These interpretative practices . . . are not political communications. By contrast the political system can connect a statute to its own communications in quite different ways. It can be described as the "will of the people". . . . These political communications do not dictate, or replicate the legal communications . . .'.

[115] John Vickers, 'Competition is for Consumers', A Speech to the Social Market Foundation, 21.02.2002 http://www.oft.gov.uk/shared_oft/speeches/spe0102.pdf, accessed on 4 August 2010, p. 1: 'Competition is increasingly being recognised as a core consumer issue'.

externality (planned economies) or an economic end in its own right (right libertarians). More humanistic disciplines can perceive competition as the right of individuals to participate in market interactions, as a significant collective interest which should be protected for its own sake inasmuch as it reflects the essence of liberal democracy or as a natural selection process. These conflicting visions of the concept do not have much in common, although all of them refer to the homonym *competition*, giving the impression of their mutual relevance.[116] They may be relevant, indeed, inasmuch as everything may depend on anything else.[117] Yet, beyond this rather general claim, their relevance becomes of a consequential nature: due to homonymy the independent concepts are treated and perceived as correlative, which creates certain theoretical connections between them. Studying the different perceptions of competition can in itself be a fruitful exercise, but it is more of an *explanandum* than an *explanans* and can be performed by separating the different phenomena from the identical phonetic form and distinctive features rather than by an uncritical interchangeable use of them depending on the context and specific interests of the decision-makers.

5.2.4 Natural Conflict of Values

Apart from epistemological discrepancies in the interpretation of different values, they also collide conceptually. No value can be protected fully without other values being sacrificed or partially excluded.[118] Tensions between the different values are irresolvable. Vickers, for instance, observes that 'tension between competition principles and property right principles . . .

---

[116] Christian Kirchner, 'Goals of Antitrust and Competition Law Revisited' in Dieter Schmidtchen, Max Albert and Stefan Voigt (eds.), *The More Economic Approach to European Competition Law*, Mohr Siebeck, Tübingen, 2007, p. 8: 'In economic theory competition and competition law are subject matters of industrial organisation. . . . But from a legal perspective goals of economic competition law are a subject matter of law. Economic and legal approaches are structurally different'.

[117] Walter Eucken, 'Die Wettbewerbsordnung und ihre Verwirklichung', Jahrbuch für die Ordnung von Wirtschaft und Gesellschaft, Vol. 2, 1949, cited in Christian Ahlborn, Carsten Grave (trans.), Walter Eucken, 'The Competitive Order and its Implementation', Competition Policy International, Vol. 2, No. 2, 2006, p. 231: 'Because of their general interdependence, every single economic policy intervention affects the economic process as a whole'.

[118] John Rawls, *Political Liberalism*, Columbia University Press, New York, 2005, p. xxvi: 'Political liberalism starts taking to heart the absolute depth of that irreconcilable latent conflict [of moral values]'.

are economic policy questions of the first order of importance'.[119] In real political life no value and no right can be fully supported, even if on the constitutional level they are declared to be absolute.[120] Values 'clash with each other . . . because they reflect the complexity of human experience'.[121] Trade-offs are unavoidable and any claim of exclusivity and absolute priority should be perceived as an internal attempt of a value to reach the highest plausible regulatory attention and the most favourable treatment. The competitive process in this respect inevitably collides with other economic values.[122] Often this discrepancy occurs between the value of competition and those societal interests which it is traditionally supposed to protect. For example, competition can sometimes be an obstacle to industrial growth or consumer welfare, but this does not mean that it is automatically vicious or unworthy of legal protection.

The tendency to protect only those values that are on average more important than the others (or as Kelsen puts it, 'social value judgements' customarily characterised with the catch-phrases 'welfare of the people', 'public interest', 'progress' and the like)[123] is epistemologically mistaken if not politically harmful. It reflects the intuitive desire of decision-makers to abandon the necessity of making hard choices and to circumscribe the decision-making process by clear-cut unambiguous rules, thereby creating an illusion of hierarchy. It might be helpful in terms of the efficient allocation of regulatory resources, but it does not reflect the interests of values that cannot be as easily converted into the most common regulatory currencies (welfare, prosperity, cohesion). The competitive process often becomes a victim of this natural optimisation (simplification) trend: inasmuch as it is difficult to measure, its societal value is either ignored or

---

119 John Vickers, 'Competition Policy and Property Rights', The Economic Journal, Vol. 120, No. 5, 2010, p. 376.

120 Aharon Barak, *The Judge in a Democracy*, Princeton University Press, Princeton, 2006, pp. 296–297: 'Any balance that is struck between security and freedom will impose certain limitations on both. . . . [T]he balance between security and freedom does not reflect the lack of a clear position. On the contrary, the proper balance is the result of a clear position'.

121 Aharon Barak, *Purposive Interpretation in Law*, Princeton University Press, Princeton, 2005, p. 176.

122 Christian Kirchner, 'Goals of Antitrust and Competition Law Revisited' in Dieter Schmidtchen, Max Albert and Stefan Voigt (eds.), *The More Economic Approach to European Competition Law*, Mohr Siebeck, Tübingen, 2007, pp. 12–13: '[C]ompetition policy is competing with other policies which may pursue conflicting ends, e.g. agricultural policy, industrial policy, environmental policy'.

123 Hans Kelsen, 'On the Theory of Interpretation', Legal Studies, Vol. 10, No. 2, 1990, p. 131.

substituted by more tangible simple benchmarks.[124] Liberal democracy embraces the idea that every value can claim protection and regulatory attention; otherwise, the rights of minorities would never be supported or taken into account. In claiming regulatory protection, non-explicitly important values rely not only on substantive arguments in their favour, but also on the argument of freedom and individual autonomy. In so doing, they seek to defend their self-identity using these universal principles as proxies at the level of balancing.

In this context, it is incorrect to juxtapose utilitarian, welfare-oriented values to deontological, rights-based values. For balancing purposes, all values contain deontological elements at the internal level of self-identification, as well as utilitarian elements at the external level of the regulatory choices. Then, wealth maximisation can be considered as an absolute value at the internal level; while externally it will be relativised and measured up against other societal values. Similarly, the purely deontological value of same-sex marriage will be treated as self-sufficient internally, but should be measured up externally. In order to ensure the commensurability of utilitarian values (like those which have easily calculable attributes) and deontological values (which are of the absolute nature and cannot be explained in other ways than self-referential), the latter should operationalise the concept of freedom and argue their case by emphasising the societal significance of diversity, liberty and human self-determination. It is the only avenue open for the values of liberal democracy to be balanced against others. However, this trade-off can be accepted by the utilitarian values only under the condition that deontological values abandon their *external* claim for exclusivity and absolute significance. They should be ready to compete with utilitarian values, which will in turn recognise some regulatory significance to absolute, non-transferable and non-convertible values. This recognition essentially reflects the dialectics of in-/commensurability described above, where each and every value is simultaneously absolute and relative, unique and comparable, calculable and immeasurable.

---

124 John J. Flynn, 'Legal Reasoning, Antitrust Policy and the Social "Science" of Economics', Antitrust Bulletin, Vol. 33, No. 4, 1988, p. 724: 'A minor premise consisting of only those "facts" the major premise permits to be "facts" is then put forward without regard to the facts of the dispute and the circumstances of the case before the court'.

5.2.5 Scarcity of Regulatory Choices

Another important aspect of the methodological autopoiesis of values is related to the application of this principle at the public regulatory level. The decision-making process is always predetermined by conflicting interests. If the *optimal* regulatory solution is considered as 100 per cent consisting of 100 regulatory units, the total amount of *reasonable* and *legitimate* solutions is 1,000 regulatory units, which entails that only 10 per cent of the reasonable, sound merits of the values can be technically protected or otherwise supported by the regulator. The regulatory units reflect the choices of the decision-makers. These choices are *external* to the values themselves. Every value has its own, *internal* (value-centric) vision of how important it is in comparison with others. This is measured by *utils* – a measure of the inherent importance of a value. The relations between the regulatory units and utils are impossible to measure *objectively*, and therefore every decision-making process holds strong elements of regulatory discretion. The task of every value is to transform its internal importance measured by utils which (unlike regulatory units) are purely value-centric and not necessarily convertible into regulatory units ('the currency' of decision-making). While the amount of preferred, selected and supported values constitutes 100 regulatory units (100 per cent optimality), the amount of reasonable, legitimate and worth being protected values is 1,000 regulatory units, the total amount of support which every value claims from the regulator (based on the internal utils which every value holds and offers in each case) is 10,000 regulatory units. And the total amount of all utils which every value internally holds is 100,000 utils. At the first, *decision-made* external level, the rate between the regulatory units and internal utils is 1 to 1. At the second, *decision-being-made* external level it is already 1 to 10. At the third *decision-should-be-made* internal level it is 1 to 100. At the fourth internal *decision-could-be-made* level it is 1 to 1,000. The trade-offs and compromises in prioritising one value over the other and a certain level of regulatory discretion are therefore unavoidable. This creates competition among the values. Economic theory has the more developed approach to the issue of measuring utility than other social sciences (the notions of cardinal and ordinal utilities inter alia), but any time the issue of quantification occurs, some subjective aspects of the value prevents the creation of a clear, predictable and homogeneous scale of values. Subsequently, they are measured like plausible presumptions rather than objective facts.

A similar process occurs at the individual level, when a person decides between different opportunities. By weighing the pros and cons of different options and by giving each of them a given amount of regulatory units the person makes a balancing act. Depending on the context the person may grant 70 units to reading a book and 30 units to listening to music. If the context changes the priorities may change as well. The choice itself is external to the value of reading and listening, which may contain different amount of utils in each case. The choice is made not between the two options only, but between many others as well (to meet friends, to watch a movie, to go for a walk). The decision-making chooses between different values which hold much more utils than the 100 units of his regulatory capacity. Furthermore, every choice allocation itself requires some time and resources which the person does not want to waste on making self-regulatory decisions. For this reason certain rules of thumb are naturally developed which do not include the least valuable alternatives (those which have less than 10 units – such as to go for community services or to write a letter to remote kinsmen). These are values as well, but they are usually ignored altogether. Furthermore the forgotten values often contain some irreplaceable (though not indispensable) elements, and even if they cannot be selected by the decision-maker, their presence on the regulatory agenda contributes to individual well-being. At the collective level this can be illustrated by the production of different forms of art: *rationally* no big producer should support art-house cinema (or only on an emotional, pro bono ground); on the contrary, he should invest in mainstream mediocrity blockbusters. Yet, art-house is generously supported by big studios, and not only for aesthetic or philanthropic purposes, but because in one out of a thousand cases the vanguard invents a new form which will be operationalised by the industry as a whole. Making an analogy with individual choices, the least important societal values (those worth less than 20 units) tend also to be ignored to avoid further difficulties in making choices. At the public level, however, this ignorance is misleading. Every value has its autopoietic sense and even the least attractive ones should be allowed to compete for prioritisation. The least attractive values often include those which have a delayed effect, are too technical or constitute only a component of broader universal values. The value of economic competition belongs to this group as well, since its significance is very difficult to articulate in each particular decision-making case. But even if it is usually outweighed by the value of consumer welfare or industrial growth, it still should be respected and analysed at the internal, autopoietic level. The internal and external levels are not under direct correlation. At a societal level a proof of the arguable *uselessness* (even if proved) or marginal significance of this value is not sufficient. While at the individual level the imaginary threshold of units which a value should possess in order to be taken into consideration is 20, at the level of public regulation it is significantly lower – say, five units; for hypothetical considerations (e.g.

science, political analysis, or brainstorming sessions) it would constitute only one unit. In other words, regardless of its usefulness in each particular case, every value should receive attention and proper (even if hypothetical) treatment. Whereas individuals engage in two types of reasoning: balanced (when the alternative x is > 20) and categorical (when an alternative x is < 20 units); reasonable public decision-makers would have a much lower balancing threshold (when x > 10 units) whereas hypothetical considerations tolerate every x > 0 situation. In this respect, the process of public decision-making is much closer to the hypothetical extreme than to the individual one. This is another way of addressing the implied hierarchy of values which suggests that 'I do not go to the movies when I have a class, and there is no balancing taking place in this case'.[125] The balancing actually does take place in this case, but since the priority of class over the cinema has reached the bifurcation point after which no explicit weighing is performed, the decision is made automatically – otherwise literarily every step would be made after making an explicit decision. But neither *automaticity* nor Nozick's notion of 'side constraints',[126] which entails that certain rules should be followed categorically without questioning their efficiency (like the rules of the game), leads to the negation of balancing. The lack of explicit deliberation and weighing in this case does not mean that some type of balancing did not occur; after all, if the quality of the movie were to be better than announced or the topic of the class to change, the considerations would be more explicit and the balancing act more visible. Balancing does occur (while deciding between two alternatives) or did occur before the act (if selecting *the right* way).

Prima facie, Rawls's idea of 'lexical order'[127] (putting the things alphabetically which implies that every Z-word follows Y-words) solves the conundrum of balancing – but it only reflects the *semantic*, the *ontology* of deontological incommensurability of values: *if* they are structured in this lexical order. But they are not, or at least the stability of such taxonomy is being constantly challenged by inferior values, seeking their promotion from Z to Y and eventually to A. Every decision-making process is predetermined by the scarcity of regulatory resources and the inevitability of making hard choices. This implies that no decision can fully reflect the internal essence of a value and that it will, on the contrary, always

[125] Stavros Tsakyrakis, 'Proportionality: An Assault on Human Rights?', International Journal of Constitutional Law, Vol. 7, No. 3, 2009, p. 473.

[126] Robert Nozick, *Anarchy, State, and Utopia*, Basic Books, New York, 1974, pp. 28–33.

[127] John Rawls, *A Theory of Justice*, Harvard University Press, Cambridge, Massachusetts, 1999, pp. 37–39.

abandon some essential elements of even the most favourably treated values, when compared with their internal self-perception.[128] This leads to the relativisation of the absoluteness of each value, but enables each of them to be pursued at the internal level as unique and absolute. Whereas absoluteness is not achievable for any value, it can be used as a cognitive tool for epistemological purposes with no reference to the outside context. The necessity of making hard choices should be perceived by each value as an inevitable component of any regulatory system. This enables them to create their own strategies seeking regulatory preferences persuading the decision-maker of the importance of the relevant value (deontological, internal approach) and demonstrating how the value will bring benefits to other important societal values (utilitarian, external stage). At the first stage the value strives to promote its own conceptual significance, while at the second stage its task is to show how its protection can be reconciled with the operability of the regulatory system as a whole. The balancing act therefore can be seen as a constant competition between different values which either individually or in alliances are constantly trying to convince the decision-maker of their significance. This explains the ad hoc nature of the balancing act, whose outcome cannot be either predetermined or predicted in advance,[129] since it significantly depends on the skilfulness of each influence-group in presenting their case to the regulator in the most attractive fashion in a given set of circumstances.

5.3 PRECONDITIONS OF THE DECISION-MAKING PROCESS

The task of this section is to assess the different preconditions of balancing from the perspective of the regulators and the representatives of the relevant values. It addresses the following issues: (1) bounded arbitrariness of a decision-maker; (2) kaleidoscopic constellation of values; (3) rock-paper-scissors effect; (4) communication between decision-makers and influence groups; (5) the value of competition and communicative problems.

---

128 Jacob Viner, 'The Short View and the Long in Economic Policy', The American Economic Review, Vol. 30, No. 1, 1940, p. 2: 'The economist conditioned to the purity of abstract thought is liable to be unreasonable in his refusal to recognize that the official, in choosing his time for action and his manner and degree of action, must give regard to their [broader] impact'.

129 Oliver Budzinski, 'Modern Industrial Economics and Competition Policy: Open Problems and Possible Limits', IME Working Paper, No. 93/09, 2009, p. 18: '[C]ompetition policy must inevitably deal with uncertainty'.

(1) The term 'bounded arbitrariness' reflects the idea that any decision should be made arbitrarily. The very semantic of the word *decision* entails it. The term *bounded* implies that arbitrariness is preconditioned by several institutional factors, which prevent the adoption of purely subjective and/or irrational decisions. (2) The decision-maker, while trying to make a proper regulatory choice encounters a kaleidoscopic constellation of values, while neither the quality of the values at stake nor their quantity and scope is known in advance with sufficient precision. This implies that every prescriptive hierarchy of values should be treated as a relative rather than a categorical requirement and that attention should be paid to the dynamism of the regulated situation. (3) The rock-paper-scissors effect is the ability of value A to outweigh value B, while being at the same time outweighed by value C, which in turn is outweighed by value B and ad infinitum. This is another feature of the volatile nature of the values that influence the decision-making process. (4) Every regulatory decision is made under the influence of representatives of those values. The task of this section is to model the communicative process between the values and regulators in order to emphasise the mechanisms ruling such interactions and the factors which can influence the process. (5) Communication between values and decision-makers can run properly only if the value itself is not internally considered as a means, but rather as an end in itself. This methodological requirement is a *conditio sine qua non*. The perspective from which the competitive process is perceived merely as an instrument to increase welfare significantly diminishes the ability of competition to communicate with decision-makers. This situation is critically explored in this subsection before analysing the alternative scenario, where the competitive process is taken as an end in itself.

5.3.1 Bounded Arbitrariness of Decision-makers

The bounded arbitrariness of decision-makers ('bounded objectivity' in Fiss's terms)[130] reflects the institutional aspects of balancing.[131] Arbitrariness is closely tied to the unavoidable relativity of values, the possibility of different interpretations and the impossibility to find a final optimum between them. In consequence, as suggested by Kelsen, some

---

130 Owen M. Fiss, 'Objectivity and Interpretation', Stanford Law Review, Vol. 34, No. 4, 1982, p. 745.

131 Fred H. Blum, 'Max Weber's Postulate of "Freedom" from Value Judgments', The American Journal of Sociology, Vol. 50, No. 1, 1944, p. 46: '[W]here human affairs are concerned, there can never be an objectivity in the sense of neutrality – even for a scientist'.

subjective judgements of value are necessary, since the difference of perceptions 'between the decision of one who considers personal freedom the highest good, and of one for whom the equality of all men is rated higher than freedom'[132] is objectively irreconcilable. According to Willoughby, 'no absolute or a priori principle can be established regarding the proper sphere of social or political control, but that in every case conditions of fact should govern'.[133] The societal significance of values is volatile; the decision-making process therefore cannot be determined ex ante, as even the most flexible hierarchical system cannot reflect the perpetual changes in the 'currency rate' of values. According to Robins, 'valuation is a subjective process. We cannot observe valuation. It is therefore out of place in a scientific explanation.'[134] As Viner points out, the decisions are usually 'reached only by vague and imperfectly communicable processes of thought',[135] and Aleinikoff suggests that '[i]n almost all conflicts, especially those that make their way into a legal system, there is something to be said in favour of two or more outcomes'.[136] This explains Schmitt's positive (not normative) claim that '[t]he decision on the exception is a decision in the true sense of the word'.[137] For Hart 'in applying legal rules, someone must take the responsibility of deciding that words do or do not cover some case in hand with all the practical consequences involved in this decision'.[138] Legal norms for him are characterised by their 'open texture'.[139] The cognitive ability of decision-makers to allocate relative weight to competing interests has been contested in the literature.[140] In addition, the more flexible the system becomes, the less imperative it

---

132 Hans Kelsen, 'The Pure Theory of Law and Analytical Jurisprudence', Harvard Law Review, Vol. 55, No. 1, 1941, p. 45.

133 Westel W. Willoughby, 'The Ethics of the Competitive Process', The American Journal of Sociology, Vol. 6, No. 2, 1900, p. 145.

134 Lionel Robbins, *An Essay on the Nature and Significance of Economic Science*, Macmillan & Co, London, 1952, p. 87.

135 Jacob Viner, 'The Short View and the Long in Economic Policy', The American Economic Review, Vol. 30, No. 1, 1940, p. 2.

136 Alexander T. Aleinikoff, 'Constitutional Law in the Age of Balancing', The Yale Law Journal, Vol. 96, No. 5, 1987, p. 943.

137 Carl Schmitt, *Political Theology – Four Chapters on the Concept of Sovereignty*, The MIT Press, Cambridge, Massachusetts, 1985, p. 6.

138 Herbert L. A. Hart, 'Positivism and the Separation of Law and Morals', Harvard Law Review, Vol. 71, No. 4, 1958, p. 607.

139 Herbert L. A. Hart, *The Concept of Law*, Oxford University Press, Oxford, 1994, pp. 124–136.

140 Alec S. Sweet and Jud Mathews, 'Proportionality Balancing and Global Constitutionalism', Columbia Journal of Transnational Law, Vol. 47, No. 1, 2008, p. 96.

should be, allowing the decision-makers greater room for discretion. Günther places the problem of the indeterminacy of norms into a broader intellectual context.[141] Comparing the positions of Durkheim and Weber in this respect, he shows that the former acknowledges indeterminacy as a distinct feature of modern societies, as 'a phenomenon, which complemented the individual autonomy',[142] juxtaposing it with mechanical obedience. Weber regards the indeterminacy of *legal* rules as a sign of the decline of modern society. 'The greater the number of arbitrarily selected ideals and irrational valuations which find their way into law, the less predictable the application and enforcement of that law'.[143] Hence, Günther connects these two diametrical views to the problem of autonomy and arbitrariness. A significant role in the articulation of the problem of indeterminacy has been played by critical legal scholars. Kress, describing their legacy, shows that law 'is indeterminate to the extent that legal questions lack single right answers. In adjudication, law is indeterminate to the extent that authoritative legal materials and methods permit multiple outcomes to lawsuits'.[144] This implies that '[i]n almost every case, except the very plainest, it would be possible to decide the issue either way with reasonable legal justification',[145] or as Kelsen put it '[i]n terms of the positive law there is simply no method according to which only one of the several readings of a norm could be distinguished as "correct"'.[146] All these claims indirectly refer to the Kantian principle of antinomies,[147] which implies the existence of competing explanatory theories for any event.

---

141 Klaus Günther, 'The Pragmatic and Functional Indeterminacy of Law', German Law Journal, Vol. 12, No. 1, 2011.

142 ibid, p. 407: 'It is hardly compatible with the ideal of individual autonomy that a society only deploys such rules as prescribe every single action in every situation down to the last detail, until they could be applied just as unconsciously as the highway code'.

143 ibid.

144 Ken Kress, 'Legal Indeterminacy', California Law Review, Vol. 77, No. 2, 1989, p. 283.

145 Lord Macmillan, *Law and Other Things*, The University Press, Cambridge, 1937, p. 38.

146 Hans Kelsen, 'On the Theory of Interpretation', Legal Studies, Vol. 10, No. 2, 1990, p. 130.

147 Karl R. Popper, 'What is Dialectic?', Mind, Vol. 49, No. 196, 1940, p. 416: '[Kant argues that] the metaphysical principle of reasonableness or self-evidence does not lead unambiguously to one and only one result, to one and only one theory. Rather, it is always possible to argue, with similar apparent reasonableness, in favour of a number of different theories, and even of opposite theories'.

Yet, arbitrariness (or discretion) is not absolute either.[148] Every decision-maker is constrained by a set of significant boundaries that limit his discretion, and require him to take them into consideration while reaching decisions.[149] These institutional requirements prevent arbitrariness from becoming a purely voluntaristic activity. It also should be distinguished from the phonetically similar term *adhocracy*, which is a managerial technique, developed in opposition to *bureaucracy*.[150] The notion of bounded arbitrariness is a positive description of the decision-making process, while adhocracy is an intentional choice of certain regulatory principles. The main boundaries in this respect are the institutional design and procedural rules that regulate the decision-making process; the substantive rules and principles that define the regulatory ambit and societal importance of each value and their main predictable constellations; economic, political, social and cultural rationale of the decision; objectives of collective policies; customs; historical and cultural traditions; rules which establish political and legal responsibility for not achieving certain goals or not protecting certain interests satisfactorily; doctrinal and practical influence from academia and interest groups; electoral accountability and coherence with ideological premises upon which the elected or appointed decision-makers regulates the relevant area. These factors, and the many other elements (like 'the Decisionmaker's experiences; i.e. his or her relationship to the community as part of the decisionmaking process')[151] influencing the decision-making process, are added up to the regulatory culture.[152] The culture is the common institutional denominator, or as Fish puts it 'the cultural assumptions within which both texts and contexts take shape for situated agents'.[153] They can be compared to

148 Owen M. Fiss, 'Objectivity and Interpretation', Stanford Law Review, Vol. 34, No. 4, 1982, p. 739: 'Interpretation, whether it be in the law or literary domains, is neither a wholly discretionary nor a wholly mechanical activity'.

149 Ronald M. Dworkin, 'The Model of Rules', The University of Chicago Law Review, Vol. 35, No. 1, 1967, p. 32: 'Discretion, like the hole in a doughnut, does not exist except as an area left open by a surrounding belt of restriction'.

150 Robert H. Waterman, *Adhocracy*, W. W. Norton & Company, New York, 1993.

151 Gerald P. Moran, 'A Radical Theory of Jurisprudence: The Decisionmaker as the Source of Law – The Ohio Supreme Court's Adoption of the Spendthrift Trust Doctrine as a Model', Akron Law Review, Vol. 30, No. 3, 1997, p. 398.

152 Lawrence M. Friedman, 'Legal Culture and Social Development', Law & Society Review, Vol. 4, No. 1, 1969, p. 34: '[The cultural elements of legal system are] the values and attitudes which bind the system together'.

153 Stanley Fish, 'Don't Know Much about the Middle Ages: Posner on Law and Literature', The Yale Law Journal, Vol. 97, No. 5, 1988, p. 783.

Alexy's 'general practical discourse',[154] or Barak's 'legal tradition'[155] in which interpretation occurs.

The influence of each institutional boundary and its particular scope depends on the circumstances of each case, but cumulatively they establish the regulatory framework that enables the decision-maker to undertake the balancing exercise in a way which corresponds to the expectations of the community. The term itself is coined by analogy with the notion of 'bounded rationality' ('limited cognitive competence')[156] as developed in particular in behavioural economics. It reflects the specificity of consumer choice, which while being rational is to a certain extent predetermined by the natural limits of complex knowledge, irrational preferences and limited information about the product. This recognition of their limits helps to continue operation within traditional rational-agent models, while at the same time taking into account the often unquantifiable specificities of the decision-making process. The significance of bounded arbitrariness (discretion) has been emphasised by Dabbah,[157] who does not reduce it to solely authorised competence of antitrust authorities, revealing the complex nature of the phenomenon in the theory of decision-making.

5.3.2 Kaleidoscopic Constellation of Values

Values, interests and rights are the main objects of economics, politics and law respectively. At the internal level they are incommensurable. At the external level they commensurate, translating their content into the relevant language. Free competition, for example, has its economic, political and legal rationales – depending on the perspective from which it is assessed.[158] This also applies to all other public values. It is the reason

---

154 Robert Alexy, 'The Special Case Thesis', Ratio Juris, Vol. 12, No. 4, 1999, p. 378: 'The general practical discourse is, in short, a discourse which combines the standpoints of expediency or utility, of value or identity, and of morality or justice. This combination, however, is not a mere addition. There exist both, a priory order and a relation of permeation between the suitable, the good and the just'.

155 Aharon Barak, *Purposive Interpretation in Law*, Princeton University Press, Princeton, 2005, p. 39.

156 Oliver E. Williamson, 'Calculativeness, Trust, and Economic Organization', Journal of Law and Economics, Vol. 36, No. 1, 1993, p. 458.

157 Maher M. Dabbah, *The Internationalisation of Antitrust Policy*, Cambridge University Press, Cambridge, 2003, pp. 70–87.

158 David J. Gerber, 'Constitutionalizing the Economy: German Neo-Liberalism, Competition Law and the "New" Europe', The American Journal of Comparative Law, Vol. 42, No. 1, 1994, p. 45: 'For the Ordoliberals [*the*

why liberal democracies protect so many values.[159] The kaleidoscope effect is another important condition that predetermines the decision-making process.[160] Its main postulate is that values are never considered by regulators separately. Every time they are explored in a connection with one another. Conversely, they are explored in connection with one another and they appear each and every time in different proportions, scales and compositions.[161] 'New situations arise – new combinations of old circumstances, or new moral and political sensibilities'.[162] As Jevons observes, a 'minute difference of quality in a commodity may . . . give rise to preference, and cause the ratio of exchange to differ'.[163] Each regulatory situation requires the decision-maker to make an individual assessment.[164] Eucken argues that '[t]he interconnections in the economic mechanism make it necessary to see every act of economic policy in the context of the whole economic process'.[165] The rate of each value is impossible to predict ex ante. It is a 'market' with very high volatility. In order to be prioritised, different values often create stable or situational alliances, which

---

Ordnungspolitik] meant that economic knowledge had to be translated into normative language'.

159 Robert Alexy, *A Theory of Constitutional Rights*, Oxford University Press, Oxford, 2002, p. 65.

160 Ian S. Forrester, 'Competition Policy Objectives', Panel Discussion, in Claus-Dieter Ehlermann and Laraine L. Laudati (eds.), *The Objectives of Competition Policy*, European Competition Law Annual 1997, Hart Publishing, Oxford, 1998, p. 16: 'It is very important to acknowledge that when law is applied, it will not be done in a scientific or universally predictable manner. It is unlike medical science or nuclear physics, because it is very highly arguable. So much depends on how the kaleidoscope is shaken'.

161 Stanley Fish, 'Don't Know Much about the Middle Ages: Posner on Law and Literature', The Yale Law Journal, Vol. 97, No. 5, 1988, p. 785: 'All shapes are interpretively produced, and since the conditions of interpretation are themselves unstable – the possibility of seeing something in a "new light", and therefore of seeing a new something, is ever and unpredictably present – the shapes that seem perspicuous to us now may not seem so or may seem differently so tomorrow'.

162 Jeremy Waldron, 'Fake Incommensurability: A Response to Professor Schauer', Hastings Law Journal, Vol. 45, No. 4, 1994, p. 822.

163 William S. Jevons, *The Theory of Political Economy*, Macmillan and Co., London, 1888, p. 77.

164 Joseph Raz, 'Legal Principles and the Limits of Law', The Yale Law Journal, Vol. 81, No. 5, 1972, p. 829–830: 'We can attend to many problems only when they arise; we are unable to decide what to do solely on the basis of previously accepted rules'.

165 Walter Eucken, 'What Kind of Economic and Social System?', in Alan T. Peacock and Hans Willgerodt (eds.), *Germany's Social Market Economy: Origins and Evolution*, Macmillan, London, 1989, p. 29.

are equally impossible to predict ex ante. The composition of the value alliances often depends on tiny proportions and nuances, which become comprehensible only if perceived at a certain point of the assessment and in a particular context. It is the reason why the same set of values does not always create the same harmonious outcomes in different contexts. This usually happens with legal transplants, 'exported' democracies or multiculturalism: because they are delicate compositions of values, they may deliver expected results in one circumstance and totally fail in another. If one of the predetermining components of these value-cocktails deviates, even slightly so, quantitatively or qualitatively from the presumed parameters, the expected harmonious outcomes can metamorphose themselves into cacophony and failure.[166]

This situation is reflected in the principles of value pluralism. According to Berlin, '[w]e are doomed to choose, and every choice may entail an irreparable loss. The . . . realisation of . . . [some of equally absolute ends] must inevitably involve the sacrifice of others . . .. The necessity of choosing between absolute claims is then an inescapable characteristic of the human condition'.[167] In addition, the mutual conflicts inevitably present between values make these alliances very unstable. The ensuing unpredictability relativises and disables the effectiveness of categorical balancing algorithms. The representatives of each set of values try to create the most attractive vision of their alliances. The decision-makers assess them from a broader regulatory perspective, suggesting different constellations of regulatory choices which can overall optimise their decisions. However, the optimisation process becomes a value in itself, obtaining thereby ontological and epistemic features. Therefore, every meta-value (prosperity, wealth maximisation, consumer welfare, peace etc.) taken separately, loses its universality to become an object of dialectical compromises. The kaleidoscopic reality is operationalised inter alia by the economic approach of Industrial Organisation.[168]

The kaleidoscopic effect model can be perceived as a theory of parentheses.[169] Its main premise is expressed in the formula $(2 \times 2) + 2 \neq$

---

166 Aharon Barak, *The Judge in a Democracy*, Princeton University Press, Princeton, 2006, p. 167: 'Balancing reflects the relativity of the clashing values'.

167 Isaiah Berlin, 'On Value Pluralism', New York Review of Books, Vol. 45, No. 8, 1998.

168 Oliver Budzinski, 'Modern Industrial Economics and Competition Policy: Open Problems and Possible Limits', IME Working Paper, No. 93/09, 2009, p. 9: '[M]odern industrial economics consists of a kaleidoscopic myriad of models in all areas of anticompetitive arrangements and conduct'.

169 Oles Andriychuk, 'Can We Protect Competition Without Protecting Consumers?', The Competition Law Review, Vol. 6, No. 1, 2009, p. 83.

2 × (2 + 2), which implies that identical variables can produce different results depending on the scope of the parentheses that reflect the exact proportion of each value in each internal composition of the values as well as the external regulatory context that predetermines the decision. As Peczenik explains, '*x* may weigh more than *y* in isolation, but in a certain situation *z* can occur and reverse the order'.[170] This reveals that various compositions of the same ingredients have different qualitative characteristics, supporting the dialectical principle that 'parts of . . . any unity . . . have higher reflective potential than the unity itself'.[171] In economics, the kaleidoscopic constellation of values is also influenced by the subjectivist law of marginal utility, according to which no value has a monolithic nominal rate, but is rather rated in relation to individual desire; a desire which oscillates depending on the context. In law, it is reflected in the notion of ad hoc balancing.[172] In the context of competition law this principle has been observed inter alia by Eucken.[173]

5.3.3 The Rock-Paper-Scissors Effect

Another aspect of indeterminacy encountered by the decision-makers in their balancing exercise can be apprehended by analogy with the game-theoretic model 'rock-paper-scissors' (non-transitivity thesis).[174] There is a mutual dependency between the values.[175] All values contain their

---

[170] Aleksander Peczenik, 'Scientia Juris: Legal Doctrine as Knowledge of Law and as a Source of Law', *Treatise of Legal Philosophy and General Jurisprudence:* Vol. 4, Springer, New York, 2007, p. 118.

[171] Niklas Luhmann, 'Deconstruction as Second-Order Observing', New Literary History, Vol. 24, No. 4, 1993, p. 770.

[172] Aharon Barak, *Purposive Interpretation in Law*, Princeton University Press, Princeton, 2005, pp. 179–181.

[173] Walter Eucken, *The Foundations of Economics: History and Theory in the Analysis of Economic Reality*, The University of Chicago Press, Chicago, 1951, p. 109: 'Just as a huge variety of words of different composition and different length can be formed out of two dozen letters, similarly an almost unlimited variety of actual economic systems can be made up out of a limited number of basic pure forms'.

[174] David Luban, 'Value Pluralism and Rational Choice', Georgetown University Law Center, Working Paper Series in Business, Economics, and Regulatory Law and Public Law and Legal Theory, Working Paper No. 264335, 2001, p. 3.

[175] Walter Eucken, 'Die Wettbewerbsordnung und ihre Verwirklichung', Jahrbuch für die Ordnung von Wirtschaft und Gesellschaft, Vol. 2, 1949, cited in Christian Ahlborn, Carsten Grave (trans.), Walter Eucken, 'The Competitive Order and its Implementation', Competition Policy International, Vol. 2, No. 2,

qualitative and quantitative potential. Some – such as competition – are difficult to quantify and therefore their independent importance tends to be ignored at the regulatory level; others – such as GDP (leaving aside Hayek's scepticism)[176] – are, on the contrary, easily quantifiable.[177] However, every single one possesses both elements. In this frame different values or their alliances create a closed epistemic cycle, with no possibility to maintain the hierarchical priority of one value over the others. Under these conditions every value is seen as more important than some conflicting values and less important than others, although those less important values outweigh values which are more important than the first ones. This creates the aporia A > B > C > A. As Sweet and Mathews argue, 'it is context that varies, and it is the judge's reading of context – the circumstances, fact patterns, and policy considerations at play in any case – that determines outcomes'.[178]

According to Alexy, a situation in which two legal principles compete does not imply that the outweighed principle is inferior to the one that is prioritised; on the contrary, 'the outweighed principle may itself outweigh the other principle in certain circumstances'.[179] Under these common circumstances in real political life, the bounded arbitrariness of regulatory choice is unavoidable.[180] The illusion of the ultimate hierarchy of values

---

2006, p. 232: 'The modern economy is a large, interrelated system. All economic-political acts thus influence the overall process and must therefore all be coordinated with each other'.

[176] Friedrich A. von Hayek, 'Competition as a Discovery Procedure', The Quarterly Journal of Austrian Economics, Vol. 5, No. 3, 2002, p. 12: 'Statistical variables such as national income, investment, price levels, and production are variables that play no role in the process of their determination itself'.

[177] John J. Flynn, 'Legal Reasoning, Antitrust Policy and the Social "Science" of Economics', Antitrust Bulletin, Vol. 33, No. 4, 1988, p. 721: 'The suggestion that . . . qualitative values are unknowable, too vague, or in mutual conflict and are therefore incapable of providing guidance for the law, and that only the quantitative guidance provided by Chicago School economic modelling can provide knowable standards for decision, is one I find unfathomable'.

[178] Alec S. Sweet and Jud Mathews, 'Proportionality Balancing and Global Constitutionalism', Columbia Journal of Transnational Law, Vol. 47, No. 1, 2008, p. 89.

[179] Robert Alexy, *A Theory of Constitutional Rights*, Oxford University Press, Oxford, 2002, p. 50.

[180] Guillermo Lariguet, 'Constitutional Dilemmas – Some criticisms of Lorenzo Zucca's Conception', in Guillermo Lariguet, David Martinez Zorilla, Silvina Alvarez with replies by Lorenzo Zucca, 'An Exchange on Constitutional Dilemmas', http://papers.ssrn.com/sol3/papers.cfm?abstract_id=1284490, accessed on 17 September 2010, pp. 3–4: '[A] right precedes another one, under certain conditions that can be altered or revised in the future'.

would be even more complicated if the qualitative aspects of the values were also influenced by their quantitative components.[181] Depending on the situation each societal value can hold different amount of *units* of the regulatory *currency*, which creates an ex ante random dice-game effect for the decision-making, further contributing to the value indeterminacy.

For instance, the significance of the competitive process may indeed be smaller than the importance of consumer welfare or industrial growth, but its ideological elements can conversely outweigh utilitarian interests. They do not necessarily have to outweigh them, but they in fact *can* do this. This means that, although externally, depending on the context of a case, the competitive process may be inferior to the interests of consumers or industrial growth, *internally* these values are in a *par in parem* relationship.[182] The rock-paper-scissors formula should not be interpreted, therefore, as a claim that all societal values are fully indeterminate and that each can outweigh any, but rather that their weight is very volatile and unpredictable in *hard cases*; the vast majority of routine, simple cases have the privilege of not being put under the pressure of such difficult choices.

5.3.4 Communication between Decision-makers and Influence Groups

Analytically, the communicative processes which influence the decision-making act can be subdivided into three stages: (i) *intra*-value communication; (ii) *inter*-value communication; (iii) *trans*-value communication (communication between the values and decision-maker). Although each decision-making act is an outcome of the three phases taken sequentially, in general the communicative process inside each phase does not stop and all of them take place at the same time. Besides, they all depend on each other and can only be separated analytically. All stages are explored as a purely theoretical 'animated' construction.

---

[181] Jeremy Waldron, 'Fake Incommensurability: A Response to Professor Schauer', Hastings Law Journal, Vol. 45, No. 4, 1994, p. 822: 'There is no final word about rights or anything else, from either legislators, judges, or philosophers. The things we want to prioritize in moral and political life . . . are the subject of constant controversy and interpretation, vision and revision'.

[182] Aharon Barak, *The Judge in a Democracy*, Princeton University Press, Princeton, 2006, pp. 164–165: '"[B]alancing" and "weighing", though neither essential nor universally applicable, are very important tools in fulfilling the judicial role. Even where applicable, however, they do not produce singular, unambiguous legal solutions . . . The concept of balancing recognises that fundamental principles may conflict with one another, and that the proper resolution of this conflict lies not in the elimination of the inferior value but in determining the proper boundary between the conflicting values'.

The first stage reflects the process of internal self-identification of the values. At this stage, each and every value is characterised by self-centricity, self-sufficiency and self-reflectivity. The communications take place only within the values' own silos by means of their own language. The only task of this communicative process is to understand the internal nature that each value holds and to analyse how other values can be used for its further improvement. At this stage the value is not interested either in its workability or its reconciliation with other values. The analysis allows some bias towards other values; its task is purely explorative, scientific, discovering, self-maintaining and positing. As a result, the value of the environment is dissociated from the values that usually counterbalance it (e.g. industrial growth, social cohesion or tax policy). These values can only be perceived as an instrument which can help to understand, improve or protect the value of the environment. A similar process is often observed in academia and can be referred to as pure science, the science which is not interested in practical outcomes, which is self-reflective and self-maintained, which operates as a closed system of knowledge, and which is the only *sensu stricto* science. At the *intra*-value communicative stage neither pure science nor any other value are interested in the outcomes which their self-centricity can cause for society; they are not selfish in this respect, they are agnostic, to the extent that each constitutes a closed circle, a self-sufficient epistemic system, and an end in itself. However, social interests consist of multiple values and society is usually sceptical – often legitimately so – of the epistemic autonomisation of its values, being aware of what pure science can lead to, and trying to impose upon them a benchmark of relevance, which is an external evaluative criterion as reflected in the question 'what's the point'? Even conceptual art as the most abstract and context-independent mode of creativity is often assessed by this yardstick, trying to evoke (as a reaction) a positive statement out of the absence of any sense rather than reaffirming its agnostic nature.

Regardless of society's scepticism towards the autonomous essence of values, this stage is inherently present in any value and cannot be avoided. The epistemological independence of values at the internal level is always determined, however, by their interaction at the external level. This is the case when the internal 'currencies', developed separately by each value in order to reflect their internal significance, become the subjects of a mutual exchange. At this *inter*-value phase, they abandon their self-centricity, trying to gain an external legitimacy by proving how they can serve the interests of other values, as well as exploring the means by which other values can be instrumentalised and creating different epistemological 'alliances' among themselves. Thus, the value of social cohesion would form sporadic alliances with fiscal, educational, international or environmental policies, depending on the context of each particular case. An important analytical distinction between the first and the second phases is the absolute nature of value in the former and its relative character in the latter situation. The interaction between them inevitably leads to their readiness to sacrifice a part of their interests or identity in order to achieve the expected support from other values in different respects.

The last communicative stage is characterised by the objectivisation of values. While at the internal level they are perceived as self-maintained and self-sufficient ends in themselves, and abandon some of their extreme subjectivity at the second stage, the third one is the most pragmatic and, hence, the most indifferent one that concerns the internal nature of each value. The last stage reveals communications between values and decision-makers. The task of the proponents of a given value is to persuade the decision-maker of the importance of each value, while the latter decides how to allocate scarce resources and to share its limited preferences in the most efficient way. Every value at this stage tries to *sell* itself to the decision-maker,[183] revealing both its own importance (as developed in the first phase) as well as its positive impact on other societal values (as discovered at the second consecutive stage).[184] The interactive exchange is influenced by the ability of the influence groups behind each value to convince the decision-maker so that the resources are allocated in the most favourable way for their preferred value. This multilogue is always pragmatic, since the choices are often hard and many values are sacrificed for the sake of others. Therefore, while at the first stage even easily commensurable values are forced to be isolated in order to explore their own nature, at the third stage, even such incommensurable values as freedom, security, justice or human rights are often required to use a pragmatic and relative language of compromises since one cannot prioritise everything and choices have to be made eventually. The second stage encompasses the possibilities of both the first and the third stages: the first reflects the awareness of each value of its internal significance (the bigger the internal self-awareness is, the higher the external price that could be required); the second demonstrates the ability of values to make compromises and

183 Alexander T. Aleinikoff, 'Constitutional Law in the Age of Balancing', The Yale Law Journal, Vol. 96, No. 5, 1987, p. 945: 'Each interest seeks recognition on its own and forces a head-to-head comparison with competing interests'.

184 James M. Buchanan, 'Post-Reagan Political Economy', in James M. Buchanan, *Constitutional Economics*, Basil Blackwell, Oxford, 1991, p. 2: 'Politics involves playing many simultaneous games with and between shifting coalitions of interests'.

create communicative alliances (the lower the external price, the higher the chances of gaining allies among other values, a step necessary for third-stage communication).

5.3.5 The Value of Competition and Communicative Problems

Concerning the interaction between competition and other economic and social goals, the task of the value of the competitive process at the *intra*-value communicative stage would be to artificially isolate itself from the closely connected legitimate societal values and to design itself independently from the real-world context. Like engineers who are trying to make the fastest car possible and neglect during that time the interests of safety and other regulatory limits, the antitrust analysis should distance itself from the influence which the competitive process has on other important values. It has been acknowledged that 'interpreters of necessity privilege passages that suggest their own substantive values'.[185] Both engineers and antitrust enforcers will come to the stage in which the requirements for the fastest car and the optimum for the competitive process will be compromised by other values under mutual agreement (the second stage) or by the regulatory decision (the third stage), but the significance of the first stage should not be underestimated, especially in cases where competition is often not perceived as an independent societal value that deserves to be protected regardless of the outcomes which it tends to generate. The task at the first stage is not declaring the dominance or independence of competition from other societal values, but to preserve the epistemological possibility to explore the competitive process within its own conceptual box, which helps to analyse its peculiarities outside of the broader regulatory level. At the second stage isolated values are compared with each other, and the value of the competitive process will try to create alliances with such values as consumer and total welfare, innovations, market integration or industrial growth. At the third stage the regulatory powers decide how many of these values (qualitatively) and how much of these values (quantitatively) will be sacrificed for the benefits of competing values.

If the competitive process is not considered as an important economic value in its own right,[186] the communication of instrumentalised competition with other values at the second stage will become a one-way process,

---

[185] Jessica Lane, 'The Poetics of Legal Interpretation', Columbia Law Review, Vol. 87, No. 1, 1987, p. 209.

[186] Wernhard Möschel, 'The Proper Scope of Government Viewed from an Ordoliberal Perspective: The Example of Competition Policy', Journal of Institutional and Theoretical Economics, Vol. 157, No. 1, 2001, p. 4: 'The actual

in which other values assess the significance of competition for them without making any attempt at contributing to the competitive process, since it is not considered as a separate value that could be taken seriously by the regulator.[187] The same problem would occur, at the third stage, were the decision-maker only to use competition for the sake of other values and not even to consider sacrificing those values for the benefits of the competitive process.

Insisting on the conceptual independence of competition is not aimed at advocating that the competitive process should be regarded as more important than the interests of consumers or market integration and that it should therefore always outweigh them. Indeed, it is impossible to establish ex ante a coherent hierarchy of values. Each regulatory choice is predetermined by an ad hoc constellation of values and interests,[188] and the situation where the competitive process will be prioritised over the interests of consumers should not be conceptually excluded. The reverse scenario, in which consumer welfare would be treated as a more significant economic value than the competitive process, appears much more plausible, but this should not undermine the mere possibility of considering the former option seriously. As Lane argues, '[e]very interpretation necessarily makes much of a text irrelevant. In the process of interpreting, key phrases come to stand paradigmatically for the text as a whole.'[189] The rhetorical and practical significance of consumer welfare can indeed play the role of a key phrase.[190] Even Ordoliberal *economists*

goal of the competition policy of ordoliberalism lies in the protection of individual economic freedom of action as a value in itself'.

[187] Dieter Wolf, 'Competition Policy Objectives', Working Paper, in Claus Dieter Ehlermann and Laraine L. Laudati (eds.), *The Objectives of Competition Policy*, European Competition Law Annual 1997, Hart Publishing, Oxford, 1998, pp. 24–25: 'In Germany, we do not favour political trade-offs and compromises in the implementation of our competition policy. Competition has no lobby. Thus, if we allow negotiations with political forces in this area to take on the same importance as political decisions in other areas, competition will always be the loser'.

[188] Günther Teubner, '"And God Laughed . . ." Indeterminacy, Self-Reference and Paradox in Law', German Law Journal, Vol. 12, No. 1, 2011, p. 400: 'Both legislatures and courts seek reactively and *ad hoc* to arrive at a precarious compromise between functional requirements of social subsystems, political control objectives and requirements internal to the legal system'.

[189] Jessica Lane, 'The Poetics of Legal Interpretation', Columbia Law Review, Vol. 87, No. 1, 1987, p. 209.

[190] Barak Y. Orbach, 'The Antitrust Consumer Welfare Paradox', Journal of Competition Law and Economics, Vol. 7, No. 1, 2010, p. 135: '[The term "consumer welfare" is] of great rhetorical power, because it combined popular appeal with a patina of economic erudition'.

recognise this role.[191] It is being used even more often in the times of economic uncertainty,[192] so 'everyone uses language of efficiency because that is, at the moment, the accepted discourse'.[193] The disadvantage of such key phrases is that their universality often leads to transformation into empty slogans.[194] Competition should not be subordinated to welfare conceptually. If the choice for societal competition is made, it becomes an independent value, which cannot be overseen anytime when it is in conflict with welfare. Bork himself, while promoting the goal of consumer welfare,[195] was sceptical of uncritical rhetorical use of the key phrases in courts.[196] Such a prioritisation would be fully consistent with the analytical model suggested in this chapter if the balancing act were to consider competition as an independent value, just like any other value. The prioritisation of one value over another does not undermine the internal features of those outweighed values and should not affect the importance of their analysis at the first stage of the communicative balancing process.

The problem of specialisation is present in every area of human activity. It is reflected in the dialectical law of correlation between the whole and its parts. Every entity simultaneously constitutes a whole and a part

---

191 Walter Eucken, Franz Böhm, 'Preface', ORDO, Vol. 1, No. 1, 1948, p. xi, translated and quoted in Nils Goldschmidt and Michael Wohlgemuth, 'Social Market Economy: Origins, Meanings, Interpretations', Constitutional Political Economy, Vol. 19, No. 3, 2008, p. 268: 'All we are asking for is the creation of an economic and social order which equally guarantees economic activity and humane living conditions. We call for competition because it can be utilized to reach this goal – in fact, the goal cannot be reached without it. It is a means, not an end in itself'.

192 Laura Parret, 'Shouldn't We Know What We Are Protecting? Yes We Should! A Plea for a Solid and Comprehensive Debate About the Objectives of EU Competition Law and Policy', European Competition Journal, Vol. 6, No. 2, 2010, p. 376.

193 Eleanor Fox, 'Competition Policy Objectives', Panel Discussion, in Claus-Dieter Ehlermann and Laraine L. Laudati (eds.), *The Objectives of Competition Policy*, European Competition Law Annual 1997, Hart Publishing, Oxford, 1998, p. 15.

194 Herbert J. Hovenkamp, *The Antitrust Enterprise*, Harvard University Press, Cambridge, Massachusetts, 2005, p. 31: 'Judges have spoken of antitrust law as a "consumer welfare prescription" for so long that the phrase seldom produces anything but yawns. . . . A statute declaring protection of consumers to be the goal of antitrust would probably pass Congress by a unanimous vote'.

195 Robert H. Bork, 'Resale Price Maintenance and Consumer Welfare', The Yale Law Journal, Vol. 77, No. 5, 1968, p. 950: 'My position is that consumer welfare is the only proper criterion for antitrust'.

196 Robert H. Bork, 'Legislative Intent and the Policy of the Sherman Act', Journal of Law and Economics, Vol. 9, 1966, p. 8.

of another entity. A screw is a separate entity and a part of an engine; an engine is a separate entity and a part of an aeroplane; an aeroplane is a separate entity and a part of a fleet of aircraft and so on. Every entity therefore should simultaneously perceive itself as a part and as an autonomy. Both stages are mutually influenced, but also analytically separable. A cosmetic surgeon being a part of the medical profession should be responsible first for a patient's health, but as a specialist in his field he should also be responsible for what the patient wants to do with his face (this is only one of many possible medical dilemmas, even if the related thought experiments are left to moral philosophy).[197] Health and beauty in this case are conflicting or, as Lianos puts it, 'the natural constraints of the language restrict the topics of conversation, its narrative'.[198] Most cosmetic interventions are unnecessary from the point of view of health. The surgeon as a *generalist* should then refuse this type of medical intervention in most cases, but as a *specialist* he does not need to.[199] The greater his expertise the bigger the physiognomic changes he can make.[200] Some of these changes can cause significant harm for the general health of the patient and the surgeon would refuse to undertake these drastic interventions. A refusal motivated on such grounds is the result of the thought process of a generalist, whereas the qualifications and expertise of a specialist enable him to intervene in the same circumstances. This implies that the specialist should know how to undertake all medical manipulations, including those which would never be allowed from the point of view of the generalist. If the goal of each patient is happiness, then the goal of each general practitioner is the patient's health and the goal of the cosmetic

197 Stephen John, 'Why "Health" is not a Central Category for Public Health Policy', Journal of Applied Philosophy, Vol. 26, No. 2, 2009, p. 129: '[T]he difficult questions for public health ethics seem to be whether we ought to focus on improving health-outcomes or individuals' opportunities for health, how we ought to distribute (opportunity for) good health, and what considerations limit this task'.

198 Ioannis Lianos, 'Lost In Translation? Towards a Theory of Economic Transplants', Current Legal Problems, Vol. 62, No. 1, 2009, p. 353.

199 Chantal Mouffe, 'Radical Democracy: Modern or Postmodern?', in Chantal Mouffe, *The Return of the Political*, Verso, London, 1993, p. 131: 'According to pluralists . . ., each individual is a member of many communities and associations [i.e. he has many identities], none of which may have priority over the others'.

200 Hideaki Kobayashi, 'Competition Policy Objectives', Panel Discussion, in Claus-Dieter Ehlermann and Laraine L. Laudati (eds.), *The Objectives of Competition Policy*, European Competition Law Annual 1997, Hart Publishing, Oxford, 1998, p. 21: 'Some doctors are modest and curing alone might satisfy them, but many doctors hope that by curing a patient, that patient will be able to work effectively, creatively, and happily. But achieving the ultimate objectives is not within the control of the doctor'.

surgeon is the patient's beauty. Yet, these various goals often conflict. In practice they are reconciled by a balancing act based on good practice and commonsense. In theory, however, they remain in conflict. Every specialist should know how to perform his central task in its wholeness, including those parts of it which he will *never* perform in real life, as this conditions his capacity to achieve a perfect expertise in the field. Similarly, the role of the theoretical analysis of the competitive process is not limited solely to those attributes of the speciality which can satisfy the generality of consumer/total welfare, but also include self-centred analytical activities, in his autonomous area of research.

5.4 THE LAW OF ECONOMICS AND THE ECONOMICS OF LAW

Political balancing is predetermined by two antagonistic views: deontology and utilitarianism. The former relies on the absolute nature of rights and is critical of the possibility to balance them. The latter believes conversely that society should seek to maximise its interests and the concept of rights should not be treated as a trump which overrules any compromise or trade-off. The task of this section is twofold. First, it analyses the main methodological inclinations of deontology and utilitarianism through the lens of their conceptual boundaries. Secondly, it illustrates their differences by exploring the polemical exchange between the representatives of both traditions.

The issue of interdisciplinarity is of paramount importance in antitrust theory. At least three disciplinary discourses – economics, law and political theory – address the problems of competition. The interactions between them illustrate the fruitfulness of interdisciplinary research. The problem of homonymy, however, is often apparent as well.[201] Stigler considers that the main problem lies in the substantive goals of each discipline and in their apparatus, submitting that '[t]he difference between a discipline that seeks to explain economic life (and, indeed, all rational behaviour) and a discipline that seeks to achieve justice in regulating all aspects of human

---

[201] Phedon Nicolaides, 'An Essay on Economics and Competition Law of the European Community', Legal Issues of Economic Integration, Vol. 27, No. 1, 2000, p. 7: 'Economists and lawyers do not often see eye to eye. They are divided by the boundaries of their respective disciplines. . . . Lawyers, for example, bemoan the "pollution" of their discipline by economists who favour the introduction of cost-benefit criteria in legal decisions, while economists find incomprehensible court rulings that appear to disregard obvious, in their eyes, economic facts'.

behaviour is profound',[202] as well as suggesting that economics and law speak different languages. Kelsen, on the other hand, observes that '[t]he sociology of law [and in the present context the economic analysis of law] cannot draw a line between its subject – law – and the other social phenomena'.[203] In their mutual attempts to internalise each other's arguments, law was originally more successive than economics, since the pre-modern culture was based on dogmas. Conversely, the age of rationality is characterised by the pervasive application of economic methods to other disciplines. Antitrust is merely an example, even if a particularly explicit one, of a much more general trend. Economics has been successfully applied to many other areas. Gauthier, for example, critically explores at least three important epistemic influences of economics on moral theory (its cognitive alma mater)[204] and philosophy in general: '[t]he first is that value is utility – a measure of subjective, individual preference. The second is that rationality is maximization. . . . The third is that interests are non-tuistic [a person is not interested in the interests of another person]'.[205] Although the centre of gravity of law and economics is primarily concerned with private law adjudication, it does not prevent its application to public law.[206] The economic analysis of the political decision-making process is reflected in public choice theory constitutional economics,[207] and more generally in social choice.[208] It would not be a big exaggeration to submit that, nowadays, one can find studies of the economics of *every* reasonable area of human practice (economics of education, religion, happiness, football, religion, recycling, art . . .).[209] The ability of economics to

---

[202] George J. Stigler, 'Law or Economics?', Journal of Law and Economics, Vol. 35, No. 2, 1992, p. 463.

[203] Hans Kelsen, 'The Pure Theory of Law and Analytical Jurisprudence', Harvard Law Review, Vol. 55, No. 1, 1941, p. 53.

[204] Ioannis Lianos, 'Lost In Translation? Towards a Theory of Economic Transplants', Current Legal Problems, Vol. 62, No. 1, 2009, p. 351.

[205] David Gauthier, 'Thomas Hobbes: Moral Theorist', The Journal of Philosophy, Vol. 76, No. 10, 1979, p. 547.

[206] Frank I. Michelman, 'Constitutions, Statutes, and the Theory of Efficient Adjudication', The Journal of Legal Studies, Vol. 9, No. 3, 1980, p. 431.

[207] James M. Buchanan and Gordon Tullock, *The Calculus of Consent: Logical Foundations of Constitutional Democracy*, University of Michigan Press, Ann Arbor, 1962.

[208] Kenneth J. Arrow, *Social Choice and Individual Values*, Yale University Press, New Haven, 1951.

[209] Francesco Parisi, 'Positive, Normative and Functional Schools in Law and Economics', European Journal of Law and Economics, Vol. 18, No. 3, 2004, p. 261: '[T]he cohesiveness of economic techniques makes it possible for economics to move successfully into another field, such as law, and dominate it intellectually'.

address legal, political and ethical questions reflects the universal symbols and interests with which it usually operates.

In legal scholarship the role of economic analysis is usually limited to its positive part.[210] It is hard to object that economics *can* indeed explain in its *intra*disciplinary way the phenomenon of law, but in addition the economic analysis often proposes the normative guidelines for the legal field.[211] Monti poses a legitimacy question: 'whether the use of economics is legitimate and . . . how economics is used'.[212] This concern is substantiated and explained by some economists as well.[213] Law and economics enthusiasts suggest that economics can 'teach' the law to be more pragmatic and respond to societal needs more rapidly and effectively. Some suggest that only economic reasoning reflects genuine relations between people.[214] More moderate authors usually acknowledge the important connections between law and economics,[215] suggesting that economics is indeed a useful tool to assess the evidence, but submit at the same time that economic analysis of law 'cannot and should not serve as a general basis

---

210 Herbert J. Hovenkamp, 'Positivism in Law & Economics', California Law Review, Vol. 78, No. 4, 1990, p. 816: 'A positive economic analysis says simply that, given a certain set of premises, A, B, and C, some conclusion D will follow'.

211 Dieter Wolf, 'Competition Policy Objectives', Working Paper, in Claus-Dieter Ehlermann and Laraine L. Laudati (eds.), *The Objectives of Competition Policy*, European Competition Law Annual 1997, Hart Publishing, Oxford, 1998, p. 24: '[E]conomists have learned to be advocates of the interests of their clients, just as lawyers have learned to do so'.

212 Giorgio Monti, 'EC Competition Law: The Dominance of Economic Analysis?', in Roger Zäch, Andreas Heinemann and Andreas Kellerhals (eds.), *The Development of Competition Law – Global Perspectives*, Edward Elgar Publishing, Cheltenham, 2010, p. 4.

213 John N. Keynes, *The Scope and Method of Political Economy*, Macmillan and Co., London, 1897, p. 8: '[T]he general tendency of popular economics is towards rash generalizations and fallacious arguments *post hoc ergo propter hoc* . . . leading to confusion of thought and the selection of false propositions as self-evident postulates; and where deductive reasoning is employed its results are often applied without regard to the conditions requisite for their valid application. To this must be added the sharp distinction drawn by opposing schools, and their narrow dogmatism' (emphasis in the original).

214 Morton J. Horwitz, 'Law and Economics: Science or Politics?', Hofstra Law Review, Vol. 8, No. 4, 1980, p. 905: 'Like . . . Marxism, law-and-economics treats law as "superstructure", merely reflecting what is "real" in the "base" of economic rationality'.

215 Herbert J. Hovenkamp, 'The Antitrust Movement and the Rise of Industrial Organisation', Texas Law Review, Vol. 68, No. 1, 1989, p. 105: 'Even though they spoke different languages, economists and lawyers derived their ideas from each other'.

of legal decision making'.[216] The sceptics make methodological observations about the mutual epistemic incompatibility of the disciplines.[217] In such technical areas of law as antitrust, economics always plays a pivotal role, but until recently it merely explained *competition,* while nowadays it often seeks to explain competition *law. Mutatis mutandis,* criminology is of paramount importance for criminal law, but it does not pretend to be its only source of interpretation or to guide its development. As some authors show, the line between positive and normative economic analysis in present-day European antitrust is blurred.[218] This trend is exacerbated by the dominance of the welfare-oriented approach, which jeopardises the other important aspects of competition law. Even if the universality of cost–benefit analysis were to enable its perception as pure *objective* science, it could not guide the law.[219]

However, even the tenets of a purist *intra*disciplinarity interpretation of law do not reject the importance of economic knowledge, claiming merely that the law *can* be defined by economics, but that the ensuing definitions can serve *only* as a theoretical modelling with no normative implications, arriving essentially at Frost's 'good fence make good neighbours'[220] conclusion. The epistemic border between disciplines implies that 'law produces by itself all the distinctions and concepts that it uses, and the unity of law is nothing but the fact of

216 Eric Engle, 'Law and Economics: Theoretical Puffery, Exaggerated Claims and Counterfactual Models', The Journal of Jurisprudence, Vol. 2, No. 2, 2009, p. 29.

217 Günther Teubner, 'The Two Faces of Janus: Rethinking legal Pluralism', Cardozo Law Review, Vol. 13, No. 5, 1992, p. 1455: 'The lawyers observe economic action under the code legal/illegal and misread economic processes and structures as sources of law. Conversely, clever economic actors misread legal norms under the economic code as bargaining chips, as new opportunities for profit-making. Again, we have a symbiosis of mutual distortion'.

218 Giorgio Monti, 'EC Competition Law: The Dominance of Economic Analysis?', in Roger Zäch, Andreas Heinemann and Andreas Kellerhals (eds.), *The Development of Competition Law – Global Perspectives,* Edward Elgar Publishing, Cheltenham, 2010, pp. 4–5: '[The Commissioner's statement that the aim of competition enforcement is to protect competition in the market as a means of enhancing consumer welfare] blurs the line between positive and normative economic analysis'.

219 Hans Kelsen, *General Theory of Law and State,* Russell & Russell, New York, 1973, p. xiv: 'One of the most difficult tasks of a general theory of law is that of determining the specific reality of its subject and of showing the difference which exists between legal and natural reality'.

220 Patrick F. Hubbard, '"Sociology of Law": One View from the Lawyer's Side of the Fence', Rutgers Law Journal, Vol. 7, No. 3, 1976, p. 458.

this self-production',[221] which means that law cannot be explained by the non-legal apparatus and, the other way around, '[p]articulars are legally relevant only inasmuch as they can be brought within juridical categories'.[222] This feature has been acknowledged by the economists as well.[223] In Kelsen's sense, purely legal silos (normative jurisprudence) recognise the importance and validity of external views on law (sociological jurisprudence),[224] suggesting that both stand side by side but 'neither can replace the other because each deals with completely different problems'.[225] The origins of this approach can be traced back – as Paulson shows[226] – at least to Jellinek.[227] Kelsen's critics also see these similarities.[228] This explains the position of legal positivism, liberating it from misinterpretation by its critics who perceive legal positivism as a claim 'that law must be strictly severed from morality . . . [and economic analysis, which denies] the possibility of any bridge between the obligation to obey law and other moral obligations'.[229]

---

221 Richard Nobles and David Schiff, 'Introduction' in Niklas Luhmann (ed.), *Law as Social System*, Oxford University Press, Oxford, 2004, p. 6.

222 Ernest J. Weinrib, 'Legal Formalism: On the Immanent Rationality of Law', The Yale Law Journal, Vol. 97, No. 6, 1988, p. 976.

223 Arthur T. Hadley, 'The Relation between Economics and Politics', The Yale Law Journal, Vol. 8, No. 4, 1899, p. 201.

224 Jack M. Balkin and Sanford V. Levinson, 'Law and the Humanities: An Uneasy Relationship', Yale Journal of Law & the Humanities, Vol. 18, No. 2, 2006, pp. 161–162: 'An externalist attitude . . . studies law as a social phenomenon, much as an anthropologist might study the ancient beliefs of the Mayan religion without adhering to them. . . . In like fashion, literary critics might be interested in the rhetorical operations of law; historians might be interested in the development of law in its social and political context, and so on'.

225 Hans Kelsen, 'The Pure Theory of Law and Analytical Jurisprudence', Harvard Law Review, Vol. 55, No. 1, 1941, p. 52.

226 Stanley L. Paulson, 'Hans Kelsen's Earliest Legal Theory: Critical Constructivism', The Modern Law Review, Vol. 59, No. 6, 1996, pp. 798–800.

227 Georg Jellinek, *System der subjektiven öffentlichen Rechte*, J.C.B. Mohr, Tübingen, 1905.

228 Carl Schmitt, *Political Theology – Four Chapters on the Concept of Sovereignty*, The MIT Press, Cambridge, Massachusetts, 1985, p. 18: 'To obtain in unadulterated purity a system of ascriptions to norms and a last uniform basic norm, all sociological elements have been left out of the juristic concept. The old contrast between *is* and *ought*, between causal and normative considerations, has been transferred to the contrast of sociology and jurisprudence, with greater emphasis and rigor than had already been done by George Jellinek and Kistiakowski, but with the same unproved certainty' (emphasis in the original).

229 Lon L. Fuller, 'Positivism and Fidelity to Law: A Reply to Professor Hart', Harvard Law Review, Vol. 71, No. 4, 1958, p. 656.

5.5 CONCLUSIONS

The task of this chapter was to explore the main theoretical approaches to the balancing act. By analysing the different epistemological conditions that predetermine regulatory choices, it is postulated that balancing is unavoidable. The relativity of values and the indeterminacy of choices make balancing the only plausible administrative exercise. This is not a normative statement. A position which relies on clear-cut hierarchies may declare that the dilemma of balancing is solved, yet the natural essence of the polysemy of values is present also in the most monolithic command systems inasmuch as 'all knowledge and all action has to be founded on paradoxes . . .; on the self-referential unity of the positive and the negative . . . [where the] paradox is the visible indicator of invisibility'.[230] The collegiate decision-making process of the EU Commission may serve as a good example of the necessity of balancing. Each Directorate is responsible for its own policy and participates in the decision-making process of the Commission as a whole body. Thereby, by trying to promote their values, the decision-makers are aware of the inevitability of reducing their absolute intentions, trying to convince other members of the importance of their proposals and accepting similar offers in turn.

Balancing takes place in all areas of life. In economics it usually takes the form of a cost–benefit analysis, in politics it is described as hard, unpopular choices, and it has been explored in law as well. This is particularly the case in constitutional jurisprudence and legal theory. The task of this chapter was to provide a positive analysis of the balancing act. Both disciplines cannot be fully coherent with each other in their understanding of the optimal competitive process.[231] The next chapter begins with an analysis of the problems of balancing from the juristic perspective, revealing the close similarities that exist between the general conceptual research of these problems and their perception in legal theory.[232]

---

230 Niklas Luhmann, 'Deconstruction as Second-Order Observing', New Literary History, Vol. 24, No. 4, 1993, p. 770.

231 Christian Kirchner, 'Goals of Antitrust and Competition Law Revisited' in Dieter Schmidtchen, Max Albert and Stefan Voigt (eds.), *The More Economic Approach to European Competition Law*, Mohr Siebeck, Tübingen, 2007, pp. 18–19: 'From an economic point of view a legal approach to competition policy appears to be sub-optimal. The application of competition law should not depend on legal interpretation of legal terms but on the effect of different problem solutions. Economics should favour an effect-based approach, which is consequentialist in nature'.

232 Samantha Besson, *The Morality of Conflict: Reasonable Disagreement and the Law*, Hart Publishing, Oxford, 2005, p. 435: 'Most of what has been said about the typology of conflicts of moral rights or rights in general applies to legal rights'.

6. The legal theoretical aspects of competition

This chapter focuses on legal theory questions relevant to antitrust. Others are left aside. The chapter starts with an analysis of the balancing act in constitutional jurisprudence reflected in the correlation between rules and principles, which conforms to a large degree with the conceptual analysis of balancing provided in the previous chapter. The interaction between law and other social norms is explored, with a particular emphasis on the relations between law and morality, which may implicitly be transposed to the domain of antitrust when the positive protection of the competitive process is juxtaposed with the utilitarian values of wealth, or when law interacts with economics. This section is followed by the analysis of the ideal and material aspects of law, which can be taken as an alternative to interdisciplinarity. The analysis of the notion of rights can be directly applied to competition law, as some antitrust schools consider competition as an important individual right. The last section is devoted to legal pluralism as the main theoretical framework to embrace the phenomenon of competition in the legal discourse.

This chapter has two main objectives: applied and normative. The first seeks to demonstrate how the analysis of the role of the competitive process and its correlation with other significant economic values can be consolidated within a legal theoretical methodology. The second is to prove that the competitive process itself constitutes an important part of analytical jurisprudence, which strives to harmonise irreconcilable visions of the essence of law and its correlation with other social norms. Against the background of legal indeterminacy the dialectical dynamics of the competitive process is perceived as an embodiment of legal pluralism anchored in the adversarial adjudicative process (dialectically combining the rationality of the logical argumentation with the inventiveness of rhetorical argumentation).[1] Alongside the economic, political and cultural

[1] Eveline T. Feteris, 'Recent Developments in Legal Argumentation Theory: Dialectical Approaches to Legal Argumentation', International Journal for the Semiotics of Law, Vol. 7, No. 20, 1994, p. 139: 'Because a purely logical or rhetorical approach seems to be too narrow as an adequate approach to argumentation,

aspects of competition it constitutes the essence of humanistic liberal democracy, taken not as a universal remedy for effective governance, but as a result of evolutionary development of the ideas of '[*f*]*reedom* [as] . . . *an artefact of civilization*',[2] performing the task of hermeneutical discovering of the actual sense of the law.

6.1 BALANCING ACT IN CONSTITUTIONAL JURISPRUDENCE

Competing interests play a pivotal role in jurisprudential analysis.[3] Metaphorically speaking, balancing 'has provided a common grammar for global constitutionalism'.[4] Many concerns are related to this legal practice. They are primarily connected to the problem of the coherence and protection of societal values. Arguably, the balancing act diminishes the significance and the absolute nature of rights. However, as Alexy points out, balancing is 'a necessary means of lending them protection and . . . [it] is not an alternative to argumentation but an indispensable form of rational practical discourse',[5] which is confirmed by Peczenik, who suggests that '[w]eighing is relevant in all juristic contexts'.[6] As Novak observes, 'balancing as a type of legal decision-making is more typical of constitutional law than of adjudication by ordinary courts'.[7] The scepticism of many deontological philosophers towards balancing[8] may be

---

in argumentation theory as well as in European legal theory a new [dialectical] approach has been developed'.

[2] Friedrich A. von Hayek, *Law, Legislation and Liberty*, Vol. 3, 'The Political Order of a Free People', Routledge & Kegan Paul, London, 1976, p. 163 (emphasis in the original).

[3] Herbert L. A. Hart, *The Concept of Law*, Oxford University Press, Oxford, 1994, p. 205.

[4] Moshe Cohen-Eliya and Iddo Porat, 'American Balancing and German Proportionality: The Historical Origins', International Journal of Constitutional Law, Vol. 8, No. 2, 2010, p. 263.

[5] Robert Alexy, 'Constitutional Rights, Balancing, and Rationality', Ratio Juris, Vol. 16, No. 2, 2003, p. 131.

[6] Aleksander Peczenik, 'Particulars and Universals in Legal Justification', in Zenon Bankowski and James MacLean (eds.), *The Universal and the Particular in Legal Reasoning*, Ashgate, Aldershot, 2006, p. 191.

[7] Marko Novak, 'Three Models of Balancing (in Constitutional Review)', Ratio Juris, Vol. 23, No. 1, 2010, p. 101.

[8] Kai Möller, 'Balancing and the Structure of Constitutional Rights', International Journal of Constitutional Law, Vol. 5, No. 3, 2007, p. 453: 'There are important differences between reasoning with constitutional rights and reasoning

explained by the methodological differences between political philosophy, which mainly operates with *ought* statements,[9] and jurisprudence, which in its theoretical mode is interested in *is* questions,[10] and in the applied form – in *how to* issues.[11] The conceptual roots and logical explanation of balancing are similar to the economic model of balancing. Although *normatively* speaking, balancing within the realm of constitutional jurisprudence is constrained by the specificities of the field, from the positive *mechanical* point of view, many principles and techniques are indirectly transposed from political economy to legal theory, which operationalises them into the constitutional adjudication process. For instance, the legal domain as a social construct faces the same dilemma of the absolute determinacy of hierarchy vs. the relative in/determinacy of choice. The more rigid and unequivocal the rules and their compliance are, the less the legal system can reflect the actual societal relations. At the same time, the more flexible and responsive the law is, the less stability and predictability can be expected from it.

Balancing by definition implies some elements of arbitrariness,[12] since often the arguments of both parties are legitimate and both may be protected by the existing legal framework.[13] The conditions for balancing

---

with moral fundamental rights. One of them is that constitutional courts around the world employ a balancing or proportionality test in order to determine the limits of rights, whereas many philosophers reject such an approach'.

9 Ronald M. Dworkin, *Taking Rights Seriously*, Harvard University Press, Cambridge, Massachusetts, 1978, p. 365: '[R]ights [are] claims of a trump over a general utilitarian justification'.

10 Hans Kelsen, *General Theory of Law and State*, Russell & Russell, New York, 1973, pp. xiii–xiv: 'A science has to describe its object as it actually is, not to prescribe how it should be or should not be from the point of view of some specific value judgements. The latter is a problem of politics, and, as such, concerns the art of government'.

11 Alexander T. Aleinikoff, 'Constitutional Law in the Age of Balancing', The Yale Law Journal, Vol. 96, No. 5, 1987, p. 945: '[Balancing is] a judicial opinion that analyses a constitutional question by identifying interests implicated by the case and reaches a decision . . . by explicitly or implicitly assigning values to the identified interests'.

12 Michal Alberstein, 'Measures of Legal Formalism', Bar-Ilan University Public Law and Legal Theory Working Paper No. 04-09, 03, 2009, p. 18: 'Discretion is an inevitable phenomenon in any decision-making'.

13 David Luban, 'Value Pluralism and Rational Choice', Georgetown University Law Center, Working Paper Series in Business, Economics, and Regulatory Law and Public Law and Legal Theory, Working Paper No. 264335, 2001, p. 2: 'In legal decision-making, courts routinely adjudicate competing value-claims by articulating tests according to which each value is assigned its proper "weight" and the weighted values are balanced against one another'.

cannot be fully anticipated in legislation, since 'balancing is an act that cannot be captured by criteria'.[14] If choices between valid norms are encompassed and predetermined in the legal system and the task of the judge is to *find* the right answer, then this practice is only covered by the balancing act implicitly reducing it to a discovery act. However, in many instances, no right answer can be derived from the literal meaning of legal texts. As Kelsen observes, insofar as the decision-maker (authority) is a human being and not a natural cause of events, every imperative norm or highest value is subjective and frequently conflicts with another imperative norm or highest value. For example, this is the case when 'personal freedom [is in conflict] with social security, the welfare of the single individual [is in conflict] with the welfare of the whole nation, in cases where the one can be reached only at the expense of the other'.[15] This leads to the bounded arbitrariness of the decision-maker, who is *bounded* by the institutional prerequisites of the system within which the decision is being made,[16] holding at the same time the significant elements of *discretion*. Sweet and Mathews observe that a 'conflict between principles places judges under a duty to balance and to optimize',[17] which means that '[l]aw is rooted in conflict'.[18] Some of these conflicts are irresolvable dilemmas or paradoxes.[19] For Alexy the balancing process has significant conceptual similarities with the economic calculus, where Pareto optimality[20] is the ideal situation. However, as economic theory shows, Pareto optimality is a theoretical construct and cannot be achieved in reality.[21] Then again,

---

[14] Zenon Bankowski, *Living Lawfully – Love in Law and Law in Love*, Kluwer, Dordrecht, 2001, p. 184.

[15] Hans Kelsen, 'The Natural-Law Doctrine before the Tribunal of Science', The Western Political Quarterly, Vol. 2, No. 4, 1949, p. 484.

[16] Stefano Bertea, 'The Arguments from Coherence: Analysis and Evaluation', Oxford Journal of Legal Studies, Vol. 25, No. 3, 2005, p. 371: '[H]owever discretional decision-making activities may be, they are never wholly arbitrary or irrational'.

[17] Alec S. Sweet and Jud Mathews, 'Proportionality Balancing and Global Constitutionalism', Columbia Journal of Transnational Law, Vol. 47, No. 1, 2008, p. 95.

[18] Lorenzo Zucca, *Constitutional Dilemmas – Conflicts of Fundamental Rights in Europe and the USA*, Oxford University Press, Oxford, 2007, p. 3.

[19] Günther Teubner, 'Dealing with Paradoxes of Law: Derrida, Luhmann, Wiethölter', in Oren Perez and Günther Teubner (eds.), *Paradoxes and Inconsistencies in Law*, Hart Publishing, Oxford, 2006, pp. 44–47.

[20] Robert Alexy, *A Theory of Constitutional Rights*, Oxford University Press, Oxford, 2002, p. 50.

[21] Guido Calabresi, 'The Pointlessness of Pareto: Carrying Coase Further', The Yale Law Journal, Vol. 100, No. 5, 1991, p. 1215: 'What is the Pareto test? It is

judges have to make practical decisions, which lead to hard choices and significant trade-offs. The conflict between legal norms is directly acknowledged not only in the pragmatic, economics-oriented part of jurisprudence, but also in legal positivism.[22]

The idea that constitutional norms are based upon a coherent hierarchical structure which foresees, encompasses and reconciles all real and potential conflicts between them is functioning in monolithic societies, which consider every constitutional uncertainty as a threat to stability (i.e. to their own existence). These models may be designed in different historical, cultural and ideological contexts and they therefore reflect different political values – from various forms of totalitarian autocracies to republican forms of democracy, and from religious fundamentalism to liberal regimes. Some features of homogeneity and hierarchical structure of constitutional norms are present in all political systems inasmuch as their main characteristics are both formal and functional. On the other hand some implicit elements of balancing, which is the alternative to monistic hierarchism, can be traced even in the most holistic, authoritarian regimes, since no hierarchy is free from indeterminacy. Balancing also harms legal certainty to some extent – a postulate of legality and legal clarity – 'a sovereign virtue in jurisprudence'.[23] Inasmuch as these elements endanger the principles upon which the hierarchies are based,[24] they are either ignored or addressed tacitly and discreetly by authorities. This research is based on the normative premise that balancing values constitutes in itself a distinctive ideological feature of liberal democracy – so that balancing values becomes a liberal value (a value of balancing). The reason for this hypothesis is reflected in the normative significance of *competition*, which constitutes the centre of gravity of this book.

Many prominent thinkers reject the idea that balancing can be an appropriate way to address constitutional dilemmas. According to

---

a simple unanimity requirement. It says that a society is not at its optimal position if there exists at least one change which would make someone in that society better off and no one in it worse off'.

22 Hans Kelsen, 'The Foundation of the Theory of Natural Law', in Hans Kelsen, *Essays in Legal and Moral Philosophy*, D. Reidel, Dordrecht, 1973, p. 116: '[C]onflicts between norms of one and the same normative order, and especially within a single legal order, . . . by no means infrequently occur'.

23 Herbert L. A. Hart, 'Positivism and the Separation of Law and Morals', Harvard Law Review, Vol. 71, No. 4, 1958, p. 593.

24 Aharon Barak, *The Judge in a Democracy*, Princeton University Press, Princeton, 2006, p. 160: 'Deviation from precedent causes damage to the legal system. It detracts from stability, certainty, and the reliance of the public on the old precedent. It obstructs the possibility of planning future activity'.

Habermas, constitutional rights, unlike economic values and political interests, cannot be balanced because their absolute nature does not accept relative measurement. Otherwise 'the fire wall erected in legal discourse by a deontological understanding of legal norms and principles collapses'.[25] The recognition of the absolute nature of rights means that they cannot be balanced against each other, let alone against other societal interests. According to Dworkin, rights 'trump' any other interest as well as the whole pragmatic reasoning of cost–benefit analysis. This vision is consistent in its rejection of the logic of pragmatism for the sake of certainty and constitutional superiority. It should be noted that balancing can take place even beyond the cost–benefit analysis *sensu stricto*. Waldron, for instance, refers to 'social utility',[26] a concept that goes beyond the utilitarian calculus. But in both cases – either openly or implicitly – the mechanics of balancing is based on trade-offs made between different rights. This is problematic from both the deontological (absolute nature of rights) and formalist (absolute determinacy of law) perspectives. The balancing process converts rights into a common regulatory currency, which increases their chances of being prioritised by the decision-maker but at the same time deprives them of their authenticity and societal significance, transforming them from *trumps* into ordinary *cards*. As a quintessential aspect of postmodern jurisprudence, balancing does not provide ultimate solutions to legal dilemmas.[27] This is the reason why emphasis is placed upon its positive aspects with the task of understanding its internal mechanisms. However, balancing also encompasses some normative elements related to the dynamics of legal conflicts, which impel the parties to develop various competitive strategies in their attempts to convince the decision-makers to ascribe a certain legal meaning to legal norms. This competitive feature of balancing goes beyond mere positive analysis.

The persistence with which the proponents of a hierarchical structure of rights advocate the principle of legal supremacy of rights and the refusal of any compromise can be compared to the determination of economists to evaluate the legitimacy of norms, facts and acts via the yardstick of cost–benefit analysis or to the toughness of politicians defending ideological beliefs. Different disciplines are cautious about permitting elements of indeterminacy and epistemological 'neighbours' to enter their field, even

---

25 Jürgen Habermas, *Between Facts and Norms – Contributions to a Discourse Theory of Law and Democracy*, Polity Press, Cambridge, 1997, pp. 258–259.

26 Jeremy Waldron, 'Rights in Conflict', Ethics, Vol. 99, No. 3, 1989, p. 508.

27 Hans Kelsen, 'On the Theory of Interpretation', Legal Studies, Vol. 10, No. 2, 1990, p. 130: 'Even the principle of so-called balancing of interests is merely a formulation of the problem . . . and not solution'.

if they know how to address the indeterminacy. Habermas, for instance, does not recognise the conceptual similarities between legal rights, economic values and political interests. For him, every value and interest is characterised by its particularity, specificity and context-dependency. This implies the ability of being balanced. On the other hand, constitutional norms 'owe their validity to a universalisation test'[28] and cannot be compromised subsequently. Zucca shares this view to a large extent and, referring to Von Wright, submits that rights are purely deontological concepts, while values are axiological.[29] Habermas accepts that political or social interests may outweigh rights in some cases provided that these collective interests are coated in the language of rights beforehand. He concludes that, '[*i*]*n the final instance*, only rights can be trumps in the argumentation game'.[30] This research shares his point, with a reservation, that the transition process between values, interests and rights is ubiquitous. This means that before any social interest outweighs another, it should be internalised by the *language* of rights. Habermas is also correct that every balancing act inevitably requires some elements of arbitrariness, suggesting that 'weighing takes place either arbitrarily or unreflectively'.[31] This research internalises and mitigates his concerns via the principle of *bounded* arbitrariness – a principle developed in the institutional legal tradition[32] which prevents decision-makers from taking positions that go beyond the constitutional interests of the polity, competition between legal interpretations playing a pivotal role in the process.

The supporters of balancing in constitutional jurisprudence suggest that it is the only plausible way to regulate conflicting societal interests reflected in the language of rights.[33] According to Alexy, '[v]alues and

---

28 Jürgen Habermas, *Between Facts and Norms – Contributions to a Discourse Theory of Law and Democracy*, Polity Press, Cambridge, 1997, p. 259.

29 Lorenzo Zucca, *Constitutional Dilemmas – Conflicts of Fundamental Rights in Europe and the USA*, Oxford University Press, Oxford, 2007, p. 21.

30 Jürgen Habermas, *Between Facts and Norms – Contributions to a Discourse Theory of Law and Democracy*, Polity Press, Cambridge, 1997, p. 259 (emphasis in the original).

31 ibid.

32 George Pavlakos, 'Normativity versus Ontology: Law, Facts and Practical Reason', Rechtstheorie, Vol. 34, No. 4, 2003, pp. 383–386: '[L]egal norms . . . exist within the coordinates of legal systems and can therefore be clearly told apart from other normative entities which are generated within different institutional frameworks (morality, ethics, courtesy, etc). . . . Normativity . . . of legal norms as institutional facts, derives from the fact that they are already embedded in an evaluative context, an institution, which is distinctly legal'.

33 Lorenzo Zucca, *Constitutional Dilemmas – Conflicts of Fundamental Rights in Europe and the USA*, Oxford University Press, Oxford, 2007, p. 3: 'When a party

principles tend to collide. A collision of principles can only be resolved by balancing'.[34] This means that the 'balancing approach is not a matter of convenience or practicability but a feature necessarily . . . connected to the nature of principles as optimisation requirements'.[35] Sweet and Mathews argue that a 'court that explicitly acknowledges that balancing inheres in rights adjudication is a more honest court than one that claims that it only enforces a constitutional code, but neither balances nor makes law'.[36]

Alexy convincingly argues that the constitutional decision-making process is necessarily accompanied by a balancing act. The argument is illustrated by the decision of the German Federal Constitutional Court in the *Lüth* case, concerning the art of German director Veit Harlan, known for the production of propaganda movies during the Second World War, who had not been the object of any criminal charges and continued to exercise his profession. Lüth called for a commercial boycott of Veit Harlan's artistic works, made after 1945 – an act prohibited by the German Civil Code. The District Court in Hamburg decided in favour of Veit Harlan, which impelled Lüth to revert to the German Federal Constitutional Court on the ground that his right to freedom of speech had been violated (but ironically arguing against the artistic right to speak freely). Freedom of speech is protected by the German Constitution and its precise limits may be circumscribed by general laws. The prohibition of boycotts in the German Civil Code is one of such general laws limiting freedom of speech. Both provisions therefore collide at the constitutional level. Alexy explains that 'the Court required that there be a balancing or weighing of the colliding constitutional principles where the application of rules of the civil law might limit a constitutional right'.[37] In fact, the Court did not balance the provisions of civil law against the provisions of constitutional law – since in this case the balancing act would be of a mechanical nature inasmuch as the provisions of the German Constitution list the conditions for the limitation of free speech and the decision would

---

has a right, then her claim must prevail over that of the opponent. In that sense, a right trumps other claims. But what if both parties have a trump card?'.

34 Robert Alexy, 'Constitutional Rights, Balancing, and Rationality', Ratio Juris, Vol. 16, No. 2, 2003, p. 133.

35 Kai Möller, 'Balancing and the Structure of Constitutional Rights', International Journal of Constitutional Law, Vol. 5, No. 3, 2007, p. 455.

36 Alec S. Sweet and Jud Mathews, 'Proportionality Balancing and Global Constitutionalism', Columbia Journal of Transnational Law, Vol. 47, No. 1, 2008, p. 89.

37 Robert Alexy, 'Constitutional Rights, Balancing, and Rationality', Ratio Juris, Vol. 16, No. 2, 2003, p. 133.

be straightforward, repeating the rationale of the District Court. The real balancing act takes place when freedom of speech is compared with public interests (namely, the prohibition of boycotts in their quality of obstacles to economic freedom). Although these interests are explicitly stated in the German Civil Code, they either directly or implicitly transpire at the constitutional level. Only then do the two norms achieve the hierarchical parity which enables the balancing to occur.

The concerns about the German constitutional style, which, according to Somek, has more 'the appearance of ad hoc divinations than of rational expositions of law',[38] have a universal nature for most legal systems.[39] For example, a disinclination of the American jurisprudence to balance values and rights, which is, according to Cohen-Eliya and Porat, a characteristic feature of US constitutional law,[40] does not render it different from the German or any other liberal democratic model. Constitutional balancing, indeed, takes place within the language of *rights*, but due to the ability of different interests to be translated from the language of one system of social norms to the other (where the interest is present as a right in jurisprudence, as a utility in economics or as a value in politics), the *exclusivity* of rights in constitutional jurisprudence should be taken as a plea for epistemological consistency and not as a normative claim. In other words, many economic, cultural and political interests compete in constitutional jurisprudence to be prioritised, but before being *taken seriously*, they are perceived in their *rights*-incarnation. On the other hand, the dogmatic approach, which perceives the concept or rights restrictively, reserving them only to a limited number of societal interests, may indeed provide to those selected interests the *trump*-protection, but at the same time it prevents those unselected interests from seeking constitutional recognition. This interpretation would disadvantage in particular those borderline interests which are not universally recognised as human rights *sensu stricto* – the economic right to compete being one of them – which diminishes their importance, since (being primarily of deontological

---

[38] Alexander Somek, 'The Indelible Science of Law', International Journal of Constitutional Law, Vol. 7, No. 3, 2009, p. 425.

[39] Winfried Brugger, 'Legal Interpretation, Schools of Jurisprudence, and Anthropology: Some Remarks from a German Point of View', The American Journal of Comparative Law, Vol. 42, No. 2, 1994, pp. 395–421.

[40] Moshe Cohen-Eliya and Iddo Porat, 'American Balancing and German Proportionality: The Historical Origins', International Journal of Constitutional Law, Vol. 8, No. 2, 2010, pp. 263–265: 'American constitutional law, relying on the absolute nature of the U.S. constitutional text, portrays itself as adhering to a categorical constitutional analysis in which the constitutional review begins and ends at the stage of identifying the infringement of a right'.

nature, but not being promoted to the formal level of rights) they are unable to use a purely utilitarian wealth maximisation calculus, which appears to be the only alternative to the rights argument in constitutional adjudicative process.

As for any balancing act, the central issue of constitutional deliberation techniques is the problem of the commensurability of values. Schauer correctly observes that, at the ontological level, 'to resolve the philosophical question whether values are or are not . . . commensurable'[41] is impossible. But his proposal to adopt an intermediate approach depending on the consequences of actions cannot be accepted inasmuch as values themselves are consequences. If so, the consequentialist approach to balancing is tautological. Waldron proposes an alternative solution, suggesting a *strong* incommensurability and a *weak* incommensurability benchmark.[42] This argument is criticised by Lariguet,[43] because of its indeterminacy. In addition, values are both commensurable and incommensurable at the same time.[44] An ultimate solution to the in-/commensurability dilemma is unreachable and it is thus *solved* in an ad hoc fashion in each particular case.[45] The argumentation of the parties and their ability to operationalise the institutional preconditions embedded in common interests (values, principles, rights, goals etc.) via the adversarial judicial (or in a broader sense any decision-making) process – often one party argues in favour of their commensurability and the other against it – is the decisive factor in

---

41 Frederick Schauer, 'Commensurability and Its Constitutional Consequences', Hastings Law Journal, Vol. 45, No. 4, 1994, p. 785.

42 Jeremy Waldron, 'Fake Incommensurability: A Response to Professor Schauer', Hastings Law Journal, Vol. 45, No. 4, 1994, p. 817: 'In a case of strong incommensurability, the competing values cannot even be brought into relation with one another: They are genuinely incomparable in the practical realm, leaving us paralysed in the face of their competition. In a case of weak incommensurability . . . the values can be brought into relation with one another. We look at them both, we consider them, and we find an immediately discernible order'.

43 Guillermo Lariguet, 'Constitutional Dilemmas – Some criticisms of Lorenzo Zucca's Conception', in Guillermo Lariguet, David Martinez Zorilla and Silvina Alvarez with replies by Lorenzo Zucca, 'An Exchange on Constitutional Dilemmas', http://papers.ssrn.com/sol3/papers.cfm?abstract_id=1284490, accessed on 17 September 2010, p. 4.

44 Jeanne L. Schroeder, 'The Laconomics of Apples and Oranges: A Speculative Analysis of the Economic Concept of Commensurability', Yale Journal of Law and Humanities, Vol. 15, No. 2, 2003, p. 350.

45 Duncan Kennedy, 'Legal Formality', The Journal of Legal Studies, Vol. 2, No. 2, 1973, p. 378: 'The heterogeneity of values and the multiplicity of factual situations, in a world of purposive actors, forces the group to admit an element of the arbitrary and irrational into its governance'.

addressing the problem of in-/commensurability.[46] This reveals the *positive* feature of the competitive process. Its *normative* significance is recognised by those societies in which the principles of individual freedom (with its apparent elements of irrationality) prevail over ersatz-religious societal beliefs in transcendental objectivity and absolute truth. The answer to Waldron's rhetorical question 'Who is this "we"' who make ultimate judgements and 'who are supposed to know in advance what beliefs about incommensurability to inculcate among "them"'[47] would have a form: the institutional foundations of liberal democracy – the competition (of lawyers, experts, doctrines, norms, values, ideas, arguments . . .) in each particular case and not of elitist philosopher-kings whom he denounces.[48] As a result, balancing should not only encompass the inevitability of the conflict in law, but should also acknowledge the ultimate irreconcilability of this conflict. Otherwise, as Zucca warns,[49] balancing could itself be transformed into another 'right answer'. This research shares only the first part of Zucca's view that 'subsumption reaches a result by using the rules of logic, while balancing interprets the premise through numbers'.[50] He basically argues that, since balancing *solves* constitutional dilemmas as the subsumption does and the dilemmas are irresolvable, balancing shares the same illusion about the clarity and ultimate coherence of law. Under such conditions, this research would agree with this argument. However, proper balancing does not claim that its outcomes are universal. Quite the contrary, it reveals the ultimate indeterminacy and polysemy of law. Balancing should not be reduced to a pragmatic calculation and it should not be seen as 'a holistic doctrine'.[51] This would indeed negate the conflicting nature of law and follow the same categorical nature as monosemic hierarchical legal architectures do. Balancing is based on the competitive process in legal reasoning. Balancing could deviate from purely normative adjudication towards broader societal interests, but these interests could never be seen as a pure cost–benefit analysis since the legal discourse will always remain averse to such an excessive pragmatism.

---

[46] Friedrich A. von Hayek, 'Competition as a Discovery Procedure', The Quarterly Journal of Austrian Economics, Vol. 5, No. 3, 2002, p. 16: 'As Adam Smith realized, . . . the situation is somewhat like agreeing to play a game based partly on skill and partly on luck'.

[47] Jeremy Waldron, 'Fake Incommensurability: A Response to Professor Schauer', Hastings Law Journal, Vol. 45, No. 4, 1994, pp. 821–823.

[48] ibid, p. 823.

[49] Lorenzo Zucca, *Constitutional Dilemmas – Conflicts of Fundamental Rights in Europe and the USA*, Oxford University Press, Oxford, 2007, p. 6.

[50] ibid, p. 20.

[51] ibid, p. 29.

6.2 CORRELATION OF LAW AND MORALITY

The main proposition of this section is that the relationship between law and economics is very similar to the relationship between law and ethics/morality. The problem of the epistemic self-sufficiency of law is not only relevant to the interaction between different disciplines (in particular, law and economics, and law and sociology), which is a relatively new trend,[52] but also with respect to morality, which claims its ultimate authority from law.[53] Unlike the interaction between disciplines, the correlation between law and morality has been at the centre of many jurisprudential debates and discussed extensively. For this purpose, morality is given a broad meaning and can encompass a variety of issues ranging from personal or religious beliefs to ideological conceptions or political necessity. Law and morality are two separate types of social norms and have strong historical and epistemic ties. Their mutual dependence could hardly be rejected. However, whether the law can regulate morally sensitive issues without referring to moral norms and be self-sufficient in this regard is more contentious. Natural law theories and legal positivism answer these questions in a radically different manner.

The natural law tradition is rooted in the idea that law originates in and is necessarily predetermined by a natural objective order. Historically, different natural law theories have derived this order from various natural, theological and humanistic preconditions. They may significantly disagree with each other on substantive matters, but they remain united as to the objective essence of law. Natural law doctrines cover the whole ideological spectrum:[54] depending on the historical and other institutional contexts,

---

[52] John C. Goodman, 'An Economic Theory of the Evolution of Common Law', The Journal of Legal Studies, Vol. 7, No. 2, 1978, p. 393: '[Until recently] judicial decisions were couched in the language of morality, fairness, and justice without explicit reference to anything resembling the modern conception of economic efficiency'.

[53] Hans Kelsen, 'Law and Morality', in Hans Kelsen, *Essays in Legal and Moral Philosophy*, D. Reidel, Dordrecht, 1973, p. 82: '[N]ot only is the methodological purity of legal science endangered by failure to observe the boundary separating it from natural science; it is still further endangered by the fact that it is not divided, or not clearly enough divided from ethics – that no sharp distinction is made between law and morality'.

[54] Albert A. Ehrenzweig, 'Psychoanalytical Jurisprudence: A Common Language for Babylon', Columbia Law Review, Vol. 65, No. 8, 1965, p. 1336: 'The god-emperor's rule in Virgil, Rome's *jus gentium*, England's common law, the Church's precepts, Islam's *Koran*, Grotius' law of nations, American "due process" – all were invoked as natural law because of their assumed positive

some claim the *naturalness* of humanism others justify with the reference to the *naturalness* various historical perversions, which incidentally explains the title of an article by Knight.[55] According to natural law theories, legal norms should conform to the requirements of the higher order which determines their legitimacy. The legal system is treated as a consequence and derivative of natural commands. Whenever the two orders collide, priority is unequivocally given to the higher ranked order. The internal legality and validity of law is always tied to its external legitimacy. In other words, *lex naturalis derogat legi generali*, because *lex iniusta non est lex*. Natural law theories are sceptical about the autopoiesis of law.[56] However, they should not be reduced to a legal form of morality.[57]

According to legal positivists, who claim that the law is what has been adopted (posited)[58] by a sovereign (be it the monarch, the parliament or the people), the law does not necessarily need to expand its boundaries by embracing the principles of morality and 'a legal system is not a phenomenon that in itself immanently embodies a moral rationality'.[59] The nineteenth century German positivistic tradition developed the notion of 'the normative power of the factual',[60] which disentangled the notions of legitimacy, legality and facticity of law. The factual *ability* to make law *legalises* the holder of power. Neither morality nor legitimacy was considered as necessary components of legality. The positivist task in this respect

---

validity, and all were invoked as positive law because of their assumed natural foundation' (emphasis in the original).

55 Frank H. Knight, 'Natural Law: Last Refuge of the Bigot', Ethics, Vol. 59, No. 2, 1949.

56 Thomas Bustamante, 'Comment on Petroski – On MacCormick's Post-Positivism', German Law Journal, Vol. 12, No. 2, 2011, p. 698: 'If the law is understood as an autopoietic social system, one cannot account for its social normativity and its proper social functions in the context of a pluralistic and secular society which can no longer rely on metaphysical arguments from natural law'.

57 Alf Ross, *Towards a Realistic Jurisprudence – A Criticism of the Dualism in Law*, Einar Munksgaard, Copenhagen, 1946, p. 22: 'Positive and natural law are united in one genus, and it is this which, by the criterion of compulsion, is opposed to morality'.

58 John Austin, *The Province of Jurisprudence Determined*, George Weidenfeld & Nicolson, London, 1954, p. 365: 'The appropriate subject of Jurisprudence, in any of its different departments, is positive law: Meaning by positive law . . . law established or "positum", in an independent political community, by the experts or tacit authority of its sovereign of supreme government'.

59 Ernest J. Weinrib, 'Legal Formalism: On the Immanent Rationality of Law', The Yale Law Journal, Vol. 97, No. 6, 1988, p. 955.

60 Ellen Kennedy, 'Introduction', in Carl Schmitt, *The Crisis of Parliamentary Democracy*, MIT University Press, Cambridge, Massachusetts, 1985, p. xxxv.

was to *explain* the relations between the sovereign and the law, rather than to *prescribe* how these relations should be formed.

From the perspective of legal positivism, the law is not directly dependent upon any external requirements.[61] This most basic characteristic of law appears to many a narrow-minded historical relict, but it is the only mode to define the concept of law in a manner, distinguishable from the concept of *good* law. This sometime is recognised even in economic analysis of law.[62] Among the main *external* requirements are political necessity, public interests, morality, economic rationality and justice. All these categories – and in particular the last one – are very closely connected to the notion of law, and sometimes law – if established and applied properly – almost coincides with them, but ontologically they are different: law sometimes may be immoral, and conversely one can potentially be moral, while acting illegally.[63] The reason for the separation is not that morality is much broader and vaguer than law. In fact '[m]oral relativism (scepticism) does not imply Legal Positivism'.[64] The reason is much more modest and unobtrusive. As Kramer puts it '[t]hough legality and morality are of course combinable, they are likewise disjoinable . . .; separability does not entail separateness'.[65] Law *can* regulate moral issues without referring to the norms of morality. Law as a cognitive system, in Luhmann's conception, should distinguish itself from every other system of norms, because '[t]he recursively interconnected operations of the system draw a boundary and thereby differentiate system and environment'.[66] Law does not make any value assessment of its internal rules and principles as long as they are adopted and applied according to the established procedure. If they are not, then the rules are either automatically null and void (which removes

---

[61] Aharon Barak, *The Judge in a Democracy*, Princeton University Press, Princeton, 2006, p. 216: 'Other branches seek to attain efficiency; the courts seek to attain legality'.

[62] John M. Clark, 'Law and Economic Life: I. The Legal Framework of Economic Life', The University Journal of Business, Vol. 3, No. 4, 1925, p. 352: 'A law is defined as a rule of action backed by that compulsory power which is an essential mark of sovereignty. Compulsion implies the power to impose virtually unlimited penalties if the rule is disregarded'.

[63] Carl Schmitt, *Political Theology – Four Chapters on the Concept of Sovereignty*, The MIT Press, Cambridge, Massachusetts, 1985, p. 7: '[W]hether the extreme exception can be banished from the world is not a juristic question'.

[64] Deryck Beyeveld and Roger Brownsword, *Law as a Moral Judgement*, Sweet & Maxwell, London, 1986, p. 277.

[65] Matthew H. Kramer, *In Defence of Legal Positivism: Law Without Trimmings*, Oxford University Press, Oxford, 1999, pp. 1–2.

[66] Niklas Luhmann, 'Deconstruction as Second-Order Observing', New Literary History, Vol. 24, No. 4, 1993, p. 772.

them from the realm of law) or the procedure is implicitly amended (the arbitrary ignorance of decision-making being such an option).

While interpreting MacCormick's statement that 'law claims nothing',[67] Alexy refers to the literal interpretation of a claim, suggesting that this claim in fact 'is by persons, in particular, though not solely . . . by officials, on behalf of the law'.[68] The *claimless* nature of law still reflects its agency feature: law can *conduct* any claim, but law itself is speechless. This feature distinguishes the law from the physical order. As Peczenik puts it, 'whereas neat calculi in natural science seem to reveal the very order of the world, neat juristic doctrines cannot reveal any such order, because there is none'.[69] In this sense legal systems may more easily regulate ex ante *random* selection as an expression of 'objective equality of opportunity from which the satisfaction of equality springs',[70] than conduct an ex post *rational* or *moral* evaluation. In this respect, the form is more important than the content. This feature of law goes beyond its inclination towards lotteries, 'a choice not to choose',[71] and other purely procedural practices: being applied to many individual transactions, the legal norm is bound to bring in some cases certain negative externalities for the actors. Law is limited in its flexibility to minimise such externalities. Their randomisation – as it is the purest case with lotteries – protects the law from being constantly challenged from the *rational* perspective. It does not mean that norms which are similar to lotteries 'generate equality, but that they may promote a conception of equality',[72] and that the law is intrinsically interested in the process of randomisation and independency of its factual content.

While natural law emphasises issues of *legitimacy*, legal positivism mostly refers to *legality*. Law is perceived as a self-sufficient discipline. It does not regulate all moral issues, but those which *are* regulated by law require a purely legal analysis. Positivists do not reject the interconnections between law and morality and accept that, in some instances, law can

---

67 Neil MacCormick, 'Why Law Makes No Claims', in George Pavlakos (ed.), *Law, Rights and Discourse*, Hart Publishing, Oxford, 2007, p. 59.

68 Robert Alexy, 'The Dual Nature of Law', Ratio Juris, Vol. 23, No. 2, 2010, p. 168.

69 Aleksander Peczenik, 'Scientia Juris: Legal Doctrine as Knowledge of Law and as a Source of Law', *Treatise of Legal Philosophy and General Jurisprudence*: Vol. 4, Springer, New York, 2007, p. 71.

70 Neil Duxbury, *Random Justice: On Lotteries and Legal Decision-Making*, Oxford University Press, Oxford, 1999, p. 62.

71 Guido Calabresi and Philip Bobbitt, *Tragic Choices*, W. W. Norton & Company, New York, 1978, p. 41.

72 Neil Duxbury, *Random Justice: On Lotteries and Legal Decision-Making*, Oxford University Press, Oxford, 1999, p. 62.

use moral norms to address specific issues. But this application should be internally *accepted* by the legal system rather than *imposed* on it from the outside. Incidentally, the origins of modern positivism and utilitarianism were developed by the same authors, primarily Bentham[73] and Austin.[74] Historically utilitarianism was developed as a reaction to legal absolutism by the modernist tradition, which can be conceptually reconciled with positivism. Nowadays these two approaches are sometimes considered to be incommensurable as utilitarian ideas are usually encompassed in natural law theories. The modern evolution of the natural law doctrine with its emphasis on human rights gave some impetus for the revival of the rights-based positivist tradition of jurisprudence.[75] Because of the place they occupy at the centre of the ideological programme of liberal democracies, human rights become defendable for different political currents and legal doctrines.

In relation to the mechanisms of this acceptance, positivists are divided into two major schools: *inclusivists* and *exclusivists*.[76] Inclusive legal positivism is a softer theory. It accepts the possibility of situations where the law can be influenced by morality, even though it requires this subordination to be explicitly acknowledged in a given legal source.[77] It is based on Hart's concept of 'the rule of recognition',[78] which can be seen as the common perceptions about the law which actually dominate in a polity. Whether the rule of recognition refers to the principles of morality or other social norms, these norms become imperative for the legal discourse. However, the validity of this subordination can be unilaterally cancelled by law; so, the law does not abandon its self-centricity but merely presumes that it should give priority to morality in certain cases.

Exclusive legal positivism is more categorical in this respect. It does not

---

[73] Jeremy Bentham, *An Introduction to the Principles of Morals and Legislation*, The Athlone Press, University of London, 1970.

[74] John Austin, *The Province of Jurisprudence Determined*, George Weidenfeld & Nicolson, London, 1954.

[75] Herbert L. A. Hart, 'Between Utility and Rights', Columbia Law Review, Vol. 79, No. 5, 1979, p. 828.

[76] Wil J. Waluchow, 'The Many Faces of Legal Positivism', The University of Toronto Law Journal, Vol. 48, No. 3, 1998, p. 394.

[77] Massimo La Torre, 'On Two Distinct and Opposing Versions of Natural Law: "Exclusive" versus "Inclusive"', Ratio Juris, Vol. 19, No. 2, 2006, p. 198: '"Inclusive" positivism allows for the possibility of moral principles to be covered or included by the sources of law and especially by the ground rule of a legal system, the rule of recognition'.

[78] Herbert L. A. Hart, *The Concept of Law*, Oxford University Press, Oxford, 1994, p. 108.

reject the argument that law can be influenced by external social norms,[79] but conditions this influence on two important requirements. First, such an influence is only accepted when it does not contradict positive law. The first condition therefore is not applicable to hard cases. Secondly, if the law has accepted the validity and legality of certain moral norms, these norms should be treated as purely *legal* norms. In other words, by their incorporation into the legal domain, moral norms cease to belong exclusively to morality and become part of legality[80] like loanwords whose adoption in the grammar leads to their perception as foreign words only etymologically and not substantively.

The two possibilities of the second condition reflect the absolutist and the relativist approaches to exclusive legal positivism respectively. The absolutist approach is a self-reflective imperative position of law which does not accept any subordination unless imposed by valid legal procedures. It is purely *intra*disciplinary in this respect. The relativist approach acknowledges the exclusivity of law but also accepts the principle of the indeterminacy of law, according to which a legal system can never be seen as a static, complete system. Its dynamics implies that different legal institutions are not always co-possible. However, the resulting incoherency does not require the law to seek a solution beyond its limits. Other social norms are even less coherent and determinate. Indeed, unlike any other social norm, the law routinely adjusts itself in order to attain some coherence and systemic harmony. According to Balkin, coherence 'is more than a property of law; it is the result of a particular way of thinking about the law'.[81] The solution can be found in the implicit ex post conversion of the social norm, which influenced the decision-making process, into the legal discourse. Legal positivism can accept this internalisation only

---

79 Matthew H. Kramer, 'Why the Axioms and Theorems of Arithmetic are not Legal Norms', Oxford Journal of Legal Studies, Vol. 27, No. 3, 2007, p. 556: 'While gladly acknowledging that moral principles often get invoked in the adjudicative and administrative activities of legal officials, the Exclusivists insist that those principles are extra-legal standards'.

80 Ota Weinberger, 'Introduction', in Hans Kelsen, *Essays in Legal and Moral Philosophy*, D. Reidel, Dordrecht, 1973, pp. x–xi: 'Kelsen, Like Max Weber, champions the notion of a value-free science, a science which seizes and sets forth what is actual, without evaluating what it finds. . . . In juristic methodology this leads to a sharp separation of considerations *de lege lata* from those *de lege ferenda* – of which only the first are in Kelsen's opinion juristic – even where questions of interpretation or discretion are concerned'.

81 Jack M. Balkin, 'Understanding Legal Understanding: The Legal Subject and the Problem of Legal Coherence', The Yale Law Journal, Vol. 103, No. 1, 1993, p. 106.

provided that it is not treated as an extra-legal norm from the moment of its legal recognition, because '[n]either an accumulation of non-legal social data nor the judge's breakfast can serve as determinants of legal development'.[82] The law thereby will reflect all the necessary requirements of flexibility and social responsiveness, while remaining at the same time a purely *intra*disciplinary phenomenon.

The moral *sterility* of the positivistic concept of law was among the main reasons for its criticism. Positivism was often accused of opportunism, in its inability to oppose immoral orders and its preparedness to serve any sovereign regardless of its moral principles. Indeed, positive law can be used by *any* political regime, however perverse the regime may be, but the same holds true for legal naturalism as well, since it is not the separability of law and morality which authorises unacceptable political regimes and practices, and these regimes can operate within the realm of morality as well as within the realm of law. Though often in these cases morality can be more humanistic than the law, the opposite is possible too, when the law serves as a restrictive boundary for the underdeveloped morality. History shows that often political dictatorships were using metaphysical, spiritual, religious and other organic theories from which to derive their *superior* sovereignty – all these explanations can be approved by the natural law as well, which is not necessarily limited to its contemporary perception. If the concept of natural law is reduced solely to its humanistic limits, then it should be perceived as a context-dependent ideological political concept only, which explains more the dominant societal values than legal mechanisms which support them. The law, which in contemporary liberal democracies is created 'by the constitutional structure itself working itself pure',[83] and the contemporary maxima that '[*t*]*he role of rules in the liberal state is to provide autonomy*'[84] can be totally different if interpreted in different historical periods or through different ideological lenses. Both scenarios, however, are irrelevant for the analysis of the essence of law, and should be addressed by political theory rather than jurisprudence. Positivism in this respect is a politically neutral concept.[85]

---

82 Günther Teubner, '"And God Laughed . . ." Indeterminacy, Self-Reference and Paradox in Law', German Law Journal, Vol. 12, No. 1, 2011, p. 377.

83 Ronald M. Dworkin, 'Law's Ambitions for Itself', Virginia Law Review, Vol. 71, No. 2, 1985, p. 175.

84 Duncan Kennedy, 'Legal Formality', The Journal of Legal Studies, Vol. 2, No. 2, 1973, p. 371 (emphasis in the original).

85 Ellen Kennedy, 'Introduction', in Carl Schmitt, *The Crisis of Parliamentary Democracy*, MIT University Press, Cambridge, Massachusetts, 1985, pp. xxxv–xxxvi.

The essence of this dialectical approach is grounded in the Hegelian philosophical tradition, according to which the whole spectrum of human relations and laws of nature is based upon contradictions. The dialectical conflict is implicitly present in everything. In jurisprudence this view is reflected in Kelsen's theory of pure law as a 'dynamic process of gradual concretisation'.[86] This point requires further clarification. Kelsen's vision of law and underlying argumentation is based on dialectical method. However, by developing his theory in the neo-Kantian dialectical tradition, he rejected some significant aspects of the Hegelian dialectics. Namely, Kelsen opposed Hegel's (and Marx's)[87] dialectical vision of history. According to Kelsen, 'Marx's historic materialism, his economic interpretation of history is an unmistakable offspring of Hegel's philosophy of history'.[88] This criticism is shared by this research. Dialectics of history clearly contradicts the main principles of dialectics as an epistemic exercise. Instead of being treated as a method of reasoning, dialectics has been transformed into a method of evolution, which is deterministic and therefore holistic, whereas holism is in methodological opposition to dialectics. Hegel's absolute spirit is non-dialectical and holistic. In this respect Leibnitz's subjective idealism reflects the notion of ideal law better than Hegel's dialectics of history. As Schroeder suggests, '[i]f antinomy is universal, then no *specific* antinomy is a problem to be *solved*. Rather, antinomy as a necessary fact of the world, is a process to be studied and *understood*.'[89] This approach does not negate action. Ultimately a choice between competing notions should be made, but this choice encompasses the final indeterminacy of law as well as that of any other system of social norms, thoughts and actions. Furthermore, it considers it as an inevitable and productive component of normative systems: by making one hard choice the regulator faces another one, which also requires proper treatment and ad infinitum.

---

86 William Ebenstein, 'The Pure Theory of Law: Demythologizing Legal Thought', California Law Review, Vol. 59, No. 3, 1971, p. 642.

87 Karl R. Popper, 'What is Dialectic?', Mind, Vol. 49, No. 196, 1940, pp. 421–423.

88 Hans Kelsen, 'The Natural-Law Doctrine before the Tribunal of Science', The Western Political Quarterly, Vol. 2, No. 4, 1949, p. 512.

89 Jeanne L. Schroeder, 'The Laconomics of Apples and Oranges: A Speculative Analysis of the Economic Concept of Commensurability', Yale Journal of Law and Humanities, Vol. 15, No. 2, 2003, p. 363 (emphasis in the original).

6.3 IDEAL AND MATERIAL LAW

The subdivision of law into an ideal and a material part is an important analytical exercise in dialectical methodology. As any other law of dialectics, the epistemological recognition of the ideal and material dimensions of social phenomena can be misinterpreted. One such wrong perception is directly related to the area of jurisprudence and reduces the material law to the written law. From this perspective, the ideal law is seen either as unwritten customary law, as 'the claim to correctness',[90] as an unachievable legal desideratum,[91] as 'idea-system',[92] motivating the law (e.g. the influence of Roman law on the development of civil codes) or as a set of legal aspirations, 'a future-oriented project and a motivating source'.[93] In the first case, ideal stands for not explicitly fixed in legal form; in the second, the ideal means the best; while the latest, and the closest to the notion of ideal as it is used in this research, still tends to go *outside* the legal discourse towards the realm of morality and can be classified as a significant institutional prerequisite of the decision-making process rather than a part of the law as such. These perceptions of the ideal would lead to the conclusion that naturalist legal theories refer to the ideal, perfect, universal dimension of law with an emphasis 'on moral values and rights',[94] while positivists support its material, written, explicit dimension. Ross has a more essentialist, dialectical view, which suggests that '[t]he law is both, valid and factual, ideal and real, physical and metaphysical',[95] but his concept of *ideal* still includes evaluative elements (ideal as being good).

---

[90] Robert Alexy, 'On the Thesis of a Necessary Connection between Law and Morality: Bulygin's Critique', Ratio Juris, Vol. 13, No. 2, 2000, p. 138.

[91] William Ebenstein, 'The Pure Theory of Law: Demythologizing Legal Thought', California Law Review, Vol. 59, No. 3, 1971, p. 623: '[Ideology] veils legal reality by justifying an existing legal order and by identifying it more or less with a higher, ideal law – the conservative version of all political ideologies and natural law doctrines'.

[92] David J. Gerber, 'Idea-Systems in Law: Nineteenth-Century German Experience', Law and History Review, Vol. 10, No. 1, 1992, pp. 153–154.

[93] Wibren Van Der Burg, 'The Importance of Ideals', The Journal of Value Inquiry, Vol. 31, No. 1, 1997, p. 25: 'Ideals are values that are implicit or latent in the law, or the public and moral culture of a society or group that usually cannot be fully realized, and that partly transcend contingent, historical formulations, and implementations in terms of rules and principles'.

[94] Sean Coyle, 'Positivism, Idealism and the Rule of Law', Oxford Journal of Legal Studies, Vol. 26, No. 2, 2006, p. 258: 'What is legal idealism? Legal idealism, or anti-positivism, or natural law theory, has to be understood as the opposite of legal positivism'.

[95] Alf Ross, *Towards a Realistic Jurisprudence – A Criticism of the Dualism in Law*, Einar Munksgaard, Copenhagen, 1946, p. 20.

The premises of this book are different. Legal idealism is by no means 'the opposite of legal positivism'.[96] The ideal is perceived here as an inherent feature of *any* law: good or bad, just or unjust. It is a *legal* component, not a moral one. The ideal and material components are considered from a dialectical perspective, which entails that every phenomenon constitutes the unity of both. It refers to a fundamental epistemological precondition of human cognition and is thus subjectivist to some extent. The idea of a thing is the proxy by which it is perceived by the subject, it is his knowledge of this particular thing at each particular moment when the thing is seen or imagined. The material aspect is the thing itself as well as its unarticulated presence in the subjective knowledge of it. This essentialist[97] view reflects the basic Platonic idea of ideal universe. As Alexy argues, '[t]he law has a dual nature . . .; [it] necessarily comprises both a . . . factual dimension and an ideal . . . one',[98] but the *ideal* does not necessarily encompass elements of morality or any other *ought to*. The ideal *is*; it is as much an *is* as the material component of the law. Alexy's perception of legal idealism[99] can then be coherently read from the perspective of legal positivism as well,[100] assuming that the descriptive part of Alexy's thesis is read separately from his prescriptive part, where he argues about an *adequate* (and therefore desirable for society, the one which does not cover the entirety of the legal domain) theory of legal argumentation.[101] Raz observes 'multiple dualities of the law'.[102]

To address a rhetorical question posed by Hart regarding a legal rule

---

[96] Bev Cluvas, 'The Sheffield School and Discourse Theory: Divergences and Similarities in Legal Idealism/Anti-Positivism', Ratio Juris, Vol. 19, No. 2, 2006, p. 230.

[97] Michael D.A. Freeman, *Lloyd's Introduction to Jurisprudence*, Sweet & Maxwell, London, 2010, p. 34: 'Essentialism . . . [reflects] the notion that every class or group of things has an essential or fundamental nature, common to every member of the class, and that the process of defining consists in isolating and identifying this common nature or intrinsic property'.

[98] Robert Alexy, 'The Dual Nature of Law', Ratio Juris, Vol. 23, No. 2, 2010, p. 167.

[99] Robert Alexy, 'The Special Case Thesis', Ratio Juris, Vol. 12, No. 4, 1999, p. 375: '[L]egal reasoning remains deeply connected with what can be called the free, discursive, or ideal side of law'.

[100] Tony Ward, 'Two Schools of Legal Idealism: A Positivist Introduction', Ratio Juris, Vol. 19, No. 2, 2006, p. 133: 'Far from being burdened with natural-law connotations, this view is perfectly compatible with positivism'.

[101] Robert Alexy, 'The Special Case Thesis', Ratio Juris, Vol. 12, No. 4, 1999, p. 375.

[102] Joseph Raz, *Between Authority and Interpretation*, Oxford University Press, Oxford, 2009, p. 1.

which forbids parking a vehicle in the public park – '[p]lainly, this forbids an automobile, but what about bicycles, roller skates, toy automobiles?'[103] – the ideal law would implicitly contain the *proper* meaning which is discovered (in the Hayekian sense of discovery procedure)[104] during each interpretation act. This 'what the law ought to be'[105] does not go beyond 'what the law is' towards 'what we would like the law to be'. On the contrary, it is embedded in legal matter and this material part – be it written or unwritten – dialectically keeps its *ideal* sense within the boundaries of the *form*. Hart underlines the danger of sliding from this position to the category of morality, which can also prescribe what the law ought to be, albeit *externally*. The ideal element of law says what the law ought to be *internally*.[106] This feature enables the law to reflect changing circumstances to cope with the 'penumbra of doubt'[107] and indeterminacy, while at the same time remaining autopoietic.[108] Recognising Alexy's thesis on the dual nature of law, it cannot be accepted that 'the dual-nature thesis implies non-positivism'.[109] The duality of law means that all legal norms and the legal system as a whole are composed of both material and ideal elements. Alexy's duality is different. By ideal dimension, he means 'the element of moral correctness'.[110]

The ideal element is an inevitable component of any legal norm – be it a rule or a principle – and cannot be seen therefore as a synonym of

---

[103] Herbert L. A. Hart, 'Positivism and the Separation of Law and Morals', Harvard Law Review, Vol. 71, No. 4, 1958, p. 607.

[104] Ernest J. Weinrib, 'Legal Formalism: On the Immanent Rationality of Law', The Yale Law Journal, Vol. 97, No. 6, 1988, p. 956: 'The paradigmatic legal function is not the manufacturing of legal norms but the understanding of what is intimated by juridical arrangements and relationships. Legal creativity here is essentially cognitive, and it is most naturally expressed in adjudication conceived more as the discovery than as the making of law'.

[105] Herbert L. A. Hart, 'Positivism and the Separation of Law and Morals', Harvard Law Review, Vol. 71, No. 4, 1958, p. 608.

[106] Ernest J. Weinrib, 'Legal Formalism: On the Immanent Rationality of Law', The Yale Law Journal, Vol. 97, No. 6, 1988, p. 956: 'Law is not so much an instrument in the service of foreign ideals as an end in itself constituting, as it were, its own ideal'.

[107] Herbert L. A. Hart, *The Concept of Law*, Oxford University Press, Oxford, 1994, p. 123.

[108] Günther Teubner, 'The King's Many Bodies: The Self-Deconstruction of Law's Hierarchy', Law & Society Review, Vol. 31, No. 4, 1997, p. 764: '[For Derrida l]aw is grounded only on itself, . . . [becoming] a deconstructed disunity of discursive fragments'.

[109] Robert Alexy, 'On the Thesis of a Necessary Connection between Law and Morality: Bulygin's Critique', Ratio Juris, Vol. 13, No. 2, 2000, p. 138.

[110] ibid, p. 167.

principle.[111] It is an immanent part of any law. Yet, its immanence by implying its inherent presence is at the same time dialectically transcendent, in the sense that the ideal part of the law cannot be fully captured by its material part, always leaving some room for interpretation. The law can be written or unwritten, valid or invalid, harmful or beneficial, well- or badly designed. Any law has an ideal component, as well as any other system of social norms. In spite of its unwritten sources, morality also has ideal and material components, and should not be treated as 'pure ideality'.[112] A *moral* norm of politeness has a formal aspect 'not to spread gossip', while its ideal aspect is subject to the context and interpretation: is this information gossip, how far is it going, how does it participate in communication etc. An identical *legal* norm has a formal aspect 'not to defame' and, here again, its ideal aspect is subject to the context and interpretation.

In fact, positivism treats the law as an autopoietic system: it does not reject the ideal elements of law, but only refuses to search for them outside the realm of law, in morality or any other cognitive source. Legal positivism should not be reduced, therefore, to a mechanical process. It is not 'a giant syllogism machine'.[113] Kelsen has criticised this reductionist perception of legal positivism.[114] *Legal* positivism should not be confused with *logical* positivism, for which the thesis of application of the syllogistic machinery would be more relevant. Kelsen's perception of law was to some extent related to logical positivism, but he did not share its vision of law as a purely societal 'one-dimensional' syllogistic construct.

As to the material element of law, it refers to the actual form in which the law is present. This premise enables the perception of positive law beyond the limits of its actual material form. Any positive law reveals itself directly in *material* sources (written or unwritten) as well as in the *idea* of what the law is. This argument should not be reduced to the origin-oriented, legal interpretation: the intentions of the law-makers do not constitute the law.[115] The scepticism towards legal originalism should not

---

111 Wibren Van Der Burg, 'The Importance of Ideals', The Journal of Value Inquiry, Vol. 31, No. 1, 1997, p. 26: 'Is there really a difference between ideals and principles? . . . The better alternative is to reserve the term principles for norms'.

112 Alf Ross, *Towards a Realistic Jurisprudence – A Criticism of the Dualism in Law*, Einar Munksgaard, Copenhagen, 1946, p. 20.

113 Burt Neuborne, 'Of Sausage Factories and Syllogism Machines: Formalism, Realism, and Exclusionary Selection Techniques', New York University Law Review, Vol. 67, No. 1, 1992, p. 421.

114 Hans Kelsen, 'Law and Logic', in Hans Kelsen, *Essays in Legal and Moral Philosophy*, D. Reidel, Dordrecht, 1973, pp. 228–253.

115 Jessica Lane, 'The Poetics of Legal Interpretation', Columbia Law Review, Vol. 87, No. 1, 1987, p. 205: 'The originalists' claim is simply one, by no means

be confused with the importance of legal hermeneutics. The former implies that those who adopted the norms not only know best what was *intended* to be achieved, but also that their intentions can guide the application of the norm in the future. The hermeneutical vision, on the contrary, is concentrated on the dynamical aspects of what the norm really means, trying to discover its sense in the rapidly changing regulatory environment. It does not glorify the views of legislators, refusing to treat the intention as a canonical imperative for the following evolvement of the norm. Law is not based on the historical preconditions of its adoption only.[116] More importantly, it requires an introspective analysis of its essence.[117] On the other hand, the ideal dimension of law is not a pure open-ended form of consequentialism, since the connection of the ideal dimension of the law to its material form does not allow any discrepancy between the two.[118] Any act of legal interpretation also contains both ideal and material dimensions. The ideal dimension of law reveals itself via legal interpretation and tolerates it as long as it corresponds to its material formal expression.

The internalisation of the dialectics of the ideal/material law is important for jurisprudence because it enables the law to operate within its natural cognitive limits, expanding beyond literalism, while remaining at the same time a closed self-referential system, as perceived by exclusive legal positivism. In turn, this demonstrates that regulation of the competitive process by law can be made in abstraction of other disciplines, like economics or political theory. An interdisciplinary study of the phenomenon of competition can be performed in order to expand the existing knowledge and to develop certain comparative postulates and this does not imply that the phenomenon cannot be addressed separately

---

necessary, conception of how intention should be stipulated for reading the Constitution'.

116 Oliver W. Holmes, 'The Theory of Legal Interpretation', Harvard Law Review, Vol. 12, No. 6, 1899, p. 419: 'We do not inquire what the legislature meant; we ask only what the statute means'.

117 Jessica Lane, 'The Poetics of Legal Interpretation', Columbia Law Review, Vol. 87, No. 1, 1987, p. 202: 'This movement involves an unobservable and often disorganized attempt to adapt various possible readings to one another and to discard those readings that are, on the whole, not as satisfying as the readings kept in play. Moreover, an interpreter must simultaneously distinguish not only which crucial passages in the text will stand for the text as a whole, but which reading of each passage is most susceptible to the exigencies of system formation'.

118 Ernest J. Weinrib, 'Legal Formalism: On the Immanent Rationality of Law', The Yale Law Journal, Vol. 97, No. 6, 1988, p. 973: '[T]he intelligibility of form is immanent to its content . . . and [this] immanent intelligibility is [sufficient] mode of understanding, no other is needed'.

by each discipline. Accordingly, interdisciplinarity is not an evolutionary epistemological step, but merely a fruitful alternative and complement to established scientific narratives.

6.4 CONCLUSIONS

The task of this chapter was to transpose the main problems addressed in the book in the domain of legal theory. The reason for this is twofold: first, to demonstrate how antitrust law and jurisprudence mutually influence each other; and secondly, to internalise the conceptual findings developed in legal theory into the area of competition law.

Because of strong economic connotations, competition law is often perceived as an applied branch of law full of technicalities, which only uses the rich legacy of legal theory as far as the jurisprudence of courts is concerned. Regardless of the eventual correctness of this common perception, legal theoretical issues are of direct relevance for antitrust too. This chapter explores some areas of legal theory which are of paramount importance for competition law and may help to address the main antitrust dilemmas and paradoxes in a more sound legal theoretical way, inasmuch as the conceptual parts of these problems are not unique to antitrust. However, the connection between competition law and jurisprudence does not only function in one direction. Legal theory can be enriched by some of the theoretical aspects of antitrust law as well. For instance, because it is predetermined by the necessity to balance law, economics and politics, competition law constitutes a unique forum for the analysis of interdisciplinarity. Yet, their mutual relevance and support go much further. Indeed, the phenomenon of competition constitutes an external element of the conflicts that define law, its internal indeterminacy and external correlation with other social norms, in which legal theory is embedded.

7. Practical conclusions

The task of this chapter is threefold: (i) to introduce a legislative proposal which invigorates the normative value of competition; (ii) to demonstrate how the constitutional perception of competition reflects antitrust practice and (iii) to summarise the main arguments of the research. These three aspects are complementary. The introduction of the normative proposal reveals a benchmark against which current antitrust problems may be addressed; it provides a more favourable legislative status for the competitive process, conceptually separating competition from its eventual market outcomes, and shows the ultimate task of the book, serving as a common denominator for the analysis provided in the previous chapters.

7.1 THE FIRST AMENDMENT OF/AND ARTICLE 101 TFEU

As argued in the chapter on the normative foundations of competition, the essence of the competitive process holds significant similarities in political, cultural and economic life. It has been shown that the dynamics of competition constitute the core normative value of liberal democracy. In politics competition is reflected in the principle of elections; in cultural life it is embedded in the notion of free speech; in economic relations it is protected by antitrust law. Competition in all these emanations is not an indispensable or optimal way to allocate resources. It is not protected due to its *effectiveness*, or as a *means*, but as a fundamental prerequisite of freedom, belonging to the main constitutional principles of liberalism. This claim neither neglects nor diminishes the important role of the competitive process in achieving political, cultural and economic *goals*, but merely underlines that such achievements cannot be considered as a unique justification for competition.

In order to illustrate the analogy, a model of three regulatory circles has been introduced[1] (see Figure 7.1). At the first (big) regulatory level *all*

---

[1] Oles Andriychuk, 'Rediscovering the Spirit of Competition: On the Normative Value of the Competitive Process', Competition Law Journal, Vol. 6, No. 3, 2010.

agreements and all types of conduct are authorised by default, revealing thereby the deontological principle of freedom. This deontological protection does not embrace all reasons for the authorisation: besides protecting the values for their own sake, they are *also* protected due to their positive contribution to societal development. This second explanation is utilitarian. Inasmuch as neither freedom nor any other public value could benefit from the full scope of regulatory protection, these expressions of freedom are limited. Limitations are illustrated by the second (middle) regulatory circle. The reason for the limitation of freedom is twofold as well: some expressions of freedom (in its political, cultural and economic senses) are prohibited either (i) because they disproportionately harm *other* public interests – for instance, when political freedom of some parties encroaches upon fundamental values of society; when freedom of expression conflicts with privacy or public morality; or when economic freedom to compete harms good business practices (unfair competition) – or (ii) because they infringe the very *same* values they are meant to promote. The second possibility is reflected in the notion of the Oroboros situation, when freedom endangers itself, thereby revealing self-destructive elements. This is the reason why in politics some parties which endanger the political system of free voting are not allowed to participate in elections; in cultural life some expressions of freedom may cause reactionary behaviours, leading to the suppression of freedom itself; in economic markets these acts endanger the competitive process. Therefore, all these *harmful* expressions of freedom are prohibited.

Due to the fact that the scope of the protected values in liberal democracies significantly expands the regulatory capacity of available protection, each decision-maker faces the necessity of reconciling these values through the balancing act. There is no possibility to design the ultimate algorithm of such reconciliations, and the elements of *bounded* arbitrariness are thus inevitable. Values *compete* at the regulatory level in order to be selected by the decision-maker on an ad hoc basis. Their normative significance varies on a case-by-case basis, depending on the numerous factual circumstances of each regulatory situation. The competition by each value enables them inter alia to claim that their outright prohibition at the second regulatory level may be re-authorised. As is the case with the former two regulatory levels, at the third (small) circle level the reason for the re-authorisation is again twofold: the prohibited expressions of freedom may be re-authorised if (i) while being harmful at the second level, they simultaneously contribute to the development of other public values or interests (the utilitarian reason for re-authorisation); or (ii) while remaining harmful to freedom itself, they still are able to outweigh this harm by significantly contributing to the development of freedom in other aspects or dimensions (the deontological reason for re-authorisation). Thus, not all political parties which violate public values are prohibited from the electoral process. Some are allowed, despite remaining actually or potentially dangerous for broader public life or political freedom itself. Likewise, not all expressions of hate speech and not all violations of privacy are prohibited, in spite of their obvious harm to the individuals concerned. Some are re-authorised, because in spite of being harmful they can contribute to public discussion, revealing the area for proper articulation of potential societal conflicts (the utilitarian justification); or due to the importance of freedom itself, which outweighs the negative impacts they cause for freedom or other public values (the deontological justification). One must emphasise that the third regulatory circle enables both deontological and utilitarian reasons for the re-authorisation of otherwise prohibited practices.

The rationale of the first circle can be found in the Preamble of the Treaty on the Functioning of the European Union (TFEU).[2] The references to the 'humanist inheritance of Europe, from which have developed the universal values of the inviolable and inalienable rights of the human person, freedom, democracy, equality and the rule of law'[3] and the 'attachment to the principles of liberty, democracy and respect for human rights and fundamental freedoms'[4] can serve as examples of the 'constitutional' significance of competition in the European context and its authorisation by default. The *deontological* reason of the second circle is encompassed in the structure of Article 101(1) TFEU, which prohibits *all* agreements which either restrict competition or *can* restrict it. As pointed out there are also other *utilitarian* reasons to prohibit economic freedom; most of them go beyond TFEU and address the issues of safety, morality or public health and are prohibited at the national level.

So far the task of the suggested model was purely descriptive. It neither introduced nor claimed any normative changes in the existing regulatory models. The description is applicable to all reasonable regulatory regimes. The task of the research up to this point was to provide a universal stylisation of the rationale of the functioning of Article 101 TFEU and not to advocate any amendments thereof. The problematic aspect of the regulation of economic competition begins at the third regulatory level. Unlike regulation of political and cultural freedom, where reasons for re-authorisation include both utilitarian and deontological grounds, the structure of Article 101(3) TFEU is limited to the former. It enables re-

---

2 ibid, p. 585.
3 Consolidated version of the Treaty on European Union, OJ, 2010/C 83/01.
4 ibid.

authorisation of anticompetitive agreements *only* if they can contribute to the utilitarian values of growth, innovation and consumer welfare. As argued (Chapter 4.3.2), the wording of Article 101(3) TFEU mentions competition only as an additional requirement, implying that re-authorised agreements should not limit competition disproportionately. In other words, the possibility for an autonomous justification of re-authorisation exclusively based on deontological grounds is not envisaged in Article 101(3) TFEU.

The following proposal can solve the existing discrepancy: alongside the existing provisions of Article 101 TFEU, it is proposed to add a paragraph 4, stating that

> The provisions of paragraph 1 may be also declared inapplicable in the case of any agreement, decision, concerted practice which while preventing, restricting or distorting some aspects of competition within the internal market, simultaneously protects, strengthens or improves others aspects of competition within the same or different part of the internal market.

The proposed amendment merely expands the possibility of re-authorisation of anticompetitive agreements on deontological grounds (Figure 7.1). It neither cancels nor diminishes the existing provisions of Article 101(3) TFEU (Figure 7.2). It provides a legal possibility for the resolution of the antitrust paradox of self-restrained freedom by applying the rationale widely accepted in political and cultural theory, as the normative analysis of this book has tried to show.

If – and only if – the observed three-circled *structure* of the primary EU antitrust rules is correct, and the *normative* claim of the constitutional status of competition developed in the book is accepted, the emerging discrepancy between regulation of political and cultural freedom on one hand and economic freedom on the other should be addressed. The observed

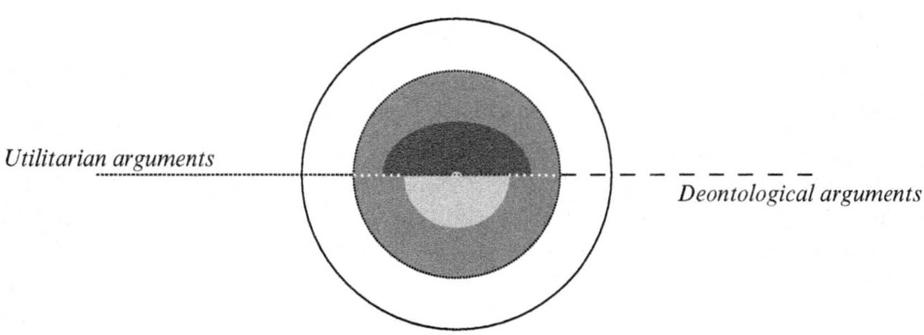

Figure 7.1 Deontological ground for re-authorisation

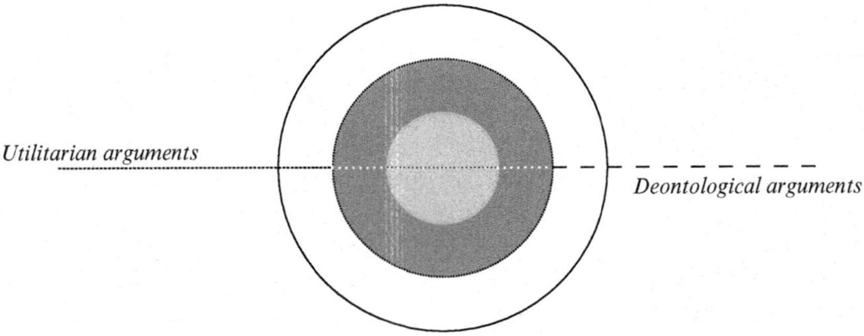

Figure 7.2 Article 101 TFEU after the proposed amendment

lacuna can be treated differently. First, it can be ignored as insignificant. This would be particularly the case if the status of the competitive process is reduced to a purely instrumental one, meaning that the importance of competition can be accepted only insofar as it contributes to other, more important economic and/or political interests. This approach is the most workable, since it ignores the existing problem altogether. It would apply, for instance, under the traditional neoclassical economic analysis, which perceives competition solely as a static method of economic reasoning, and not as a public value. Competition, according to this view, is accepted insofar as it benefits consumer or total welfare. It is only a means to other ends, and not an end in itself. Second, the problem can be solved at the practical level. This approach does not reject the normative value of competition, but limits it solely to the first and second regulatory circles, implying that competition is important indeed, and it is exactly the reason why its restriction is not allowed by Article 101(1) TFEU. Unlike the former, this approach dominates the legal community. Both visions mentioned above were able to regulate competition in a reasonably good manner for many decades, and there is nothing to presume that such a strong situational alliance of *economics* and *law* cannot continue to remain effective in regulating competition in the future. In addition, there is no realistic *political* possibility to imply that any changes in the current antitrust regime are plausible, particularly those which address the wording of the primary EU sources. The proposed amendment therefore is offered solely as a theoretical solution, for the sake of methodological clarity, and only serves purely academic purposes.

7.2 PRACTICAL IMPLICATIONS OF THE CONSTITUTIONAL APPROACH TO COMPETITION

The proposed constitutional treatment of competition has a number of practical implications. Since the primary task of the book was to offer a theoretical analysis of the normative status of the competitive process, it is beyond its methodological limits to provide a comprehensive contextualisation of the proposed vision to the realm of the existing case law, which would require a different comparative approach. This subsection sketches out three main practical implications of the suggested proposal. (i) Despite the suggestions that the current status of competition has been implicitly downgraded by the Lisbon Treaty, it is argued that the current provisions of the EU Treaties provide sufficient scope for constitutional interpretation of competition. Constitutionality does not imply exclusivity, and neither competition nor any other European value can be granted full protection. Different values *compete* for prioritisation by the decision-maker. (ii) Although the amendment concerns Article 101 TFEU, its normative underlying premises also cover the provisions of Article 102 TFEU. (iii) The last paragraph of this subsection addresses the situation where some aspects of competition are balanced against others, exploring the provisions of the EU rules on vertical and horizontal restraints, and concluding that although the algorithm that balances different aspects of competition corresponds to the principle suggested in the proposed Article 101(4) TFEU, the real assessment of pro- and anticompetitive effects is still performed from a monistic *either-or* perspective.

7.2.1 The Concept of *Internal* Competition

The perception of competition as an independent value goes beyond the scope of Article 101 TFEU and covers situations of abuse of market power, as well as some aspects of mergers regulation. The central element of its application is the concept of an undertaking. To the extent that antitrust law gives priority to the economic definition of an undertaking (the functional approach), which significantly differs from the purely formal, registration-based principle, the application of the same approach can be expanded for the benefits of the competitive process. This implies that the competitive process can be potentially maintained both *between* the different market agents, as well as *within* the legal or economic framework of undertakings. This situation is particularly relevant for large economic entities. While preserving strong legal and economic control over its subsidiaries, a large entity can enable them to develop different commercial strategies, thereby enhancing not only competition with other undertakings, but also internal (inter-affiliate)[5] competition within a given entity.

The different divisions of an undertaking can compete with each other, enhancing the competitive process. The societal value of competition, perceived separately from other legitimate public goals deserves public protection. This situation constitutes an independent ground for authorisation of anticompetitive agreements, abusive practices and mergers alongside other legitimate justifications for antitrust immunity. The notion of undertaking is taken in the case law as 'a relative concept in the sense that a given entity might be regarded as an undertaking for one part of its activities while the rest fall outside the competition rules',[6] and its meaning is 'not identical to the question of legal personality for the purposes of company law or fiscal law';[7] therefore the concept embraces 'every entity in an economic activity, regardless of its status and the way in which it is financed'.[8] For the purposes of the hypothesis that the *internal* aspects of competition have some potential value, the separation between the legal and economic concepts of undertakings can be operationalised towards a perception of different subsidiaries of big undertakings as independent economic entities, provided they compete with each other under the control of the parent company. This can lead to the creation of two scenarios for immunisation of anticompetitive practices from the antitrust sanctions within the framework of Article 101 TFEU and in particular Article 102 TFEU, although the structure of the latter Article would not require any changes, since its wording is more flexible than that of Article 101 TFEU. First, an undertaking can mitigate the severity of restriction of *external* competition by showing that the practice simultaneously contributes to the improvement of *internal* competition. Second, in some cases an undertaking can claim that economic dominance does not prevent competition (but replaces its *external* aspects with *internal* ones) and ask for another dominance test, submitting that one legal entity consists of several economic entities which compete with each other. In addition,

---

[5] John J. Brennan, 'The Sherman Act and Multi-Corporate Single-Traders: Competition among Affiliates?', University of Pennsylvania Law Review, Vol. 100, No. 7, 1952, p. 1006.

[6] Case C–475/99, *Ambulanz Glöckner v. Landkreis Südwestpfalz* ECR 2001 p. I-08089, Jacobs AG, para. 72.

[7] 86/398/EEC, Commission Decision relating to a proceeding under Article 85 of the EEC Treaty (IV/31.149 – Polypropylene), [1986] OJ L230/1, [1988] 4 CMLR 347, para. 99.

[8] Case C-41/90, *Höfner and Elser v. Macrotron GmbH* ECR1991 p. I-1979, para. 21.

if the competitive process is perceived as a methodologically separate value, the duty to promote *internal* competition can also be carried out as a commitment decision (mainly behaviourally, but also with a remedy of accounting separation) pursuant to Article 9 of Regulation 1/2003.[9] Easterbrook argues that the difference between cooperation *inside* the firm and competition *between* the firms 'is just a convenient shorthand for a far more complicated continuum',[10] explaining that some companies have both the structure and capacity to develop internal competition, and claiming that the firm itself 'is just a legal name for a complicated set of contractual arrangements among workers, managers, and contributors of capital'.[11]

The concept of internal competition can be addressed in antitrust by analogy with similar regulatory notions, developed in sports and media industries. In the former, the professional sports leagues are often perceived as single entities. This does not prevent them from promoting competition between their members. Inasmuch as the competitive process is the essence of any sport, one could argue against the possibility to extrapolate from the analogy to other industries, where the competitive process is not seen by its participants as inevitable. This argument would be correct if antitrust expected dominant companies on the market to promote internal competition *voluntarily*. The peculiarity of sports leagues does not allow them to eliminate competition between their participants, while the members of other industries do not depend directly on the successful performance of their rivals. For this reason the analogy has more limited purposes. Professional sports, being among the major entertainment sectors of the economy, may be useful for an analysis of the mechanisms which the sports leagues apply in order to protect and promote the competitive process. These mechanisms go far beyond the generality of ex post rules. The dominant undertakings from other industries may also have the elements of similar mechanisms of internal competition between their subsidiaries, which could be further enhanced if these companies were to be encouraged to promote the competitive process within their own realm. Neither the scope nor the nature of internal competition can substitute for the necessity of external competition, yet in some cases – particularly under the suggested model of a perpetual balancing – some elements of

[9] Council Regulation (EC) No 1/2003 of 16 December 2002 on the implementation of the rules on competition laid down in Articles 81, OJ L1, 4.1.2003.

[10] Frank H. Easterbrook, 'The Limits of Antitrust', Texas Law Review, Vol. 63, No. 1, 1984, p. 1.

[11] ibid, pp. 1–2.

internal competition can serve as an additional criterion for immunisation from antitrust sanctions.

The North American system of distribution of sports media rights provides an example of cooperative competition. Individual clubs are united into professional leagues, which are closed to entry for any other sports clubs, regardless of their sportive performance or levels of income. This format of cooperation between undertakings has many attributes akin to cartels. It cannot be explained by the peculiarity of professional sport alone, since European leagues allow entrance to all clubs, based on their performance and minimal financial solvency. The North American model is very competitive in both senses of the word: (a) its clubs are very strong and demonstrate very high sporting and financial performance and (b) the level of competition between the members of these 'cartels' is very high too. It could be argued that the prime purpose of their consolidation into closed groups is not the elimination of competition from the outside, but the creation of enhanced competition within the group. Assuming that competition is a multifaceted phenomenon, it is possible to demonstrate that by limiting competition in one aspect, closed leagues simultaneously promote competition in the other. It would be possible to argue that the level of competition which has been achieved due to the limitation of competition is indeed higher than the level of competition which has been sacrificed. This would imply that such practice can be potentially re-authorised. In this sense, the term 'harmful/illegal cartel' is not a tautology, as the term 'illegal crime' is. The history of the evolution of antitrust proves this presumption.[12]

A similar principle exists in the media industry, which encompasses the notion of media pluralism. The plurality of media is assessed in two ways: externally and internally. Both formats significantly contribute to the development of the competitive process in cultural life, enhancing the diversity of views and the free circulation of ideas. Traditionally it has been assumed that external media pluralism plays a more important role, since it enables the existence of different voices, which independently compete on the media market. The independence of the media companies is, however, not the exclusive way to enhance the plurality of opinions and freedom of speech. Some countries – including many European

---

[12] Herbert J. Hovenkamp, 'The Antitrust Movement and the Rise of Industrial Organisation', Texas Law Review, Vol. 68, No. 1, 1989, pp. 143–144: 'Neoclassicists such as Arthur Twining Hadley wrote of the trusts as if their potential to achieve economies of scale was infinite, while their threat to competition was negligible. Even progressive Richard T. Ely was overwhelmed by the trusts' ability to achieve cost reductions through large-scale production and distribution'.

ones – have a more concentrated industry, particularly in the broadcasting sector, which is explained by the historical and cultural peculiarities of the development of public media. This format is not necessarily anticompetitive. Single ownership and control alone do not necessarily lead to censorship or other *anticompetitive* practices. Both the journalists in the media or different subsidiaries of the media holdings can effectively compete with each other. This situation is particularly visible in competition between the different channels of the same broadcasting company. Regardless of how specific the audience of these channels is, its partial overlapping is inevitable, which impels the heads of the channels to develop different competitive strategies against their counterparts of the same parent company. The level of media pluralism and competition between different channels and/or individual journalists cannot be defined by the assessment of the ownership or control, but by the level of the 'effective competitive process',[13] or by the test of 'significant impediment of effective competition',[14] which is not necessarily higher under the system of *external* media pluralism, which promotes the legal independence of the companies.

Among the most important obstacles to this regulatory format is the issue of jurisdiction. If internal competition belongs to the realm of antitrust authorities, then another parent company can be questioned by antitrust enforcers regarding its eventual 'anticompetitive' behaviour towards its subsidiaries. The commitment to develop internal competition can be regulated as a separate legal area, implying that the obligation is of a voluntary nature, and it is not for the public to decide upon the level of the competitive process which an undertaking may freely develop and restrict *internally*. Also it would be disproportional to claim that the promotion of internal competition by a dominant undertaking provides sufficient reason for the re-qualification of its conduct from the scope of Article 102 TFEU to that of Article 101 TFEU.

7.2.2 Pro-competitiveness of Anticompetitive Agreements

Traditionally the Commission applies a monistic approach to Article 101 TFEU. It leads to assess justifications under Article 101(3) TFEU in the *words* of competition, but within the *logic* of welfare. Thus, according to the guidelines on the application of Article 101(3) TFEU, the task

---

[13] Guidance on the Commission's enforcement priorities in applying Article 82 of the EC Treaty to abusive exclusionary conduct by dominant undertakings, Brussels, OJ C 045, 24/02/2009, para. 6.

[14] Council Regulation (EC) No 139/2004 on the control of concentrations between undertakings, OJ L, 20.1.2004, para. 25.

of Article 101(3) TFEU is 'to determine the pro-competitive benefits produced by that agreement and to assess whether these pro-competitive effects outweigh the anti-competitive effects'.[15] Similarly, according to the EU guidelines on horizontal agreements, the task of Article 101(3) TFEU is 'to determine the pro-competitive benefits produced by that [anti-competitive] agreement and to assess whether those pro-competitive effects outweigh the restrictive effects on competition'.[16] Inasmuch as the wording of Article 101(3) TFEU is not designed in terms of competition, but addresses the issues of immunisation from antitrust sanctions of those *anticompetitive* agreements which have beneficial effects on consumers, growth and innovation, it becomes clear that the Commission applies the more economic approach not only to its assessment of the technical aspects of agreements, but also to the very definition of competition. For equilibrium economics the sole goal of competition is its effectiveness, which is reflected in positive outcomes for consumers, growth and innovation. These consequences not only *justify* competition normatively, they *explain* it positively.[17] According to this approach, competition is a perfect condition of equilibrium between the atomistic market actors.

If in order to be considered pro-competitive an agreement has to be in fact pro-consumer, then conversely, all pro-competitive agreements automatically become pro-consumer, and welfare-enhancing provisions in Article 101(3) TFEU can be perceived as pro-competitive, inasmuch as the competitive effects are relevant only in terms of welfare generation. This approach misinterprets Article 101 TFEU twice: at the level of paragraph 1 it provides a consumer-centred interpretation of competition, shifting the centre of gravity from the competitive process to the welfare effects; and then, after *deactivating* all aspects of rivalry, making competition purely instrumental, it provides the competition-centred interpretation of paragraph 3, the provisions of which mention competition only sporadically, and the very logic of which is in balancing the anticompetitive effects of Article 101(1) TFEU with some socially important aspects of Article

---

[15] Communication from the Commission, Guidelines on the application of Article 81(3) of the Treaty, 2004/C 101/08, OJ C 101/97, 27. 4. 2004, para. 11.

[16] Communication from the Commission, Guidelines on the Applicability of Article 101 of the Treaty on the Functioning of the European Union to Horizontal Co-operation Agreements, OJ, 2011/C 11/01, 2011, para. 20.

[17] Communication from the Commission, Guidelines on the application of Article 81(3) of the Treaty, 2004/C 101/08, OJ C 101/97, 27.4.2004, para. 33: 'The aim of the Community competition rules is to protect competition on the market as a means of enhancing consumer welfare and of ensuring an efficient allocation of resources'.

101(3) TFEU. Thus a misinterpretation of competition at the level of Article 101(1) TFEU leads to the same mistreatment at the level of Article 101(3) TFEU.

An anticompetitive practice *may* indeed have pro-competitive elements, yet such pro-competitiveness can only be assessed from a pluralistic and not a monistic perspective. This rationale is embedded in the structure of the proposed Article 101(4) TFEU, and unlike the previous approach it requires a genuine assessment of competition as such and not only as the reduced welfare-enhancing efficiency effects of itself.[18] Current provisions of Article 101(3) TFEU mention competition only as a reservation that it should not be restrained more than absolutely necessary for the achievements of positive effects. This formula alone does not render the immunised anticompetitive agreements pro-competitive. A proposal for a similar form has been made by Monti,[19] though its substantive nature was related to the more articulated correlation between efficiency concerns and other EU objectives and not to the epistemological independency and normative improvement of the competitive process as such.

7.2.3 Reconciling Theory with Practice

It could be said that the proposed changes are primarily of a conceptual nature. It is simply absurd to identify one policy via the other. The suggested changes do not encourage a dystopian version of black letter law. It became clear after 1897 that literarily *any* market transaction in one form or another affects competition and that competition law deals only with reasonable situations.[20]

To illustrate this point one can look at the Commission's application of the rationale of Article 101 TFEU to 'object' restrictions. Inasmuch as they are known to be anticompetitive per se, the literal interpretation would require the Commission to investigate a significant number of agreements. This would be administratively ineffective. Therefore, a conceptual proxy has been developed that is reasonable de facto, but formally is illogical: an agreement that is likely to pass the efficiency test is not considered as restrictive to competition at all, even though the anticompetitive elements in such an agreement could be quite explicit. This is illogical. The conceptual proposal, suggested in this book is that *all* anticompetitive

18 ibid: 'Agreements that restrict competition may at the same time have pro-competitive effects by way of efficiency gains'.

19 Giorgio Monti, 'Article 81 EC and Public Policy', Common Market Law Review, Vol. 39, No. 5, 2002, pp. 1096–1097.

20 *United States v. Trans-Missouri Freight Ass'n*, 166 U.S. 290, 346 (1897).

agreements should be captured by Article 101(1) TFEU and then *most* of them would pass the threshold of Articles 101(3) or 101(4) automatically – as is currently the case. In other words, those formally restrictive agreements which are currently considered as being outside the scope of Article 101(1) can either be captured by Article 101(3) and 101(4) or even remain beyond the scope of Article 101(1), based on a reasonability test. But they should not be labelled as '*procompetitive* and immune as such from the sanctions of Article 101'. This is logical fallacy.

The suggested approach to balancing between the pro- and anticompetitive elements of an agreement is more closely related to the model developed by the Commission with respect to analysing inter- and intra-brand competition within the vertical restraint practices. Both the Regulation[21] and Guidelines[22] provide conditions for differentiation of competition. This approach deviates from the neoclassical monism in respect to the formalistic definition of competition in terms of welfare. The technical ability to distinguish between inter- and intra-brand competition alone does not solve the theoretical conundrum of the eventual pro-competitiveness of anticompetitive practices, continuing the analysis of competition through the lens of consumers,[23] but it provides some instruments for further separation of competition from its welfare-generating effects. Thus, according to the Guidelines, '[w]here there is no residual competition and no foreseeable threat of entry, the protection of rivalry and the competitive process outweighs possible efficiency gains',[24] and conversely, the mere fact that a restrictive agreement is likely to have efficiency gains is not considered as a sufficient ground for re-authorisation.[25] This part of the Guidelines shows that the ethos of consumer welfare and efficiency is not always the *ultima ratio* of European antitrust policy, and that the competitive process itself deserves to be protected even to the detriment of welfare.[26] However,

---

[21] Commission Regulation (EU) No. 330/2010 of April 2010, 'On the Application of Article 101(3) of the Treaty on the Functioning of the European Union to Categories of Vertical Agreements and Concerted Practices', OJ L 102, 23.4.2010.

[22] Commission Notice 'Guidelines on Vertical Restraints', European Commission, Brussels, 10 May 2010, SEC (2010).

[23] ibid, I 1 (7): '[The task of regulation is] to ensure that undertakings do not use agreements . . . to restrict competition on the market to the detriment of consumers'.

[24] ibid, VI 1 (127).

[25] ibid.

[26] Oles Andriychuk, 'New Bottles – Same Wine? A Critical Assessment of the Reformed EU Rules on Vertical Restraints', Concorrenza e Mercato, Rivista Annuale di Concorrenza, Vol. 18, No. 1, 2011, p. 659.

the methodology of balancing of pro- and anticompetitive effects remains problematic because the Guidelines explicitly equate pro-competitive effects with efficiency gains.[27] The EU approach in this respect is consonant with the US vision of intra-brand competition, both at the judicial[28] and the doctrinal level.[29]

The monistic perception of the balancing act acknowledges the trade-offs between the different types of competition, but limits it solely to the compromise between intra- and inter-brand competition, considering the former as less important than the latter. According to the guidelines, 'the loss of intra-brand competition can only be problematic if inter-brand competition is limited',[30] which implies that the losses of intra-brand competition can be recovered by sufficient inter-brand competition. Without denying the significance of the latter, the importance of the former should not be underestimated. The suggested formula does not address the intensity of the competitive process as such, but merely evaluates its external impact on other economic values. From the perspective of Article 101(4) TFEU, whether competition takes place on the intra- or inter-brand level would not be decisive. Both types of competition are equally important, and the fact that the value of inter-brand competition is appreciated more is related to the utilitarian essence of Article 101(3) TFEU.

7.3 CONCLUSION

As argued in Chapter 5, the history of liberal democracies shows that a variety of values and interests has been recognised either directly or implicitly at the constitutional level. Pluralistic societies tend to expand the scope of protected values, which widens the realm of constitutionality for the multiplicity of interests, covering also those which are not in conformity with the preferences of the majority, providing protection for a diversity of views, interests and beliefs. On the one hand such pluralism of values is beneficial for society; on the other hand, granting virtually all

---

27 Commission Notice 'Guidelines on Vertical Restraints', European Commission, Brussels, 10 May 2010, SEC (2010), VI 1 (122).

28 *Continental T.V., Inc., v. G.T.E. Sylvania Inc.*, 694 F.2d 1132, 1137 (9th Cir.1982): '[A] vertical restraint may be reasonable if it is likely to promote inter-brand competition without overly restricting intrabrand competition'.

29 Herbert Hovenkamp, *Federal Antitrust Policy: The Law of Competition and Its Practice*, Thomson West, St. Paul, 2005, pp. 483–484.

30 Commission Notice 'Guidelines on Vertical Restraints', European Commission, Brussels, 10 May 2010, SEC (2010), VI 2 (153).

tolerable interests some constitutional recognition may cause an *inflation* in rights and permanent conflicts. Societies aware of these potential difficulties may either reject the pluralistic democratic principles, or develop mechanisms for their reconciliation. Liberal democracies adopt the second option, which requires them to balance conflicting views and interests, covered by broad terms such as 'human dignity, freedom, democracy, equality, the rule of law and respect for human rights, including the rights of persons belonging to minorities . . .; pluralism, non-discrimination, tolerance, justice, solidarity and equality between women and men'.[31] Tiedeman observes in this respect that 'the fragility and instability of a constitution are in direct proportion to the multiplicity of its written rules',[32] putting the main emphasis on their contextual interpretation and a balanced rather than literal application.

Following the adoption of the Lisbon Treaty, the formal EU provisions on competition have undergone some changes. The provisions of Article 3(1)(g) TEU including 'a system ensuring that competition in the internal market is not distorted'[33] among the activities of the Community have been removed. Drexl explains the initial removal of this provision by the rearrangement of the structure of the Treaties related to purely organisational issues, as it has been decided that Article 3 TEU will not reappear in the new Treaty, 'the reference to the protection of competition had initially been deleted from the Treaty text accidentally and without further consideration',[34] and that the subsequent reluctance of the French delegation to reintroduce the omitted provision into Article 3(3) TEU emerged only afterwards. The elimination of the provision on undistorted competition from the objectives of the EU would have a direct impact on the subsequent implementation of new antitrust policies (as was the case with the implementation of EU merger rules),[35] as the provisions of Article 352 TFEU limit the introduction of new policies only to the framework of EU goals, and the references to freedom and democracy in Article 2 TEU as common values (and not objectives) can substitute this formal require-

31 Article 2, TEU, Consolidated versions of the Treaty on European Union and the Treaty on the Functioning of the European Union, OJ C 83, 30.3.2010.

32 Christopher G. Tiedeman, *The Unwritten Constitution of the United States: A Philosophical Inquiry into the Fundamentals of American Constitutional Law*, G.P. Putnam's Sons, New York, 1890, p. 43.

33 Consolidated versions of the Treaty on European Union and of the Treaty Establishing the European Community, OJ C, 29.1.2006.

34 Josef Drexl, 'Competition Law as Part of the European Constitution', in Armin von Bogdandy and Jürgen Bast (eds.), *Principles of European Constitutional Law*, Hart Publishing, Oxford, Verlag CH Beck, Munich, 2010, p. 661.

35 ibid.

ment only partially. This disadvantage of competition can also be partially replaced in conjunction with the provisions of the Preamble to the TFEU, which refers to values like liberty and fair competition, as 'Article [101] as a whole should be read in the context of the provisions of the Preamble to the Treaty'.[36] The final reconciliation has still been provided in Protocol 27 on The Internal Market and Competition, which foresees the possibility of necessary actions being taken by the Union in order to ensure a system of internal market with undistorted competition. In addition, the reference to free competition remains in Article 119 TFEU. Drexl points out in this respect that in fact the protection of competition 'is challenged more by the disappearance of the hierarchy of objectives which was essential for the development of the case law, than by the transferral of the objective to the Protocol'.[37]

From a broader methodological perspective reliance on a hierarchical reconciliation of the conflicts between these values with a reference to their concretisation in the subsequent provisions of the Treaty is only partially accurate. The fact that some provisions have not been sufficiently clarified may cause difficulties at the level of their *application*, but it does not deprive or diminish their *normative* recognition in the first place. The principle of hierarchical taxonomy should then be complemented by the rationale of balancing, which by weighing the importance and proportionality of each constitutional value in each particular case enables their ad hoc reconciliation, but also brings elements of indeterminacy and vagueness to the apparently coherent taxonomy of a hierarchical order of values. In turn, this leads to the abandoning of the holistic perception of a harmonious coexistence of values and a naive/radical belief in the omnipotence of decision-makers who can reconcile the real and potential conflicts between equally important values. Conflicts can be only solved on an ad hoc basis, they cannot be eliminated outright. It requires the analysis of intra- as well as inter-value multilogues and the existence of internal *lobbies* for each value, i.e. those doctrinal interest groups which perceive the development of the broad societal policies through the lens of these values. As pointed out by Wolf, competition does not have such a lobby,[38] as the value of the competitive process is difficult to *translate* into the universal language of welfare which dominates the European political

---

36 Case 32/65, *Italy v. Council and Commission*, ECR 1966 p. 389, pp. 403–407.

37 Josef Drexl, 'Competition Law as Part of the European Constitution', in Armin von Bogdandy and Jürgen Bast (eds.), *Principles of European Constitutional Law*, Hart Publishing, Oxford, Verlag CH Beck, Munich, 2010, p. 665.

38 Dieter Wolf, 'Competition Policy Objectives', Panel Discussion, in Claus-Dieter Ehlermann and Laraine L. Laudati (eds.), *The Objectives of Competition*

discourse. As a result, competition is usually perceived only from the perspective of its positive impact upon welfare. This implies abandoning the *specification* stage of the balancing procedure, and redirecting the analysis at the second, *universal* level. This research argues against such a holistic approach. The fact that the competitive process itself has neither priority nor much use divorced from welfare concerns does not imply – on both methodological and normative levels – that it should not be addressed and protected separately, rather than as a part of the welfare-generation process. Therefore antitrust should reassess its doctrinal priorities; alongside intellectual efforts in promoting consumer welfare or other utilitarian goals, it should also enhance the analysis of purely internal, competition-centred narratives, developing both the research and political agendas for the improvement of the competitive process as a legitimate academic and practical goal, implying that a 'competition policy that focuses on the protection of the competitive process conforms with the objectives of the Union's constitutional order'.[39] The constitutional status of competition does not entail its universality or its priority over other values, but a constant *competition* with them. So far the value of the competitive process cannot *compete* with other values, because it is not seen as an independent value, but as predetermined by and even defined by welfare-enhancing goals.

The second aspect of the constitutionality of competition is related to the normative status and competences of antitrust regulators and their interaction with other regulators. The former aspect is important for the definition of the essence of the competitive process as a normatively independent value, while the latter is relevant to the process of communication between different societal values. The independent status of antitrust regulators provides a possibility for the proper articulation of the specificity of the competitive process, as well as administrative autonomy in dealing with politically sensitive issues. Wolf convincingly argues that 'as long as competition authorities are not independent, the risk is always present that specific interests will influence their decisions'.[40] The idea of an

---

Policy, European Competition Law Annual 1997, Hart Publishing, Oxford, 1998, pp. 24–25.

[39] Josef Drexl, 'Competition Law as Part of the European Constitution', in Armin von Bogdandy and Jürgen Bast (eds.), *Principles of European Constitutional Law*, Hart Publishing, Oxford, Verlag CH Beck, Munich, 2010, p. 697.

[40] Dieter Wolf, 'Competition Policy Objectives', Panel Discussion, in Claus-Dieter Ehlermann and Laraine L. Laudati (eds.), *The Objectives of Competition Policy*, European Competition Law Annual 1997, Hart Publishing, Oxford, 1998, pp. 24–25.

independent antitrust organ was originally developed by the Ordoliberal School.[41] According to Eucken, the 'monopoly supervision should thus be transferred to a state monopoly office . . . [which] should not be . . . a department of the economic ministry'.[42] This implies that the institutional independence of antitrust enforcers should be established and protected. On the other hand, this situation could lead to the regulatory isolation of antitrust from the broader set of political and economic issues. Assuming that no societal value is granted a clear-cut priority over other values and that the context of each particular situation requires a thorough examination of the unique circumstances in hand, values and their advocates face the necessity of delicate political negotiations. Grassroots politics is based more upon compromises than on principles, and the more explicitly this regulatory reality is articulated, the higher the potential for success each policy has. The possibility to explore economic reality through the prism of the interests of the competitive process does not provide a warranty for the success of antitrust at the broader regulatory level.[43] The specificity of the competitive process does not deprive it of the opportunity to defend its societal importance at the governmental level. Competition in one way or another has to be reconciled with other values. The more distant it is from the broader regulatory priorities, the less its chances of receiving political support in the long term. It can be done either by direct compromises between the interests of competition and other social values, or implicitly, by reducing the very meaning of competition to the universal regulatory priority. The trend that perceives competition in terms of consumer welfare belongs to the latter option, while the perception of competition as an independent value in the broader frame of regulatory compromises belongs to the former.

---

[41] David J. Gerber, 'Constitutionalizing the Economy: German Neo-Liberalism, Competition Law and the "New" Europe', The American Journal of Comparative Law, Vol. 42, No. 1, 1994, p. 54.

[42] Walter Eucken, 'Die Wettbewerbsordnung und ihreVerwirklichung', Jahrbuchfür die Ordnung von Wirtschaft und Gesellschaft, Vol. 2, 1949, cited in Christian Ahlborn, Carsten Grave (trans.), Walter Eucken, 'The Competitive Order and its Implementation', Competition Policy International, Vol. 2, No. 2, 2006, p. 241.

[43] Claus-Dieter Ehlermann, 'Introduction, Objectives of Competition Policy in General', in Claus-Dieter Ehlermann and Laraine L. Laudati (eds.), *The Objectives of Competition Policy*, European Competition Law Annual 1997, Hart Publishing, Oxford, 1998, p. xi: 'The broader the objectives, the greater is the need for a centralised political body to pursue them. On the contrary, narrower objectives will facilitate the transfer of responsibilities from the central government to an independent agency and/or courts'.

The main objective of this book was to offer an account of competition which goes beyond its purely welfare-oriented goals. While offering some *original* ideas and solutions, the added value of the book was in reviving and consolidating *existing* ideas, developed beyond orthodox economic schools as well as in such disciplines as philosophy and law. The normative proposal developed in this book emanates from the research which has been done. It is not driven by a political agenda. It is a logical consequence of the research, not its navigator.

Bibliography

Ackerman, Bruce A., *Private Property and the Constitution*, Yale University Press, New Haven, 1978.

Adams, Walter, 'The "Rule of Reason": Workable Competition or Workable Monopoly?', The Yale Law Journal, Vol. 63, No. 3, 1954.

Adams, Walter and James W. Brock, 'Antitrust and Efficiency: A Comment', New York University Law Review, Vol. 62, No. 5, 1987.

Adler, Joseph A., 'Zhou Dunyi: The Metaphysics and Practice of Sagehood', in William Theodore De Bary and Irene Bloom (eds.), *Sources of Chinese Tradition*, Vol. 1, Columbia University Press, New York, 1999.

Adler, Matthew D., 'Incommensurability and Cost-Benefit Analysis', University of Pennsylvania Law Review, Vol. 146, No. 5, 1998.

Adler, Matthew D., 'Rights against Rules: The Moral Structure of American Constitutional Law', Michigan Law Review, Vol. 97, No. 1, 1998.

Adler, Matthew D., 'Bounded Rationality and Legal Scholarship', in Mark D. White (ed.) *Theoretical Foundations of Law and Economics*, Cambridge University Press, 2009.

Adler, Mortimer J., 'The Idea of Dialectic', in Mortimer J. Adler, Robert M. Hutchins and John Van Doren (eds.), *The Great Ideas Today*, Encyclopaedia Britannica, Chicago, 1986.

Ben Ahmed, Walid and Bernard Yannou, 'Polysemy of Values or Conflict of Interests: A Multi-Disciplinary Analysis', International Journal of Value-Based Management, Vol. 16, No. 2, 2003.

Ahlborn, Christian and Carsten Grave, 'Walter Eucken and Ordoliberalism: An Introduction from a Consumer Welfare Perspective', Competition Policy International, Vol. 2, No. 2, 2006.

Ahlborn, Christian and A. Jorge Padilla, '*From* Fairness *To* Welfare: Implications for the Assessment of Unilateral Conduct under EC Competition Law', in Claus-Dieter Ehlermann and Mel Marquis (eds.), *European Competition Law Annual 2007: A Reformed Approach to Article 82 EC*, Hart Publishing, Oxford, 2008.

Akman, Pinar, 'Searching for the Long-Lost Soul of Article 82EC', Oxford Journal of Legal Studies, Vol. 29, No. 2, 2009.

Akman, Pinar, *The Concept of Abuse in EU Competition Law: Law and Economic Approaches*, Hart Publishing, Oxford, 2012.

Akman, Pinar, 'The Role of "Freedom" in EU Competition Law', Legal Studies, Vol. 34, No. 2, 2014.

Akman, Pinar, 'The Tests of Illegality under Articles 101 and 102 TFEU', The Antitrust Bulletin, Vol. 61, No. 1, 2016.

Alberstein, Michal, 'Measures of Legal Formalism', Bar-Ilan University Public Law and Legal Theory Working Paper No. 04–09, 03, 2009.

Aleinikoff, Alexander T., 'Constitutional Law in the Age of Balancing', The Yale Law Journal, Vol. 96, No. 5, 1987.

Alexander, Larry, 'What are Constitutions, and What Should (and Can) They Do?', San Diego Legal Studies Paper, No. 10-005, 2010.

Alexy, Robert, 'On Necessary Relations between Law and Morality', Ratio Juris, Vol. 2, No. 2, 1989.

Alexy, Robert, 'The Special Case Thesis', Ratio Juris, Vol. 12, No. 4, 1999.

Alexy, Robert, 'On the Structure of Legal Principles', Ratio Juris, Vol. 13, No. 3, 2000.

Alexy, Robert, 'On the Thesis of a Necessary Connection between Law and Morality: Bulygin's Critique', Ratio Juris, Vol. 13, No. 2, 2000.

Alexy, Robert, *A Theory of Constitutional Rights*, Oxford University Press, Oxford, 2002.

Alexy, Robert, 'Constitutional Rights, Balancing, and Rationality', Ratio Juris, Vol. 16, No. 2, 2003.

Alexy, Robert, 'On Balancing and Subsumption: A Structural Comparison', Ratio Juris, Vol. 16, No. 4, 2003.

Alexy, Robert, 'The Dual Nature of Law', Ratio Juris, Vol. 23, No. 2, 2010.

Allan, Trevor R. S., 'Constitutional Justice and the Concept of Law', in Grant Huscroft (ed.), *Expounding the Constitution: Essays in Constitutional Theory*, Cambridge University Press, Cambridge, 2008.

Alter, Max, 'Aristotle and the Metallist Tradition: A Note', History of Political Economy, Vol. 14, No. 2, 1982.

Amato, Giuliano, *Antitrust and the Bounds of Power: The Dilemma of Liberal Democracy in the History of the Market*, Hart Publishing, Oxford, 1997.

Andriychuk, Oles, 'Can We Protect Competition Without Protecting Consumers?', The Competition Law Review, Vol. 6, No. 1, 2009.

Andriychuk, Oles, 'Dialectical Antitrust: An Alternative Insight into the Methodology of the EC Competition Law Analysis in a Period of Economic Downturn', European Competition Law Review, Vol. 31, No. 4, 2010.

Andriychuk, Oles, 'Economic Freedom as Political Virtue: An Insight from the Perspective of Value Pluralism', European Journal of Legal Studies, Vol. 3, No. 1, 2010.

Andriychuk, Oles, 'Rediscovering the Spirit of Competition: On the Normative Value of the Competitive Process', Competition Law Journal, Vol. 6, No. 3, 2010.

Andriychuk, Oles, 'New Bottles – Same Wine? A Critical Assessment of the Reformed EU Rules on Vertical Restraints', Concorrenza e Mercato, Rivista Annuale di Concorrenza, Vol. 18, No. 1, 2011.

Andriychuk, Oles, 'The Concept of Perfect Competition as the Law of Economics: Addressing the Homonymy Problem', Northern Ireland Legal Quarterly, Vol. 62, No. 4, 2011.

Andriychuk, Oles, 'The Dialectics of Competition Law: Sketching the Ordo-Austrian Approach to Antitrust', World Competition: Law and Economics Review, Vol. 35, No. 2, 2012.

Andriychuk, Oles, 'Thinking Inside the Box: Why Competition as a Process is a *Sui Generis* Right – a Methodological Observation' in Daniel Zimmer (ed.), *The Goals of Competition Law*, Edward Elgar Publishing, Cheltenham, 2012.

Andriychuk, Oles, 'The Law – Morality Conundrum: On the Multifaceted Sources of Normativity', Rechtstheorie, Vol. 44, No. 1, 2013.

Andriychuk, Oles, 'Exclusive Legal Positivism and Legal Autopoiesis: Towards a Theory of Dialectical Positivism', Rechtstheorie, Vol. 46, No. 1, 2015.

Armentano, Dominick T., 'Time to Repeal Antitrust Regulation?', The Antitrust Bulletin, Vol. 35, No. 2, 1990.

Arrow, Kenneth J., *Social Choice and Individual Values*, Yale University Press, New Haven, 1951.

Arthur, Thomas C., 'Farewell to the Sea of Doubt: Jettisoning the Constitutional Sherman Act', California Law Review, Vol. 74, No. 2, 1986.

Asso, Pier F. and Luca Fiorito, 'Human Nature and Economic Institutions: Instinct Psychology, Behaviorism, and the Development of American Institutionalism', Journal of the History of Economic Thought, Vol. 26, No. 4, 2004.

Audretsch, David B., William J. Baumol and Andrew E. Burke, 'Competition Policy in Dynamic Markets', International Journal of Industrial Organisation, Vol. 19, No. 5, 2001.

Austin, John, *The Province of Jurisprudence Determined*, George Weidenfeld & Nicolson, London, 1954.

Avbelj, Matej and Jan Komárek, 'Introduction', in Matej Avbelj and Jan Komárek (eds.), 'Four Visions of Constitutional Pluralism', EUI Working Papers, Law 2008/21, Florence, 2008.

Baker, Edwin C., 'Starting Points in Economic Analysis of Law', Hofstra Law Review, Vol. 8, No. 4, 1980.

Baker, Jonathan B., 'A Preface to Post-Chicago Antitrust', in Antonio Cucinotta, Roberto Pardolesi and Roger Van den Bergh (eds.), *Post-Chicago Developments in Antitrust Law*, Edward Elgar Publishing, Cheltenham, 2002.

Baker, Jonathan B., 'Beyond Schumpeter vs. Arrow: How Antitrust Fosters Innovation', Antitrust Law Journal, Vol. 74, No. 3, 2007.

Baker, Jonathan B., 'Economics and Politics: Perspectives on the Goals and Future of Antitrust', Fordham Law Review, Vol. 81, No. 5, 2013.

Ballard, Edward G., 'On the Nature and Use of Dialectic', Philosophy of Science, Vol. 22, No. 3, 1955.

Balkin, Jack M., 'Understanding Legal Understanding: The Legal Subject and the Problem of Legal Coherence', The Yale Law Journal, Vol. 103, No. 1, 1993.

Balkin, Jack M., 'Interdisciplinarity as Colonisation', Washington and Lee Law Review, Vol. 53, No. 3, 1995.

Balkin, Jack M. and Sanford V. Levinson, 'Law and the Humanities: An Uneasy Relationship', Yale Journal of Law & the Humanities, Vol. 18, No. 2, 2006.

Bankowski, Zenon, *Living Lawfully – Love in Law and Law in Love*, Kluwer, Dordrecht, 2001.

Bankowski, Zenon, 'In the Judgement Space: The Judge and the Anxiety of the Encounter', in Zenon Bankowski and James MacLean (eds.), *The Universal and the Particular in Legal Reasoning*, Ashgate, Aldershot, 2006.

Barber, William J., 'American Economics to 1900', in Warren J. Samuels, Jeff E. Biddle and John B. Davis (eds.), *A Companion to The History of Economic Thought*, Blackwell Publishing, Oxford, 2003.

Barak, Aharon, *Purposive Interpretation in Law*, Princeton University Press, Princeton, 2005.

Barak, Aharon, *The Judge in a Democracy*, Princeton University Press, Princeton, 2006.

Barnes, David W., 'Antitrust Dialogue on Social Science, Cultural Values, and Merger Law', Antitrust Bulletin, Vol. 33, No. 4, 1988.

Barnes, David W., 'Antitrust, the Rule of Reason, and Democracy', Review of Industrial Organization, Vol. 14, No. 2, 1999.

Barry, Norman P., 'The New Liberalism', British Journal of Political Science, Vol. 13, No. 1, 1983.

Barry, Norman P., 'Unanimity, Agreement, and Liberalism: A Critique of James Buchanan's Social Philosophy', Political Theory, Vol. 12, No. 4, 1984.

Barry, Norman P., 'Political and Economic Thought of German Neo-Liberals', in Alan Peacock and Hans Willgerodt (eds.), *German Neo-*

Liberals, and the Social Market Economy, The Macmillan Press, London, 1989.

Barry, Norman P., *Welfare*, Open University Press, Buckingham, 1999.

Baumol, William J., John C. Panzar and Robert D. Willig, 'Contestable Markets: An Uprising in the Theory of Industry Structure', The American Economic Review, Vol. 73, No. 3, 1983.

Bebchuk, Lucian A., 'The Pursuit of a Bigger Pie: Can Everyone Expect a Bigger Slice?', Hofstra Law Review, Vol. 8, No. 3, 1980.

Behlke, Reinhard, *Der Neoliberalismus und die Gestaltung der Wirtschaftsverfassung in der Bundesrepublik Deutschland*, Duncker & Humblot, Berlin, 1961.

Ben Ahmed, Walid and Bernard Yannou, 'Polysemy of Values or Conflict of Interests: A Multi-Disciplinary Analysis', International Journal of Value-Based Management, Vol. 16, No. 2, 2003.

Bentham, Jeremy, 'Anarchical Fallacies: Being an examination of the Declaration of Rights issued during the French Revolution', 1843 http://www.law.georgetown.edu/Faculty/lpw/documents/Bentham_Anarchical_Fallacies.pdf.

Bentham, Jeremy, *An Introduction to the Principles of Morals and Legislation*, The Athlone Press, University of London, 1970.

Berdyaev, Nicolas, 'The Metaphysical Problem of Freedom', Put, Vol. 9, No. 1, 1928, http://www.berdyaev.com/berdiaev/berd_lib/1928_329.html.

Berdyaev, Nicolas, *Freedom and the Spirit*, The Centenary Press, London, 1935.

Berdyaev, Nicolas, *Spirit and Reality*, The Centenary Press, London, 1939.

Berdyaev, Nicolas, *Slavery and Freedom*, The Centenary Press, London, 1943.

Berdyaev, Nicolas, *The Meaning of the Creative Act*, Victor Gollancz Ltd, London, 1955.

Bergson, Henri, *Creative Evolution*, Hern Hold, New York, 1911.

Berlin, Isaiah, *Four Essays on Liberty*, Oxford University Press, Oxford, 1990.

Berlin, Isaiah, 'On Value Pluralism', 'New York Review of Books', Vol. 45, No. 8, 1998.

Berlin, Isaiah, 'Two Concepts of Liberty', in Isaiah Berlin, *Liberty*, Oxford University Press, Oxford, 2002.

Bertea, Stefano, 'The Arguments from Coherence: Analysis and Evaluation', Oxford Journal of Legal Studies, Vol. 25, No. 3, 2005.

Berti, Enrico, 'Ancient Greek Dialectic as Expression of Freedom of Thought and Speech', Journal of the History of Ideas, Vol. 39, No. 3, 1978.

Besson, Samantha, *The Morality of Conflict: Reasonable Disagreement and the Law*, Hart Publishing, Oxford, 2005.
Beyeveld, Deryck and Roger Brownsword, *Law as a Moral Judgement*, Sweet & Maxwell, London, 1986.
Binmore, Ken, 'Modelling Rational Players: Part I', Economics and Philosophy, Vol. 3, No. 2, 1987.
Bix, Brian, 'H. L. A. Hart and "The Open Texture" of Language', Law and Philosophy, Vol. 10, No. 1, 1991.
Bix, Brian, '"Positively Positivism": Book Review, Anthony J. Sebok, "Legal Positivism in American Jurisprudence" Cambridge University Press, Cambridge, 1996', Virginia Law Review, Vol. 85, No. 5, 1999.
Black, Oliver, *Conceptual Foundations of Antitrust*, Cambridge University Press, Cambridge, 2005.
Bladel, John P., 'Against Polanyi-Centrism: Hayek and the Re-Emergence of "Spontaneous Order"', The Quarterly Journal of Austrian Economics, Vol. 8, No. 4, 2005.
Blair, Roger D. and Daniel Sokol, 'Welfare Standards in U.S. and E.U. Antitrust Enforcement', Fordham Law Review, Vol. 81, No. 5, 2013.
Blaug, Mark, 'Is Competition Such a Good Thing? Static Efficiency versus Dynamic Efficiency', Review of Industrial Organization, Vol. 19, No. 1, 2001.
Blake, Harlan M., William K. Jones, 'Toward a Three-Dimensional Antitrust Policy', Columbia Law Review, Vol. 65, No. 3, 1965.
Blum, Fred H., 'Max Weber's Postulate of "Freedom" from Value Judgments', The American Journal of Sociology, Vol. 50, No. 1, 1944.
Böhm, Franz, *Wettbewerb und Monopolkampf: Eine Untersuchung zur Frage des wirtschaftlichen Kampfrechts und zur Frage der rechtlichen Struktur der geltenden Wirtschaftsordnung*, Carl Heymanns Verlag, Berlin, 1933.
Böhm, Franz, *Die Ordnung der Wirtschaft als geschichtliche Aufgabe und rechtsschöpferische Leistung*, W. Kohlhammer, Stuttgart, 1937.
Böhm, Franz, *Wirtschaftsordnung und Staatsverfassung*, Mohr Siebeck, Tübingen, 1950.
Böhm, Franz, Walter Eucken and Hans Grossmann-Doerth, 'The Ordo Manifesto of 1936', in Alan T. Peacock and Hans Willgerodt (eds.), *Germany's Social Market Economy: Origins and Evolution*, Macmillan, London, 1989.
von Böhm-Bawerk, Eugen, *The Positive Theory of Capital*, Macmillan and Co., London, 1888.
Boettke, Peter J., 'The Use and Abuse of the History of Economic Thought within the Austrian School of Economics', History of Political Economy, Vol. 34, No. 2, 2002.

Bonefeld, Werner, 'Free Economy and the Strong State: Some Notes on the State', Capital & Class, Vol. 34, No. 1, 2010.

Bork, Robert H., 'Contrasts in Antitrust Theory: I', Columbia Law Review, Vol. 65, No. 3, 1965.

Bork, Robert H., 'Legislative Intent and the Policy of the Sherman Act', Journal of Law and Economics, Vol. 9, 1966.

Bork, Robert H., 'The Rule of Reason and the Per Se Concept: Price Fixing and Market Division', The Yale Law Journal, Vol. 75, No. 3, 1966.

Bork, Robert H., 'The Goals of Antitrust Policy', The American Economic Review, Vol. 57, No. 2, 1967.

Bork, Robert H., 'Resale Price Maintenance and Consumer Welfare', The Yale Law Journal, Vol. 77, No. 5, 1968.

Bork, Robert H., *The Antitrust Paradox: A Policy at War with Itself*, Basic Books, New York, 1978.

Bork, Robert H. and Ward S. Bowman, Jr., 'The Crisis in Antitrust', Columbia Law Review, Vol. 65, No. 3, 1965.

Boyd White, James, 'The Ethics of Argument: Plato's *Gorgias* and the Modern Lawyer', University of Chicago Law Review, Vol. 50, No. 3, 1983.

Branco, Manuel C., *Economics Versus Human Rights*, Routledge, London, 2009.

Brandon, James R., 'Kabuki and Shakespeare: Balancing Yin and Yang', TDR, Vol. 43, No. 2, 1999.

Brennan, John J., 'The Sherman Act and Multi-Corporate Single-Traders: Competition among Affiliates?', University of Pennsylvania Law Review, Vol. 100, No. 7, 1952.

Brest, Paul, 'Interpretation and Interest', Stanford Law Review, Vol. 34, No. 4, 1982.

Brietzke, Paul H., 'The Constitutionalisation of Antitrust: Jefferson, Madison, Hamilton and Thomas C. Arthur', Valparaiso University Law Review, Vol. 22, No. 2, 1988.

Bright, Christopher, 'EU Competition Policy: Rules, Objectives and Deregulation', Oxford Journal of Legal Studies, Vol. 16, No. 4, 1996.

Brodley, Joseph F., 'The Economic Goals of Antitrust: Efficiency, Consumer Welfare, and Technological Progress', New York University Law Review, Vol. 62, No. 5, 1987.

Broyer, Sylvian, 'German Contemporary Analyses of Economic Order: Standard Ordnungstheorie, Ordoliberalism and Ordnungsökonimik in Perspective', in Agnès Labrousse and Jean-Daniel Weisz (eds.), *Institutional Economics in France and Germany: German Ordoliberalism versus the French Regulation School*, Springer, Berlin, 2001.

Brugger, Winfried, 'Legal Interpretation, Schools of Jurisprudence, and

Anthropology: Some Remarks from a German Point of View', The American Journal of Comparative Law, Vol. 42, No. 2, 1994.
Buchanan, James M., 'Positive Economics, Welfare Economics, and Political Economy', in James Buchanan, *Fiscal Theory and Political Economy*, University of North Carolina Press, Durham, 1960.
Buchanan, James M., *Liberty, Market and the State*, Wheatsheaf Books, Brighton, 1986.
Buchanan, James M., 'Post-Reagan Political Economy', in James M. Buchanan, *Constitutional Economics*, Basil Blackwell, Oxford, 1991.
Buchanan, James M., 'Lagged Implementation as an Element in Constitutional Strategy', European Journal of Political Economy, Vol. 10, No. 1, 1994.
Buchanan, James M. and Gordon Tullock, *The Calculus of Consent: Logical Foundations of Constitutional Democracy*, University of Michigan Press, Ann Arbor, 1962.
Buchanan, James M., Richard E. Wagner and John Burton, 'The Consequences of Mr Keynes', in James M. Buchanan, *Constitutional Economics*, Basil Blackwell, Oxford, 1991.
Budzinski, Oliver, 'Cognitive Rules, Institutions, and Competition', Constitutional Political Economy, Vol. 14, No. 3, 2003.
Budzinski, Oliver, 'An Evolutionary Theory of Competition', University of Southern Denmark – Department of Environmental and Business Economics Working Paper, 2004, http://papers.ssrn.com/sol3/papers.cfm?abstract_id=534862.
Budzinski, Oliver, 'Monoculture versus Diversity in Competition Economics', Cambridge Journal of Economics, Vol. 32, No. 2, 2008.
Budzinski, Oliver, 'Modern Industrial Economics and Competition Policy: Open Problems and Possible Limits', IME Working Paper, No. 93/09, 2009.
Bulygin, Eugenio, 'Alexy's Thesis on the Necessary Connection between Law and Morality', Ratio Juris, Vol. 13, No. 2, 2000.
Bustamante, Thomas, 'Comment on Petroski – On MacCormick's Post-Positivism', German Law Journal, Vol. 12, No. 2, 2011.
Buttigieg, Eugène, *Competition Law: Safeguarding the Consumer Interest. A Comparative Analysis of US Antitrust Law and EC Competition Law*, Kluwer, Alphen aan den Rijn, 2009.
Calabresi, Guido, 'Some Thoughts on Risk Distribution and the Law of Torts', The Yale Law Journal, Vol. 70, No. 4, 1961.
Calabresi, Guido, 'About Law and Economics: A Letter to Ronald Dworkin', Hofstra Law Review, Vol. 8, No. 3, 1980.
Calabresi, Guido, 'The Pointlessness of Pareto: Carrying Coase Further', The Yale Law Journal, Vol. 100, No. 5, 1991.

Calabresi, Guido and Philip Bobbitt, *Tragic Choices*, W. W. Norton & Company, New York, 1978.

Campbell, William F., 'The Free Market for Goods and the Free Market for Ideas in the Platonic Dialogues', History of Political Economy, Vol. 17, No. 2, 1985.

Cantor, Paul A. and Stephen Cox, 'Preface', in Paul A. Cantor and Stephen Cox (eds.), *Literature and the Economics of Liberty: Spontaneous Order in Culture*, Ludwig von Mises Institute, Auburn, Alabama, 2009.

Carroll, Lewis, 'Sylvie and Bruno Concluded', in *The Complete Works of Lewis Carroll*, The Nonesuch Press, London, 1939.

Cave, Martin and Robert W. Crandall, 'Sports Rights and the Broadcast Industry', The Economic Journal, Vol. 111, No. 2, 2001.

Chamberlin, Edward H., 'Monopolistic Competition Revisited', Economica, New Series, Vol. 18, No. 72, 1951.

Cherniss, Harold, 'The Characteristics and Effects of Presocratic Philosophy', Journal of the History of Ideas, Vol. 12, No. 3, 1951.

Chirita, Anca D., 'A Legal-Historical Review of the EU Competition Rules', International & Comparative Law Quarterly, Vol. 63, No. 2, 2014.

Christensen, Paul P., 'Epicurean and Stoic Sources for Boisguilbert's Physiological and Hippocratic Vision of Nature and Economics', History of Political Economy, Vol. 35, No. 5 (annual supplement), 2003.

Christiansen, Arndt and Wolfgang Kerber, 'Competition Policy with Optimally Differentiated Rules Instead of "Per se Rules vs. Rule of Reason"', Marburg Papers on Economics, No. 6, 2006.

van Cise, Jerrold G., 'The Future of Per Se in Antitrust Law', Virginia Law Review, Vol. 50, No. 7, 1964.

Clark, John B., 'The Limits of Competition', Political Science Quarterly, Vol. 2, No. 1, 1887.

Clark, John B., *The Federal Trust Policy*, Johns Hopkins University Press, Baltimore, 1931.

Clark, John M., 'Law and Economic Life: I. The Legal Framework of Economic Life', The University Journal of Business, Vol. 3, No. 4, 1925.

Clark, John M., 'What Is Competition?', The University Journal of Business, Vol. 3, No. 3, 1925.

Clark, John M., 'Toward a Concept of Workable Competition', The American Economic Review, Vol. 30, No. 2, 1940.

Clark, John B. and John M. Clark, *The Control of Trusts*, Macmillan, New York, 1911.

Clark, Roger and Angela Lang, 'Balancing Yin and Yang: Teaching and Learning Qualitative Data Analysis within an Undergraduate Quantitative Data Analysis Course', Teaching Sociology, Vol. 30, No. 3, 2002.

Claassen, Rutger and Anna Gerbrandy, 'Rethinking European Competition Law: From a Consumer Welfare to a Capability Approach', Utrecht Law Review, Vol. 12, No. 1, 2016.

van Cleynenbreugel, Pieter, *Market Supervision in the European Union: Integrated Administration in Constitutional Context*, Brill Nijhoff, Leiden, 2014.

Cluvas, Bev, 'The Sheffield School and Discourse Theory: Divergences and Similarities in Legal Idealism/Anti-Positivism', Ratio Juris, Vol. 19, No. 2, 2006.

Coase, Ronald H., 'The Problem of Social Costs', Journal of Law and Economics, Vol. 3, No. 1, 1960.

Coase, Ronald, 'The New Institutional Economics', The American Economic Review, Vol. 88, No. 2, 1998.

Coate, Malcolm B. and Jeffrey H. Fischer, 'Can Post-Chicago Economics Survive *Daubert*?', Akron Law Review, Vol. 34, No. 4, 2001.

Cohen-Eliya, Moshe and Iddo Porat, 'American Balancing and German Proportionality: The Historical Origins', International Journal of Constitutional Law, Vol. 8, No. 2, 2010.

Coleman, Jules L., 'Efficiency, Exchange, and Auction: Philosophic Aspects of the Economic Approach to Law', California Law Review, Vol. 68, No. 2, 1980.

Coleman, Jules L., 'Efficiency, Utility, and Wealth Maximisation', Hofstra Law Review, Vol. 8, No. 3, 1980.

Collins English Dictionary and Thesaurus, Harper-Collins Publishers, Glasgow, 2006.

Collins, Wayne D., 'Trusts and the Origins of Antitrust Legislation', Fordham Law Review, Vol. 81, No. 5, 2013.

Colomo, Pablo I., 'On the Application of Competition Law as Regulation: Elements for a Theory', Yearbook of European Law, Vol. 29, No. 1, 2010.

Colomo, Pablo I., 'Article 101 TFEU and Market Integration', Journal of Competition Law and Economics, Vol. 12, No. 4, 2016.

Coyle, Sean, 'Positivism, Idealism and the Rule of Law', Oxford Journal of Legal Studies, Vol. 26, No. 2, 2006.

Crane, Daniel A., 'Rules Versus Standards in Antitrust Adjudication', Washington and Lee Law Review, Vol. 64, No. 1, 2007.

Crane, Daniel A., 'Chicago, Post-Chicago, and Neo-Chicago', The University of Chicago Law Review, Vol. 76, No. 4, 2009.

Crane, Daniel A., 'The Tempting of Antitrust: Robert Bork and the Goals of Antitrust Policy', Antitrust Law Journal, Vol. 79, No. 3, 2014.

Crocker, Lawrence, *Positive Liberty: An Essay in Normative Political Philosophy*, Martinus Nijhoff Publishers, The Hague, 1980.

Cruz, Julio Baquero, 'Discussion', in Matej Avbelj and Jan Komárek (eds.), *Four Visions of Constitutional Pluralism*, EUI Working Papers, Law 2008/21, Florence, 2008.

Dabbah, Maher M., *The Internationalisation of Antitrust Policy*, Cambridge University Press, Cambridge, 2003.

Dani, Marco, 'Economic Constitutionalism(s) in a Time of Uneasiness – Comparative Study on the Economic Constitutional Identities of Italy, the WTO and the EU', Jean Monnet Working Paper 08/05, 2008.

Daskalova, Victoria, 'Consumer Welfare in EU Competition Law: What Is It (Not) About?', Competition Law Review, Vol. 11, No. 1, 2015.

Davies, Gareth, 'Constitutional Disagreement in Europe and the Search for Pluralism', Eric Stein Working Paper No 1/2010, 2010.

Demsetz, Harold, 'Economic, Legal and Political Dimensions of Competition', University of California, Los Angeles Discussion Paper, No. 209, 1981.

Dewey, Donald, 'The Economic Theory of Antitrust: Science or Religion?', Virginia Law Review, Vol. 50, No. 3, 1964.

Dibadj, Reza, 'Postmodernism, Representation, Law', University of San Francisco Law Research Papers, No. 2009-03, 2009.

Dimova-Cookson, Maria, 'A New Scheme of Positive and Negative Freedom – Reconstructing T. H. Green on Freedom', Political Theory, Vol. 31, No. 4, 2003.

Dietsch, Peter, 'The Market, Competition, and Equality', Politics Philosophy Economics, Vol. 9, No. 2, 2010.

Diver, Colin S., 'The Optimal Precision of Administrative Rules', The Yale Law Journal, Vol. 93, No. 1, 1983.

Dobson, Stephen and John Goddard, 'Performance, Revenue, and Cross Subsidization in the Football League, 1927–1994', The Economic History Review, New Series, Vol. 51, No. 4, 1998.

Dolmans, Maurits, Robert O'Donoghue and Paul-John Loewenthal, 'Are Article 82 EC and Intellectual Property Interoperable? The State of the Law Pending the Judgment in Microsoft v. Commission', Competition Policy International, Vol. 3, No. 1, 2007.

Don, Henk, Ron Kemp and Jarig Van Sinderen, 'Measuring the Economic Effects of Competition Law Enforcement', De Economist, Vol. 156, No. 4, 2008.

Dorf, Michael C., 'Truth, Justice, and the American Constitution', Columbia Law Review, Vol. 97, No. 1, 1997.

Drexl, Josef, 'Competition Law as Part of the European Constitution', in Armin von Bogdandy and Jürgen Bast (eds.), *Principles of European Constitutional Law*, Hart Publishing, Oxford, Verlag CH Beck, Munich, 2010.

Duxbury, Neil, 'Faith in Reason: The Process Tradition in American Jurisprudence', Cardozo Law Review, Vol. 15, No. 3, 1993.

Duxbury, Neil, *Random Justice: On Lotteries and Legal Decision-Making*, Oxford University Press, Oxford, 1999.

Dworkin, Ronald M., 'The Model of Rules', The University of Chicago Law Review, Vol. 35, No. 1, 1967.

Dworkin, Ronald M., 'Hard Cases', Harvard Law Review, Vol. 88, No. 6, 1975.

Dworkin, Ronald M., *Taking Rights Seriously*, Harvard University Press, Cambridge, Massachusetts, 1978.

Dworkin, Ronald M., 'Is Wealth a Value?', The Journal of Legal Studies, Vol. 9, No. 2, 1980.

Dworkin, Ronald M., 'Why Efficiency? A Response to Professors Calabresi and Posner', Hofstra Law Review, Vol. 8, No. 3, 1980.

Dworkin, Ronald M., 'Law's Ambitions for Itself', Virginia Law Review, Vol. 71, No. 2, 1985.

Easterbrook, Frank H., 'Antitrust and the Economics of Federalism', Journal of Law and Economics, Vol. 26, No. 1, 1983.

Easterbrook, Frank H., 'The Limits of Antitrust', Texas Law Review, Vol. 63, No. 1, 1984.

Easterbrook, Frank H., 'Workable Antitrust Policy', Michigan Law Review, Vol. 84, No. 8, 1986.

Easterbrook, Frank H., 'Does Antitrust Have a Comparative Advantage?', Harvard Journal of Law & Public Policy, Vol. 23, No. 1, 1999.

Ebenstein, William, 'The Pure Theory of Law: Demythologizing Legal Thought', California Law Review, Vol. 59, No. 3, 1971.

Ebner, Alexander, 'The Intellectual Foundations of the Social Market Economy: Theory, Policy, and Implications for European Integration', Journal of Economic Studies, Vol. 33, No. 3, 2006.

Edwards, Corwin D., *Big Business and the Policy of Competition*, The Press of Western Reserve University, Cleveland, 1956.

Ehlermann, Claus-Dieter, 'Introduction, Objectives of Competition Policy in General', in Claus-Dieter Ehlermann and Laraine L. Laudati (eds.), *The Objectives of Competition Policy*, European Competition Law Annual 1997, Hart Publishing, Oxford, 1998.

Ehrenzweig, Albert A., 'Psychoanalytical Jurisprudence: A Common Language for Babylon', Columbia Law Review, Vol. 65, No. 8, 1965.

Einaudi, Luigi, *Selected Economic Essays*, Palgrave Macmillan, New York, 2006.

Eleftheriadis, Pavlos, 'Pluralism and Integrity', Ratio Juris, Vol. 23, No. 3, 2010.

Ely, Richard T., 'Competition: Its Nature, Its Permanency, and Its

Beneficence', Publications of the American Economic Association, 3rd Series, Vol. 2, No. 1, 1901.
Engle, Eric, 'Law and Economics: Theoretical Puffery, Exaggerated Claims and Counterfactual Models', The Journal of Jurisprudence, Vol. 2, No. 2, 2009.
Eucken, Walter, 'Die Wettbewerbsordnung und ihre Verwirklichung', Jahrbuch für die Ordnung von Wirtschaft und Gesellschaft, Vol. 2, 1949.
Eucken, Walter, *The Foundations of Economics: History and Theory in the Analysis of Economic Reality*, The University of Chicago Press, Chicago, 1951.
Eucken, Walter, *Grundsätze der Wirtschaftspolitik*, Rohwolt Verlag, Hamburg, 1959.
Eucken, Walter, 'What Kind of Economic and Social System?', in Alan T. Peacock and Hans Willgerodt (eds.), *Germany's Social Market Economy: Origins and Evolution*, Macmillan, London, 1989.
Eucken, Walter, 'Die Wettbewerbsordnung und ihre Verwirklichung', Jahrbuch für die Ordnung von Wirtschaft und Gesellschaft, Vol. 2, 1949, in Christian Ahlborn, Carsten Grave (trans.), Walter Eucken, 'The Competitive Order and its Implementation', Competition Policy International, Vol. 2, No. 2, 2006.
Eucken, Walter and Franz Böhm, 'Preface', ORDO, Vol. 1, No. 1, 1948.
Farrell, Joseph, 'Complexity, Diversity and Antitrust', Antitrust Bulletin, Vol. 51, No. 1, 2006.
Faull, Jonathan, 'Competition Policy Objectives', Panel Discussion, in Claus-Dieter Ehlermann and Laraine L. Laudati (eds.), *The Objectives of Competition Policy*, European Competition Law Annual 1997, Hart Publishing, Oxford, 1998.
Feteris, Eveline T., 'Recent Developments in Legal Argumentation Theory: Dialectical Approaches to Legal Argumentation', International Journal for the Semiotics of Law, Vol. 7, No. 20, 1994.
Fikentscher, Wolfgang, *Wirtschaftsrecht*, C.H. Beck, Munich, 1983.
Finlayson, James G., 'Conflict and Reconciliation in Hegel's Theory of the Tragic', Journal of the History of Philosophy, Vol. 37, No. 3, 1999.
Finnis, John M., '"Reason and Passion": The Constitutional Dialectic of Free Speech and Obscenity', University of Pennsylvania Law Review, Vol. 116, No. 2, 1967.
Finnis, John M., 'Natural Law and Legal Reasoning', Cleveland State Law Review, Vol. 38, No. 1, 1990.
First, Harry and Spencer Weber Waller, 'Antitrust's Democracy Deficit', Fordham Law Review, Vol. 81, No. 5, 2013.
Fiss, Owen M., 'Objectivity and Interpretation', Stanford Law Review, Vol. 34, No. 4, 1982.

Fish, Stanley, 'Fish v. Fiss', Stanford Law Review, Vol. 36, No. 6, 1984.

Fish, Stanley, 'Don't Know Much about the Middle Ages: Posner on Law and Literature', The Yale Law Journal, Vol. 97, No. 5, 1988.

Flynn, John J., 'The Misuse of Economic Analysis in Antitrust Litigation', Southwestern University Law Review, Vol. 12, No. 2, 1980.

Flynn, John J. and James F. Ponsoldt, 'Legal Reasoning and the Jurisprudence of Vertical Restraints: The Limitations of Neoclassical Economic Analysis in the Resolution of Antitrust Disputes', New York University Law Review, Vol. 62, No. 5, 1987.

Flynn, John J., 'Discussion' in David W. Barnes, 'Antitrust Dialogue on Social Science, Cultural Values, and Merger Law', Antitrust Bulletin, Vol. 33, No. 4, 1988.

Flynn, John J., 'Legal Reasoning, Antitrust Policy and the Social "Science" of Economics', Antitrust Bulletin, Vol. 33, No. 4, 1988.

Flynn, John J., 'Antitrust Policy and the Concept of A Competitive Process', New York Law School Law Review, Vol. 35, No. 4, 1990.

Foer, Albert A., 'The Political-Economic Nature of Antitrust', Saint Louis University Law Journal, Vol. 27, No. 2, 1983.

Forget, Evelyn L., 'Jean-Baptiste Say and Spontaneous Order', History of Political Economy, Vol. 33, No. 2, 2001.

Forrester, Ian S., 'Competition Policy Objectives', Panel Discussion, in Claus-Dieter Ehlermann, Laraine L. Laudati (eds.), *The Objectives of Competition Policy*, European Competition Law Annual 1997, Hart Publishing, Oxford, 1998.

Foucault, Michel, *Geschichte der Gouvernementalität II: Die Geburt der Biopolitik*, Suhrkamp, Frankfurt, 2004.

Fox, Eleanor M., 'The Modernization of Antitrust: A New Equilibrium', Cornell Law Review, Vol. 66, No. 6, 1981.

Fox, Eleanor M., 'Consumer Beware Chicago', Michigan Law Review, Vol. 84, No. 8, 1986.

Fox, Eleanor M., 'The Battle for the Soul of Antitrust', California Law Review, Vol. 75, No. 3, 1987.

Fox, Eleanor M. and Lawrence A. Sullivan, 'Antitrust – Retrospective and Prospective: Where Are We Coming From? Where are We Going?', New York University Law Review, Vol. 62, No. 5, 1987.

Fox, Eleanor M., 'Competition Policy Objectives', Panel Discussion, in Claus-Dieter Ehlermann and Laraine L. Laudati (eds.), *The Objectives of Competition Policy*, European Competition Law Annual 1997, Hart Publishing, Oxford, 1998.

Fox, Eleanor M., 'The Efficiency Paradox', New York University Centre for Law, Economics and Organisation, Law & Economics Research Paper Series, Working Paper No. 09–26, 2009.

Fox, Eleanor M., 'Against Goals', Fordham Law Review, Vol. 81, No. 5, 2013.
Frantz, Laurent B., 'The First Amendment in the Balance', The Yale Law Journal, Vol. 71, No. 8, 1962.
Frantz, Laurent B., 'Is The First Amendment Law? A Reply to Professor Mendelson', California Law Review, Vol. 51, No. 4, 1963.
Freeman, Michael D.A., *Lloyd's Introduction to Jurisprudence*, Sweet & Maxwell, London, 2010.
Freedman, Monroe H., 'Our Constitutionalized Adversary System', Chapman Law Review, Vol. 1, No. 1, 1998.
Friedman, Lawrence M., 'Legal Culture and Social Development', Law & Society Review, Vol. 4, No. 1, 1969.
Friedman, Milton, 'The Methodology of Positive Economics' in Milton Friedman (ed.), *Essays in Positive Economics*, University of Chicago Press, 1953.
Friedman, Milton, 'Capitalism and Freedom', The University of Chicago Press, Chicago, 1962.
Friedrich, Carl J., 'The Political Thought of Neo-Liberalism', The American Political Science Review, Vol. 49, No. 2, 1955.
Fruehwald, Edwin, 'Postmodern Legal Thought and Cognitive Science', Hofstra University School of Law Legal Studies Research Paper Series, Research Paper No. 06–31, 2006.
Fuller, Lon L., 'The Case of the Speluncean Explorers', Harvard Law Review, Vol. 62, No. 4, 1949.
Fuller, Lon L., 'Positivism and Fidelity to Law: A Reply to Professor Hart', Harvard Law Review, Vol. 71, No. 4, 1958.
Fuller, Lon L., *The Morality of Law*, Yale University Press, New Haven, 1969.
Gadamer, Hans-Georg, 'Heidegger as Rhetor: Hans-Georg Gadamer Interviewed by Ansgar Kemmann', in Daniel M. Gross and Ansgar Kemmann (eds.), *Heidegger and Rhetoric*, State University of New York Press, Albany, 2005.
Gadamer, Hans-Georg, *Philosophical Hermeneutics*, University of California Press, 2008.
Gaffard, Jean-Luc and Michel Quéré, 'What's the Aim for Competition Policy: Optimizing Market Structure or Encouraging Innovative Behaviours?', Journal of Evolutionary Economics, Vol. 16, No. 1, 2006.
Gardner, John, 'The Virtue of Justice and the Character of Law', Current Legal Problems, Vol. 53, No. 1, 2000.
Gardner, John, 'Legal Positivism: 5 1/2 Myths', The American Journal of Jurisprudence, Vol. 46, No. 1, 2001.

Gardner, John, 'Can There Be a Written Constitution?', University of Oxford Legal Research Paper Series, Paper No. 17, 2009.

Gauthier, David, 'Thomas Hobbes: Moral Theorist', The Journal of Philosophy, Vol. 76, No. 10, 1979.

Geistfeld, Mark A., 'Efficiency, Fairness and the Economic Analysis of Tort Law', in Mark D. White (ed.), *Theoretical Foundations of Law and Economics*, Cambridge University Press, 2009.

Gerber, David J., 'Idea-Systems in Law: Nineteenth-Century German Experience', Law and History Review, Vol. 10, No. 1, 1992.

Gerber, David J., 'The Origins of European Competition Law in Fin-de-Siècle Austria', The American Journal of Legal History, Vol. 36, No. 4, 1992.

Gerber, David J., 'Constitutionalizing the Economy: German Neo-Liberalism, Competition Law and the "New" Europe', The American Journal of Comparative Law, Vol. 42, No. 1, 1994.

Gerber, David J., 'Prometheus Born: Shaping the Relationship Between Law and Economic Conduct', St. Louis University Law Journal, Vol. 38, No. 3, 1994.

Gerber, David J., *Law and Competition in Twentieth Century Europe: Protecting Prometheus*, Oxford University Press, Oxford, 2001.

Gerber, David J., 'Convergence in the Treatment of Dominant Firm Conduct: The United States, the European Union, and the Institutional Embeddedness of Economics', Vol. 76, No. 3, 2010.

Gerber, David J. and Richard Azarnia, 'Dirigisme and the Challenge of Competition Law in France', Cardozo Journal of International & Comparative Law, Vol. 9, No. 1, 1995.

Giocoli, Nicola, 'Competition versus Property Rights: American Antitrust Law, the Freiburg School, and the Early Years of European Competition Policy', Journal of Competition Law and Economics, Vol. 5, No. 4, 2009.

Goldman, Calvin, 'Competition Policy Objectives', Panel Discussion, in Claus-Dieter Ehlermann and Laraine L. Laudati (eds.), *The Objectives of Competition Policy*, European Competition Law Annual 1997, Hart Publishing, Oxford, 1998.

Goldschmidt, Nils and Hermann Rauchenschwandtner, 'The Philosophy of Social Market Economy: Michel Foucault's Analysis of Ordoliberalism', Freiburg Discussion Papers on Constitutional Economics, 07/04, 2007.

Goldschmidt, Nils and Michael Wohlgemuth, 'Social Market Economy: Origins, Meanings, Interpretations', Constitutional Political Economy, Vol. 19, No. 3, 2008.

Gottlieb, Stephen E., 'The Paradox of Balancing Significant Interests', Hastings Law Journal, Vol. 45, No. 4, 1994.

Grengs, Christopher M., 'Verizon v. Trinko: From Post-Chicago Antitrust to Resource-Advantage Competition', Journal of Law, Economics and Policy, Vol. 2, No. 1, 2006.

Goldschmidt, Jona, 'The Pro Se Litigant's Struggle for Access to Justice: Meeting the Challenge of Bench and Bar Resistance', Family Court Review, Vol. 40, No. 1, 2002.

Goodman, John C., 'An Economic Theory of the Evolution of Common Law', The Journal of Legal Studies, Vol. 7, No. 2, 1978.

Gray, John, *Isaiah Berlin*, Harper Collins, London, 1995.

Grimes, Warren S., 'Fifteen Years of Supreme Court Antitrust Jurisprudence: The Defendant Always Wins', in Roger Zäch, Andreas Heinemann and Andreas Kellerhals (eds.), *The Development of Competition Law – Global Perspectives*, Edward Elgar Publishing, Cheltenham, 2010.

Grimm, Dieter, 'Does Europe Need a Constitution?', European Law Journal, Vol. 1, No. 3, 1995.

Grimm, Dieter, 'Freedom of Speech in a Globalized World', in Ivan Hare and James Weinstein (eds.), *Extreme Speech and Democracy*, Oxford University Press, Oxford, 2009.

Groenewegen, Peter, 'English Marginalism: Jevons, Marshall, Pigou', in Warren J. Samuels, Jeff E. Biddle and John B. Davis (eds.), *A Companion to The History of Economic Thought*, Blackwell Publishing, Oxford, 2003.

Grossekettler, Heinz G., 'On Designing an Institutional Infrastructure for Economies', Journal of Economic Studies, Vol. 21, No. 4, 1994.

Günther, Klaus, *Der Sinn für Angemessenheit*, Suhrkamp, Frankfurt, 1988.

Günther, Klaus, 'The Pragmatic and Functional Indeterminacy of Law', German Law Journal, Vol. 12, No. 1, 2011.

Haakonssen, Knud, *The Science of a Legislator: The Natural Jurisprudence of David Hume and Adam Smith*, Cambridge University Press, Cambridge, 1981.

Habermas, Jürgen, *Between Facts and Norms – Contributions to a Discourse Theory of Law and Democracy*, Polity Press, Cambridge, 1997.

Hadley, Arthur T., 'The Relation between Economics and Politics', The Yale Law Journal, Vol. 8, No. 4, 1899.

Halme, Lasse, *The Polarity of Dynamics and Form: The Basic Tension in Paul Tillich's Thinking*, Lit Verlag, Helsinki, 2003.

Hamilton, Walton H., 'The Institutional Approach to Economic Theory', The American Economic Review, Vol. 9, No. 1, Supplement, 1919.

Hammer, Peter J., 'Free Speech and the "Acid Bath": An Evaluation and Critique of Judge Richard Posner's Economic Interpretation of the First Amendment', Michigan Law Review, Vol. 87, No. 2, 1988.

Hammer, Peter J., 'Antitrust beyond Competition: Market Failures, Total Welfare, and the Challenge of Intramarket Second-Best Tradeoffs', Michigan Law Review, Vol. 98, No. 4, 2000.

Harlow, Carol, 'Voices of Difference in a Plural Community', The American Journal of Comparative Law, Vol. 50, No. 2, 2002.

Hardin, Russell, 'The Morality of Law and Economics', Law and Philosophy, Vol. 11, No. 4, 1992.

Hart, Herbert L. A., 'Positivism and the Separation of Law and Morals', Harvard Law Review, Vol. 71, No. 4, 1958.

Hart, Herbert L. A., 'Book Review: Lon L. Fuller, "The Morality of Law"', Harvard Law Review, Vol. 78, No. 6, 1965.

Hart, Herbert L. A., 'Rawls on Liberty and Its Priority', The University of Chicago Law Review, Vol. 40, No. 3, 1973.

Hart, Herbert L. A., 'American Jurisprudence Through English Eyes: The Nightmare and the Noble Dream', Georgia Law Review, Vol. 11, No. 5, 1977.

Hart, Herbert L. A., 'Between Utility and Rights', Columbia Law Review, Vol. 79, No. 5, 1979.

Hart, Herbert L. A., *The Concept of Law*, Oxford University Press, Oxford, 1994.

Harvey, David, *A Brief History of Neoliberalism*, Oxford University Press, Oxford, 2009.

Hausman, Daniel M., 'Economic Methodology in a Nutshell', The Journal of Economic Perspectives, Vol. 3, No. 2, 1989.

Hausman, Daniel M. and Michael S. McPherson, 'Taking Ethics Seriously: Economics and Contemporary Moral Philosophy', Journal of Economic Literature, Vol. 31, No. 2, 1993.

Hausman, Daniel M., 'Introduction', in Daniel M. Hausman (ed.), *The Philosophy of Economics – An Anthology*, Cambridge University Press, Cambridge, 2008.

von Hayek, Friedrich A., *Monetary Theory and the Trade Cycle*, Sentry Press, New York, 1933.

von Hayek, Friedrich A., 'The Use of Knowledge in Society', The American Economic Review, Vol. 35, No. 4, 1945.

von Hayek, Friedrich A., *Individualism and Economic Order*, The University of Chicago Press, Chicago, 1948.

von Hayek, Friedrich A., '"Free" Enterprise and Competitive Order', in Friedrich A. von Hayek, *Individualism and Economic Order*, The University of Chicago Press, Chicago, 1958.

von Hayek, Friedrich A., 'Freedom, Reason and Tradition', Ethics, Vol. 68, No. 4, 1958.

von Hayek, Friedrich A., 'The Meaning of Competition', in Friedrich

A. von Hayek, *Individualism and Economic Order*, The University of Chicago Press, Chicago, 1958.
von Hayek, Friedrich A., 'The Use of Knowledge in Society', in Friedrich A. von Hayek, *Individualism and Economic Order*, The University of Chicago Press, Chicago, 1958.
von Hayek, Friedrich A., *The Constitution of Liberty*, Routledge & Kegan Paul, London, 1960.
von Hayek, Friedrich A., *Law, Legislation and Liberty*, Vol. 2, 'The Mirage of Social Justice', Routledge & Kegan Paul, London, 1976.
von Hayek, Friedrich A., *Law, Legislation and Liberty*, Vol. 3, 'The Political Order of a Free People', Routledge & Kegan Paul, London, 1976.
von Hayek, Friedrich A., 'Competition as a Discovery Procedure', The Quarterly Journal of Austrian Economics, Vol. 5, No. 3, 2002.
Hazard, Geoffrey C., *Ethics in the Practice of Law*, Yale University Press, New Haven, 1978.
Heimler, Alberto, 'Competition Policy Objectives', Panel Discussion, in Claus-Dieter Ehlermann and Laraine L. Laudati (eds.), *The Objectives of Competition Policy*, European Competition Law Annual 1997, Hart Publishing, Oxford, 1998.
Hein, Hilde, 'Molecular Biology vs. Organicism: The Enduring Dispute between Mechanism and Vitalism', Synthese, Vol. 20, No. 2, 1969.
Heinemann, Andreas, 'The Impact of Innovation – Comments on Uwe Canter and Wolfgang Kerber', in Josef Drexl, Wolfgang Kerber and Rupprecht Podszun (eds.), *Competition Policy and the Economic Approach: Foundations and Limitations*, Edward Elgar Publishing, Cheltenham, 2011.
Henkin, Louis, 'Infallibility under Law: Constitutional Balancing', Columbia Law Review, Vol. 78, No. 5, 1978.
Herbeck, Dale A., 'Critical Legal Studies and Argumentation Theory', Argumentation, Vol. 9, No 5, 1995.
Hesiod, 'Works and Days'.
Hicks, John R., *Wealth and Welfare*, Basil Blackwell, Oxford, 1981.
Hodgson, Geoffrey M., 'Thorstein Veblen and Post-Darwinian Economics', Cambridge Journal of Economics, Vol. 16, No. 3, 1992.
El-Hodiri, Mohamed and James Quirk, 'An Economic Model of a Professional Sports League', The Journal of Political Economy, Vol. 79, No. 6, 1971.
Holmes, Oliver W., 'The Theory of Legal Interpretation', Harvard Law Review, Vol. 12, No. 6, 1899.
Holmes, Oliver W., *The Common Law*, Dover Publications, New York, 1991.
Honig, Bonnie, *Political Theory and the Displacement of Politics*, Cornell University Press, Ithaca, 1993.

Honig, Bonnie, 'The Politics of Agonism: A Critical Response to "Beyond Good and Evil: Arendt, Nietzsche, and the Aestheticization of Political Action" by Dana R. Villa', Political Theory, Vol. 21, No. 3, 1993.

Hoppmann, Erich, 'Wettbewerb als Norm der Wettbewerbspolitik', Ordo – Jahrbuch für die Ordnung von Wirtschaft und Gesellschaft, Vol. 18, No. 1, 1967.

Horwitz, Morton J., 'Law and Economics: Science or Politics?', Hofstra Law Review, Vol. 8, No. 4, 1980.

Hovenkamp, Herbert J., 'Distributive Justice and the Antitrust Laws', George Washington Law Review, Vol. 51, No. 1, 1982.

Hovenkamp, Herbert J., 'Antitrust Policy after Chicago', Michigan Law Review, Vol. 84, No. 2, 1985.

Hovenkamp, Herbert J. 'The Antitrust Movement and the Rise of Industrial Organization', Texas Law Review, Vol. 68, No. 1, 1989.

Hovenkamp, Herbert J., 'Positivism in Law & Economics', California Law Review, Vol. 78, No. 4, 1990.

Hovenkamp, Herbert J., 'The First Great Law & Economics Movement', Stanford Law Review, Vol. 42, No. 4, 1990.

Hovenkamp, Herbert J., 'Post-Chicago Antitrust: A Review and Critique', Columbia Business Law Review, Vol. 16, No. 2, 2001.

Hovenkamp, Herbert J., 'The Reckoning of Post-Chicago Antitrust', in Antonio Cucinotta, Roberto Pardolesi and Roger Van den Bergh (eds.), *Post-Chicago Developments in Antitrust Law*, Edward Elgar Publishing, Cheltenham, 2002.

Hovenkamp, Herbert J., *Federal Antitrust Policy: The Law of Competition and Its Practice*, Thomson West, St. Paul, 2005.

Hovenkamp, Herbert J., *The Antitrust Enterprise*, Harvard University Press, Cambridge, Massachusetts, 2005.

Hovenkamp, Herbert J., 'Antitrust and the Costs of Movement', University of Iowa Legal Studies Research Paper, 12, 2010.

Hovenkamp, Herbert J., 'Implementing Antitrust's Welfare Goals', Fordham Law Review, Vol. 81, No. 5, 2013.

Hovenkamp, Herbert J., 'Antitrust Balancing', New York University Journal of Law and Business, Vol. 12, No. 1, 2016.

Hubbard, Patrick F., '"Sociology of Law": One View from the Lawyer's Side of the Fence', Rutgers Law Journal, Vol. 7, No. 3, 1976.

Hughes, Edwin J., 'The Left Side of Antitrust: What Fairness Means and Why It Matters', Marquette Law Review, Vol. 77, No. 2, 1993.

Huscroft, Grant, 'Introduction', in Grant Huscroft (ed.), *Expounding the Constitution: Essays in Constitutional Theory*, Cambridge University Press, Cambridge, 2008.

Hyman, David A. and William E. Kovacic, 'Institutional Design, Agency Life Cycle, and the Goals of Competition Law', Fordham Law Review, Vol. 81, No. 5, 2013.

Ikeda, Sanford, 'Market Process', in Peter J. Boettke (ed.), *The Elgar Companion to Austrian Economics*, Edward Elgar Publishing, Cheltenham, 1994.

Ilyenkov, Evald V., *The Dialectics of the Abstract and the Concrete in Marx's Capital*, Progress, Moscow, 1982.

Immenga, Ulrich, 'Future Competition Law', Working Paper, in Claus-Dieter Ehlermann and Laraine L. Laudati (eds.), *The Objectives of Competition Policy*, European Competition Law Annual 1997, Hart Publishing, Oxford, 1998.

Jellinek, Georg, *System der subjektiven öffentlichen Rechte*, J.C.B. Mohr, Tübingen, 1905.

Jenny, Frederic, 'Competition Policy Objectives', Panel Discussion, in Claus-Dieter Ehlermann and Laraine L. Laudati (eds.), *The Objectives of Competition Policy*, European Competition Law Annual 1997, Hart Publishing, Oxford, 1998.

Jevons, William S., 'Brief Account of a General Mathematical Theory of Political Economy', Journal of the Royal Statistical Society, Vol. 29, No. 3, 1866.

Jevons, William S., *The Theory of Political Economy*, Macmillan and Co., London, 1888.

Joerges, Christian, 'The Law in the Process of Constitutionalizing Europe', European University Institute Working Paper, No. 2002/4, 2002.

Joerges, Christian and Florian Rödl, '"Social Market Economy" as Europe's Social Model?', European University Institute Working Paper, Law, No. 2004/8, 2004.

John, Klaus Dieter, 'The German Social Market Economy – (Still) a Model for the European Union?', Theoretical and Applied Economics, Vol. 3, No. 3, 2007.

John, Stephen, 'Why "Health" is not a Central Category for Public Health Policy', Journal of Applied Philosophy, Vol. 26, No. 2, 2009.

Johnson, Daniel, 'Exiles and Half-exiles: Wilhelm Röpke, Alexander Rüstow and Walter Eucken', in Alan Peacock and Hans Willgerodt (eds.), *German Neo-Liberals, and the Social Market Economy*, The Macmillan Press, London, 1989.

Jones, Franklin D., 'Historical Development of the Law of Business Competition', The Yale Law Journal, Vol. 35, No. 8, 1926.

Kant, Immanuel, *Critique of Pure Reason*, Palgrave Macmillan, London, 2007.

Kaplow, Louis, 'On the Choice of Welfare Standards in Competition Law' in Daniel Zimmer (ed.), *The Goals of Competition Law*, Edward Elgar Publishing, Cheltenham, 2012.

Kaplow, Louis and Carl Shapiro, 'Antitrust', John M. Olin Center for Law, Economics and Business, Discussion Paper No. 575, 2007.

Kaplow, Louis and Steven Shavell, 'Economic Analysis of Law', http://papers.ssrn.com/sol3/papers.cfm?abstract_id=226405.

Karsten, Siegfried G., 'Eucken's "Social Market Economy" and Its Test in Post-War West Germany: The Economist as Social Philosopher Developed Ideas That Paralleled Progressive Thought in America', American Journal of Economics and Sociology, Vol. 44, No. 2, 1985.

Katz, Avery W., 'Positivism and the Separation of Law and Economics', Michigan Law Review, Vol. 94, No. 7, 1996.

Keenan, Donald, 'Value Maximization and Welfare Theory', The Journal of Legal Studies, Vol. 10, No. 2, 1981.

Kekes, John, *The Morality of Pluralism*, Princeton University Press, Princeton, 1993.

Kelsen, Hans, 'The Pure Theory of Law and Analytical Jurisprudence', Harvard Law Review, Vol. 55, No. 1, 1941.

Kelsen, Hans, 'The Natural-Law Doctrine before the Tribunal of Science', The Western Political Quarterly, Vol. 2, No. 4, 1949.

Kelsen, Hans, 'On the Pure Theory of Law', Israel Law Review, Vol. 1, No. 1, 1966.

Kelsen, Hans, *Pure Theory of Law*, University of California Press, 1967.

Kelsen, Hans, *General Theory of Law and State*, Russell & Russell, New York, 1973.

Kelsen, Hans, 'Law and Logic', in Hans Kelsen, *Essays in Legal and Moral Philosophy*, D. Reidel, Dordrecht, 1973.

Kelsen, Hans, 'Law and Morality', in Hans Kelsen, *Essays in Legal and Moral Philosophy*, D. Reidel, Dordrecht, 1973.

Kelsen, Hans, 'The Foundation of the Theory of Natural Law', in Hans Kelsen, *Essays in Legal and Moral Philosophy*, D. Reidel, Dordrecht, 1973.

Kelsen, Hans, 'What Is Justice?', in Hans Kelsen, *Essays in Legal and Moral Philosophy*, D. Reidel, Dordrecht, 1973.

Kelsen, Hans, 'On the Theory of Interpretation', Legal Studies, Vol. 10, No. 2, 1990.

Kelsen, Hans and Albert A. Ehrenzweig, 'Professor Stone and the Pure Theory of Law', Stanford Law Review, Vol. 17, No. 6, 1965.

Kennedy, Duncan, 'Legal Formality', The Journal of Legal Studies, Vol. 2, No. 2, 1973.

Kennedy, Ellen, 'Introduction', in Carl Schmitt, *The Crisis of Parliamentary Democracy*, MIT University Press, Cambridge, Massachusetts, 1985.

Kerber, Wolfgang, 'German Market Process Theory', in Peter J. Boettke (ed.), *The Elgar Companion to Austrian Economics*, Edward Elgar Publishing, Cheltenham, 1994.

Kerber, Wolfgang, 'Should Competition Law Promote Efficiency? Some Reflections of an Economist on the Normative Foundations of Competition Law', Marburg Papers on Economics, No. 09, 2007.

Kerber, Wolfgang, 'Competition, Innovation and Maintaining', in Josef Drexl, Wolfgang Kerber and Rupprecht Podszun, *Competition Policy and the Economic Approach: Foundations and Limitations*, Edward Elgar Publishing, Cheltenham, 2011.

Kerber, Wolfgang and Ulrich Schwalbe, 'Economic Principles of Competition Law', in Günther Hirsch, Frank Montag, Franz Jürgen Säcker (eds.), *Competition Law: European Community Practice and Procedure – Article-by-Article Commentary*, Sweet & Maxwell, London, 2008.

Kern, William, 'Returning to the Aristotelian Paradigm: Daly and Schumacher', History of Political Economy, Vol. 15, No. 4, 1983.

Késenne, Stefan, 'The Impact of Salary Caps in Professional Team Sports', Scottish Journal of Political Economy, Vol. 47, No. 4, 2000.

Keynes, John N., *The Scope and Method of Political Economy*, Macmillan and Co., London, 1897.

Khosla, Madhav, 'Proportionality: An Assault on Human Rights?: A Reply', International Journal of Constitutional Law, Vol. 8, No. 2, 2010.

Kirchner, Christian, 'Future Competition Law', Working Paper, in Claus-Dieter Ehlermann and Laraine L. Laudati (eds.), *The Objectives of Competition Policy*, European Competition Law Annual 1997, Hart Publishing, Oxford, 1998.

Kirchner, Christian, 'Goals of Antitrust and Competition Law Revisited' in Dieter Schmidtchen, Max Albert and Stefan Voigt (eds.), *The More Economic Approach to European Competition Law*, Mohr Siebeck, Tübingen, 2007.

Kirkwood, John B. and Robert H. Lande, 'The Chicago School's Foundation Is Flawed: Antitrust Protects Consumers, Not Efficiency', University of Baltimore Legal Studies Research Paper No. 2009–17, 2009.

Kirzner, Israel M., *The Economics Point of View*, Van Nostrand, Princeton, 1960.

Kirzner, Israel M., 'Entrepreneurial Discovery and the Competitive Market Process: An Austrian Approach', Journal of Economic Literature, Vol. 35, No. 1, 1997.

Kirzner, Israel M., 'Creativity and/or Alertness: A Reconsideration of the Schumpeterian Entrepreneur', Review of Austrian Economics, Vol. 11, No. 1, 1999.

Kirzner, Israel M., *How Markets Work: Disequilibrium, Entrepreneurship and Discovery*, Institute of Economic Affairs, London, 2000.

Klamer, Arjo, 'Formalism in Twentieth-Century Economics', in Peter J. Boettke (ed.), *The Elgar Companion to Austrian Economics*, Edward Elgar Publishing, Cheltenham, 1994.

Klimkiewicz, Beata, 'Media Pluralism: European Regulatory Policies and the Case of Central Europe', European University Institute Working Papers, RSCAS No. 2005/19, 2005.

Kloten, Norbert, 'Role of the Public Sector in the Social Market Economy', in Alan Peacock and Hans Willgerodt (eds.), *German Neo-Liberals, and the Social Market Economy*, The Macmillan Press, London, 1989.

Knight, Frank H., 'The Ethics of Competition', The Quarterly Journal of Economics, Vol. 37, No. 4, 1923.

Knight, Frank H., 'Economists on Economic Ethics', International Journal of Ethics, Vol. 48, No. 1, 1937.

Knight, Frank H., 'Lippmann's The Good Society', The Journal of Political Economy, Vol. 46, No. 6, 1938.

Knight, Frank H., 'Human Nature and World Democracy', The American Journal of Sociology, Vol. 49, No. 5, 1944.

Knight, Frank H., 'Immutable Law in Economics: Its Reality and Limitations', The American Economic Review, Vol. 36, No. 2, 1946.

Knight, Frank H., 'The Sickness of Liberal Society', Ethics, Vol. 56, No. 2, 1946.

Knight, Frank H., 'Natural Law: Last Refuge of the Bigot', Ethics, Vol. 59, No. 2, 1949.

Knight, Frank H., 'The Rôle of Principles in Economics and Politics', The American Economic Review, Vol. 41, No. 1, 1951.

Knox, Bernard, 'Always To Be Best: The Competitive Spirit in Ancient Greek Culture', The Professor John C. Rouman Classical Lecture Series, University of New Hampshire, Durham, 1999, www.helleniccomserve.com/images/Knox%20Lecture.pdf.

Kobayashi, Hideaki, 'Competition Policy Objectives', Panel Discussion, in Claus-Dieter Ehlermann and Laraine L. Laudati (eds.), *The Objectives of Competition Policy*, European Competition Law Annual 1997, Hart Publishing, Oxford, 1998.

Kolakowski, Leszek, *Husserl and the Search for Certitude*, Yale University Press, New Haven, 1975.

Kolev, Stefan, 'F. A. Hayek as an Ordo-Liberal', Hamburg Institute of International Economics Research Paper, 5–11, 2010.

Kramer, Matthew H., *In Defence of Legal Positivism: Law Without Trimmings*, Oxford University Press, Oxford, 1999.

Kramer, Matthew H., 'Why the Axioms and Theorems of Arithmetic are not Legal Norms', Oxford Journal of Legal Studies, Vol. 27, No. 3, 2007.

Kress, Ken, 'Legal Indeterminacy', California Law Review, Vol. 77, No. 2, 1989.

Kronman, Anthony T., 'Wealth Maximization as a Normative Principle', The Journal of Legal Studies, Vol. 9, No. 2, 1980.

Krotoszynski, Ronald J., 'The New Legal Process: Games Peoples Play and the Quest for Legitimate Judicial Decision Making', Washington University Law Quarterly, Vol. 77, No. 4, p. 1999.

Krygier, Martin, '"The Concept of Law" and Social Theory', Oxford Journal of Legal Studies, Vol. 2, No. 2, 1982.

Kuhn, Thomas S., *The Structure of Scientific Revolution*, University of Chicago Press, 1962.

Kuhn, Thomas S., 'Commensurability, Comparability, Communicability', PSA: Proceedings of the Biennial Meeting of the Philosophy of Science Association, Vol. 2, 1982.

Künzler, Adrian, 'Economic Content of Competition Law: the Point of Regulating Preferences' in Daniel Zimmer (ed.), *The Goals of Competition Law*, Edward Elgar Publishing, Cheltenham, 2012.

Künzler, Adrian, 'Dilution Law, Vertical Agreements, and the Construction of Consumption', Oxford Journal of Legal Studies, Vol. 36, No. 1, 2016.

Labrousse, Agnès and Jean-Daniel Weisz (eds.), *Institutional Economics in France and Germany: German Ordoliberalism versus the French Regulation School*, Springer, Berlin, 2001.

Lachmann, Ludwig, *Capital and Its Structure*, Universal Press, Kansas, 1978.

Ladeur, Karl-Heinz, 'From Universalistic Law to the Law of Uncertainty: On the Decay of the Legal Order's "Totalizing Teleology" as Treated in the Methodological Discussion and its Critique from the Left', German Law Journal, Vol. 12, No. 1, 2011.

Lahav, Alexandra D., 'Recovering the Social Value of Jurisdictional Redundancy', Tulane Law Review, Vol. 82, No. 6, 2008.

Lamberton, Robert, *Hesiod*, Yale University Press, New Haven, 1988.

Lande, Robert H., 'The Rise and (Coming) Fall of Efficiency as the Rules of Antitrust', The Antitrust Bulletin, Vol. 33, No. 3, 1988.

Lande, Robert H., 'A Traditional and Textualist Analysis of the Goals of Antitrust: Efficiency, Preventing Theft from Consumers, and Consumer Choice', Fordham Law Review, Vol. 81, No. 5, 2013.

Lane, Jessica, 'The Poetics of Legal Interpretation', Columbia Law Review, Vol. 87, No. 1, 1987.

Lange, Bettina, 'Understanding Regulatory Law: Empirical versus Systems-Theoretical Approaches?', Oxford Journal of Legal Studies, Vol. 18, No. 3, 1998.

Langholm, Odd, 'Economic Freedom in Scholastic Thought', History of Political Economy, Vol. 14, No. 2, 1982.

LaPiana, William P., 'The Legal Culture of the Formative Period in Sherman Act Jurisprudence', New York Law School Law Review, Vol. 35, No. 4, 1990.

Lariguet, Guillermo, 'Constitutional Dilemmas – Some criticisms of Lorenzo Zucca's Conception', in Guillermo Lariguet, David Martinez Zorilla, Silvina Alvarez with replies by Lorenzo Zucca, 'An Exchange on Constitutional Dilemmas', http://papers.ssrn.com/sol3/papers.cfm?abstract_id=1284490.

Laski, Harold J., *Liberty in the Modern State*, Faber & Faber, London, 1930.

Lasswell, Harold D. and Abraham Kaplan, *Power and Society: A Framework for Political Inquiry*, Yale University Press, New Haven, 1950.

Lazzarato, Maurizio, 'Neoliberalism in Action: Inequality, Insecurity and the Reconstruction of the Social', Theory Culture Society, Vol. 26, No. 6, 2009.

Leary, Thomas B., 'Freedom as the Core Value of Antitrust in the New Millennium', Antitrust Law Journal, Vol. 68, No. 2, 2001.

Legrand, Pierre, 'Econocentrism', University of Toronto Law Journal, Vol. 59, No. 2, 2009.

Lemley, Mark A. and Christopher R Leslie, 'Categorical Analysis in Antitrust Jurisprudence', Iowa Law Review, Vol. 93, No. 4, 2008.

Lenel, Hans Otto, 'Evolution of the Social Market Economy', in Alan Peacock and Hans Willgerodt (eds.), *German Neo-Liberals, and the Social Market Economy*, The Macmillan Press, London, 1989.

Leucht, Brigitte, 'How German Is It? The Emergence of European Union Competition Policy and the Ordo-Liberal Model', in Eric Bussière, Michel Dumoulin and Sylvain Schirmann (eds.), *Intégration Économique et Gouvernance Européenne Depuis les Années Cinquante*, L'Harmattan, Paris, 2014.

Levi, Edward H., 'The Antitrust Laws and Monopoly', The University of Chicago Law Review, Vol. 14, No. 2, 1947.

Levy, David, 'Rational Choice and Morality: Economics and Classical Philosophy', History of Political Economy, Vol. 14, No. 1, 1982.

Lianos, Ioannis, 'Lost In Translation? Towards a Theory of Economic Transplants', Current Legal Problems, Vol. 62, No. 1, 2009.

Lianos, Ioannis, 'Some Reflections on the Question of the Goals of EU Competition Law' in Ioannis Lianos and Damien Geradin (eds.), *Handbook on European Competition Law: Substantive Aspects*, Edward Elgar Publishing, Cheltenham, 2013.

Liefmann, Robert, 'Monopoly and Competition as the Basis of a

Government Trust Policy', Quarterly Journal of Economics, Vol. 29, No. 2, 1915.

Lind, Allan, John Thibaut and Laurens Walker, 'A Cross-Cultural Comparison of the Effect of Adversary and Inquisitorial Processes on Bias in Legal Decision Making', Virginia Law Review, Vol. 62, No. 2, 1976.

Lippmann, Walter, *The Good Society*, Transaction Publishers, New Brunswick, 2005.

Lorenz, Edward M., 'Deterministic Nonperiodic Flow', Journal of the Atmospheric Sciences, Vol. 20, No. 2, 1963.

Di Lorenzo, Thomas J. and Jack C. High, 'Antitrust and Competition, Historically Considered', Economic Inquiry, Vol. 26, No. 3, 1988.

Lovdahl Gormsen, Lisa, *A Principled Approach to Abuse of Dominance in European Competition Law*, Cambridge University Press, Cambridge, 2010.

Lowry, Todd, 'The Economic and Jurisprudential Ideas of the Ancient Greeks: Our Heritage from Hellenic Thought', in S. Todd Lowry and Gordon (eds.), *Ancient and Medieval Economic Ideas and Concepts of Social Justice*, Brill Publishing, Leiden, 1998.

Lowry, Todd, 'Ancient and Medieval Economics', in Warren J. Samuels, Jeff E. Biddle, John B. Davis (eds.), *A Companion to The History of Economic Thought*, Blackwell Publishing, Oxford, 2003.

Luban, David, 'Value Pluralism and Rational Choice', Georgetown University Law Center, Working Paper Series in Business, Economics, and Regulatory Law and Public Law and Legal Theory, Working Paper No. 264335, 2001.

Luhmann, Niklas, 'Deconstruction as Second-Order Observing', New Literary History, Vol. 24, No. 4, 1993.

Luhmann, Niklas, *Law as a Social System*, Oxford University Press, Oxford, 2003.

Lutz, Friedrich A., 'Introduction', in Walter Eucken, *The Foundations of Economics: History and Theory in the Analysis of Economic Reality*, The University of Chicago Press, Chicago, 1951.

Ma, Tay-Cheng, 'Antitrust and Democracy: Perspectives from Efficiency and Equality', Journal of Competition Law & Economics, Vol. 12, No. 2, 2016.

Macagno, Fabrizio and Douglas Walton, 'Dichotomies and Oppositions in Legal Argumentation', Ratio Juris, Vol. 23, No. 2, 2010.

MacCallum, Gerald C., 'Negative and Positive Freedom', The Philosophical Review, Vol. 76, No. 3, 1967.

MacCormick, Neil, 'Reconstruction after Deconstruction: A Response to CLS', Oxford Journal of Legal Studies, Vol. 10, No. 4, 1990.

MacCormick, Neil, *Institutions of Law, An Essay on Legal Theory*, Oxford University Press, Oxford, 2007.
MacCormick, Neil, 'Why Law Makes No Claims', in George Pavlakos (ed.), *Law, Rights and Discourse*, Hart Publishing, Oxford, 2007.
Lord Macmillan, *Law and Other Things*, The University Press, Cambridge, 1937.
Madison, Gary B., 'Phenomenology and Economics', in Peter J. Boettke (ed.), *The Elgar Companion to Austrian Economics*, Edward Elgar Publishing, Cheltenham, 1994.
Maduro, Miguel Poiares, 'What is Constitutional Pluralism?' Discussion in Matej Avbelj and Jan Komárek (eds.), *Four Visions of Constitutional Pluralism*, EUI Working Papers, Law 2008/21, Florence, 2008.
Maher, Imelda, 'Re-imagining the Story of European Competition Law', Oxford Journal of Legal Studies, Vol. 20, No. 1, 2000.
Maier-Rigaud, Frank, 'Efficiency, Political Freedom and the Freedom to Competition' in Daniel Zimmer (ed.), *The Goals of Competition Law*, Edward Elgar Publishing, Cheltenham, 2012.
Manson, Daniel D., 'What Is the Sports Product and Who Buys It? The Marketing of Professional Sports Leagues', European Journal of Marketing, Vol. 33, Nos. 3–4, 1999.
Cristina Marcuzzo, Maria, 'The "First" Imperfect Competition Revolution', in Warren J. Samuels, Jeff E. Biddle and John B. Davis (eds.), *A Companion to the History of Economic Thought*, Blackwell Publishing, 2003.
Markham, Jesse W., 'An Alternative Approach to the Concept of Workable Competition', The American Economic Review, Vol. 40, No. 3, 1950.
Markovits, Richard S., 'Legal Analysis and The Economic Analysis of Allocative Efficiency', Hofstra Law Review, Vol. 8, No. 4, 1980.
Markovits, Richard S., 'On the Inevitable Arbitrariness of Market Definitions', The Antitrust Bulletin, Vol. 47, No. 4, 2002.
Malloy, Robin P., 'Truth and Law: Economics and Legal Interpretation', Syracuse University College of Law Public Law & Legal Theory Research Paper Series, Research Paper No. 05–02, 2002.
Márkus, György, 'On Freedom: Positive and Negative', Constellations, Vol. 6, No. 3, 1999.
Marmor, Andrei, 'On the Limits of Rights', Law and Philosophy, Vol. 16, No. 1, 1997.
Martin, Stephen, 'The Goals of Antitrust Policy', in Wayne D. Collins (ed.), *Issues in Competition Law and Policy*, American Bar Association Publishing, Chicago, 2008.
Marx, Karl, 'Letter to Pavel Vasilyevich Annenkov', in *Marx Engels Collected Works*, Vol. 38, International Publishers, 1975, http://www.marxists.org/archive/marx/works/1846/letters/46_12_28.htm.

Mason, Edward S., 'Monopoly in Law and Economics', The Yale Law Journal, Vol. 47, No. 1, 1937.

Maturana, Humberto and Francisco Varela, *Autopoiesis and Cognition: The Realization of the Living*, Kluwer, Dordrecht, 1972.

McNulty, Paul J., 'A Note on the History of Perfect Competition', The Journal of Political Economy, Vol. 75, No. 4, 1967.

McNulty, Paul J., 'Economic Theory and the Meaning of Competition', The Quarterly Journal of Economics, Vol. 82, No. 4, 1968.

Meese, Alan J., 'Reframing the (False?) Choice Between Purchaser Welfare and Total Welfare', Fordham Law Review, Vol. 81, No. 5, 2013.

Megay, Edward N., 'Treitschke Reconsidered: The Hegelian Tradition of German Liberalism', Midwest Journal of Political Science, Vol. 2, No. 3, 1958.

Megay, Edward N., 'Anti-Pluralist Liberalism: The German Neoliberals', Political Science Quarterly, Vol. 85, No. 3, 1970.

Melsheimer, Thomas M., 'Economics and Ideology: Antitrust in the 1980s', Stanford Law Review, Vol. 42, No. 5, 1990.

Menger, Carl, *Principles of Economics*, Ludwig von Mises Institute, Auburn, Alabama, 2007.

Mercuro, Nicholas, 'The Jurisprudential Niche Occupied by Law and Economics', The Journal Jurisprudence, Vol. 2, No. 1, 2009.

Mestmäcker, Ernst-Joachim, 'A Legal Theory Without Law: Posner v. Hayek on Economic Analysis of Law', Walter Eucken Institut, Beiträge zur Ordnungstheorie und Ordnungspolitik 174, Tübingen, Mohr Siebeck, 2007.

Mestmäcker, Ernst-Joachim, 'The Development of German and European Competition Law with Special Reference to the EU Commission's Article 82 Guidance of 2008', Max Planck Private Law Research Paper No. 10/1, 2010.

Mestmäcker, Ernst-Joachim, 'Towards a Concept of Workable European Competition Law: Revisiting the Formative Period' in Kiran Patel and Heike Schweitzer (eds.), *The Historical Foundations of EU Competition Law*, Oxford University Press, 2013.

Metcalfe, Stan, Ronald Ramlogan, Elvira Uyarra, 'Economic Development and the Competitive Process', Centre on Regulation and Competition Working Paper Series, No. 36, 2002.

Michelman, Frank I., 'Constitutions, Statutes, and the Theory of Efficient Adjudication', The Journal of Legal Studies, Vol. 9, No. 3, 1980.

Michelon, Claudio, 'MacCormick's Institutionalism between Theoretical and Practical Reason', Diritto & Questioni Pubbliche, Vol. 9, No. 1, 2009.

Mill, John S., *Principles of Political Economy*, University of Toronto Press, 1965.

Mill, John S., *Principles of Political Economy*, Oxford University Press, Oxford, 1998.

von Mises, Ludwig, *Human Action – A Treatise on Economics*, William Hodge and Co., 1949.

von Mises, Ludwig, 'Planning for Freedom', in Ludwig von Mises, *Planning for Freedom and Twelve Other Essays and Addresses*, Libertarian Press, Illinois, 1974.

Molle, Alexander and Franz Jürgen Säcker, 'Anti-Competitive and Pro-Competitive Elements of an Agreement', in Günther Hirsch, Frank Montag and Franz Jürgen Säcker (eds.), *Competition Law: European Community Practice and Procedure – Article-by-Article Commentary*, Sweet & Maxwell, London, 2008.

Möller, Kai, 'Balancing and the Structure of Constitutional Rights', International Journal of Constitutional Law, Vol. 5, No. 3, 2007.

Möller, Kai, 'Two Conceptions of Positive Liberty: Towards an Autonomy-based Theory of Constitutional Rights', Oxford Journal of Legal Studies, Vol. 29, No. 4, 2009.

Monti, Giorgio, 'Article 81 EC and Public Policy', Common Market Law Review, Vol. 39, No. 5, 2002.

Monti, Giorgio, 'EC Competition Law: The Dominance of Economic Analysis?', in Roger Zäch, Andreas Heinemann and Andreas Kellerhals (eds.), *The Development of Competition Law – Global Perspectives*, Edward Elgar Publishing, Cheltenham, 2010.

Moran, Gerald P., 'A Radical Theory of Jurisprudence: The Decisionmaker as the Source of Law – The Ohio Supreme Court's Adoption of the Spendthrift Trust Doctrine as a Model', Akron Law Review, Vol. 30, No. 3, 1997.

Morgan, John, 'Financing Public Goods by Means of Lotteries', The Review of Economic Studies, Vol. 67, No. 4, 2000.

Morgan, Mary S., 'Competing Notions of "Competition" in Late Nineteenth-Century American Economics', History of Political Economy, Vol. 25, No. 4, 1993.

Möschel, Wernhard, 'Competition Policy from an Ordo Point of View', in Alan Peacock and Hans Willgerodt (eds.), *German Neo-Liberals, and the Social Market Economy*, The Macmillan Press, London, 1989.

Möschel, Wernhard, 'The Proper Scope of Government Viewed from an Ordoliberal Perspective: The Example of Competition Policy', Journal of Institutional and Theoretical Economics, Vol. 157, No. 1, 2001.

Motta, Massimo, *Competition Policy: Theory and Practice*, Cambridge University Press, Cambridge, 2004.

Mouffe, Chantal, 'Radical Democracy: Modern or Postmodern?', in Chantal Mouffe, *The Return of the Political*, Verso, London, 1993.

Mouffe, Chantal, 'Carl Schmitt and the Paradox of Liberal Democracy', in Chantal Mouffe (ed.), *The Challenge of Carl Schmitt*, Verso, London, 1999.

Mouffe, Chantal, 'Introduction: Schmitt's Challenge', in Chantal Mouffe (ed.), *The Challenge of Carl Schmitt*, Verso, London, 1999.

Mouffe, Chantal, *On the Political*, Routledge, London, 2005.

Müller-Armack, Alfred, *Stabilität in Europa: Strategien und Institutionen für eine europäische Stabilitätsgemeinschaft*, Econ Verlag, Düsseldorf, 1971.

Müller-Armack, Alfred, *Religion und Wissenschaft: Geistesgeschichtliche Hintergründe unserer Europäischen Lebensform*, Bern, Stuttgart, 1981.

Müller-Armack, Alfred, 'The Meaning of the Social Market Economy', in Alan T. Peacock and Hans Willgerodt (eds.), *Germany's Social Market Economy: Origins and Evolution*, Macmillan, London, 1989.

Nachbar, Thomas B., 'Monopoly, Mercantilism & the Politics of Regulation', University of Virginia Law School, Public Law and Legal Theory Working Paper Series, No. 32, 2005.

Edgar Nawroth, Egon, *Die Sozial- und Wirtschaftsphilosophie des Neoliberalismus*, Heidelberg and Löwen, Kerle, 1961.

Nazzini, Renato, 'Article 81 EC between Time Present and Time Past: A Normative Critique of "Restriction of Competition" in EU Law', Common Market Law Review, Vol. 43, No. 2, 2006.

Nelson, Eric, 'Liberty: One Concept Too Many?', Political Theory, Vol. 33, No. 1, 2005.

Nelson, Richard R., 'Recent Evolutionary Theorizing About Economic Change', Journal of Economic Literature, Vol. 33, No. 1, 1995.

Neuborne, Burt, 'Of Sausage Factories and Syllogism Machines: Formalism, Realism, and Exclusionary Selection Techniques', New York University Law Review, Vol. 67, No. 1, 1992.

Neves, Marcelo, 'From the Autopoiesis to the Allopoiesis of Law', Journal of Law and Society, Vol. 28, No. 2, 2001.

Niblett, Anthony, Richard A. Posner and Andrei Shleifer, 'The Evolution of a Legal Rule', The Journal of Legal Studies, Vol. 39, No. 2, 2010.

Nietzsche, Friedrich, 'Homer's Contest', in Friedrich Nietzsche, *On the Genealogy of Morality*, Cambridge University Press, Cambridge, 2007.

Nicholson, Peter P., 'The Internal Morality of Law: Fuller and His Critics', Ethics, Vol. 84, No. 4, 1974.

Nicolaides, Phedon, 'An Essay on Economics and Competition Law of the European Community', Legal Issues of Economic Integration, Vol. 27, No. 1, 2000.

Nobles, Richard and David Schiff, 'Introduction' in Niklas Luhmann (ed.), *Law as Social System*, Oxford University Press, Oxford, 2004.

Nockleby, John T., 'Two Theories of Competition in The Early 19th Century Labour Cases', The American Journal of Legal History, Vol. 38, No. 4, 1994.

Noll, Roger G., 'The Economics of Promotion and Relegation in Sports Leagues: The Case of English Football', Journal of Sports Economics, Vol. 3, No. 2, 2002.

Wolfgang Nörr, Knut, 'On the Concept of "Economic Constitution" and the Importance of Franz Böhm from the Viewpoint of Legal History', European Journal of Law and Economics, Vol. 3, No. 4, 1996.

Wolfgang Nörr, Knut and 'Franz Böhm and the Theory of the Private Law Society', in Peter Koslowski (ed.), *The Theory of Capitalism in the German Economic Tradition: Historism, Ordo-liberalism, Critical Theory, Solidarism*, Springer, Hannover, 2000.

Novak, Marko, 'Three Models of Balancing (in Constitutional Review)', Ratio Juris, Vol. 23, No. 1, 2010.

Nozick, Robert, *Anarchy, State, and Utopia*, Basic Books, New York, 1974.

Nygren, Anders, *Agape and Eros*, The University of Chicago Press, Chicago, 1982.

O'Driscoll, Gerald P., 'Justice, Efficiency, and the Economic Analysis of Law: A Comment on Fried', The Journal of Legal Studies, Vol. 9, No. 2, 1980.

Oetken, Paul, 'Form and Substance in Critical Legal Studies', The Yale Law Journal, Vol. 100, No. 7, 1991.

Oliver, Henry M., 'German Neoliberalism', The Quarterly Journal of Economics, Vol. 74, No. 1, 1960.

Orbach, Barak Y., 'The Antitrust Consumer Welfare Paradox', Journal of Competition Law and Economics, Vol. 7, No. 1, 2011.

Orbach, Barak Y., 'How Antitrust Lost Its Goal', Fordham Law Review, Vol. 81, No. 5, 2013.

Owens, Lewis, '"Does This One Exist"? The Unveiled Abyss of Nikos Kazantzakis', Journal of Modern Greek Studies, Vol. 16, No. 2, 1998.

Owens, Patricia, *The Ethic of Reality in Hannah Arendt*, Oxford University Press, Oxford, 2008.

Özbideciler, Umut Devrim, 'Social Market Economy: An Inquiry into the Theoretical Bases of German Model of Capitalism', http://etd.lib.metu.edu.tr/upload/1041896/index.pdf.

Page, William H., 'The Chicago School and the Evolution of Antitrust: Characterization, Antitrust Injury, and Evidentiary Sufficiency', Virginia Law Review, Vol. 75, No. 7, 1989.

Page, William H., 'Ideological Conflict and the Origins of Antitrust Policy', Tulane Law Review, Vol. 66, No. 1, 1991.

Page, William H., 'Legal Realism and the Shaping of Modern Antitrust', Emory Law Journal, Vol. 44, No. 1, 1995.

Page, William H., 'The Ideological Origins and Evolution of U.S. Antitrust Law', in Wayne D. Collins (ed.), *Issues in Competition Law and Policy*, American Bar Association Publishing, Chicago, 2008.
Parisi, Francesco, 'Positive, Normative and Functional Schools in Law and Economics', European Journal of Law and Economics, Vol. 18, No. 3, 2004.
Parret, Laura, 'Shouldn't We Know What We Are Protecting? Yes We Should! A Plea for a Solid and Comprehensive Debate About the Objectives of EU Competition Law and Policy', European Competition Journal, Vol. 6, No. 2, 2010.
Paulson, Stanley L., 'The Neo-Kantian Dimension of Kelsen's Pure Theory of Law', Oxford Journal of Legal Studies, Vol. 12, No. 3, 1992.
Paulson, Stanley L., 'Radbruch on Unjust Laws: Competing Earlier and Later Views?', Oxford Journal of Legal Studies, Vol. 15, No. 3, 1995.
Paulson, Stanley L., 'Hans Kelsen's Earliest Legal Theory: Critical Constructivism', The Modern Law Review, Vol. 59, No. 6, 1996.
Paulson, Stanley L., 'Introduction', in Stanley L. Paulson and Bonnie Litschewski Paulson (eds.), *Normativity and Norms: Critical Perspectives on Kelsenian Themes*, Clarendon Press, Oxford, 1998.
Pavlakos, George, 'Normativity versus Ontology: Law, Facts and Practical Reason', Rechtstheorie, Vol. 34, No. 4, 2003.
Peacock, Alan and Hans Willgerodt, 'Overall View of the German Liberal Movement', in Alan Peacock and Hans Willgerodt (eds.), *German Neo-Liberals, and the Social Market Economy*, The Macmillan Press, London, 1989.
Peck, Jamie, *Constructions of Neoliberal Reason*, Oxford University Press, Oxford, 2010.
Peczenik, Aleksander, 'Particulars and Universals in Legal Justification', in Zenon Bankowski and James MacLean (eds.), *The Universal and the Particular in Legal Reasoning*, Ashgate, Aldershot, 2006.
Peczenik, Aleksander, 'Scientia Juris: Legal Doctrine as Knowledge of Law and as a Source of Law', *Treatise of Legal Philosophy and General Jurisprudence*: Vol. 4, Springer, New York, 2007.
Peeters, Jan, 'The Rule of Reason Revisited: Prohibition on Restraints of Competition in the Sherman Act and the EEC Treaty', The American Journal of Comparative Law, Vol. 37, No. 3, 1989.
Pera, Alberto, 'Changing Views of Competition, Economic Analysis and EC Antitrust Law', European Competition Journal, Vol. 4, No. 1, 2008.
Perelman, Michael, 'Classical Political Economy and Primitive Accumulation: the Case of Smith and Steuart', History of Political Economy, Vol. 15, No. 3, 1983.
Peritz, Rudolph J. R., 'The "Rule of Reason" in Antitrust Law: Property

Logic in Restraint of Competition', Hastings Law Journal, Vol. 40, No. 2, 1989.
Peritz, Rudolph J. R., 'A Counter-History of Antitrust Law', Duke Law Journal, Vol. 39, No. 2, 1990.
Peritz, Rudolf J. R., 'Three Visions of Managed Competition, 1920–1950', The Antitrust Bulletin, Vol. 39, No. 1, 1994.
Peritz, Rudolph J. R., *Competition Policy in America: History, Rhetoric, Law*, Oxford University Press, Oxford, 1996.
Perrot, Anne, 'Appropriation of the Legal System by Economic Concepts: Should Conflicting Goals Be Considered?', in Josef Drexl, Laurence Idot and Joël Monéger (eds.), *Economic Theory and Competition Law*, Edward Elgar Publishing, Cheltenham, 2009.
Perrotta, Cosimo, 'The Legacy of the Past: Ancient Economic Thought on Wealth and Development', The European Journal of the History of Economic Thought, Vol. 10, No. 2, 2003.
Petrochilos, George A., '*Kalokagathia*: The Ethical Basis of Hellenic Political Economy and Its Influence from Plato to Ruskin and Sen', History of Political Economy, Vol. 34, No. 3, 2002.
Petroski, Karen, 'Is Post-Positivism Possible?', German Law Journal, Vol. 12, No. 2, 2011.
Peukert, Helge, 'Walter Eucken (1891–1950) and the Historical School', in Peter Koslowski (ed.), *The Theory of Capitalism in the German Economic Tradition: Historism, Ordo-liberalism, Critical Theory, Solidarism*, Springer, Hannover, 2000.
Pildes, Richard H., 'Avoiding Balancing: The Role of Exclusionary Reasons in Constitutional Law', Hastings Law Journal, Vol. 45, No. 4, 1994.
Pintore, Anna, 'Law as Fact? MacCormick's Institutional Theory of Law: Between Legal Positivism and Sociological Jurisprudence', International Journal for the Semiotics of Law, Vol. 4, No. 3, 1991.
Piraino, Thomas A., 'Reconciling the Harvard and Chicago Schools: A New Antitrust Approach for the 21st Century', Indiana Law Journal, Vol. 82, No. 2, 2007.
Polanyi, Karl, 'Aristotle Discovers the Economy', in George Dalton (ed.), *Primitive, Archaic, and Modern Economics*, Doubleday, Garden City, 1968.
Polanyi, Michael, 'The Value of the Inexact', Philosophy of Science, Vol. 3, No. 2, 1936.
Polanyi, Michael, 'The Growth of Thought in Society', Economica, New Series, Vol. 8, No. 32, 1941.
Polanyi, Michael, 'The Logic of Liberty', Routledge, London, 1951.
Popper, Karl R., 'What is Dialectic?', Mind, Vol. 49, No. 196, 1940.
Popper, Karl R., *Conjectures and Refutations: The Growth of Scientific Knowledge*, Routledge, London, 2003.

Posner, Richard A., 'The Rule of Reason and the Economic Approach: Reflections on the *Sylvania* Decision', The University of Chicago Law Review, Vol. 45, No. 1, 1977.

Posner, Richard A., 'Utilitarianism, Economics, and Legal Theory', The Journal of Legal Studies, Vol. 8, No. 1, 1979.

Posner, Richard A., 'The Ethical and Political Basis of the Efficiency Norm in Common Law Adjudication', Hofstra Law Review, Vol. 8, No. 3, 1980.

Posner, Richard A., 'The Value of Wealth: A Comment on Dworkin and Kronman', The Journal of Legal Studies, Vol. 9, No. 2, 1980.

Posner, Richard A., *The Economics of Justice*, Harvard University Press, Cambridge, Massachusetts, 1981.

Posner, Richard A., 'The Problematics of Moral and Legal Theory', Harvard Law Review, Vol. 111, No. 7, 1998.

Posner, Richard A., 'Kelsen versus Hayek: Pragmatism, Economics, and Democracy', in Richard A. Posner, *Law, Pragmatism and Democracy*, Harvard University Press, Cambridge, Massachusetts, 2003.

Posner, Richard A., 'Law and Economics in Common-Law, Civil-Law, and Developing Nations', Ratio Juris, Vol. 17, No. 1, 2004.

Posner, Richard A., *A Failure of Capitalism: The Crisis of '08 and the Descent into Depression*, Harvard University Press, Cambridge, Massachusetts, 2009.

Post, Robert C., 'Community and the First Amendment', Arizona State Law Journal, Vol. 29, No. 3, 1997.

Poster, Mark, 'Interpreting Texts: Some New Directions', Southern California Law Review, Vol. 58, No. 3, 1985.

Pound, Roscoe, 'Mechanical Jurisprudence', Columbia Law Review, Vol. 8, No. 8, 1908.

Pound, Roscoe, 'The Theory of Judicial Decision I. The Materials of Judicial Decision', Harvard Law Review, Vol. 36, No. 6, 1923.

Pound, Roscoe, 'Law and the Science of Law in Recent Theories', The Yale Law Journal, Vol. 43, No. 4, 1934.

Prosser, Tony, *The Limits of Competition Law: Markets and Public Services*, Oxford University Press, Oxford, 2005.

Radbruch, Gustav, 'Legal Philosophy', in Emil Lask and Edwin Patterson (eds.), *The Legal Philosophies of Lask Radbruch and Dabin*, Harvard University Press, Cambridge, Massachusetts, 1950.

Radbruch, Gustav, 'Statutory Lawlessness and Supra-Statutory Law', 1946, translated by Bonnie Litschewski Paulson and Stanley L. Paulson, Oxford Journal of Legal Studies, Vol. 26, No. 1, 2006.

Ramirez Perez, Sigfrido and Sabastien van de Scheur, 'The Evolution of the Law on Articles 101 and 102 TFEU: Ordoliberalism and Its

Keynesian Challenge' in Kiran Patel and Heike Schweitzer (eds.), *The Historical Foundations of EU Competition Law*, Oxford University Press, 2013.
Rawls, John, 'Two Concepts of Rules', The Philosophical Review, Vol. 64, No. 1, 1955.
Rawls, John, *A Theory of Justice*, Harvard University Press, Cambridge, Massachusetts, 1999.
Rawls, John, *Political Liberalism*, Columbia University Press, New York, 2005.
Raz, Joseph, 'Legal Principles and the Limits of Law', The Yale Law Journal, Vol. 81, No. 5, 1972.
Raz, Joseph, *The Concept of a Legal System*, Clarendon Press, Oxford, 1980.
Raz, Joseph, *The Morality of Freedom*, Clarendon Press, Oxford, 1986.
Raz, Joseph, 'Free Expression and Personal Identification', Oxford Journal of Legal Studies, Vol. 11, No. 3, 1991.
Raz, Joseph, *Between Authority and Interpretation*, Oxford University Press, Oxford, 2009.
Raz, Joseph, 'The Rule of Law and Its Virtue', in Joseph Raz, *The Authority of Law, Essays on Law and Morality*, Oxford University Press, Oxford, 2009.
Rittershausen, Johannes R. B., 'The Postwar West German Economic Transition: From Ordoliberalism to Keynesianism', Institut für Wirtschaftspolitik an der Universität zu Köln Working Paper, No. 07/1, 2007.
Robbins, Lionel, *An Essay on the Nature and Significance of Economic Science*, Macmillan & Co, London, 1952.
Robinson, Joan, *The Economics of Imperfect Competition*, Macmillan and Co., London, 1933.
Robinson, Joan, *Essays in the Theory of Economic Growth*, Macmillan, London, 1962.
de Roover, Raymond, 'Monopoly Theory Prior to Adam Smith: A Revision', The Quarterly Journal of Economics, Vol. 65, No. 4, 1951.
Röpke, Wilhelm, *Civitas humana – Grundfragen der Gesellschafts- und Wirtschaftsreform*, Rentsch-Zürich, Erlenbach, 1949.
Röpke, Wilhelm, 'Liberalism and Christianity', Modern Age, Vol. 1, No. 2, 1957.
Röpke, Wilhelm, 'Wirtschaftlicher Liberalismus und Staatsgedank', in Wilhelm Röpke, *Gegen die Brandung*, Rentsch-Zürich, Erlenbach, 1959.
Rosenfeld, Michel, 'Hate Speech In Constitutional Jurisprudence: A Comparative Analysis', Cardozo Law Review, Vol. 24, No. 4, 2003.
Ross, Alf, *Towards a Realistic Jurisprudence – A Criticism of the Dualism in Law*, Einar Munksgaard, Copenhagen, 1946.

Roth, Wulf-Henning, 'Strategic Competition Policy: A Comment on EU Competition Policy' in Hanns Ullrich (ed.), *The Evolution of European Competition Law: Whose Regulation, Which Competition*, Edward Elgar Publishing, Cheltenham, 2006.

Rothbard, Murray N., *Man, Economy and State – A Treatise on Economic Principles*, Ludwig von Mises Institute, Auburn, Alabama, 2009.

Rousseau, Jean-Jacques, *The Social Contract*, Oxford University Press, Oxford, 1994.

Rowe, Frederick M., 'The Decline of Antitrust and the Delusions of Models: The Faustian Pact of Law and Economics', Georgetown Law Journal, Vol. 72, No. 4, 1984.

Royall, Sean M., 'Editor's Note: Symposium Post-Chicago Economics', Antitrust Law Journal, Vol. 63, No. 2, 1995.

Rubin, Paul H., 'Why Is the Common Law Efficient?', The Journal of Legal Studies, Vol. 6, No. 1, 1977.

Rubinfeld, Daniel L. and Peter O. Steiner, 'Quantitative Methods in Antitrust Litigation', Law and Contemporary Problems, Vol. 46, No. 4, 1983.

Russell, Bertrand, 'Vagueness', in *Collected Papers of Bertrand Russell*, Vol. 9, Unwin Hyman, London, 1988.

Rüstow, Alexander, 'Weltpolitische Folgerunge', in *Hat der Westen eine Idee?*, Aktionsgemeinschaft Soziale Marktwirtschaft Tagung, Protokoll No. 7, 1957.

Säcker, Franz Jürgen, 'Legal Foundations of Competition', in Günther Hirsch, Frank Montag and Franz Jürgen Säcker (eds.), *Competition Law: European Community Practice and Procedure – Article-by-Article Commentary*, Sweet & Maxwell, London, 2008.

Sagers, Chris, 'Proliferating Rules of Per Se Legality in Antitrust: The Great Swiss Cheese and the Myth of Theoretical Unification', Cleveland-Marshall College of Law, Research Paper 09–177, 2009.

Samuels, Warren J., 'The Physiocratic Theory of Economic Policy', The Quarterly Journal of Economics, Vol. 76, No. 1, 1962.

Sartor, Giovanni, 'A Formal Model of Legal Argumentation', Ratio Juris, Vol. 7, No. 2, 1994.

Sartor, Giovanni, 'A Teleological Approach to Legal Dialogues', EUI Working Paper, Law, No. 2006/28, Florence, 2006.

Schaub, Alexander, 'Competition Policy Objectives', Working Paper, in Claus-Dieter Ehlermann and Laraine L. Laudati (eds.), *The Objectives of Competition Policy*, European Competition Law Annual 1997, Hart Publishing, Oxford, 1998.

Schauer, Frederick, 'Commensurability and Its Constitutional Consequences', Hastings Law Journal, Vol. 45, No. 4, 1994.

Schauer, Frederick, 'Fuller's Internal Point of View', Law and Philosophy, Vol. 13, No. 3, 1994.
Schauer, Frederick, 'Balancing, Subsumption, and the Constraining Role of Legal Text', Symposium on Rights, Law, and Morality: Themes from the Legal Philosophy of Robert Alexy, New College, Oxford University, 10–11 September 2008.
Schmalbeck, Richard, 'The Justice of Economics: An Analysis of Wealth Maximization as a Normative Goal', Columbia Law Review, Vol. 83, No. 2, 1983.
Schmitt, Carl, *Political Theology – Four Chapters on the Concept of Sovereignty*, The MIT Press, Cambridge, Massachusetts, 1985.
Schmitt, Carl, *The Crisis of Parliamentary Democracy*, MIT University Press, Cambridge, Massachusetts, 1985.
Schopenhauer, Arthur, *The Art of Controversy*, Kessinger Publishing, Whitefish, Montana, 2004.
Jeanne L. Schroeder, 'The End of the Market: A Psychoanalysis of Law and Economics', Harvard Law Review, Vol. 112, No. 2, 1998.
Schroeder, Jeanne L., 'Fear of Freedom: A Polemic Against Policy Scholarship', Cardozo Law School, Jacob Burns Institute for Advanced Legal Studies, Working Paper Series No. 35, 2001.
Schroeder, Jeanne L., 'The Laconomics of Apples and Oranges: A Speculative Analysis of the Economic Concept of Commensurability', Yale Journal of Law and Humanities, Vol. 15, No. 2, 2003.
Schumpeter, Joseph A., *History of Economic Analysis*, Routledge, London, 1994.
Schwartz, Louis B., '"Justice" and other Non-Economic Goals of Antitrust', University of Pennsylvania Law Review, Vol. 127, No. 4, 1979.
Schwartz, Barry, *The Paradox of Choice: Why More is Less*, HarperCollins, London, 2005.
Schweitzer, Heike, 'Competition Law and Public Policy: Reconsidering an Uneasy Relationship: The Example of Art. 81', EUI Working Paper, Law, 2007/30, 2007.
Schweitzer, Heike, 'Parallels and Differences in the Attitudes towards Single-Firm Conduct: What are the Reasons? The History, Interpretation and Underlying Principles of Sec. 2 Sherman Act and Art. 82 EC', EUI Working Paper, Law, 2007/32, 2007.
Schweitzer, Heike, 'The Role of Consumer Welfare in EU Competition Law', in Josef Drexl, Reto M. Hilty, Laurence Boy, Christine Godt and Bernard Remiche (eds.), *Technology and Competition: Contributions in Honour of Hanns Ullrich*, Larcier, Brussels, 2009.
Schwenk, Allen J., 'What Is the Correct Way To Seed a Knockout

Tournament?', The American Mathematical Monthly, Vol. 107, No. 2, 2000.

Sebok, Anthony J., *Legal Positivism in American Jurisprudence*, Cambridge University Press, Cambridge, 1998.

Semmelmann, Constanze, 'The Future Role of the Non-Competition Goals in the Interpretation of Article 81 EC', Global Antitrust Review, Vol. 1, No. 1, 2008.

Sen, Amartya, 'Freedom of Choice: Concept and Content', European Economic Review, Vol. 32, No. 2–3, 1988.

Shooshan, Harry M., 'Confrontation with Congress: Professional Sports and the Television Antiblackout Law', Syracuse Law Review, Vol. 25, No. 3, 1974.

Siems, Mathias, 'Legal Originality', Oxford Journal of Legal Studies, Vol. 28, No. 1, 2008.

da Silva, Virgílio Afonso, 'Comparing the Incommensurable: Constitutional Principles, Balancing and Rational Decision', Oxford Journal of Legal Studies, Vol. 31, No. 2, 2011.

Silver, Charles, 'Elmer's Case: A Legal Positivist Replies to Dworkin', Law and Philosophy, Vol. 6, No. 3, 1987.

Silvermintz, Daniel, 'Plato's Supposed Defense of the Division of Labor: A Reexamination of the Role of Job Specialization in the *Republic*', History of Political Economy, Vol. 42, No. 4, 2010.

Simon, Herbert A., *Models of Man: Social and Rational*, Wiley Publishing, Oxford, 1957.

Singer, Joseph W., 'Legal Realism Now', California Law Review, Vol. 76, No. 2, 1988.

Skinner, Andrew S., 'Adam Smith (1723–1790): Theories of Political Economy', in Warren J. Samuels, Jeff E. Biddle, John B. Davis (eds.), *A Companion to The History of Economic Thought*', Blackwell Publishing, Oxford, 2003.

Sleat, Matt, 'Liberalism, Fundamentalism and Truth', Journal of Applied Philosophy, Vol. 23, No. 4, 2006.

Small, Albion W., *The Cameralists: The Pioneers of German Social Polity*, Batoche Books, Kitchener, 2001.

Šmejkal, Václav, 'Competition Law and the Social Market Economy Goal of the EU', International Comparative Jurisprudence, Vol. 1, No. 1, 2015.

Smith, Adam, *An Inquiry into the Nature and Causes of the Wealth of Nations*, Edwin Cannan (ed.), Methuen & Co, London, 1904.

Smith, Adam, *The Theory of Moral Sentiments*, Prometheus Books, Amherst, 2000.

Smith, Barry, 'Aristotelianism, Apriorism, Essentialism', in Peter J. Boettke (ed.), *The Elgar Companion to Austrian Economics*, Edward Elgar Publishing, Cheltenham, 1994.

Somek, Alexander, 'The Indelible Science of Law', International Journal of Constitutional Law, Vol. 7, No. 3, 2009.

Soper, Philip, 'Critical Notice: Legal Systems, Normative Systems, and the Paradoxes of Positivism', Canadian Journal of Law and Jurisprudence, Vol. 8, No. 2, 1995.

Sosnick, Stephen H., 'A Critique of Concepts of Workable Competition', The Quarterly Journal of Economics, Vol. 72, No. 3, 1958.

de Soto, Jesus Huerta, 'Economic Thought in Ancient Greece', Mises Daily, 15 September 2010.

de Sousa Santos, Boaventura, 'Law: A Map of Misreading. Toward a Postmodern Conception of Law', Journal of Law and Society, Vol. 14, No. 3, 1987.

Spaak, Torben, 'Moral Relativism and the *Rechtsstaat*', ssrn.com/abstract=923435.

Spector, Horacio, 'Legal Fictionalism and the Economics of Normativity', in Mark D. White (ed.), *Theoretical Foundations of Law and Economics*, Cambridge University Press, Cambridge, 2009.

Spencer, Herbert, *First Principles*, D. Appleton and Co., New York, 1914.

Spengler, Joseph J., 'The Physiocrats and Say's Law of Markets. II', The Journal of Political Economy, Vol. 53, No. 4, 1945.

Stalin, Joseph, 'Dialectical and Historical Materialism', 1938, http://www.marxists.org/reference/archive/stalin/works/1938/09.htm.

von Stein, Lorenz, *Geschichte der sozialen Bewegung in Frankreich von 1789 bis auf unsre Tage*, O. Wigand, Leipzig, 1850.

Stigler, George J., 'Perfect Competition, Historically Contemplated', The Journal of Political Economy, Vol. 65, No. 1, 1957.

Stigler, George J., 'The Goals of Economic Policy', The Journal of Business, Vol. 31, No. 3, 1958.

Stigler, George J., 'Economic Competition and Political Competition', Public Choice, Vol. 13, No. 1, 1972.

Stigler, George J., 'Economics or Ethics', The Tanner Lectures on Human Values, Harvard University, 1980 http://www.tannerlectures.utah.edu/lectures/documents/stigler81.pdf.

Stigler, George J., 'The Economists and the Problem of Monopoly', The American Economic Review, Vol. 72, No. 2, 1982.

Stigler, George J., 'The Origin of the Sherman Act', The Journal of Legal Studies, Vol. 14, No. 1, 1985.

Stigler, George J., 'Law or Economics?', Journal of Law and Economics, Vol. 35, No. 2, 1992.

Stocking, George W., 'The Rule of Reason, Workable Competition, and the Legality of Trade Association Activities', The University of Chicago Law Review, Vol. 21, No. 4, 1954.

Stocking, George W., 'Economic Change and the Sherman Act: Some Reflections on "Workable Competition"', Virginia Law Review, Vol. 44, No. 4, 1958.

Streit, Manfred E., 'Economic Order, Private Law and Public Policy: the Freiburg School of Law and Economics in Perspective', Journal of Institutional and Theoretical Economics, Vol. 148, No. 4, 1992.

Streit, Manfred E. and Werner Mussier, 'The Economic Constitution of the European Community', Constitutional Political Economy, Vol. 5, No. 3, 1994.

Streit, Manfred E., 'The Freiburg School of Law and Economics', in Peter J. Boettke (ed.), *The Elgar Companion to Austrian Economics*, Edward Elgar Publishing, Cheltenham, 1994.

Streit, Manfred E. and Michael Wohlgemuth, 'The Market Economy and the State: Hayekian and Ordoliberal Conceptions', Max-Planck-Institut zur Erforschung von Wirtschaftssystemen, Discussion paper, 06/97, 1997.

Stucke, Maurice E., 'What is Competition?' in Daniel Zimmer (ed.), *The Goals of Competition Law*, Edward Elgar Publishing, Cheltenham, 2012.

Stucke, Maurice E., 'Should Competition Policy Promote Happiness?', Fordham Law Review, Vol. 81, No. 5, 2013.

Sullivan, Lawrence A., 'Economics and More Humanistic Disciplines: What Are the Sources of Wisdom for Antitrust?', University of Pennsylvania Law Review, Vol. 125, No. 6, 1977.

Sullivan, Lawrence A., *Handbook of the Law of Antitrust*, West Publishing, St. Paul, 1977.

Sullivan, Lawrence A., 'The Viability of the Current Law on Horizontal Restraints', California Law Review, Vol. 75, No. 3, 1987.

Sullivan, Lawrence A., 'Post-Chicago Economics: Economists, Lawyers, Judges and Enforcement Officials in a Less Determinate Theoretical World', Antitrust Law Journal, Vol. 63, No. 2, 1995.

Sullivan, Lawrence A. and Wolfgang Fikentscher, 'On the Growth of the Antitrust Idea', Berkeley Journal of International Law, Vol. 16, No. 2, 1998.

Summers, Robert S., 'Professor H. L. A. Hart's "Concept of Law"', Duke Law Journal, Vol. 12, No. 4, 1963.

Svetiev, Yane, 'Antitrust Governance: The New Wave of Antitrust', Loyola University Chicago Law Journal, Vol. 38, No. 3, 2007.

Sward, Ellen E., 'Values, Ideology, and the Evolution of the Adversary System', Indiana Law Journal, Vol. 64, No. 2, 1989.

Sweet, Alec S. and Jud Mathews, 'Proportionality Balancing and Global

Constitutionalism', Columbia Journal of Transnational Law, Vol. 47, No. 1, 2008.

Szymanski, Stefan and Stefan Késenne, 'Competitive Balance and Gate Revenue Sharing in Team Sports', The Journal of Industrial Economics, Vol. 52, No. 1, 2004.

Talbot, Conor, 'Ordoliberalism and Balancing Competition Goals in the Development of the European Union', The Antitrust Bulletin, Vol. 61, No. 2, 2016.

Tamanaha, Brian Z., 'The Folly of the "Social Scientific" Concept of Legal Pluralism', Journal of Law and Society, Vol. 20, No. 2, 1993.

Tamanaha, Brian Z., 'A Non-Essentialist Version of Legal Pluralism', Journal of Law and Society, Vol. 27, No. 2. 2000.

Tamanaha, Brian Z., 'The Bogus Tale About the Legal Formalists', St. John's University, Legal Studies Research Working Paper Series, Paper No. 08-0130, 2008.

Taylor, Hunter E., 'H. L. A. Hart's Concept of Law in the Perspective of American Legal Realism', The Modern Law Review, Vol. 35, No. 6, 1972.

Temple Lang, John and Robert O'Donoghue, 'The Concept of an Exclusionary Abuse under Article 82 EC', Global Competition Law Centre Research Papers on Article 82 EC, 2005.

Teubner, Günther, 'Autopoiesis in Law and Society: A Rejoinder to Blankenburg', Law & Society Review, Vol. 18, No. 2, 1984.

Teubner, Günther, *Autopoietic Law: A New Approach to Law and Society*, Walter de Gruyter & Co., Berlin, 1987.

Teubner, Günther, 'The Two Faces of Janus: Rethinking Legal Pluralism', Cardozo Law Review, Vol. 13, No. 5, 1992.

Teubner, Günther, 'The King's Many Bodies: The Self-Deconstruction of Law's Hierarchy', Law & Society Review, Vol. 31, No. 4, 1997.

Teubner, Günther, 'Dealing with Paradoxes of Law: Derrida, Luhmann, Wiethölter', in Oren Perez and Gunther Teubner (eds.), *Paradoxes and Inconsistencies in Law*, Hart Publishing, Oxford, 2006.

Teubner, Günther, '"And God Laughed . . ." Indeterminacy, Self-Reference and Paradox In Law', German Law Journal, Vol. 12, No. 1, 2011.

Thaler, Richard H. and Cass R. Sunstein, *Nudge: Improving Decisions about Health, Wealth, and Happiness*, Yale University Press, New Haven, 2008.

Thalmann, William G., '"The Most Divinely Approved and Political Discord": Thinking about Conflict in the Developing Polis', Classical Antiquity, Vol. 23, No. 2, 2004.

Thiele, Leslie P., 'The Agony of Politics: The Nietzschean Roots of Foucault's Thought', The American Political Science Review, Vol. 84, No. 3, 1990.

Thomasberger, Claus, 'The Two Utopias of Economics: Human Freedom and the Mechanism of Competition', www.f3.htw-berlin.de/Professoren/Thomasberger/pdf/Theorie3.pdf.

Thorelli, Hans, *The Federal Antitrust Policy: Origination of an American Tradition*, Johns Hopkins University Press, Baltimore, 1955.

Tiedeman, Christopher G., *The Unwritten Constitution of the United States: A Philosophical Inquiry into the Fundamentals of American Constitutional Law*, G.P. Putnam's Sons, New York, 1890.

Tillich, Paul, *The Courage to Be*, Yale University Press, New Haven, 1952.

La Torre, Massimo, 'On Two Distinct and Opposing Versions of Natural Law: "Exclusive" versus "Inclusive"', Ratio Juris, Vol. 19, No. 2, 2006.

Townley, Christopher, 'Co-ordinated Diversity: Revolutionary Suggestions for EU Competition Law (and for EU Law Too)', Yearbook of European Law, Vol. 33, No. 1, 2014.

Tribe, Laurence H., 'Constitutional Calculus: Equal Justice or Economic Efficiency?', Harvard Law Review, Vol. 98, No. 3, 1985.

Tsakyrakis, Stavros, 'Proportionality: An Assault on Human Rights?', International Journal of Constitutional Law, Vol. 7, No. 3, 2009.

Tschentscher, Axel, 'Interpreting Fundamental Rights: Freedom vs. Optimization', http://papers.ssrn.com/sol3/papers.cfm?abstract_id=163 0393.

Tugwell, Rexford G., 'Human Nature in Economic Theory', The Journal of Political Economy, Vol. 30, No. 3, 1922.

Tumlir, Jan, 'Franz Böhm and the Development of Economic-constitutional Analysis', in Alan Peacock and Hans Willgerodt (eds.), *German Neo-Liberals, and the Social Market Economy*, The Macmillan Press, London, 1989.

Valcke, Catherine, 'Comparative Law as Comparative Jurisprudence: The Comparability of Legal Systems', The American Journal of Comparative Law, Vol. 52, No. 3, 2004.

Vanberg, Viktor V., 'Markets and Regulation: On the Contrast Between Free-Market Liberalism and Constitutional Liberalism', Constitutional Political Economy, Vol. 10, No. 3, 1999.

Vanberg, Viktor J., 'The Freiburg School: Walter Eucken and Ordoliberalism', Freiburg Discussion Papers on Constitutional Economics, 04/11, 2004.

Vanberg, Viktor J., 'Consumer Welfare, Total Welfare and Economic Freedom – On the Normative Foundations of Competition Policy', Freiburg Discussion Papers on Constitutional Economics, 09/3, 2009.

Vanberg, Viktor J., 'Liberal Constitutionalism, Constitutional Liberalism and Democracy', Freiburg Discussion Papers on Constitutional Economics, 09/04, 2009.

Vanberg, Viktor J., 'Constitutionalism, Federalism, and Limited Government: Hayekian Arguments in Political Scientists' Perspective', in Peter J. Boettke and Virgil Henry Storr (eds.), *Revisiting Hayek's Political Economy, Advances in Austrian Economics*, Vol. 21 Emerald Group Publishing, 2016.

Van den Bergh, Roger J. and Peter D. Camesasca, *European Competition Law and Economics: A Comparative Perspective*, Sweet & Maxwell, London, 2006.

Van der Burg, Wibren, 'The Importance of Ideals', The Journal of Value Inquiry, Vol. 31, No. 1, 1997.

Vaubel, Roland, 'The Role of Competition in the Rise of Baroque and Renaissance Music', Journal of Cultural Economics, Vol. 29, No. 4, 2005.

Del Vecchio, Giorgio, 'Truth and Untruth in Morals and Law' in Paul Sayre (ed.), *Interpretations of Modern Legal Philosophies: Essays in Honour of Roscoe Pound*, Oxford University Press, Oxford, 1981.

Vermeule, Adrian, 'The Invisible Hand in Legal Theory', Harvard Public Law Working Paper, No. 09–43, 2009.

Vickers, John, 'Concepts of Competition', Oxford Economic Papers, New Series, Vol. 47, No. 1, 1995.

Vickers, John, 'Competition is for Consumers', A Speech to the Social Market Foundation, 21.02.2002 http://www.oft.gov.uk/shared_oft/speeches/spe0102.pdf.

Vickers, John, 'Competition Policy and Property Rights', The Economic Journal, Vol. 120, No. 5, 2010.

Viner, Jacob, 'The Utility Concept in Value Theory and Its Critics', The Journal of Political Economy, Vol. 33, No. 4, 1925.

Viner, Jacob, 'Adam Smith and Laissez Faire', The Journal of Political Economy, Vol. 35, No. 2, 1927.

Viner, Jacob, 'The Short View and the Long in Economic Policy', The American Economic Review, Vol. 30, No. 1, 1940.

Viner, Jacob, 'Schumpeter's History of Economic Analysis', The American Economic Review, Vol. 44, No. 5, 1954.

Viner, Jacob, 'The Intellectual History of Laissez-Faire', Journal of Law and Economics, Vol. 3, No. 1, 1960.

Vysheslavtsev, Boris, *Etika Preobrazhennogo Erosa (The Ethics of Transformed Eros)*, Republic, Moscow, 1994.

Waismann, Friedrich, 'Verifiability', Proceedings of the Aristotelian Society, Supplementary Vol. 19, 1945.

Waismann, Friedrich, 'Language Strata', in Antony G. N. Flew (ed.), *Logic and Language* (Second Series), Basil Blackwell, Oxford, 1953.

Waldenfels, Hans, 'Absolute Nothingness. Preliminary Considerations on

a Central Notion in the Philosophy of Nishida Kitaro and the Kyoto School', Monumenta Nipponica, Vol. 21, No. 3/4, 1966.
Waldron, Jeremy, 'Rights in Conflict', Ethics, Vol. 99, No. 3, 1989.
Waldron, Jeremy, 'Fake Incommensurability: A Response to Professor Schauer', Hastings Law Journal, Vol. 45, No. 4, 1994.
Waldron, Jeremy, 'Can There Be a Democratic Jurisprudence?', New York University School of Law Public Law & Legal Theory Research Paper Series, Working Paper No. 08–35, 2008.
Waller, Spencer S., 'Market Talk: Competition Policy in America', Law & Social Inquiry, Vol. 22, No. 2, 1997.
Waluchow, Wil J., 'The Many Faces of Legal Positivism', The University of Toronto Law Journal, Vol. 48, No. 3, 1998.
Ward, Tony, 'Two Schools of Legal Idealism: A Positivist Introduction', Ratio Juris, Vol. 19, No. 2, 2006.
Waterman, Robert H., *Adhocracy*, W. W. Norton & Company, New York, 1993.
Weber, Max, *On Law in Economy and Society*, Harvard University Press, Cambridge, Massachusetts, 1954.
Weber, Max, 'Science as a Vocation', Daedalus, Vol. 87, No. 1, 1958.
Weikart, Richard, 'The Origins of Social Darwinism in Germany, 1859–1895', Journal of the History of Ideas, Vol. 54, No. 3, 1993.
Weinberger, Ota, 'Introduction', in Hans Kelsen, *Essays in Legal and Moral Philosophy*, D. Reidel, Dordrecht, 1973.
Weinrib, Ernest J., 'Utilitarianism, Economics, and Legal Theory', The University of Toronto Law Journal, Vol. 30, No. 3, 1980.
Weinrib, Ernest J., 'Legal Formalism: On the Immanent Rationality of Law', The Yale Law Journal, Vol. 97, No. 6, 1988.
Weiss, Edoardo, *Principles of Psychodynamics*, Grune & Stratton, New York, 1950.
West, Robin, 'Authority, Autonomy, and Choice: The Role of Consent in the Moral and Political Visions of Franz Kafka and Richard Posner', Harvard Law Review, Vol. 99, No. 2, 1985.
Whish, Richard, '*Intel v Commission*: Keep Calm and Carry on!', Journal of European Competition Law & Practice, Vol. 6, No. 1, 2015.
von Wieser, Friedrich, *Social Economics*, Adelphi Company, New York, 1927.
Wigger, Angela, 'Competition for Competitiveness: The Politics of the Transformation of the EU Competition Regime', dare.ubvu.vu.nl/bitstream/1871/15601/5/8237.pdf.
Willgerodt, Hans and Alan T. Peacock, 'German Liberalism and Economic Revival', in Alan T. Peacock and Hans Willgerodt (eds.), *Germany's Social Market Economy: Origins and Evolution*, Macmillan, London, 1989.

Williams, Joan C., 'Culture and Certainty: Legal History and the Reconstructive Project', Virginia Law Review, Vol. 76, No. 3, 1990.
Williamson, Oliver E., 'Calculativeness, Trust, and Economic Organization', Journal of Law and Economics, Vol. 36, No. 1, 1993.
Willoughby, Westel W., 'The Ethics of the Competitive Process', The American Journal of Sociology, Vol. 6, No. 2, 1900.
Wiseman, Jack, 'Social Policy and the Social Market Economy', in Alan Peacock and Hans Willgerodt (eds.), *German Neo-Liberals, and the Social Market Economy*, The Macmillan Press, London, 1989.
Witt, Ulrich, 'Evolutionary Economics', in Peter J. Boettke (ed.), *The Elgar Companion to Austrian Economics*, Edward Elgar Publishing, Cheltenham, 1994.
Wittgenstein, Ludwig, *Philosophical Grammar*, Basil Blackwell, Oxford, 1974.
Wohlgemuth, Michael, 'A European Social Model of State-Market Relations – The Ethics of Competition from a "Neo-liberal" Perspective', Zeitschrift für Wirtschafts- und Unternehmensethik – Journal for Business, Economics & Ethics, Vol. 9, No. 1, 2008.
Wolf, Dieter, 'Competition Policy Objectives', Working Paper, in Claus-Dieter Ehlermann and Laraine L. Laudati (eds.), *The Objectives of Competition Policy*, European Competition Law Annual 1997, Hart Publishing, Oxford, 1998.
Wolff, Jonathan, 'The Ethics of Competition', in Geraint Parry, Asif Qureshi and Hillel Steiner (eds.), *The Legal and Moral Aspects of International Trade: Freedom and Trade*, Vol. 3, Routledge, London, 1998.
Wolff, Jonathan, 'Libertarianism, Utility and Economic Competition', Virginia Law Review, Vol. 92, No. 7, 2006.
Wright, Joshua D., 'The Roberts Court and the Chicago School of Antitrust: The 2006 Term and Beyond', Competition Policy International, Vol. 3, No. 2, 2007.
Wright, Joshua D. and Douglas H. Ginsburg, 'The Goals of Antitrust: Welfare Trumps Choice', Fordham Law Review, Vol. 81, No. 5, 2013.
Yankwich, Leon R., 'Competition, Real or Soft – Or What Have You? Observations on Competition and Antitrust Policy', American Bar Association Section of Antitrust Law Proceedings at the Annual Meeting, 1952.
Young, Crawford, 'The Dialectics of Cultural Pluralism: Concept and Reality', in Crawford Young (ed.), *The Rising Tide of Cultural Pluralism: The Nation-State at Bay?*, The University of Wisconsin Press, Madison, 1993.
Young, Jeffrey T. and Barry Gordon, 'Distributive Justice as a Normative

Criterion in Adam Smith's Political Economy', History of Political Economy, Vol. 28, No. 1, 1996.

Zäch, Roger, 'Competition Law Should Promote Economic and Social Welfare by Ensuring the Freedom to Compete – a Lawyer's View', in Josef Drexl, Laurence Idot and Joël Monéger (eds.), *Economic Theory and Competition Law*, Edward Elgar Publishing, Cheltenham, 2009.

Zäch, Roger and Adrian Künzler, 'Efficiency or Freedom to Compete? Towards an Axiomatic Theory of Competition Law', Zeitschrift für Wettbewerbsrecht, Vol. 7, No. 3, 2009.

Zäch, Roger and Adrian Künzler, 'Freedom to Compete or Consumer Welfare: The Goal of Competition Law According to Constitutional Law' in Roger Zäch, Andreas Heinemann and Andreas Kellerhals (eds.), *The Development of Competition Law – Global Perspectives*, Edward Elgar Publishing, Cheltenham, 2010.

Zamir, Eyal and Barak Medina, 'Law, Morality, and Economics: Integrating Moral Constraints with Economic Analysis of Law', California Law Review, Vol. 96, No. 2, 2008.

Zimmer, Daniel, 'Protection of Competition v. Maximizing (Consumer) Welfare', in Jürgen Basedow and Wolfgang Wurmnest (eds.), *Structure and Effects in EU Competition Law: Studies on Exclusionary Conduct and State Aid*, Kluwer, Alphen aan den Rijn, 2011.

Zucca, Lorenzo, *Constitutional Dilemmas – Conflicts of Fundamental Rights in Europe and the USA*, Oxford University Press, Oxford, 2007.

Zywicki, Todd J. and Anthony B. Sanders, 'Posner, Hayek & the Economic Analysis of Law', George Mason University Law and Economics Research Paper Series, 07–05, 2007.

Index

Printed by Printforce, United Kingdom